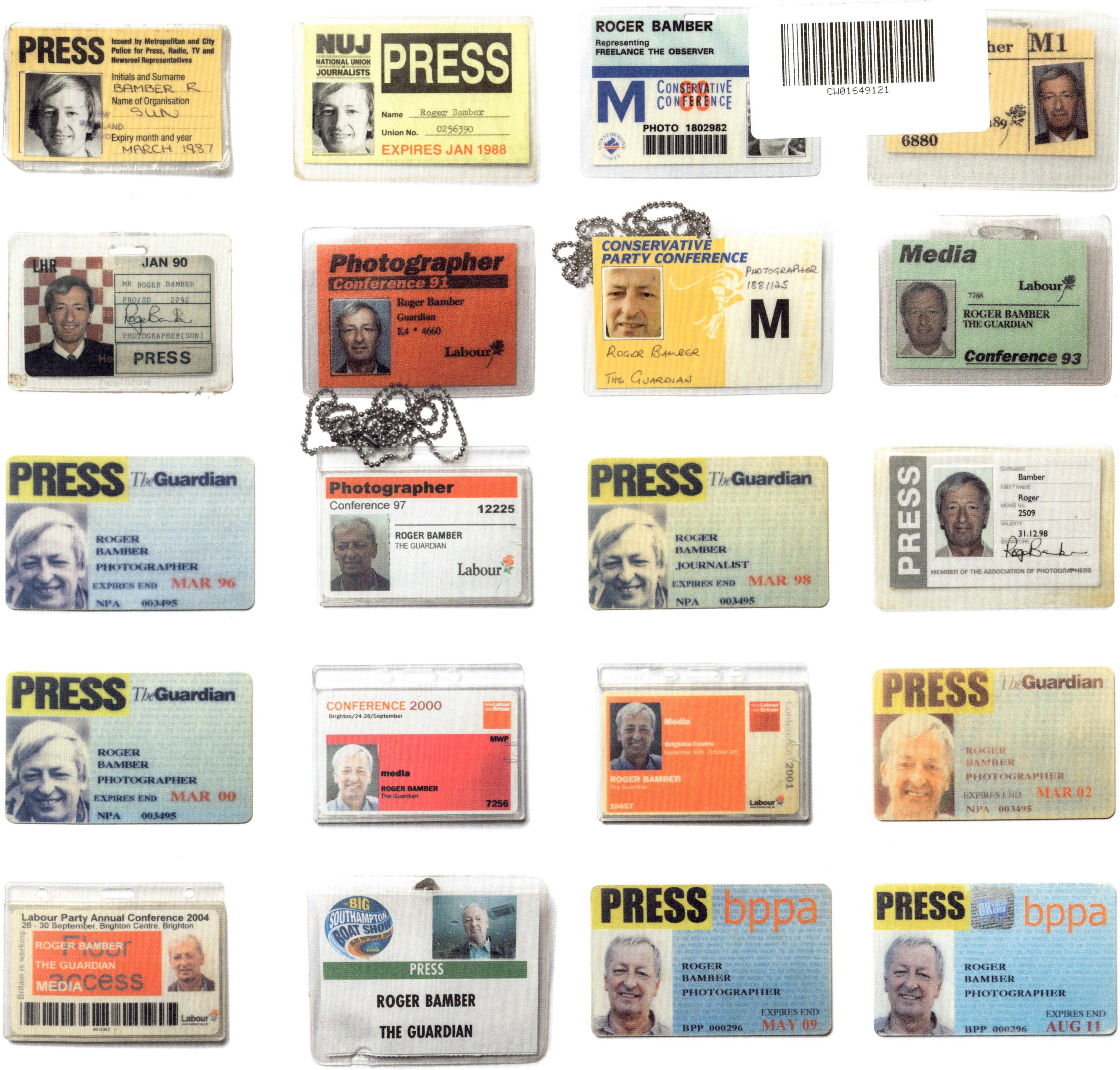
PRESS
Issued by Metropolitan and City Police for Press, Radio, TV and Newsreel Representatives
Initials and Surname
BAMBER R
Name of Organisation
SUN
Expiry month and year
MARCH 1987
NUJ
NATIONAL UNION OF JOURNALISTS
PRESS
Name Roger Bamber
Union No. 0256390
EXPIRES JAN 1988
ROGER BAMBER
Representing
FREELANCE THE OBSERVER
M
CONSERVATIVE CONFERENCE
PHOTO 1802982
M1
6880
LHR
JAN 90
MR ROGER BAMBER
PRO/SD 2292
PHOTOGRAPHER(SUN)
PRESS
Photographer
Conference 91
Roger Bamber
Guardian
K4 * 4660
Labour
CONSERVATIVE PARTY CONFERENCE
PHOTOGRAPHER
188/125
M
ROGER BAMBER
THE GUARDIAN
Brighton 1992
Media
Labour
7788
ROGER BAMBER
THE GUARDIAN
Conference 93
PRESS The Guardian
ROGER
BAMBER
PHOTOGRAPHER
EXPIRES END MAR 96
NPA 003495
Photographer
Conference 97
12225
ROGER BAMBER
THE GUARDIAN
Labour
PRESS The Guardian
ROGER
BAMBER
JOURNALIST
EXPIRES END MAR 98
NPA 003495
PRESS
SURNAME Bamber
FIRST NAME Roger
MEMB No. 2509
VALIDITY 31.12.98
SIGNATURE
MEMBER OF THE ASSOCIATION OF PHOTOGRAPHERS
PRESS The Guardian
ROGER
BAMBER
PHOTOGRAPHER
EXPIRES END MAR 00
NPA 003495
CONFERENCE 2000
Brighton/24-28/September
MWP
media
ROGER BAMBER
The Guardian
7256
Media
Brighton Centre
ROGER BAMBER
The Guardian
10457
Labour
2001
PRESS The Guardian
ROGER
BAMBER
PHOTOGRAPHER
EXPIRES END MAR 02
NPA 003495
Labour Party Annual Conference 2004
26 - 30 September, Brighton Centre, Brighton
ROGER BAMBER
THE GUARDIAN
MEDIA
Floor access
Britain is working
Labour
BIG SOUTHAMPTON BOAT SHOW
PRESS
ROGER BAMBER
THE GUARDIAN
PRESS bppa
ROGER
BAMBER
PHOTOGRAPHER
EXPIRES END MAY 09
BPP 000296
PRESS bppa
ROGER
BAMBER
PHOTOGRAPHER
EXPIRES END AUG 11
BPP 000296

ROGER BAMBER

Out of the Ordinary

A picture editor's dream

Eamonn McCabe

Roger Bamber covered music, riots and politics for British newspapers from the *Sun* to the *Guardian.* He won photographer of the year for both of those newspapers – a unique achievement.

While at the *Sun,* he snapped one of the defining images of Freddie Mercury performing at Live Aid in 1985. Among his many memorable photographs for the *Guardian* is a black-and-white image of a lone boy on a Brighton Beach, pointing and laughing at a Punch and Judy show. The simple, yet perfect image was part of Roger's portfolio when he won the Ilford Press Photographer of the Year for the *Guardian* in 1992.

Roger had begun working as a freelance for the Observer in 1988, then the Guardian soon after I had arrived to run the picture desk and was charged by the then editor, Peter Preston, to take on the Independent – which had made a name for itself with its great photography.

Through his slew of awards and accolades, as well as his eye for a good picture and endless energy and enthusiasm, Roger helped our team to do just that. It was my belief that readers of the *Guardian* visited art galleries and watched good television and films, and as such, they deserved to be stimulated by the photographs they looked at in the *Guardian.* Bamber's pictures made the reader think and smile and even look twice. He was a picture editor's dream.

A true pictorialist, he enjoyed capturing the beauty of shape and form, always with a wry sense of humour and even a twist of anarchy. He specialised in finding quirky people in arts and crafts up and down the country who he instinctively knew would make great photographs. Roger was a lover of trains, and one of his best photographs, entitled *The Station Under the Station,* shows an avid collector as a giant, looking through a miniature station at his beloved train set. The sense of scale in the image is extraordinary and looked incredible in the paper.

He would photograph the same scene fifty times from ever so slightly different angles. To me it often looked like the same picture on six different contact sheets – sometimes I just used a pin and randomly chose one; they were all great.

In 1965 he got his first Fleet Street job, covering news and features for the *Daily Mail,* then a broadsheet. While there, he won Commercial and Industrial Photographer of the Year in the 1967 British Press Awards. In November 1969, he was poached for Rupert Murdoch's new project – the tabloid *Sun* newspaper. Over the nineteen years he spent there he covered news and features all over the world, and won many awards, including News Photographer of the Year for his 1973 image of a bloodied, injured barrister being helped to safety after the IRA bombed the Old Bailey.

During this time, he hung out on tour with the likes of David Bowie, and the Rolling Stones. A handwritten note on hotel stationery from 1976 confirms the Stones granted him permission to photograph rehearsals for the first night of their European tour, at the Festhalle, Frankfurt. A 1983 image of Mick Jagger and Jerry Hall in Barbados depicts Jagger strumming a guitar and laughing his head off – not because Hall is pregnant with their first child, Elizabeth, but because Roger had been swallowed up by a huge wave. Nevertheless he got his picture.

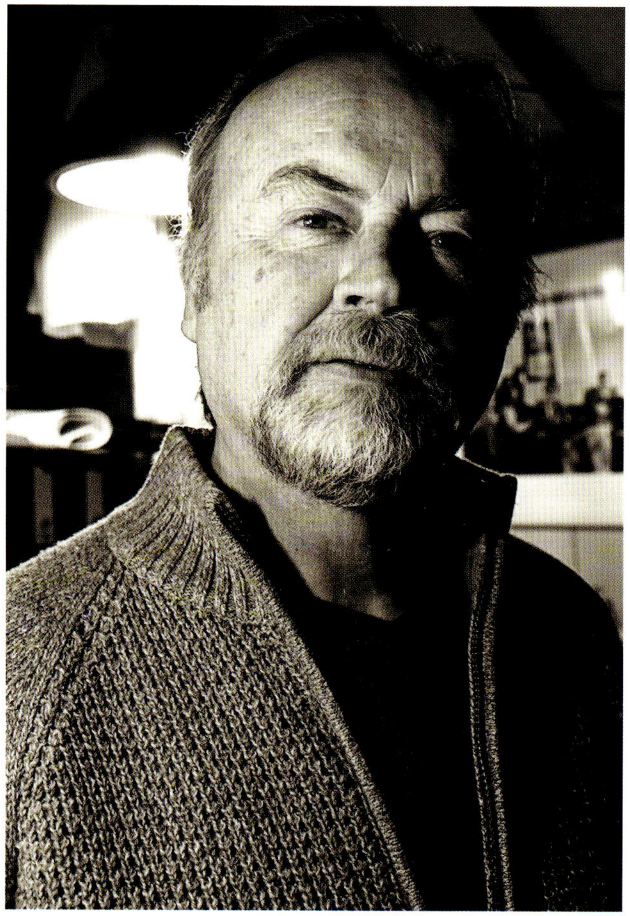

Eamonn McCabe, photographed by Bill Jackson

Roger moved to Brighton in 1973, and in 1999 he worked with Brighton and Hove Council in its bid for city status, his portraits and images of favourite places contributing to its success.

Roger's work was used so regularly in the *Guardian,* and featured so many Brighton images, that in 2005 he was awarded an Honorary Master of Arts degree from the University of Brighton 'for his distinguished photo-journalism and the wealth of images of Brighton inspired by the City.' Sometimes I seriously thought that he was employed by the Brighton Tourist Board. He was genuinely chuffed to receive this honour, given that he had left school without a single O-level.

Despite living in Brighton, Roger was usually seen in a Leicester Cricket Club sweater under a sports jacket, even though he hated cricket – Leicester City FC was his first love.

Roger continued to win awards while at the *Guardian,* until his retirement from newspapers in 2009. But he never put his camera down, continuing to snap anything and everything that caught his eye, and encouraged young photographers with endless patience. In the days before he died Roger was thrilled to see (and was correcting to the last) the proofs of his aptly named forthcoming book, *Out of the Ordinary.*

He married his long-term partner, Shân Lancaster, a journalist, in 2004. The couple met while both working for the *Sun* in the late '70s. They were together for forty years.

This was written as Roger Bamber's obituary for the Guardian *and published on* Guardian Online *on 22 September 2022*

Rebecca Smithers adds:

This book – a showcase of Roger Bamber's wonderful and award-winning photography over an extraordinary fifty-year career – has been a long time in the planning. Better late than never.

It is a truly well-deserved tribute to his talents but very sad that Roger himself will not get to see the completed result despite working on the final proofs until the day before he died. My husband, Eamonn McCabe, should have written this introduction – and opened the accompanying exhibition in 2023 – but by a dreadful coincidence he also died, very suddenly, a month after Roger. He only had time to complete this obituary, which still serves as a memoir of a wonderful working relationship.

For twenty years – evidently the happiest segment of his career – Roger bombarded the *Guardian* with photographs, typically delivered to the offices in London's Farringdon Road in bulk by Red Star, the pre-digital way via the UK's network of railway stations. His packages were, not surprisingly, more bulky than most and Eamonn said his staff groaned in despair when they were delivered. The content, however, never failed to delight.

Eamonn hired and commissioned hundreds of photographers during his time as picture editor at the *Guardian,* but there were very few who he would describe as a picture editor's dream. Roger was most definitely that, as well as being a very decent bloke.

Eamonn McCabe, photographer
Born 28 July 1948; died 2 October 2022

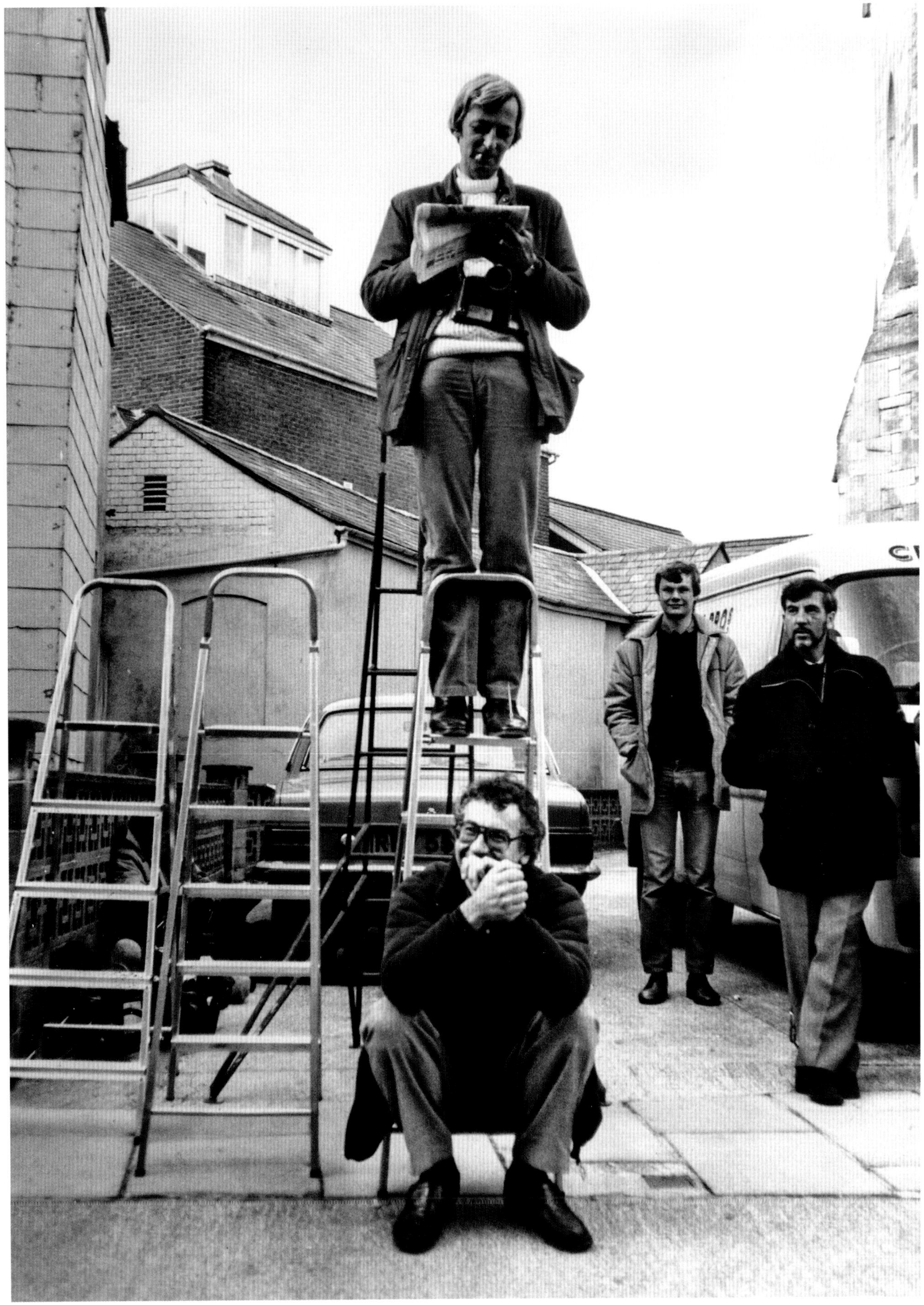

Roger waiting for the action, crossword in hand, on one of his five invaluable ladders.

The sewer and the tank: working with Roger Bamber

Maev Kennedy

When I first met Roger Bamber he could have been wearing black Levi 501s with a denim jacket or perhaps white Levi 501s with a denim shirt; double denim held no terrors for a man who once walked through Carnaby Street wearing a copy of Mick Jagger's flouncy white minidress. In truth I can't remember, but it must have been the black: he knew where we were going. I was wearing a pair of brand new white espadrilles myself, which was a serious mistake.

Obviously, I already knew Bamber's name and his work – he was one of the few photographers whose work I recognise upside down and at a distance – but he was a bit of a puzzle to me. In my long experience as the reporter with the wire-bound notebook lurking in their shadow, press photographers came in three quite distinct varieties: the globe-hopping adrenaline-crazed combat junkies with family lives like a post-apocalyptic disaster movie; the chain-smoking, moaning door-steppers lurking for days at a time behind a thicket of aluminium ladders – 'turn the little fecker's face around!!!!' one bellowed by my ear, when Kate Middleton first emerged from hospital carrying the tiny bundle of Prince George; and the arty ones working entirely in black and white, whose ideal subject is a ballerina visible only as a blur of movement.

Bamber's work seemed to cross all the genres. He kept several aluminium ladders in the bowels of his black Land Rover, and as far as I knew he had an irreproachable home life in Brighton, but before coming to the *Guardian* he had served years before the mast on the red tops on breaking news, features, celebrity chasing, tough overseas stints, and the odd black and white blurry ballerina. His eye was distinctive, shrewd, original and – very much not a given in his trade – strikingly kind. His people, and unpeopled landscapes, were rare in his work, often captured in moments when they appeared vulnerable, odd, or endearingly eccentric, but they were never mocked.

I wasn't sure whether I would meet a rugger-shouldered bruiser or a wispy aesthete. As it turned, out he was neither, a skinny streak of a man with a youthful face and a thatch of white hair, smoking Gauloises in those days, remorselessly charming but with a down to earth friendly manner which won over the shyest subjects. He liked people. It's a good trick.

Even on that first day, I rapidly learned how he achieved his dazzling results: obsessive perfectionism, causing him to fizz with nervous energy until he knew he had that one frame

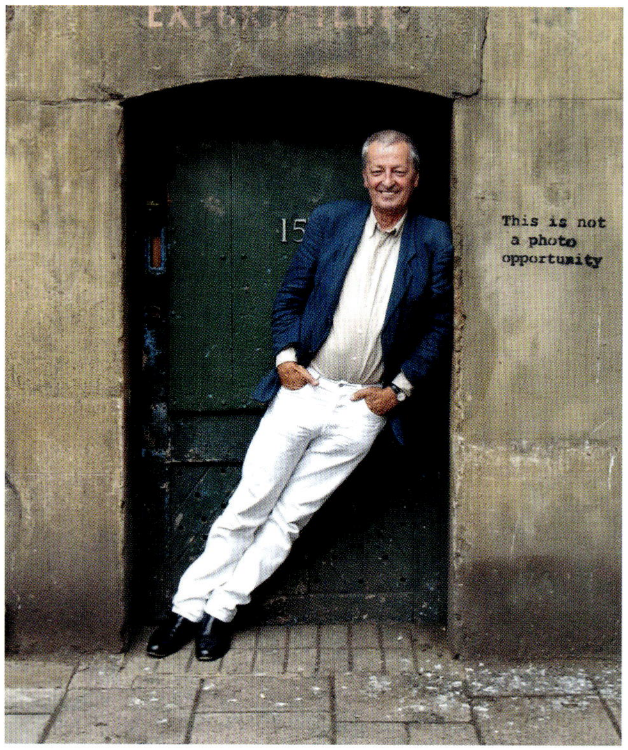

matching the perfect image in his mind's eye. He could work fast if forced to, but if he had time he was quite untroubled by minor considerations such as falling rain or rising tides, or a subject or reporter weak with thirst and hunger by his side. He was a very late adopter of digital, so I learned to do my interviews in snatched minutes as he changed film, since he rarely bothered to use more than one camera. Camera recharged, subject and reporter silenced, I held reflectors or flash guns, seasick, blinded by steam coal smoke, sinking gradually into gravel, mud or sewage, frozen or parboiled as the season dictated. He could use fifty rolls of film. It could take hours.

On occasions I was in the office to see a picture editor dive a hand into a fat padded bag of rolls of film – in those pre-ping days when on edition work from out of town was usually collected as unprocessed film from the nearest railway station Red Star depot – and pull one out at random. I knew it would have wounded Bamber.

There was collateral damage from this relentless pursuit of the perfect image. On one occasion a sweet-natured caretaker, required to stand twisted at a killer angle on top of the aluminium ladder, apparently taking a feather duster (another prop from the unsavoury depths of PAP 2X, 'The Tank' as I always rudely called the cherished black Land Rover) to the angels above him on the domed roof, eventually meekly asked if we could help him down, as he had a bad back and feared he could no longer move. We had to carefully lift him down by the elbows.

We truly had some grand days out stalking stately homes and windmills, towers and tunnels, plasterers and poets – including Sebastian Barker ostensibly reading his new poem to celebrate the restored bandstand in Brighton. How to photograph a poem? Bamber's inspired solution was a sheaf of computer paper streaming away from the poet on the wind – a stiff wind, and after the first couple of hours, a bloody cold one.

I only saw the charm fail once, ironically on a story close to his heart, a steam railway line where the volunteers had managed to build a new station. Bamber wanted the loco steaming, obviously, past the new station with a castle in the background. The train crew couldn't have been less helpful if we'd been undercover investigators from Inland Revenue. He wore them down over hours and eventually got his pic in the last rays of sunset – after uniquely, in our experience, we'd been required to buy tickets for the ride. We both cared very much about our work, but we wouldn't have minded if that one had been spiked – of course it sailed straight into the paper.

My favourite photograph, of scores of stories

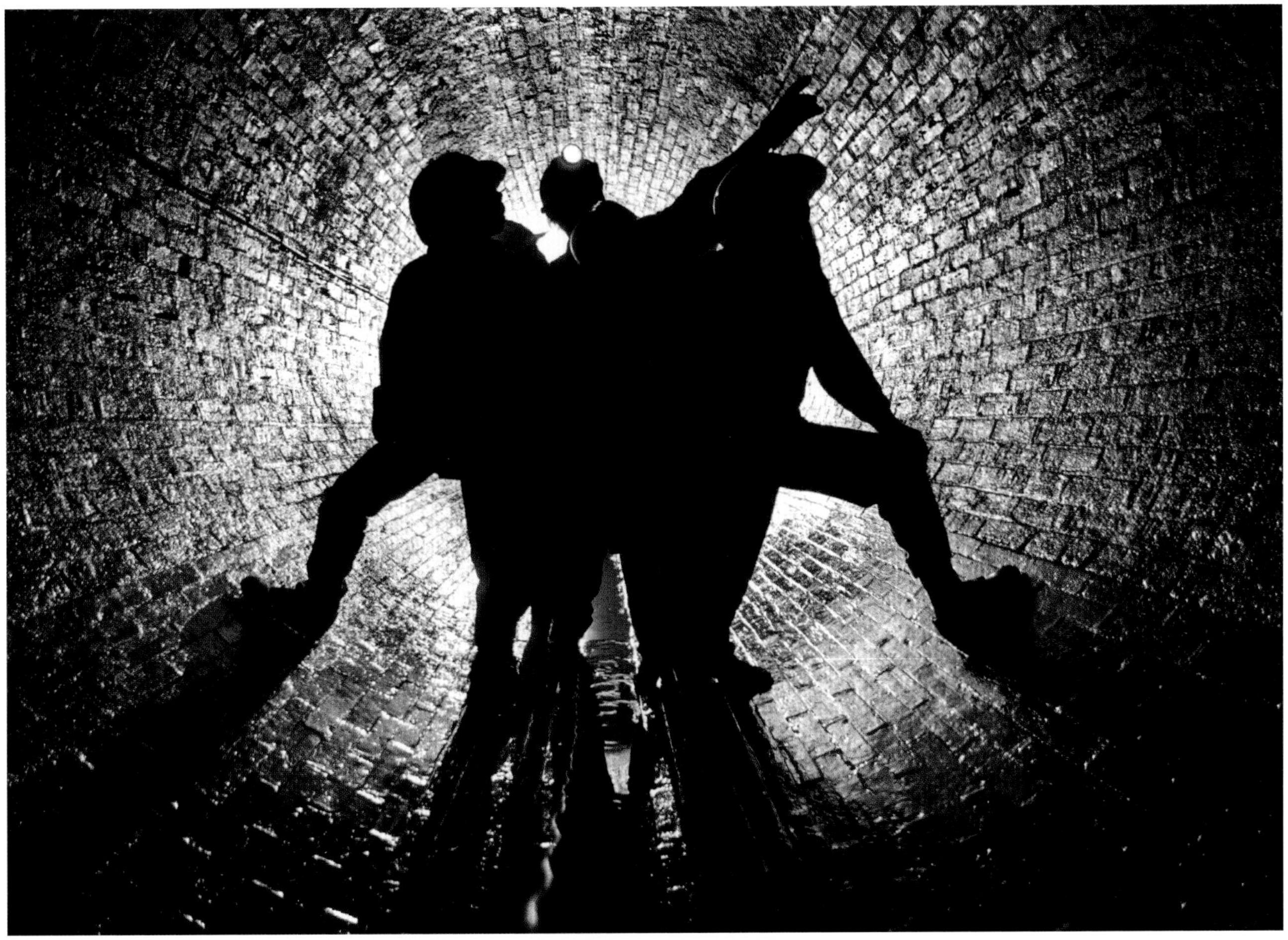

we worked on, was his portrait of the astronomer Sir Patrick Moore. Moore, much like Bamber, no longer saw any need to travel further from his own front door than absolutely essential. We visited as the BBC's *Sky at Night,* long since the world's longest-running science show, clocked up another anniversary. The show was filmed in Moore's garden, living room and study at his home in Selsey, a few miles from Bamber's home in Brighton, so it suited both men well.

Moore, by then quite deaf but very vain about it, and with a dim view of all reporters and most women, was not an easy interview. Sitting down for a formal Q&A was out of the question: half the village seemed to wander through the house, including schoolchildren on their way home who just came in, took a book off the shelves, and settled down to read in the most comfortable available chair. A star-gazing man from Peterborough turned up, a regular visitor who came on leave days to help with the sacks of correspondence from all over the world.

However, Bamber loved cats, and Moore loved kit. While they chatted about fur and lens apertures, Bamber dismantled and reconstructed Moore's study – the astronomer waged a running battle over the BBC crew daring to move so much as a paper clip in the house – filling his enormous desk with globes, medals, books, star maps, telescopes, and one of the current cats at his elbow. I just lurked in the background and took notes. The resulting portrait still seems to me a miracle, recalling a Flemish Golden Age painting, every detail in sharp focus, including the famous eyebrows, while nailing Moore's intelligence, wit and studied eccentricity.

On that very first meeting, we had been granted a sneak preview – thanks to Bamber's impeccable local contacts – of Brighton's sewers, where the council was about to admit the public for the first time. Our trot around the underworld was supposed to last half an hour. I first noted the expression on Bamber's face that would become very familiar on countless later jobs, a look of gnawing discomfort, like a man reminded of a recent encounter with a dodgy oyster.

We emerged into the light of the Brighton seafront three hours later. I squelched across the boardwalk to a rubbish bin, disposed of the brand new white espadrilles, bought a pair of flip-flops from one of the bucket and spade shops, and in those ancient times settled down to write in longhand, before phoning the words to a copy taker in the office from the nearby red phone box. In our long working relationship, it was a severe irritation that I often felt Bamber's fifty-word captions, in impeccably art school black felt-tip block capitals, told the story as completely and perhaps better than my laboured 750 words.

Every place on the sewer tours sold out as soon as his beautiful photographs appeared, and I still regularly see them reproduced on cards and calendars. We were friends ever after, despite the fact that his sewer won the Canon Picture of the Month Award and the covetable prize of a portable electric typewriter for which I would have given at least one eye tooth, while my attempt to charge the white espadrilles to expenses was turned down like a blanket.

It's no part of this story that Bamber was one of the kindest men who ever drew a grumbling breath. He was a proper genius, and you don't get many of those to the kilo, particularly wearing double denim.

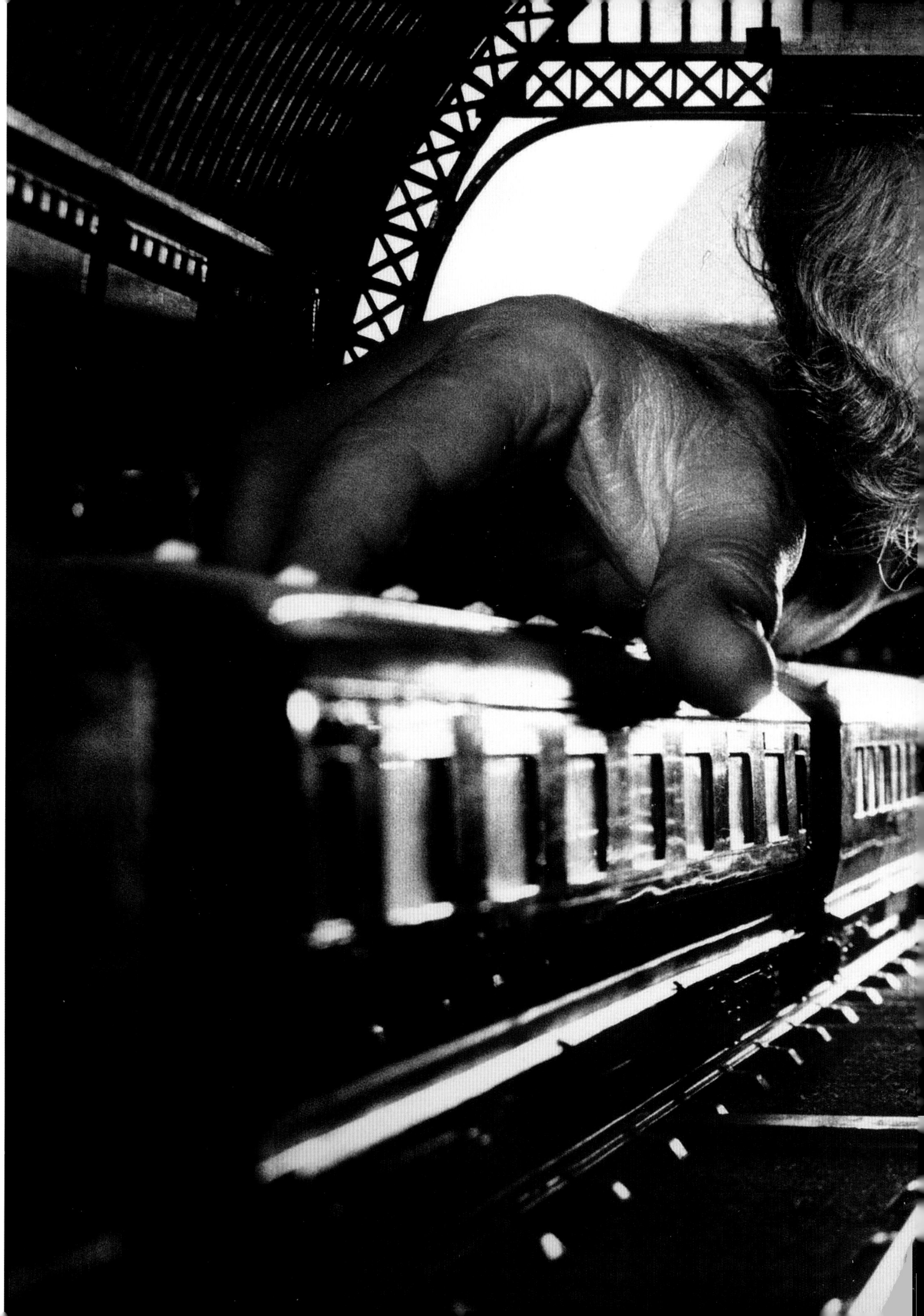

The Station Under the Station

The Guardian, 1991

Curator Chris Littledale arranging Bassett-Lowke O gauge model steam locomotives on a tinplate model station for the opening of the Toy and Model Museum in the Victorian cellars under Brighton Station in 1991. It is now one of the world's great toy collections, with more than 10,000 exhibits from the eighteenth to the twentieth centuries, but its model trains are still the most popular attraction.

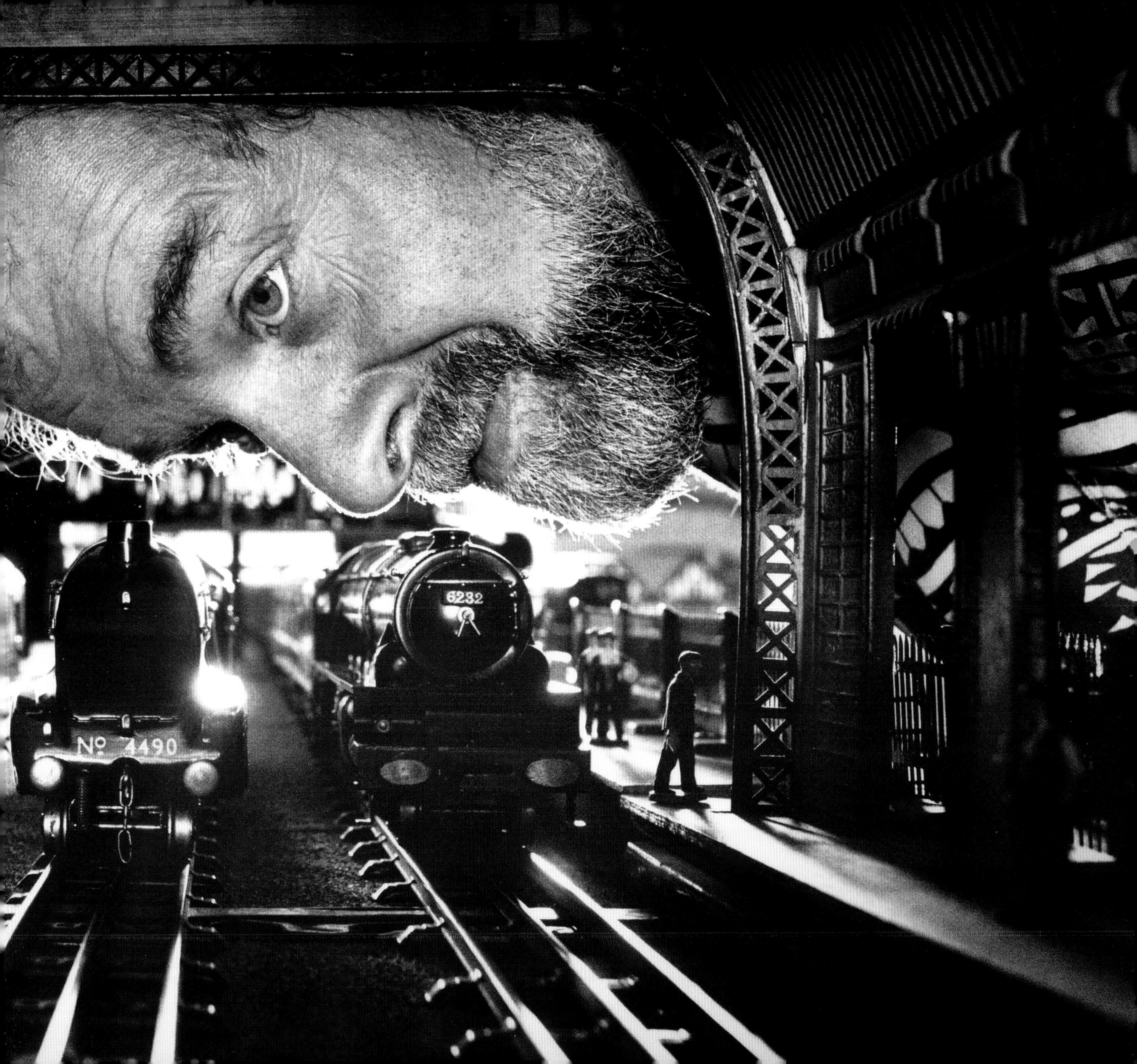
6232
Nº 4490

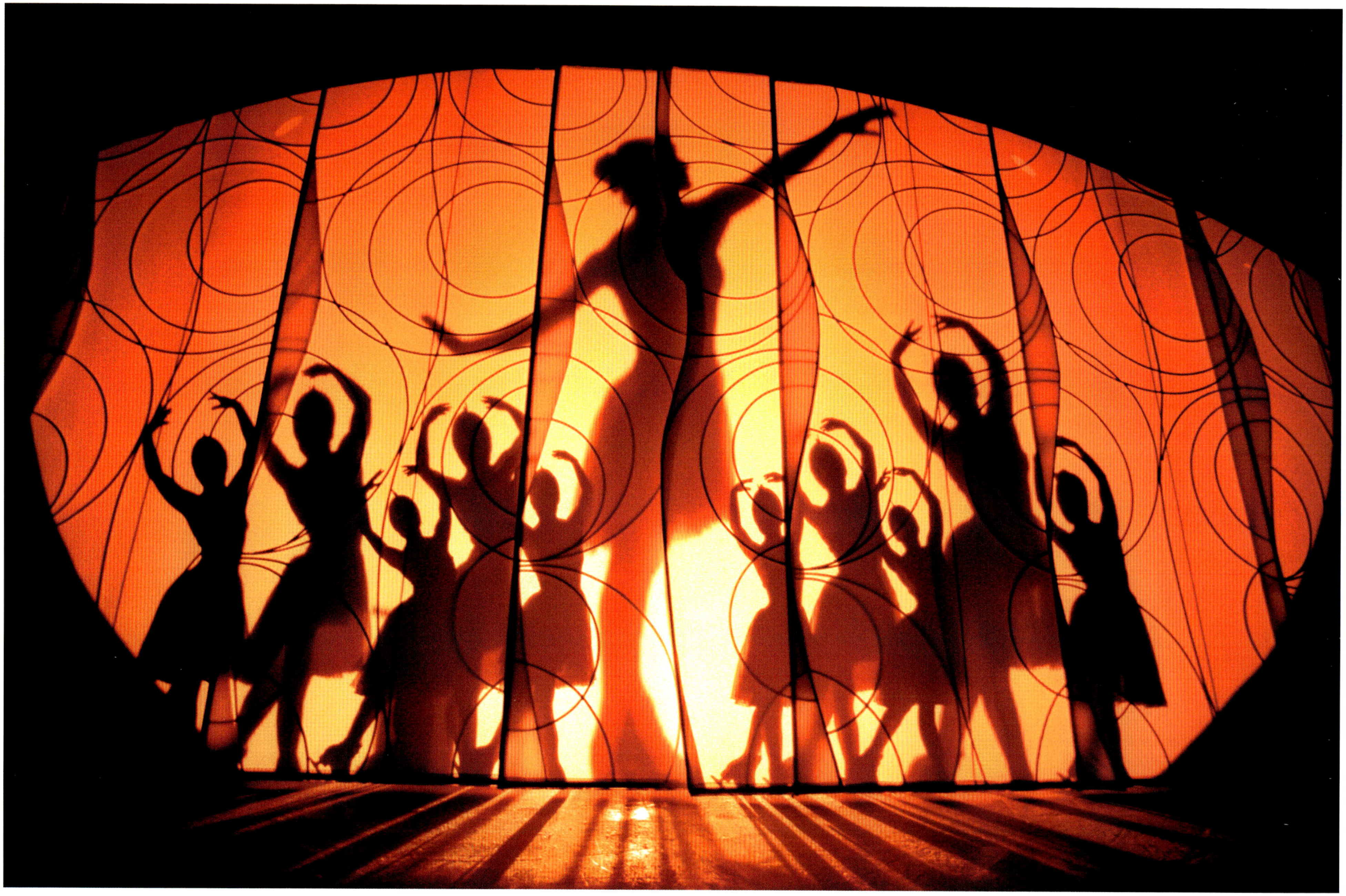

Shadow Skaters

The Guardian, 2001

Driving along Brighton seafront, I noticed the Holiday on Ice show had arrived for its annual winter visit. The stage doors of the Brighton Centre were open and there was a strange orange glow. Being nosy, I went to have a look. The rear of the stage curtain revealed the shadows of skaters rehearsing, backlit by the stage spotlights. Thinking that it could make a picture, I met the show's director and arranged to see the rehearsals. After a bit of persuasion, one of the show's stars, Czech Olympic skater Lenka Kulovana, and a corps de ballet swung into action for me and this was the result. It was used in the *Guardian* the next day.

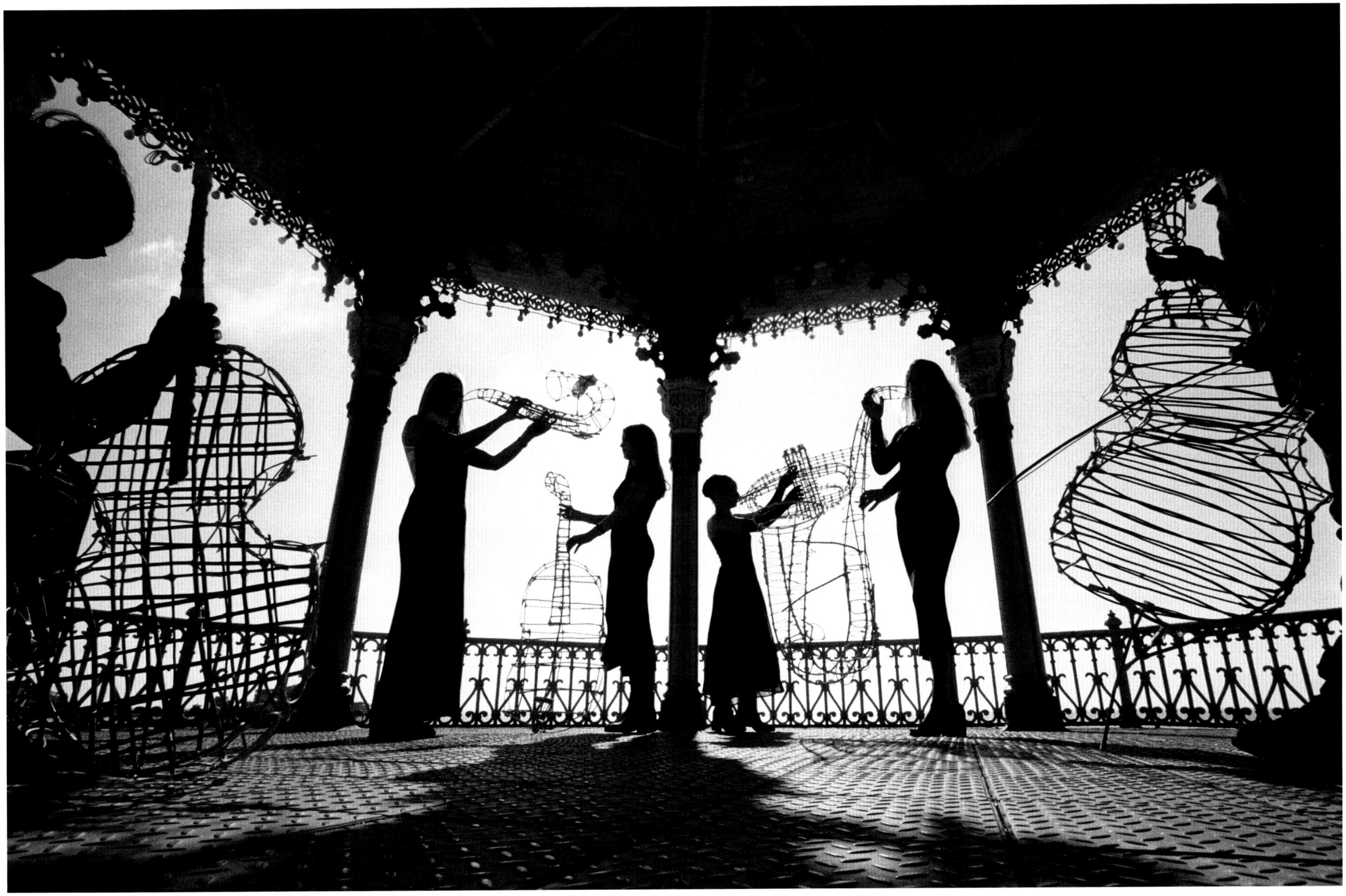

Orchestral Manoeuvres

The Guardian, 1996

Students from City Technical College of Further Education were given a project by their art teacher, sculptor Jane Lister, to make musical instruments out of willow and wicker to hang in the railway station during the Brighton Festival. The designs, including a guitar, cellos, saxophones, bassoons and a double bass were great but the display was a bit dull, so I persuaded the students to wear evening dress and move their silent orchestra to the bandstand on the seafront. They drew an audience who all seemed happy to imagine the music.

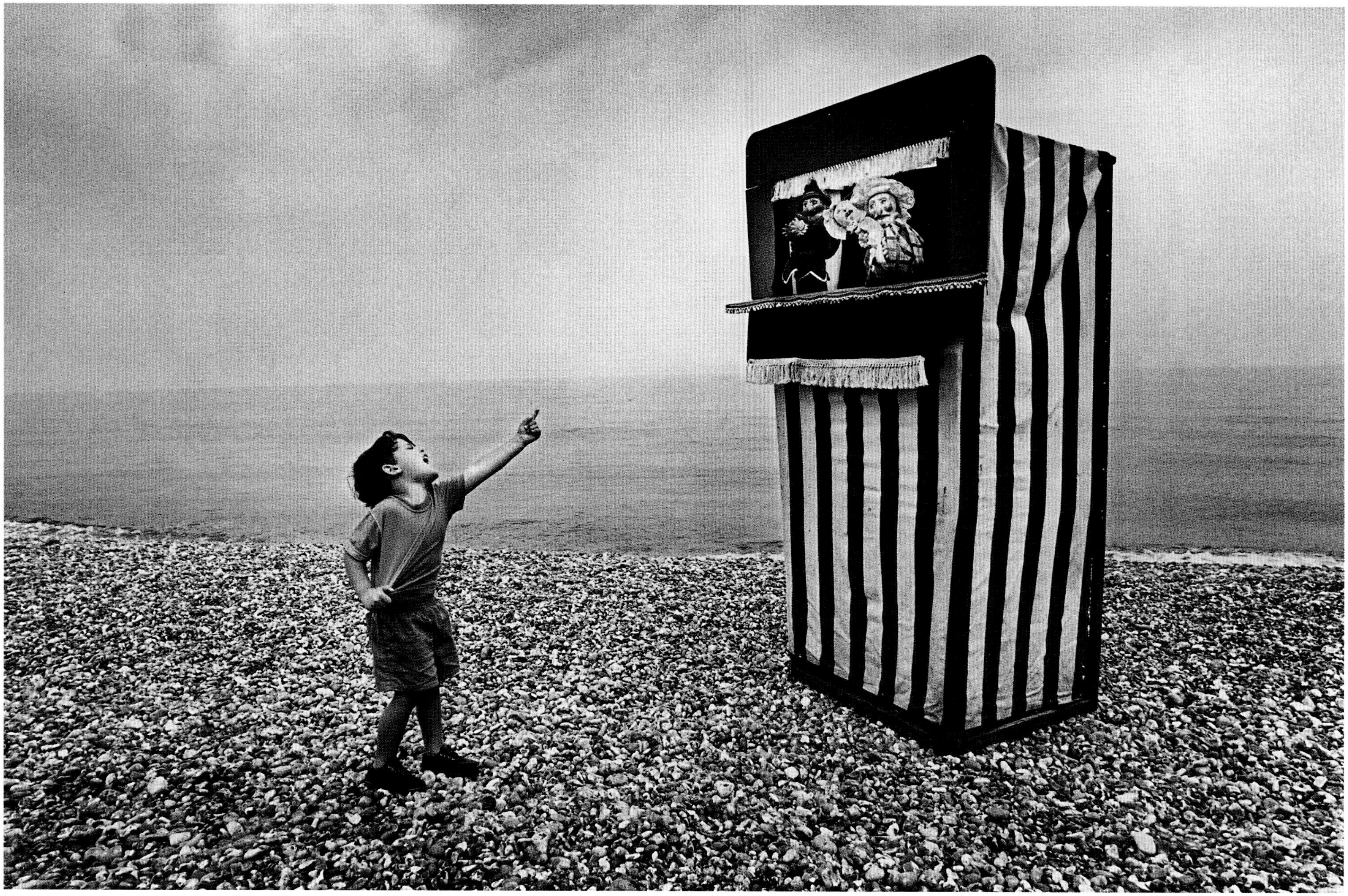

Punch Line

The Guardian, 1992

Brighton's Punch and Judy man Sergeant Stone, was setting up shop when four-year-old Jermaine Briffa wandered along the deserted beach with his father and provided him with a small but enthusiastic audience. I was on the beach too, looking for a picture that would mark the start of the school summer holidays.

The child was so enthralled with his one-to-one with Mr Punch, that he totally ignored me speaking to his dad, then clicking away, and urging Sergeant Stone to keep the banter going. Everything just fell into place.

The photograph was part of a portfolio that won the Ilford Press Photographer of the Year in 1992 and Ilford later used it as a poster for Ilford film, with the slogan 'That's the Way to Do It'. Michael Stone's tent and puppets are now on display at Brighton Museum & Art Gallery.

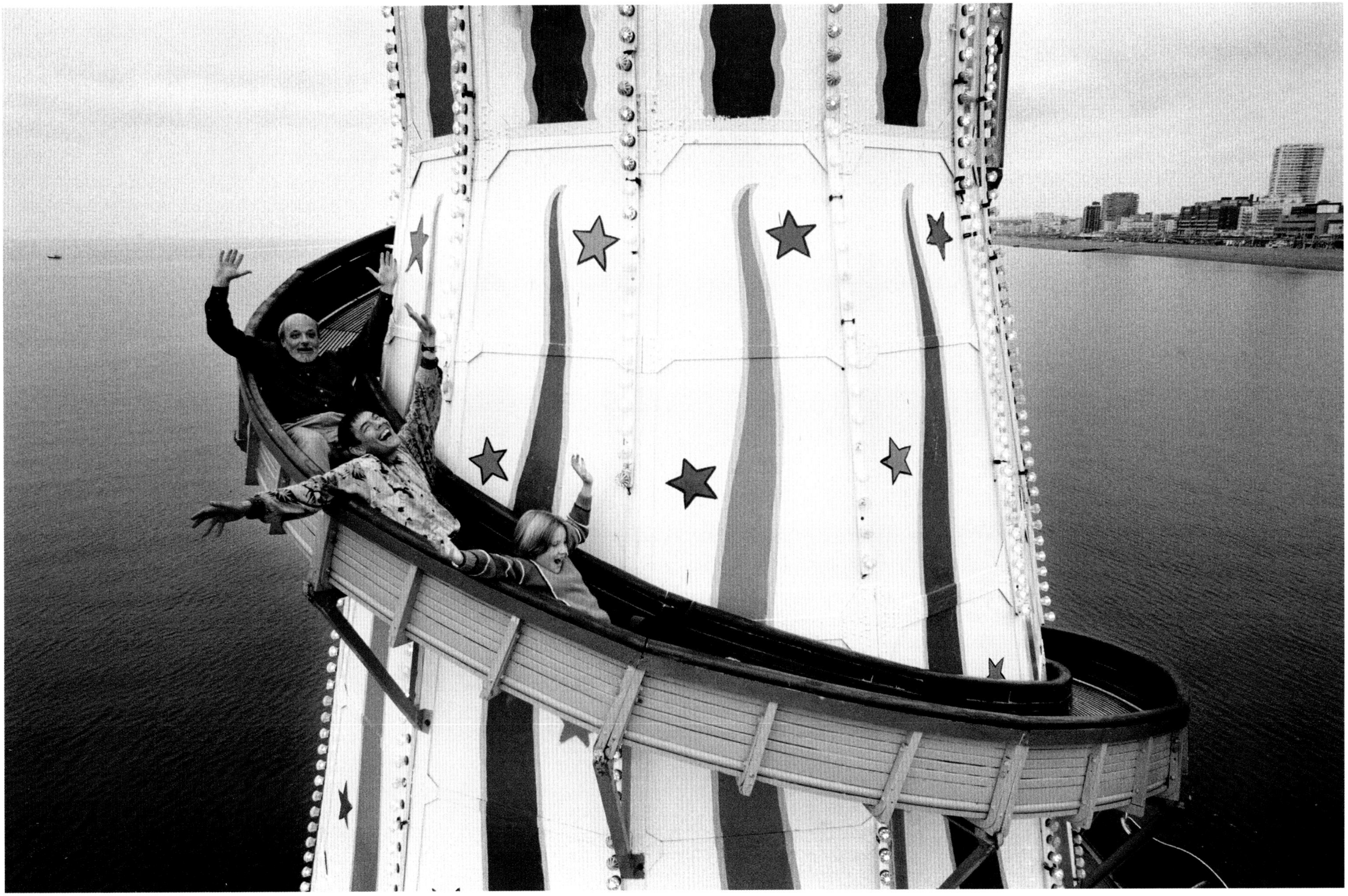

Helter-Skelter

The Guardian, 1994

Artist Philip Dunn, Punch and Judy man Mike Stone and Brighton schoolgirl Jessica Holloway on the helter-skelter ride on Brighton Pier in 1994. They were all taking part in the My Brighton project where Brightonians recorded their personal stories for posterity and named their favourite place. These three were all big fans of the funfair on the pier.

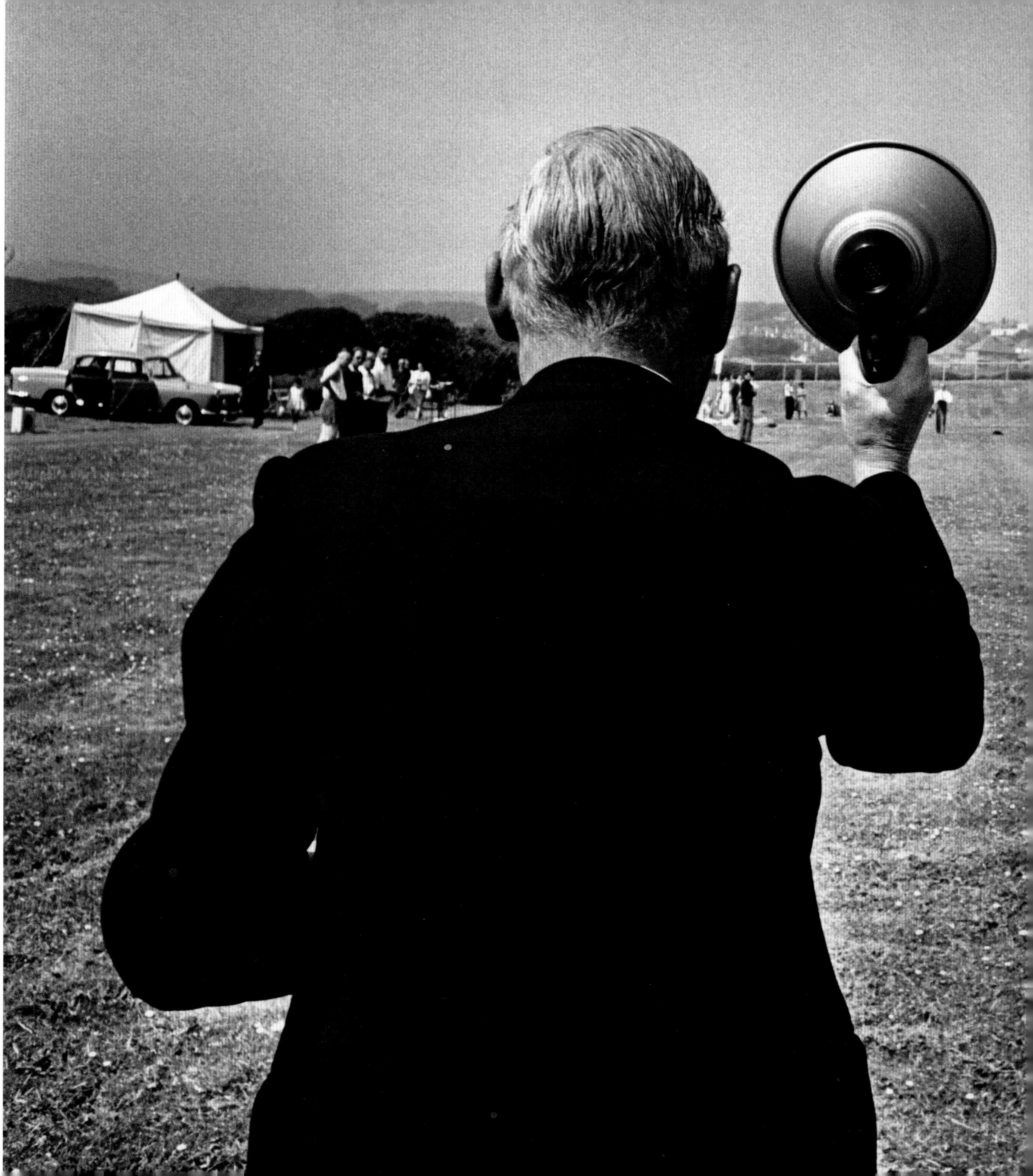

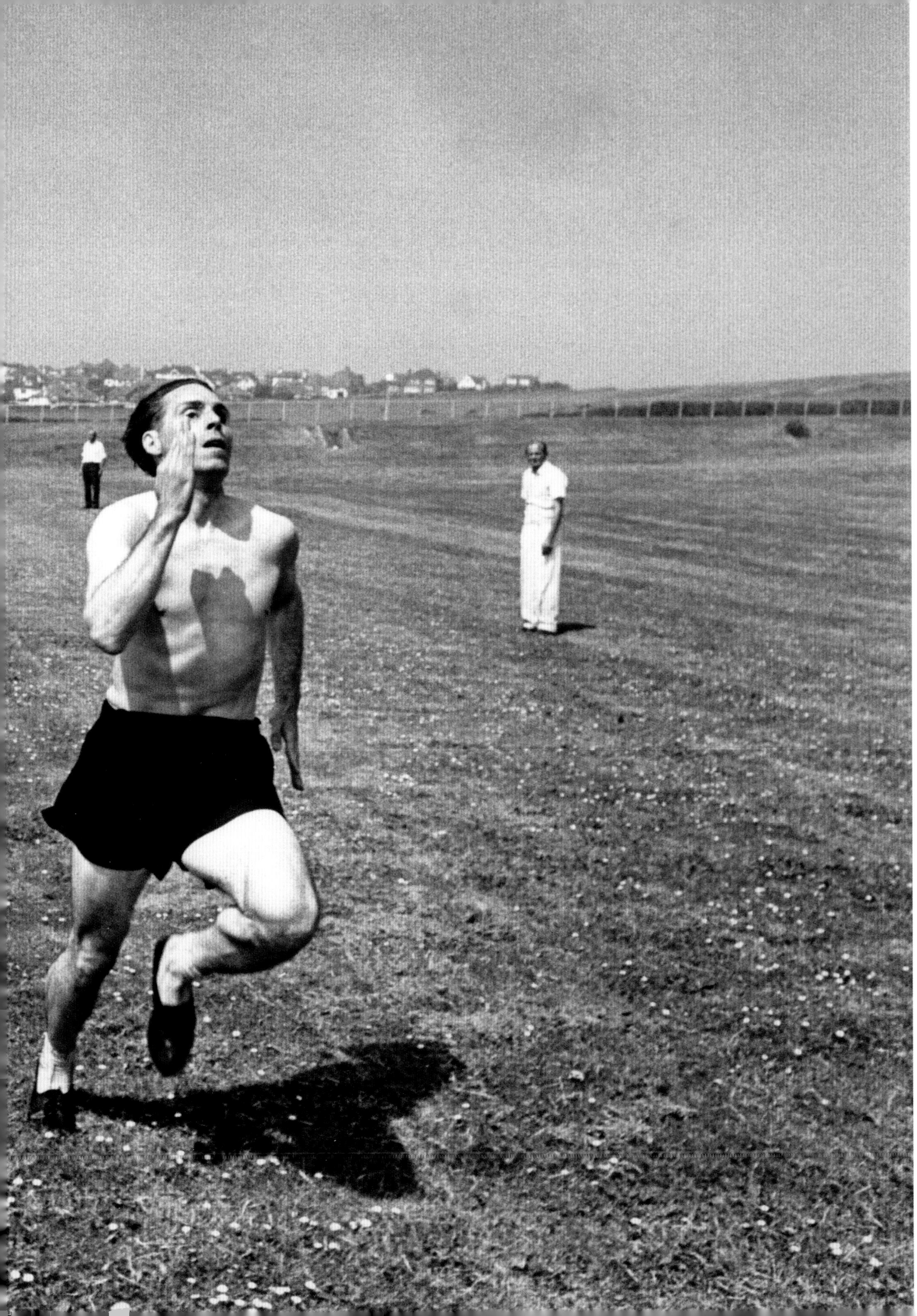

Running Blind

The Daily Mail, 1967

Although I'd visited Brighton as a child in the 1950s, the first time I came to the town as a photographer was in 1967, to cover the annual sports day at St Dunstans home for war-blinded army veterans. It produced remarkable feats of courage. Nothing demonstrated this better than the 100-yard dash, in which each runner ran full pelt towards an official holding a megaphone emitting a bleeping sound to guide them. This runner was the winner, the only one to come straight to the finishing line.
It was used in the then broadsheet *Daily Mail.* Forty-eight years later, in 2015, I had an exhibition at Brighton Photography Gallery which included this image and got a call from the gallery owner, asking to come quickly and meet someone important. Waiting for me was an elderly lady who told me she was Pat Fulling and the runner about to win the race was her late husband, Captain Jack Fulling. He served with the 22nd SAS and was blinded in Malaya in 1952. She also said that he went on to be a very successful physiotherapist, they had a family and a long and happy marriage, and he only died in 2007 in their home in Argyll, Scotland. The family still had a tattered copy of the picture in the *Mail*. I gave her a hug, took the print off the wall and gave it to her.

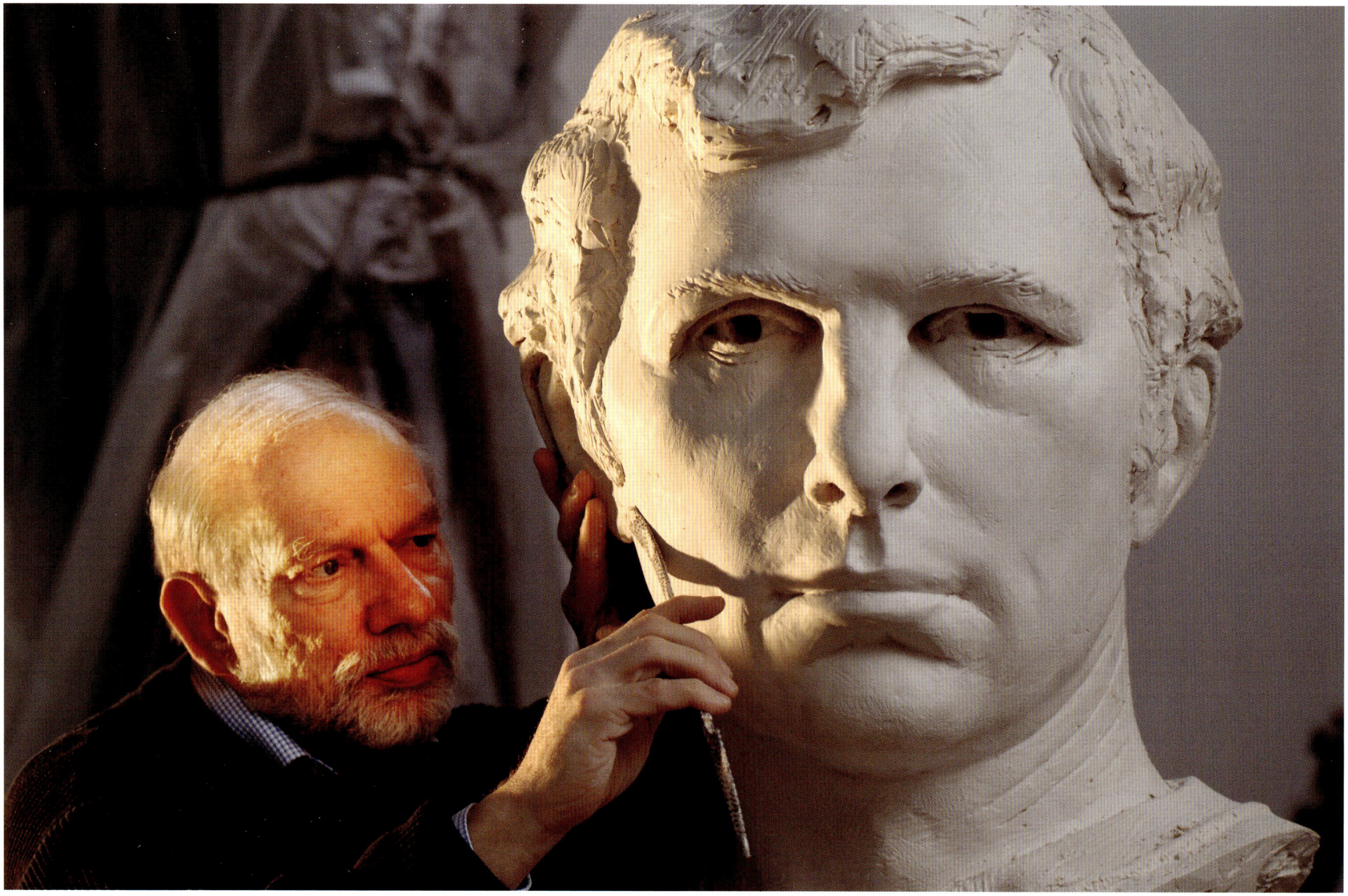

World Cup Hero

The Guardian, 2006

Philip Jackson, one of Britain's leading contemporary figurative sculptors, working on his commission to create a Bobby Moore sculpture for Wembley Stadium. It was unveiled there in 2007.

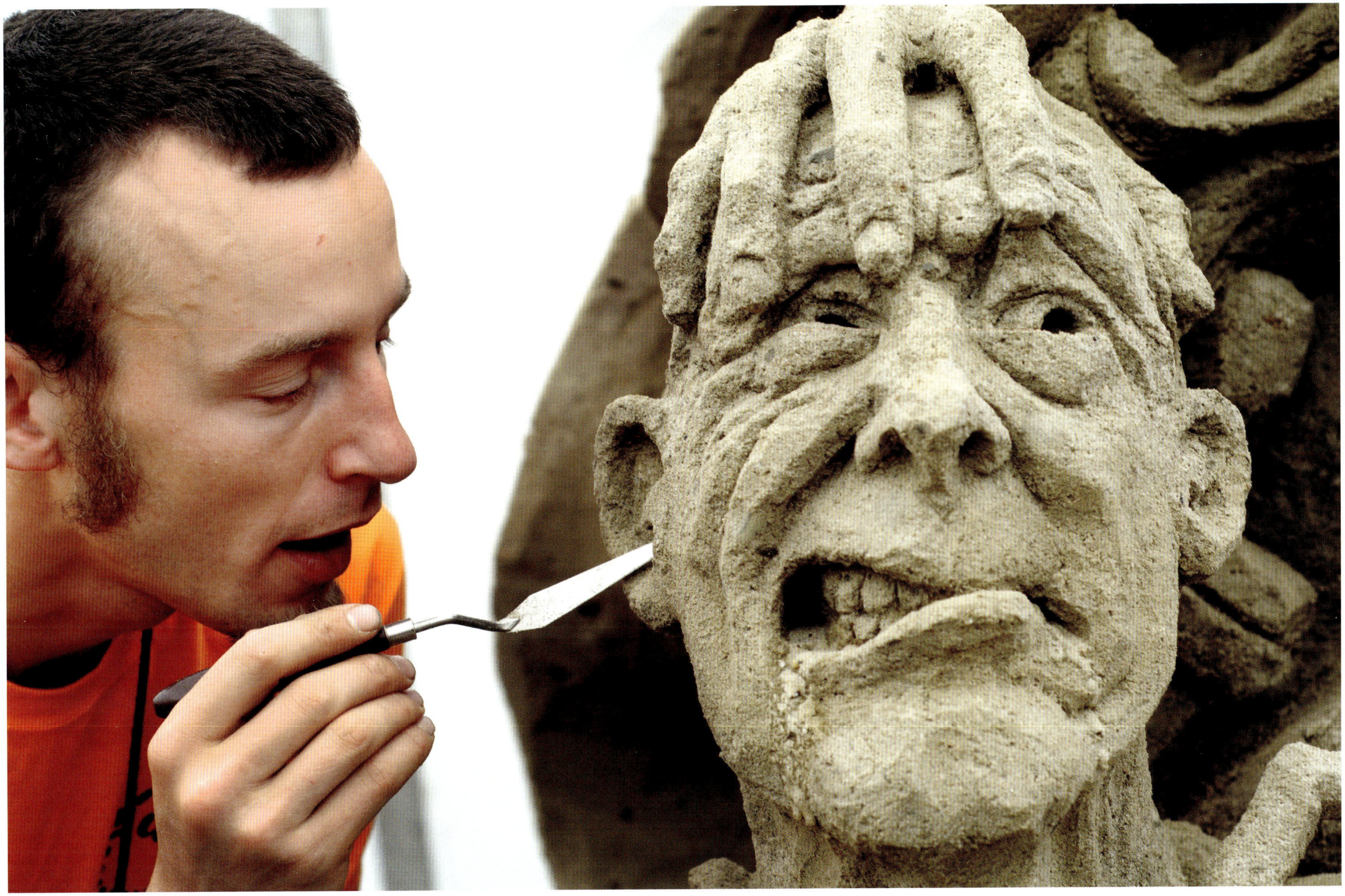

Poking Fun At

The Guardian, 2006

Dutch sculptor Johannes Hogebrink, was painstakingly carving the details of one of an army of larger-than-life barbarian hordes attacking Rome. His warrior was part of a huge artwork showing the rise and fall of the Roman Empire. It wasn't quite working as a picture until I asked him to put the tip of his trowel very gently into the ear of his creation.

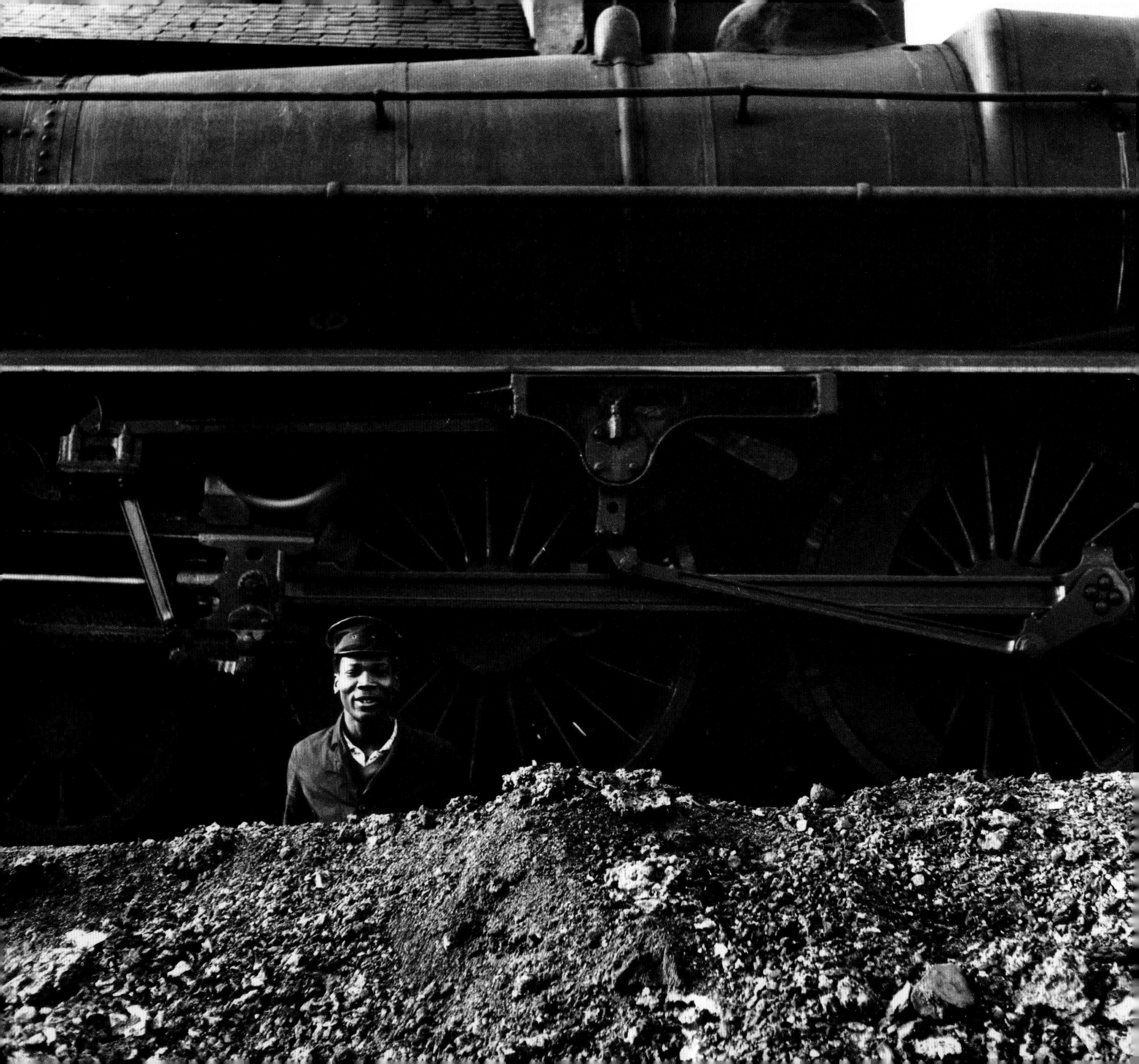

Ashpit Cleaner

Student portfolio, 1968

I was still at Leicester College of Art when I met this young Caribbean railway worker. He was working as a shed cleaner at Leicester Central Station and one of his responsibilities was to clear away the spent ash from the steam locomotives, after they finished their journeys and dumped the remains of their fires into the ashpit. Here he is, demonstrating that it was a very deep pit indeed. The loco behind him is an LMS Stanier Class 5, known to railwaymen as a Black Five.

It was a filthy job but he managed to do it with a smile that lit up the picture, which in turn became part of the portfolio that landed me my first newspaper job.

More recently, in 2022, his portrait became part of an installation of photographs from the TopFoto archive with new poems and curation by Rommi Smith, called *Changing The Story: Photographs of British Life in Black and White, 1917-1962.*

Laid Off

The Sun, 1969

Off-shift Welsh miners at the pithead of Clydach Vale coal mine, Tonypandy. They had just learned their mine was to be the latest victim in a long line of closures in the Rhonda Valley.

Today, former miner's cottages still stand all along the 12-mile-long valley but the old mines have been landscaped almost out of existence, along with industry that once defined the area.

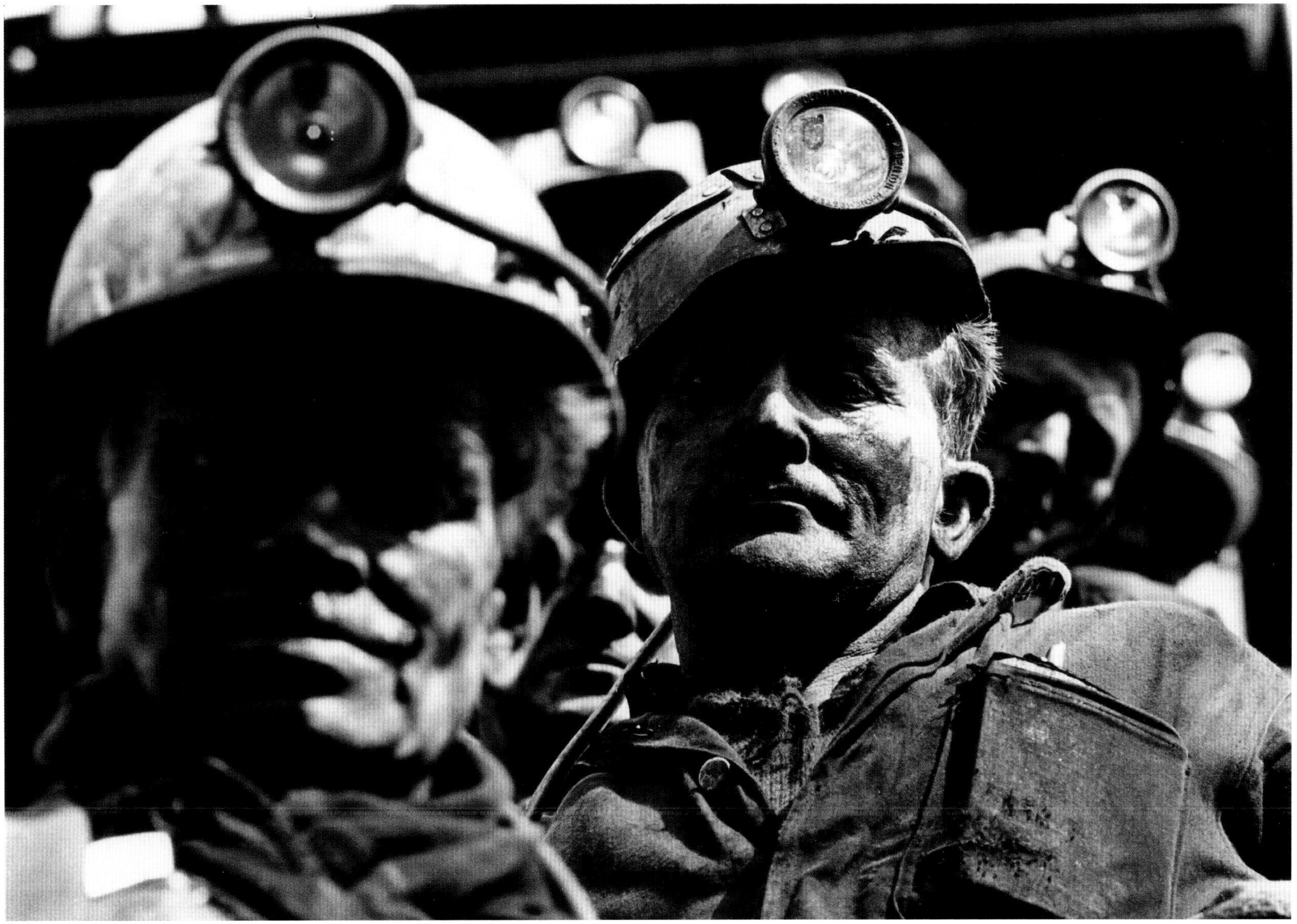

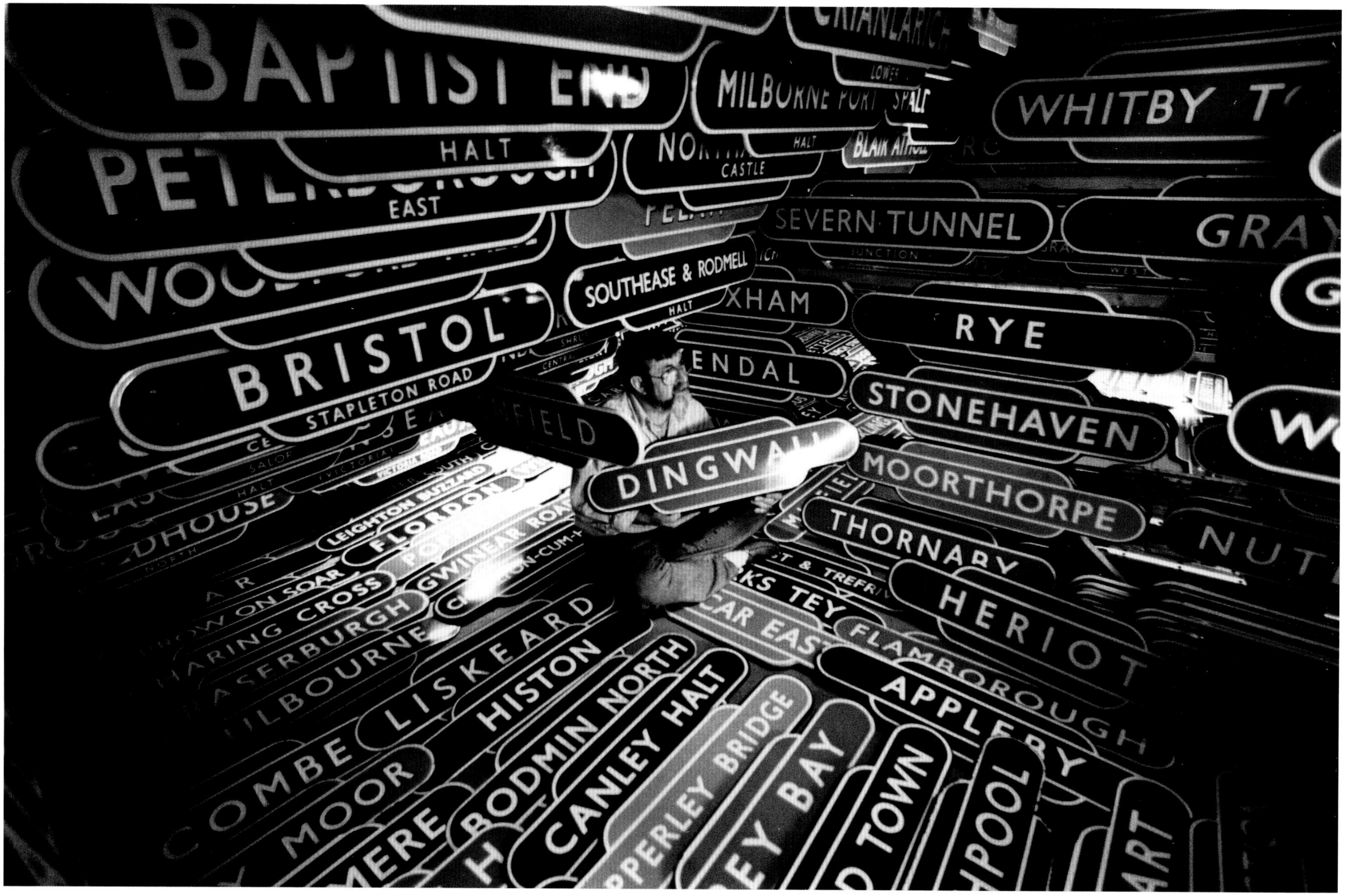

Where Are We?

The Guardian, 1993

For some passionate collectors there is simply no such thing as enough. Ian Faulkner knew no bounds in his love for these small station signs, known as totems. The attic of his home in South Norwood, London was crammed with the bulk of his enormous collection of more than 2,000 of the things but there were always more to find.
He was well aware that a challenging total of 2,857 stations in the UK were issued with them. Small stations had two or maybe four but grand ones like Waterloo or King's Cross had eighty or ninety displayed across their concourses and buildings. Each region had its own totem colour – Southern was green, Eastern was blue, Scottish was light blue, Western was brown. All were represented in Ian's vast collection. They were everywhere in his attic: on the floor, the ceiling, on every beam. He also had backup. There were 900 spares, all ready for swaps, in a shed in the garden.

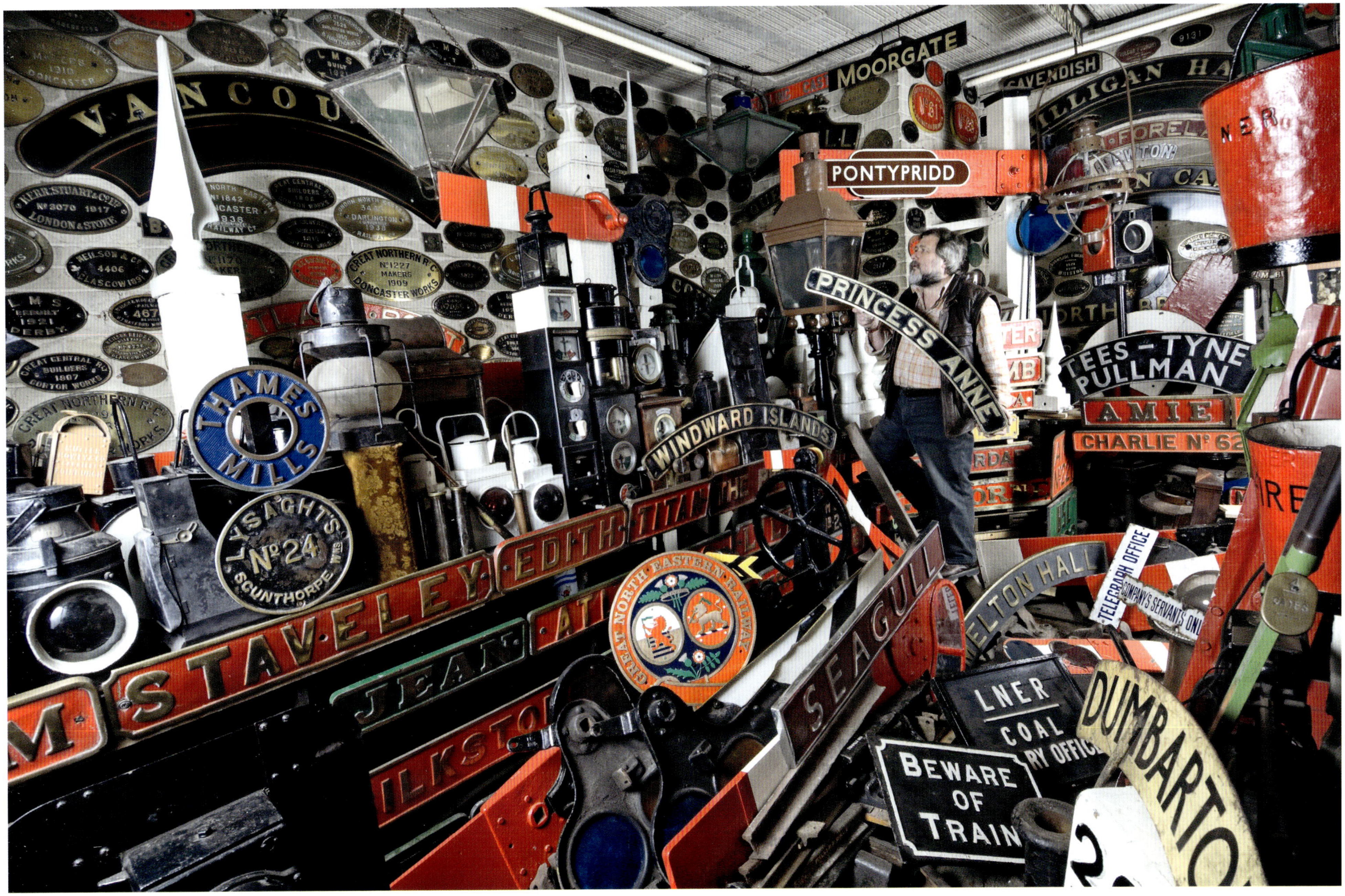

Schoolboy Treasures

The Guardian, 2009

Pupils and teachers at Doncaster Grammar School started a railway society in the 1930s and began collecting everything from lamps and buckets to whole bits of old locomotives. They housed their treasures in the school's water tower and it grew and it grew and it grew.

By the 1970s, the schoolboys had lost interest in old trains and the school society was disbanded, but the old tower with its narrow spiral staircase was so already crammed with artefacts it was almost impossible to turn round.

When I went to try to photograph it, my lighting had to be tied on to the exhibits themselves and the curator Peter Sargieson had to move a dozen exhibits just to give himself room to stand (uncomfortably) holding the locomotive nameplate, Princess Anne, for me. There were other nameplates, builders' works-plates, cast brass numbers from steam engines, express titles, station totems, lamps, signals trespass warnings, rail chairs, fire buckets, finials, crests and more everywhere you looked.

Doncaster got a purpose-built Rail Heritage Centre in 2012 and the whole collection is housed there now. I was glad to have seen it in all its chaotic glory in the water tower.

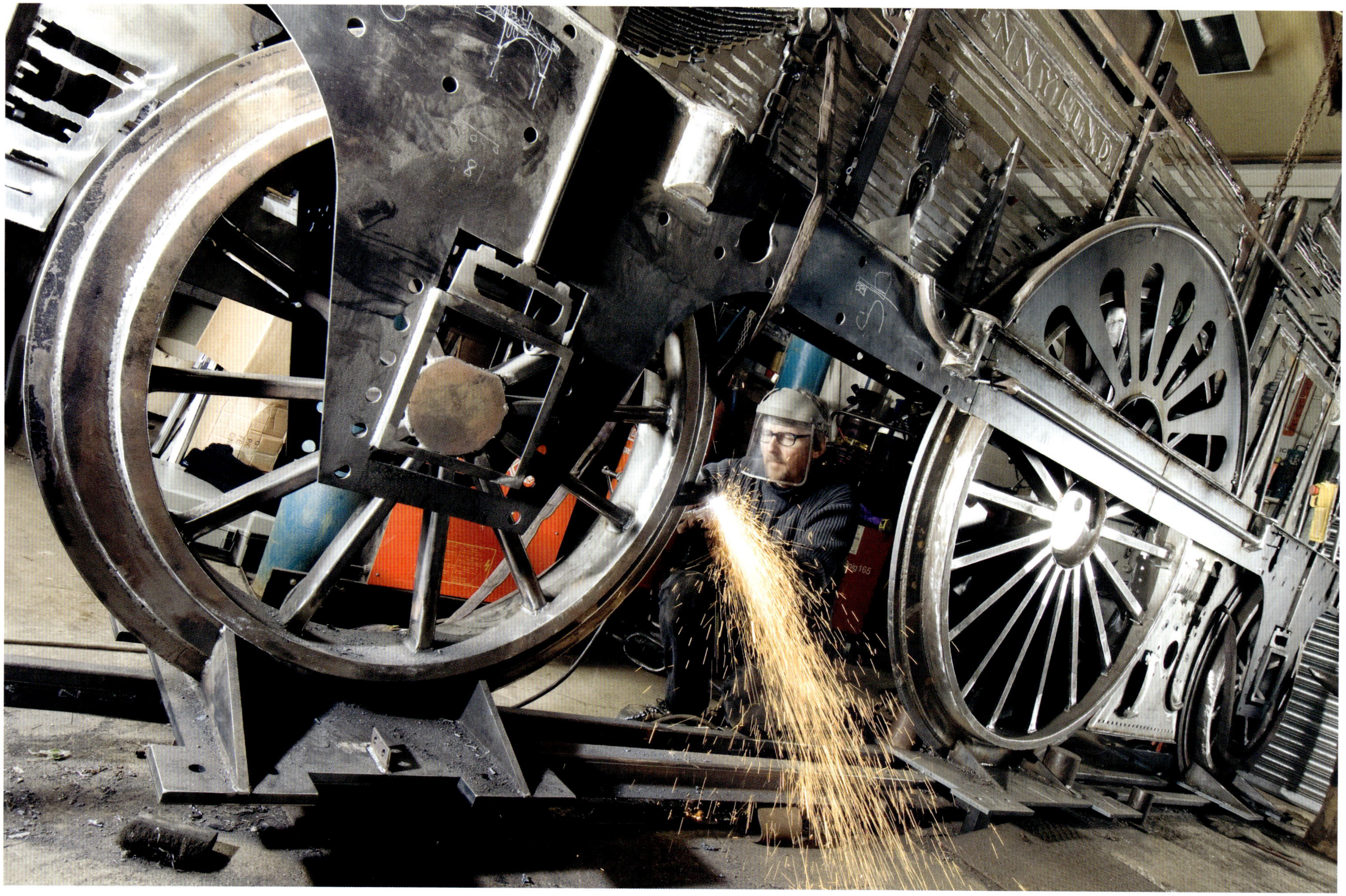

Welding a Ghost

The Guardian, 2014

Sculptor Jon Mills was commissioned to make an artwork to stand high on an old railway bridge in Brighton. I went to see him welding the driving wheels of his Ghost Train – a delicate full size etching-like replica of the silhouette of an 1847 engine called 'Jenny Lind'.
The original 'Jenny', named after a famous opera singer, became the most popular engine used on the line and her 'ghost' can now be seen on the bridge where the London, Brighton and South Coast Railway used to run.

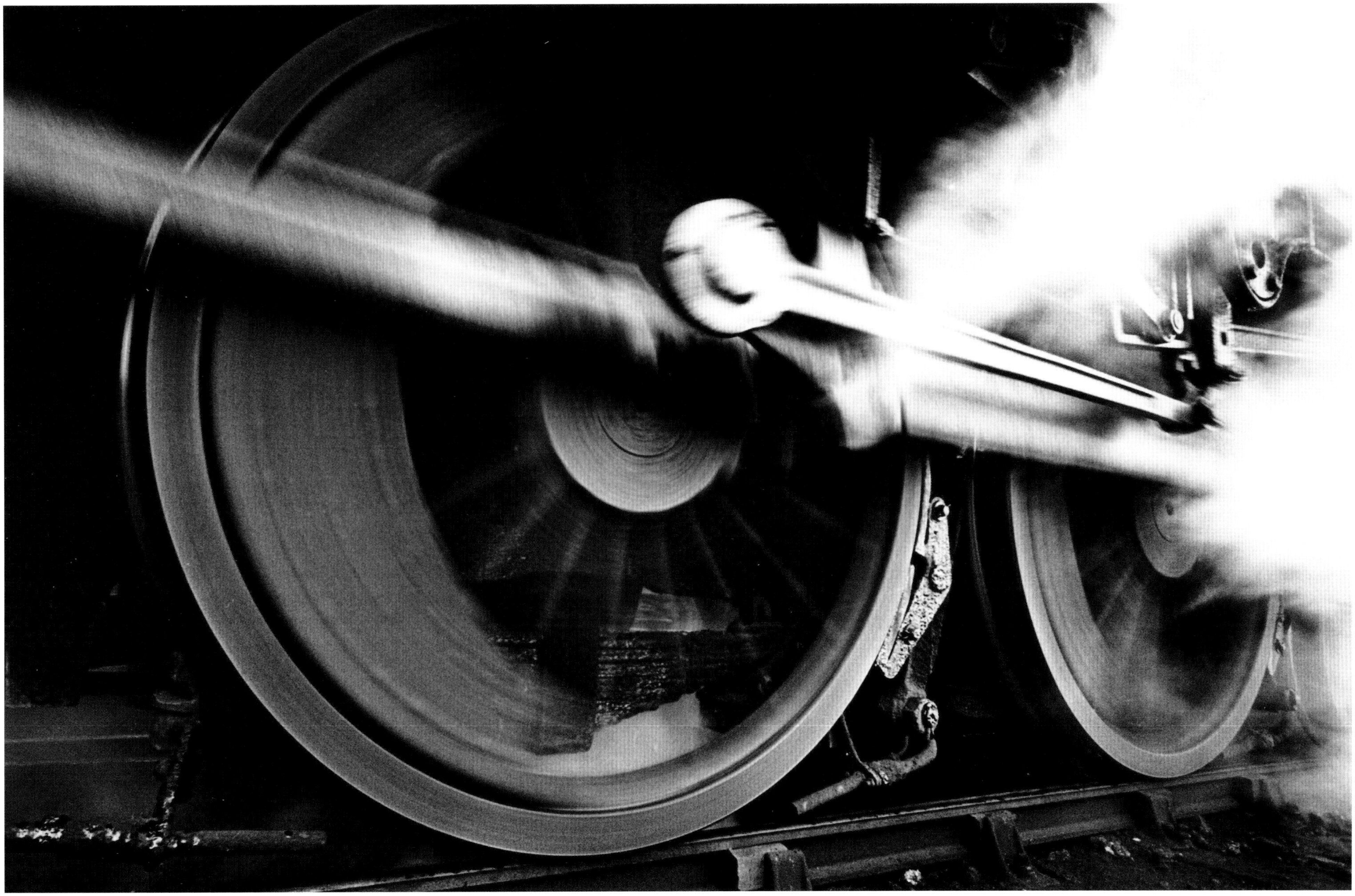

Going Nowhere

The Illustrated London News, 1968

The driving wheels of steam locomotives often slipped on wet or greasy rails when hauling heavy trains. I wanted to get this effect when I was trying to document the last days of steam, so I persuaded the footplate crew of this freight locomotive to grease the rails on a length of track at Carnforth engine shed and open the regulator. The 90-ton steam engine just stood there with its wheels racing and slipping on the spot. The smoke from the huge engine labouring in vain obliterated the sun from the best part of the town while I worked and the driver and his fireman went off for a cup of tea.

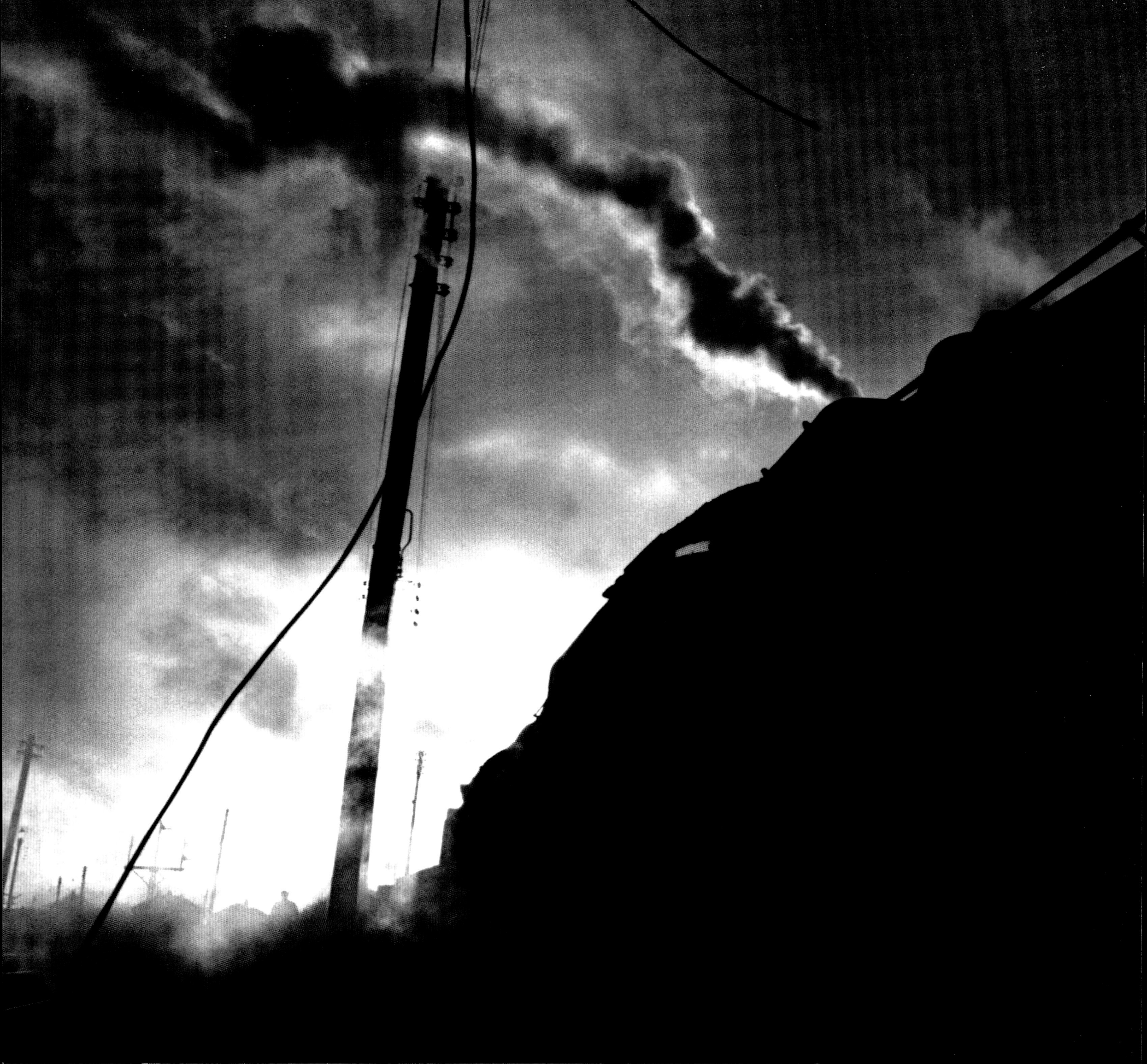

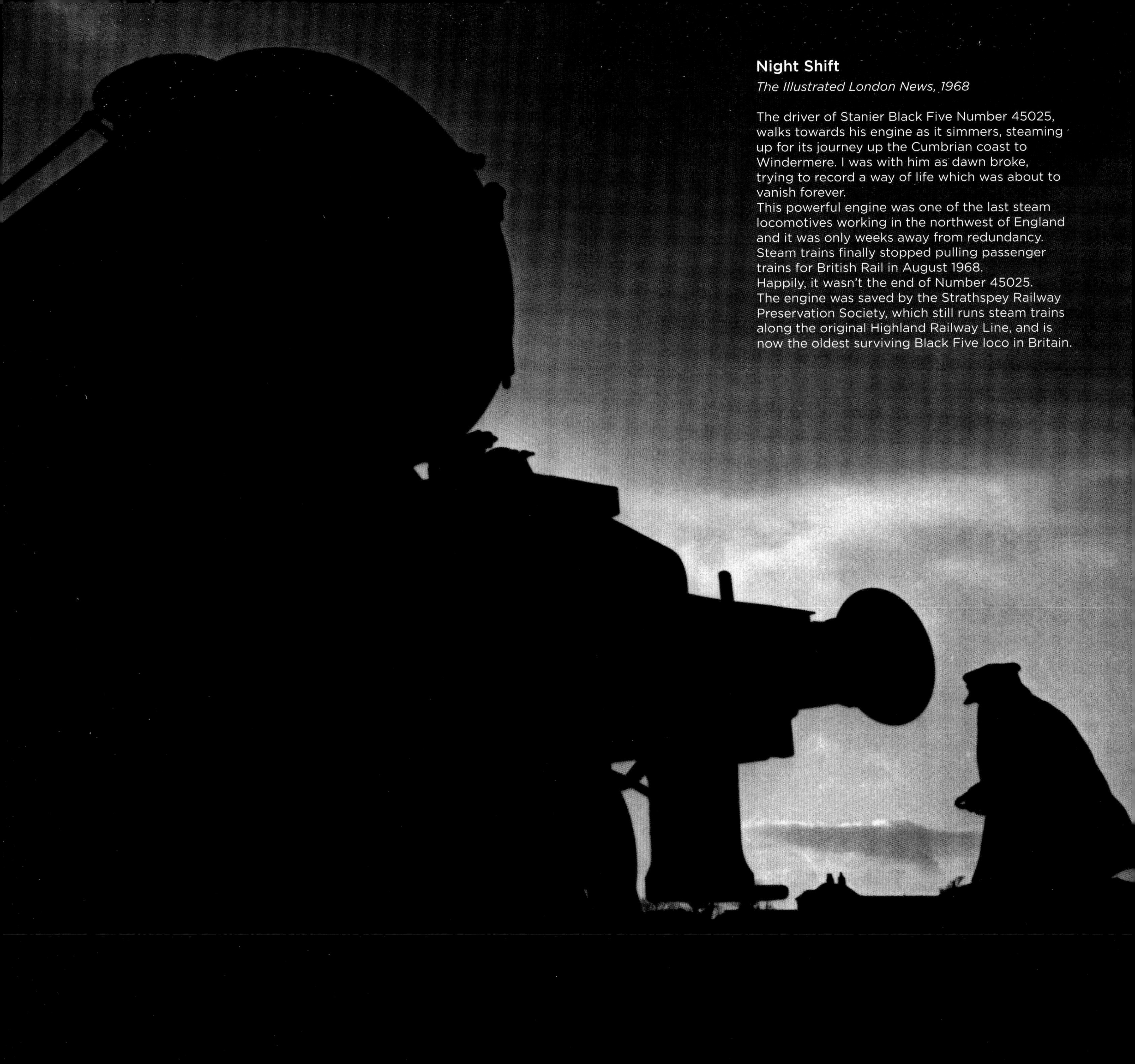

Night Shift

The Illustrated London News, 1968

The driver of Stanier Black Five Number 45025, walks towards his engine as it simmers, steaming up for its journey up the Cumbrian coast to Windermere. I was with him as dawn broke, trying to record a way of life which was about to vanish forever.
This powerful engine was one of the last steam locomotives working in the northwest of England and it was only weeks away from redundancy. Steam trains finally stopped pulling passenger trains for British Rail in August 1968.
Happily, it wasn't the end of Number 45025. The engine was saved by the Strathspey Railway Preservation Society, which still runs steam trains along the original Highland Railway Line, and is now the oldest surviving Black Five loco in Britain.

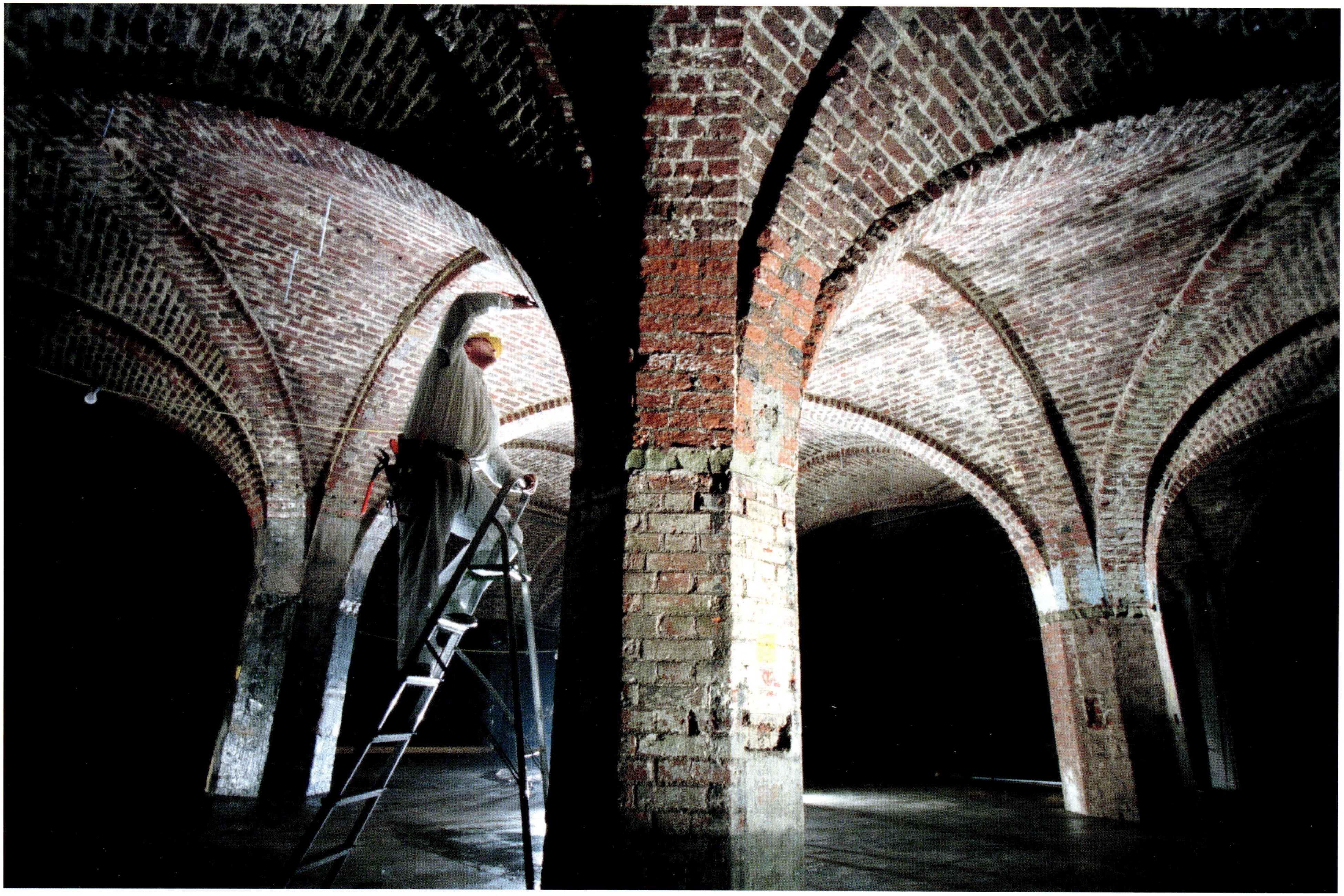

Underneath the Arches

The Guardian, 1998

For decades this huge space under the promenade at Brighton was a dull series of storage rooms. When work began on refurbishing it for use as a café bar, it was stripped out and I got a call – 'come and see this beautiful brickwork'. Behind false walls and low ceilings were glorious arches, wonderful ornate Victorian brickwork, gothic pillars and all. Electrician Mark Earnshaw was busy fitting plugs and power points and his working lights provided perfect illumination.

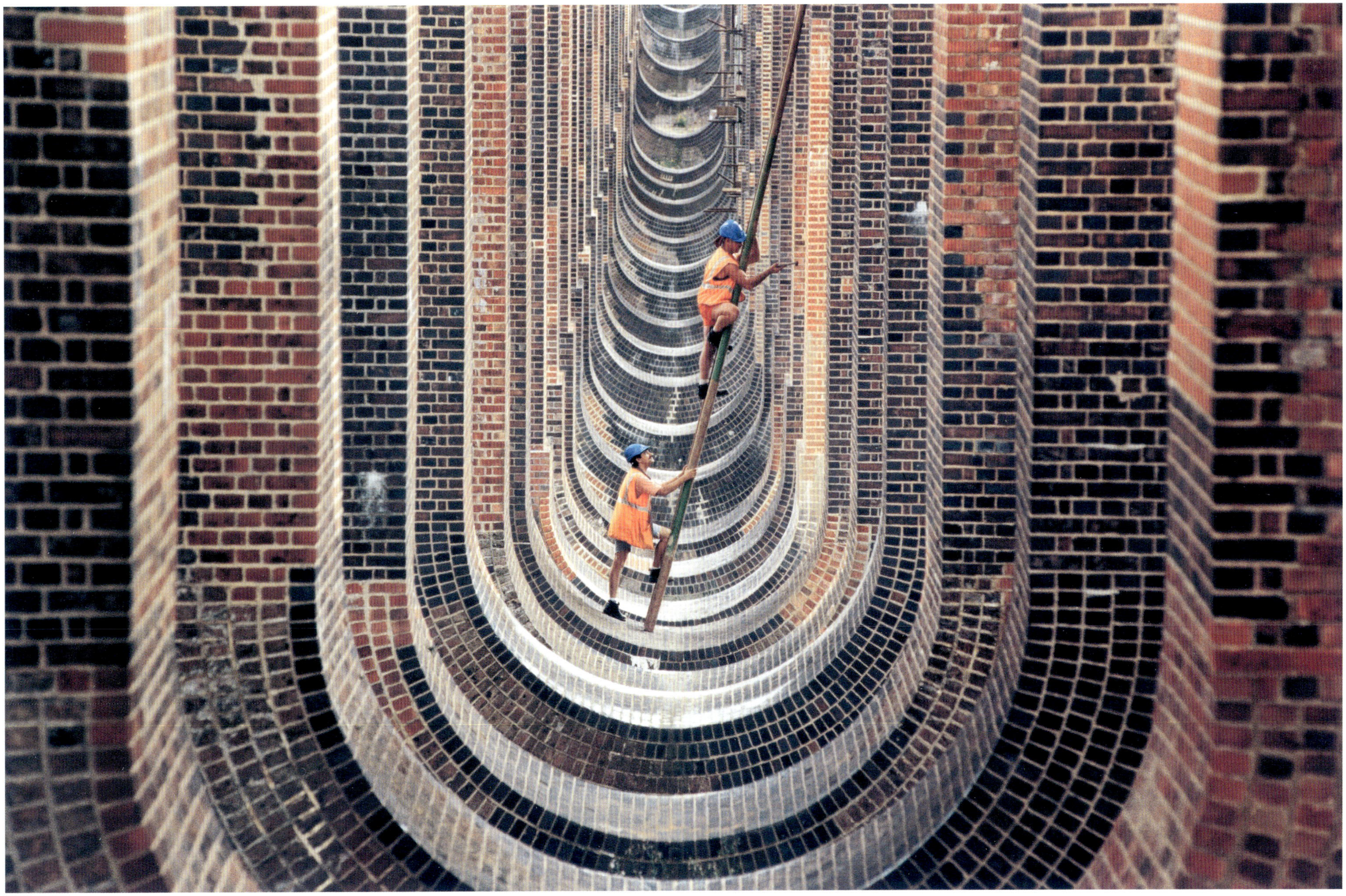

Another Brick in the Wall

The Guardian, 1998

Bricklayers John and Wayne had the mammoth job of re-pointing patches of wear and tear round the 11 million bricks in the thirty-seven arches of the Ouse Valley Viaduct at Balcombe, near Haywards Heath. They seemed to welcome the break when I focused on them halfway through the work. I've always admired this extraordinary structure, designed by John Rastrick and built in 1841 to carry the London-Brighton and South Coast Railway line across a deep valley between Brighton and London. I doubt if many of the hundreds of thousands of commuters who travel over it daily realise that their train is going over such a beautiful example of industrial architecture.

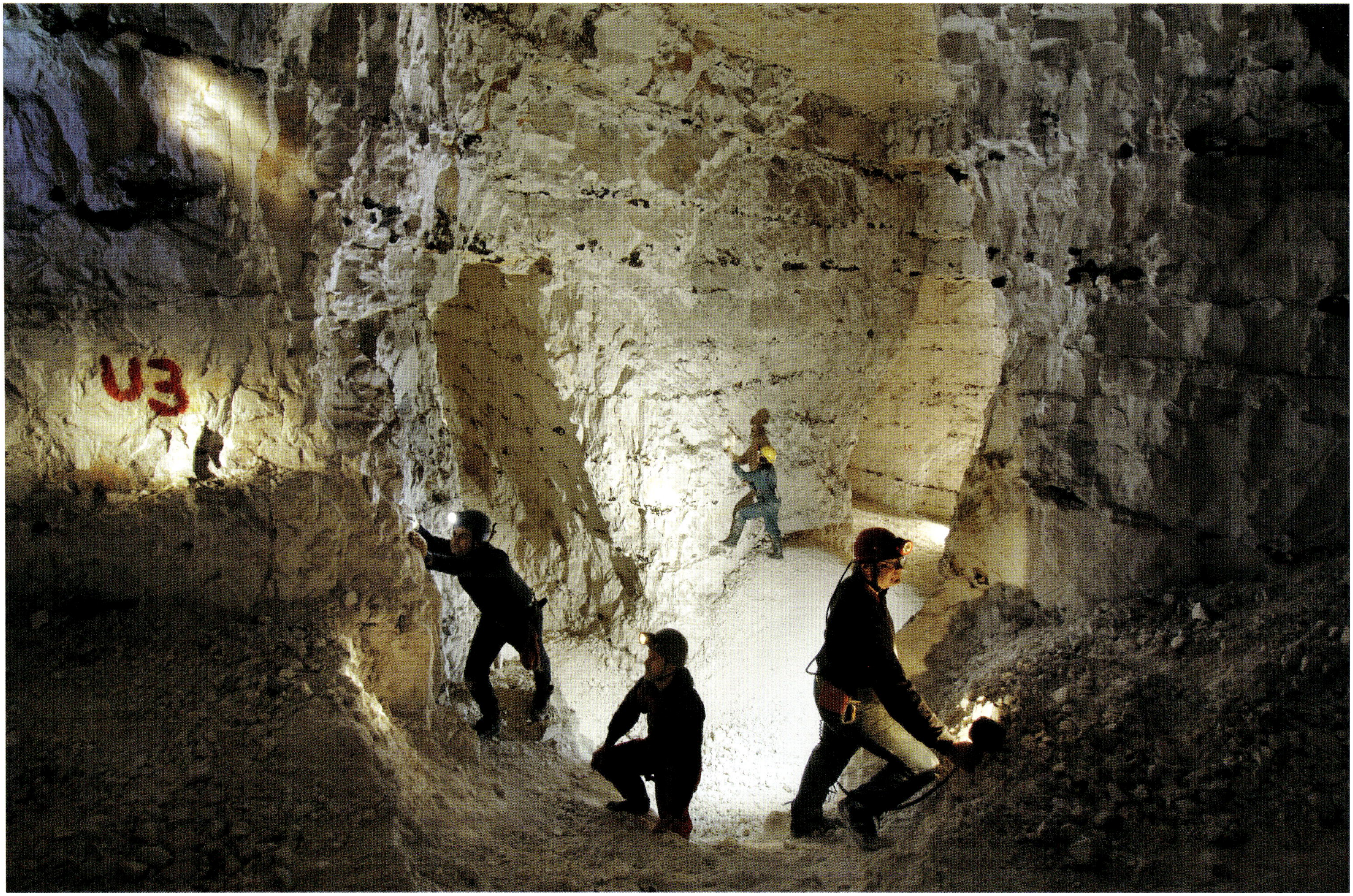

Undermining

The Guardian, 2007

Under Reading, Berkshire lies a warren of eighteenth- and nineteenth-century chalk mines, all of them gently deteriorating. I'd seen on the news that a house in the town had been destroyed when an abandoned mine suddenly collapsed, and I wanted to see what was down there.

A caving society agreed to take me to Emmer Green South Mine under a housing development in the north of the town. Access was via an old ventilation shaft and down a 50-ft ladder, slimy with wet chalk. Below was an enormous chalk mine being explored and mapped by the cavers. They had already mapped thirty mines like this with miles of linking passages, many of them crumbling away beneath modern homes.

While we were down there it rained. Getting down was precarious but climbing back up an even wetter and more slippery ladder with all my gear was something I never want to repeat.

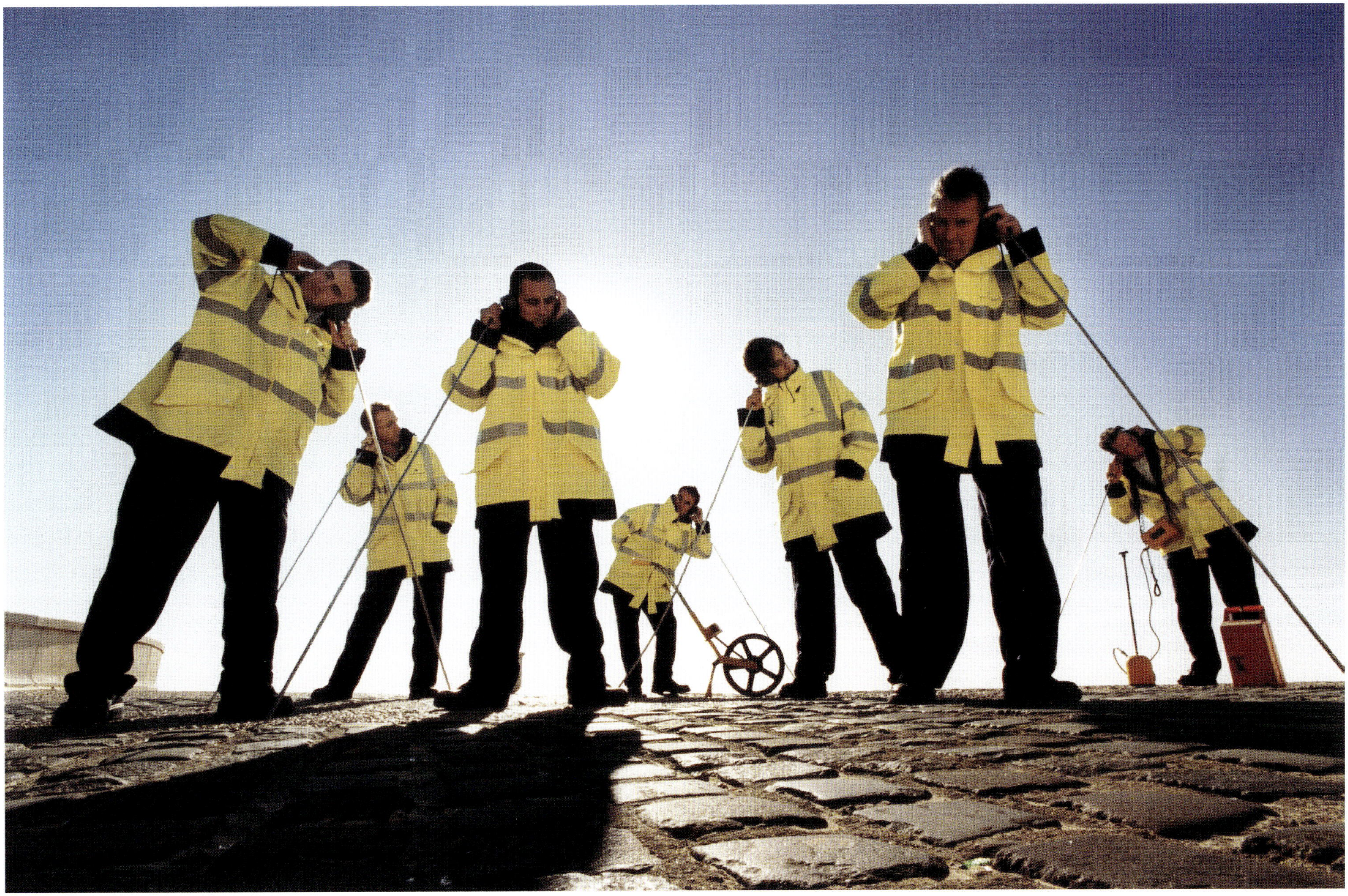

Leakbusters

The Guardian, 2005

Water companies have masses of high-tech equipment to help them in the battle against leaks but many leak detection crews still carry listening sticks – lengths of thin metal piping with a wooden ear cone on one end – alongside their acoustic sensors and tiny pipe-checking cameras. Sometimes a pair of ears and a listening stick is the fastest way to check for a leak at close range. Here, seven Southern Water board inspectors were on a listening stick training course, pressing the cups to their ears as they tried to isolate a leak somewhere in the maze of water supplies below them.

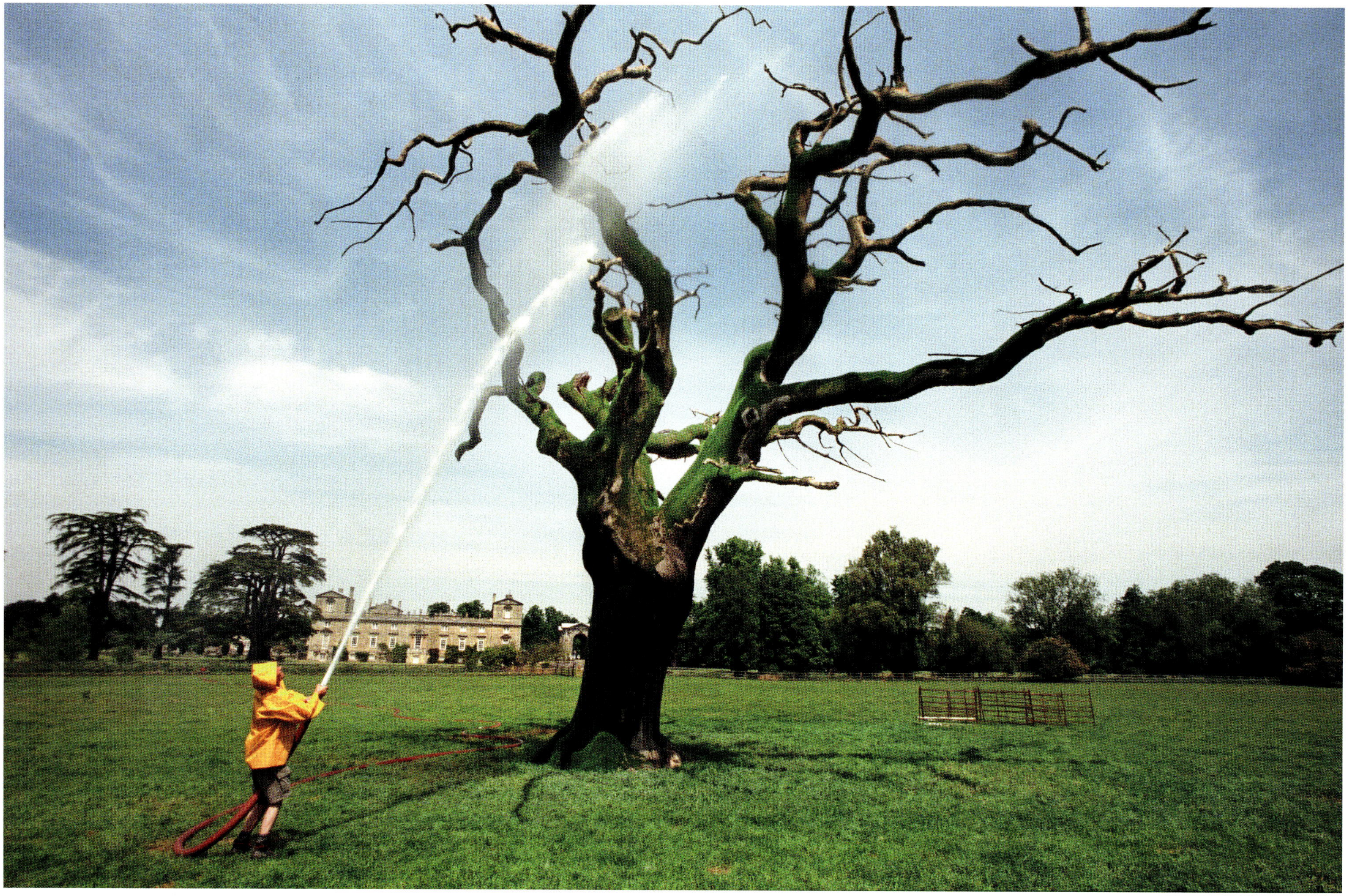

Branching Out

The Guardian, 2009

This is not a fireman, it's an artist at work. Dan Harvey was watering his 'Blasted Oak', a dead oak tree in the grounds of Wilton house near Salisbury, Wiltshire that he had transformed by covering it in yoghurt and sprinkling it with grass seed to turn it green and hairy. After that it just needed to be kept damp enough to keep the grass green.

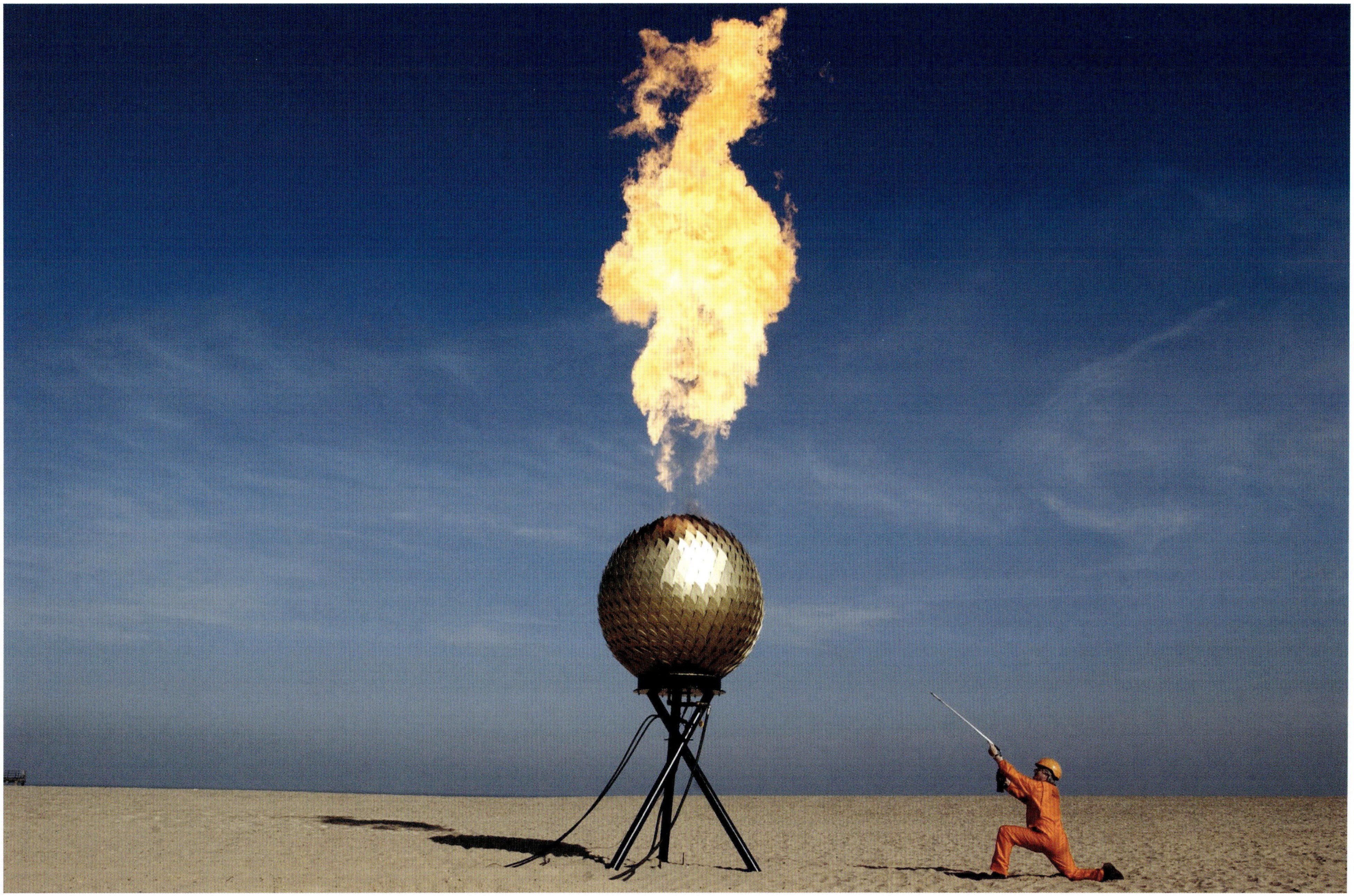

Light my Fire

The Guardian, 1995

Pageant master Bruno Peek rehearses lighting the first of the Queen's Diamond Jubilee Beacons on the sandy beach at Great Yarmouth, Norfolk, in preparation for the lighting of 1,589 beacons throughout the Commonwealth. The test was a big success, except that the fierce 30-ft-high flame singed off his eyebrows.

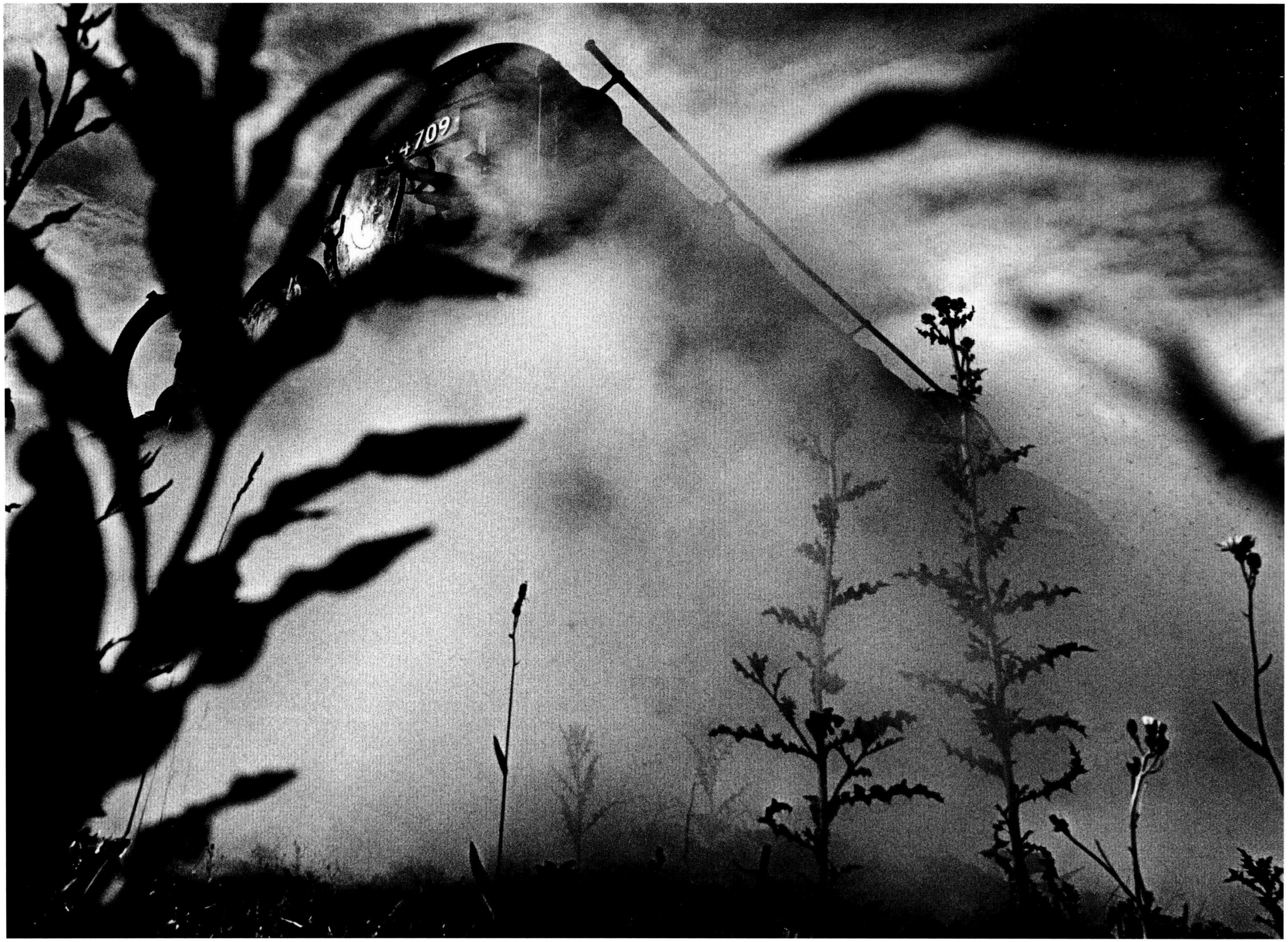

Heading for the Scrapheap

The Illustrated London News, 1968

One of the last steam locomotives operating on British Railways, before they were all finally taken out of service in August 1968, was rumbling through a gloomy trackbed full of weeds, thistles and dandelions. This grimy workhorse was one of only a couple of hundred left at the very end, although less than a decade earlier there had been more than 20,000 steam engines serving the rail network. The picture was taken in Carnforth, Lancashire, where there is now a restoration centre for the few preserved steam locomotives which escaped the scrapyards.

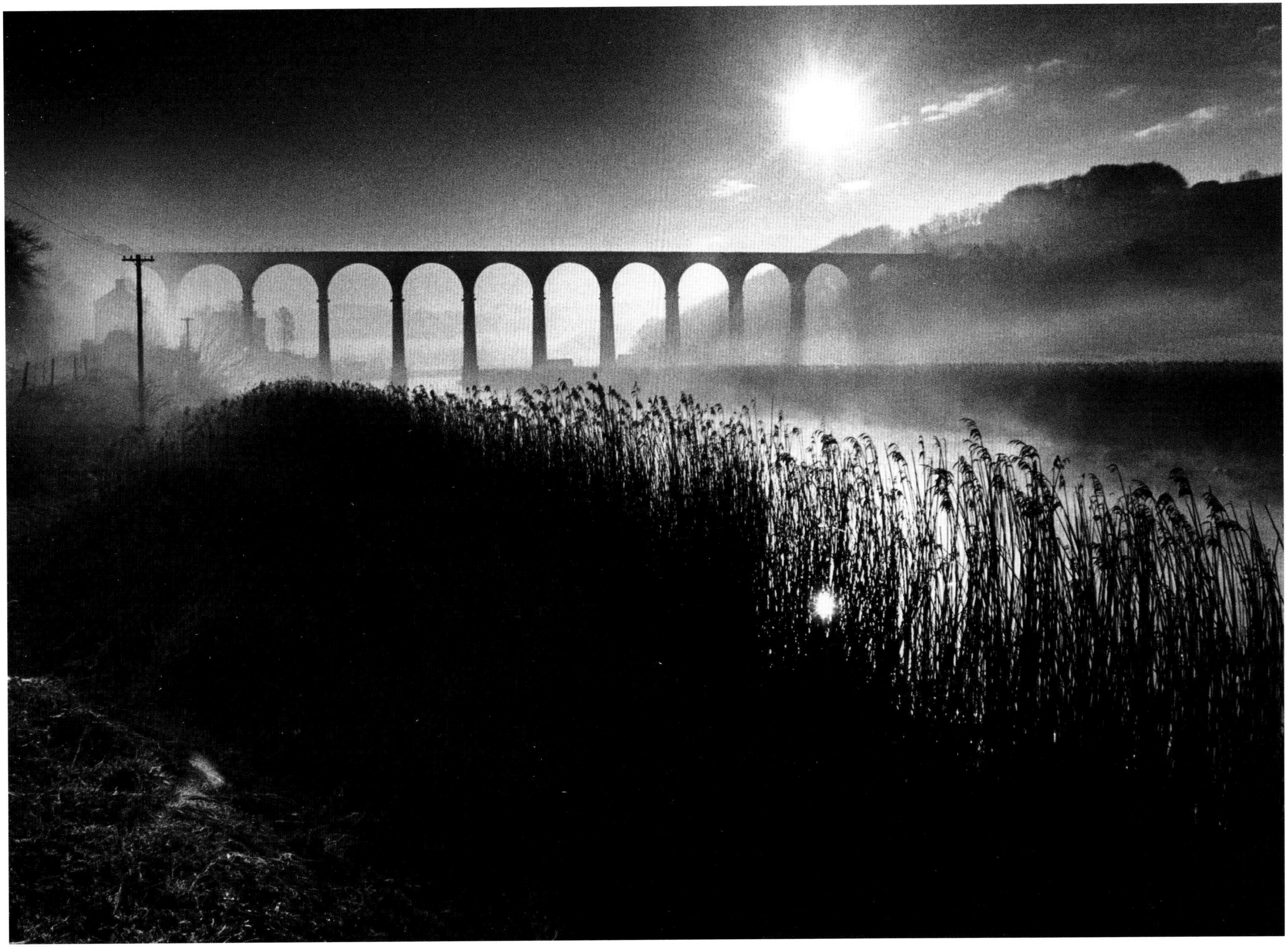

Calstock Viaduct

The Sun, 1977

The scene is beautiful but this was a sad job. I was illustrating a feature about the slow decline of the rail service in the West Country. The lovely twelve-arch Calstock Viaduct was carrying an ever-dwindling number of trains over the River Tamar between Devon and Cornwall, so I took a nostalgic picture at 6am, with the mist still lying on the river.

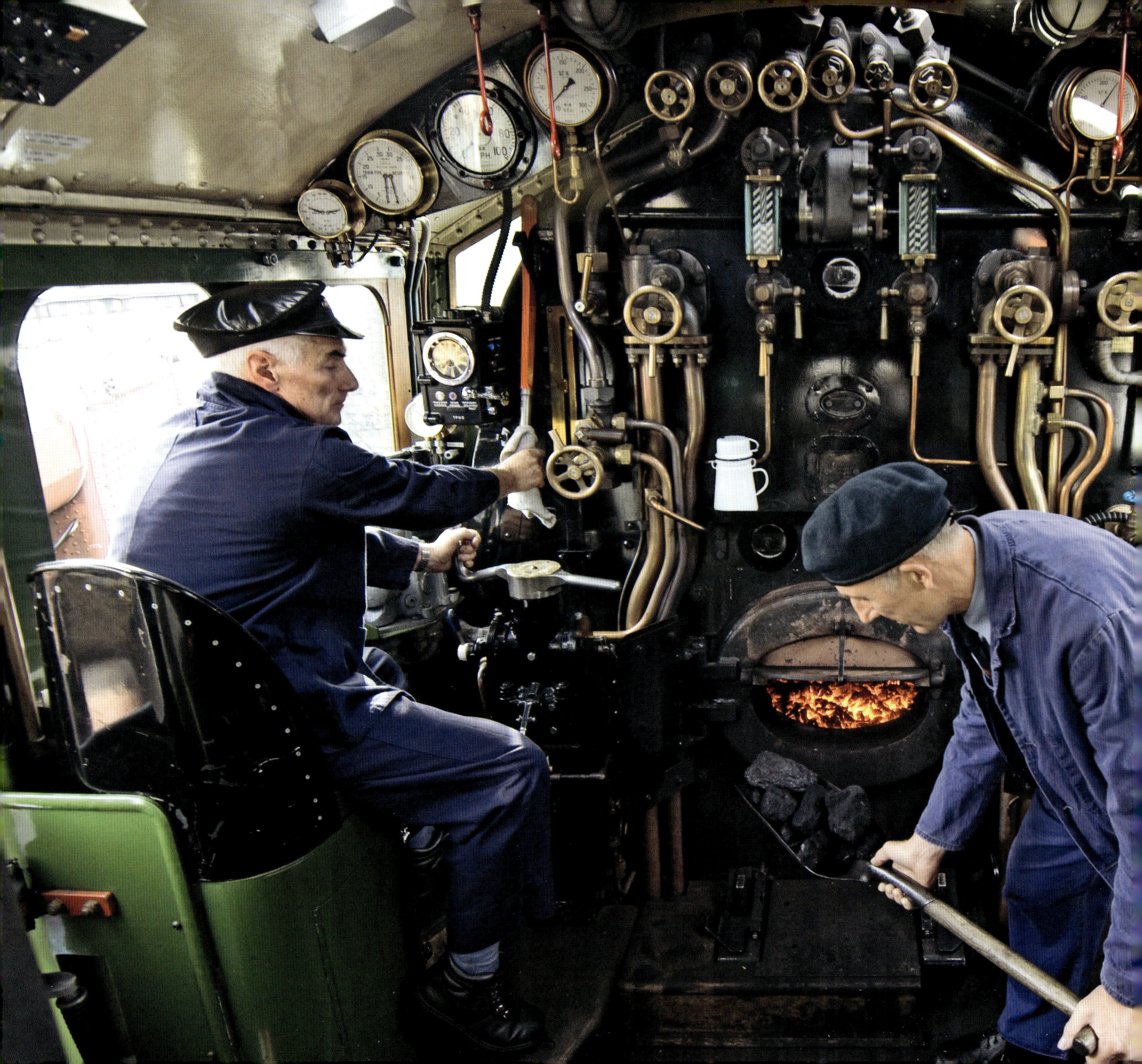

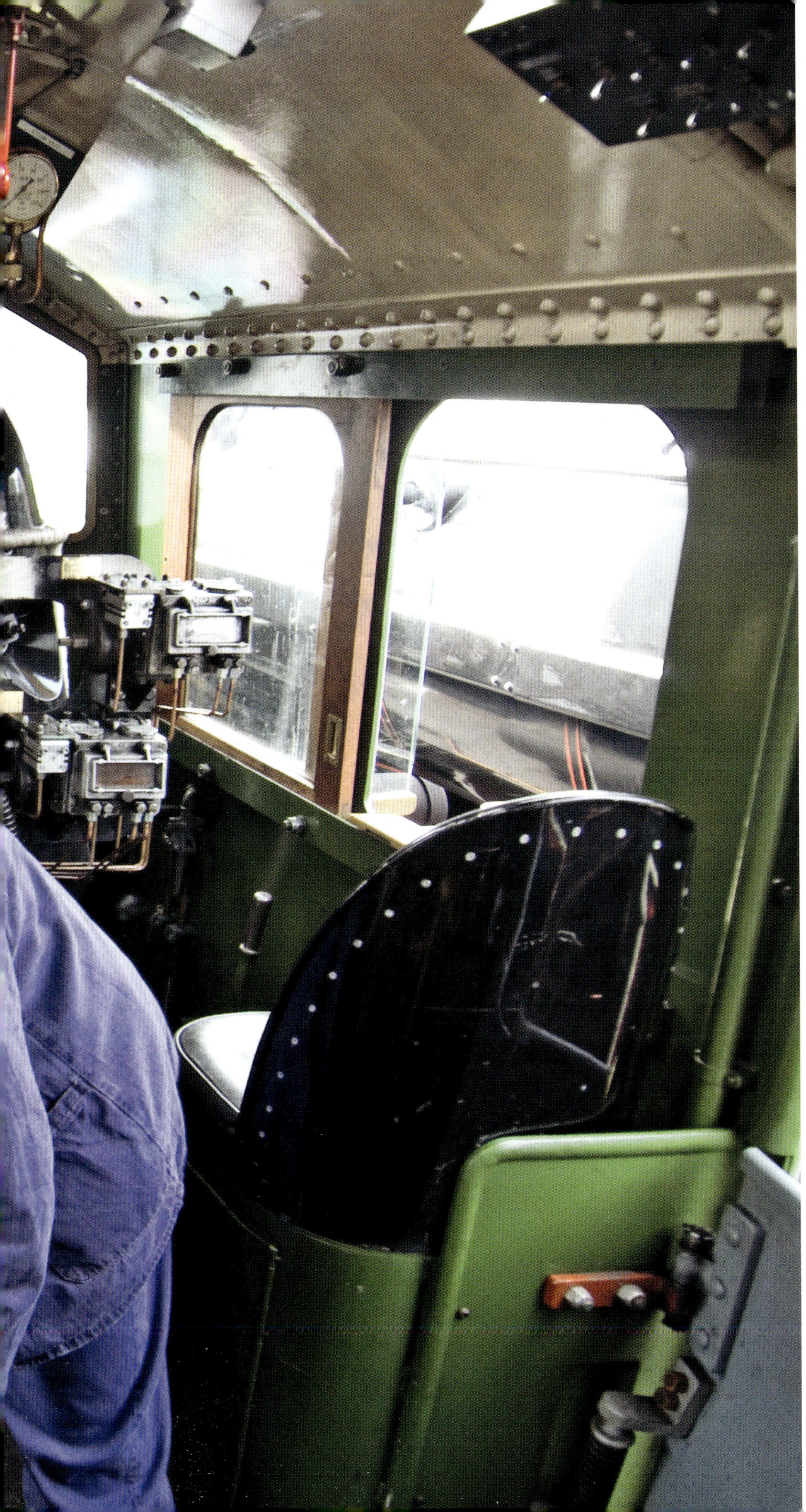

Full Steam Ahead

The Guardian and many other papers, 2008

This was the cab of Tornado (No 60163 A1 class Pacific 4-6-2 to its many fans) a brand-new mainline steam locomotive. It was the first to be built in Britain in fifty years, the culmination of eighteen years of fundraising which raised £3 million to reconstruct an original 1940s design by Arthur Peppercorn - but with the extra water capacity and latest railway safety electronics which qualified it to run on today's main line railways. Driver Cliff Perry and his fireman, Peter Buckley, were picking up speed for the inaugural steam test, speed and brake trials. It passed without a hitch and a few months later Tornado was passed as fully fit to let off steam and reached a speed of 100mph on mainline tracks, north of York.
This picture was widely used for features on the almost forgotten art of how to drive a loco, annotated with notes on everything from the regulator to the reverser, to the steam injector, right down to the drivers' mash can, seen here perched above the fire to keep their tea warm.

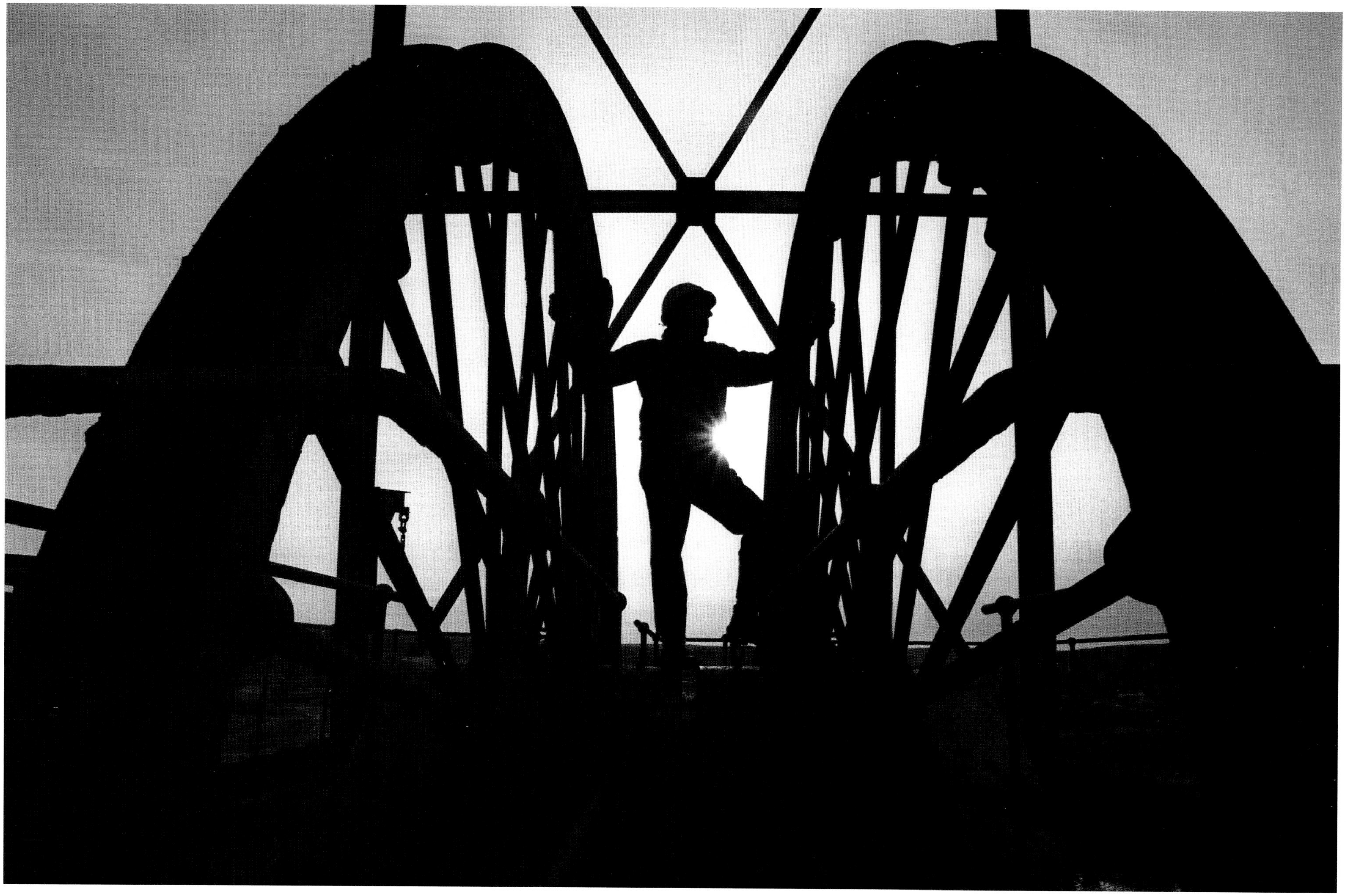

Last Tin Mine Pithead

The Guardian, 1994

South Crofty was the last surviving tin mine in Britain and fighting for survival when I visited it in 1994. The mine, just outside Camborne, Cornwall was more than 400 years old and the giant sheave wheels on the pithead already looked more like a nostalgic reminder of a quaint old industry than a going concern. The miners had just taken a voluntary pay cut to try to save their jobs but South Crofty seemed to be doomed. Four years later it did close. But there was huge local belief in it and support for it which never wavered and in 2022, with growing demand for tin for electronics and solar cells, drilling began again. The pithead gear is going to look very different but the old mine may have a future after all.

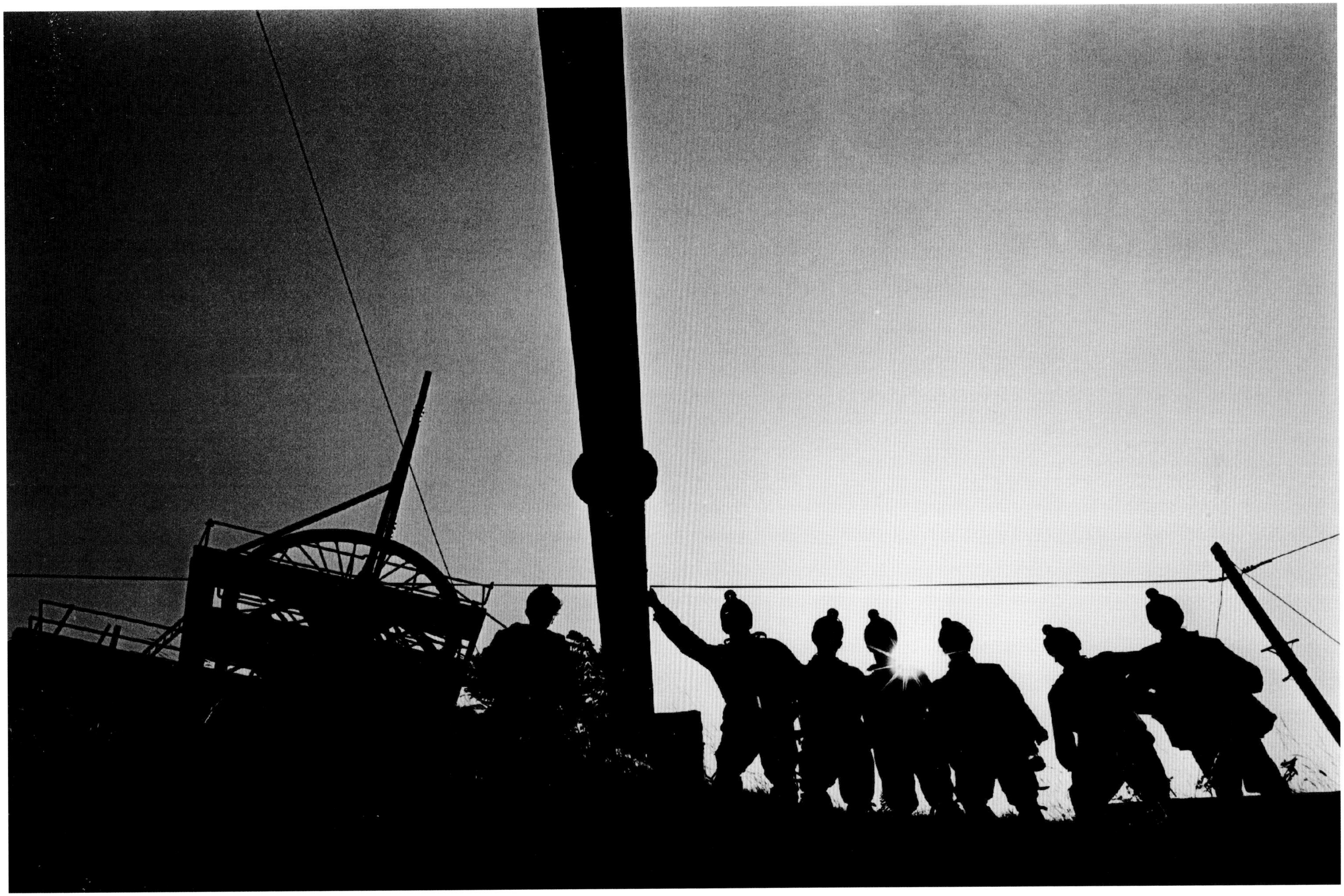

Dirty Work

The Sun, 1969

The Welsh valleys were facing a bleak future as the 1960s drew to an end. Once one of the world's most important coal-mining regions, cheap coal from abroad made them unprofitable. Pits were closing but not everyone was sad to see them go. Coal-mining was filthy, dangerous work and when this picture was taken, working pits like this one in Rhondda were still taking on fifteen-year-old boys to work long, dark, dangerous shifts underground alongside their fathers. In the 1950s and '60s almost half the miners in the area had some form of lung disease and pit disasters regularly caused death or serious injuries. The real tragedy was that there were no alternative jobs to be had in the area as the dirty work ended.

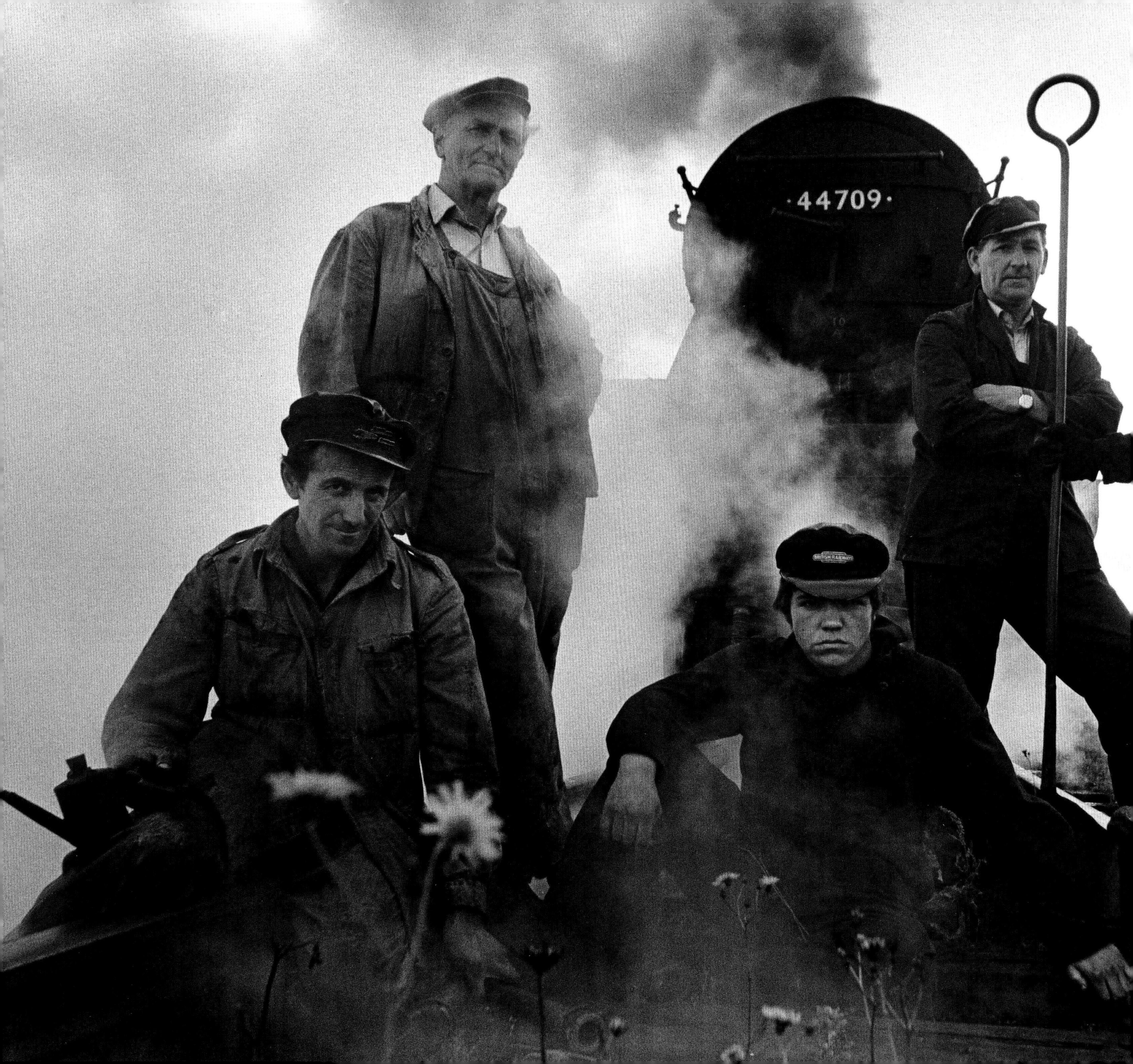
·44709·

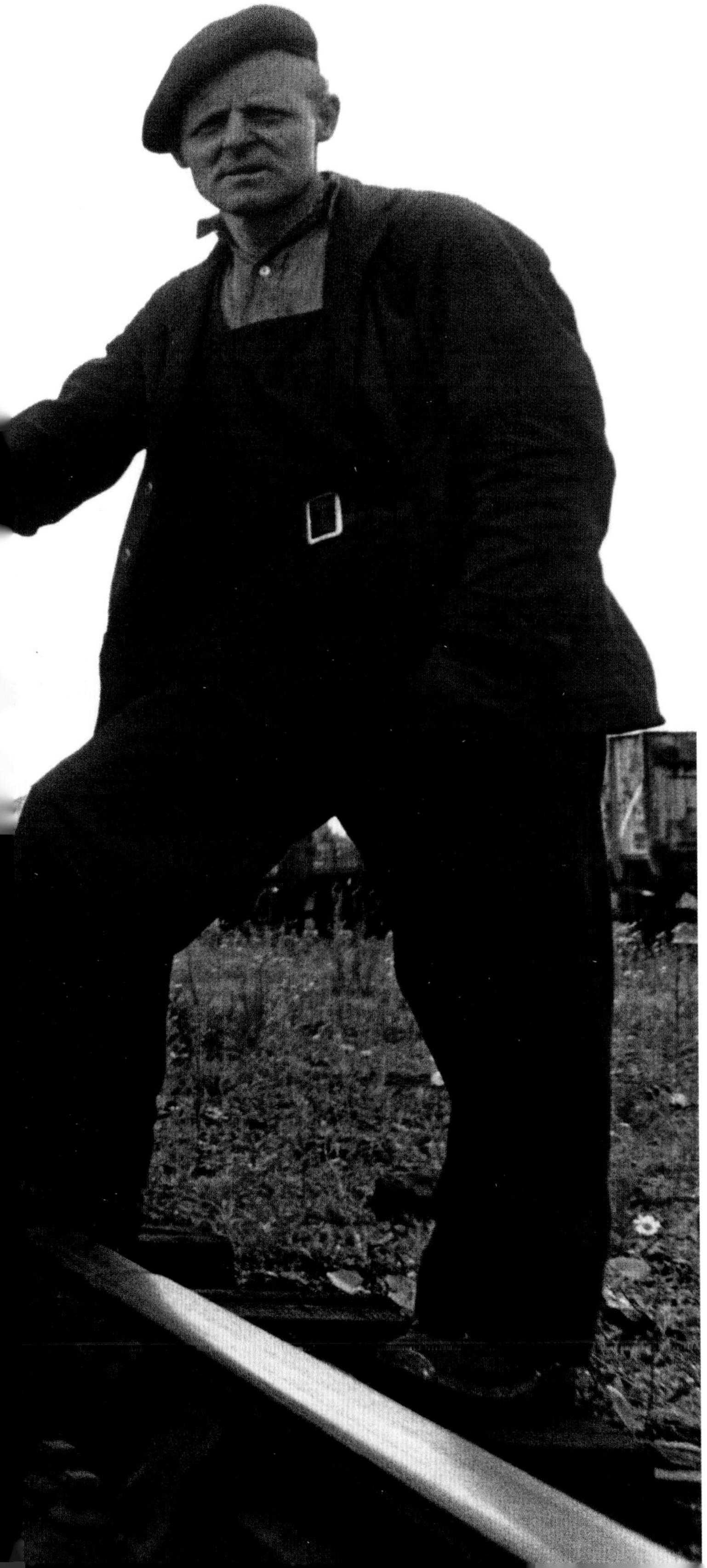

Running out of Steam

The Daily Mail and The Illustrated London News, 1968

A farewell portrait of five railwaymen whose jobs disappeared with the end of steam on British Railways on 17 August 1968. Boiler washer Norman Wilson, firedropper John Cottier, bar lad Tommy Longstaff, driver Joe Harrison and steamraiser Fred Scott pose with LMS Black Five No 44709 at Carnforth Locomotive shed, near Preston, Lancashire. The dandelions in the foreground are hand-held. This was my first award-winning picture. It got a gong for Commercial and Industrial Photographer of the Year in the British Press Awards.

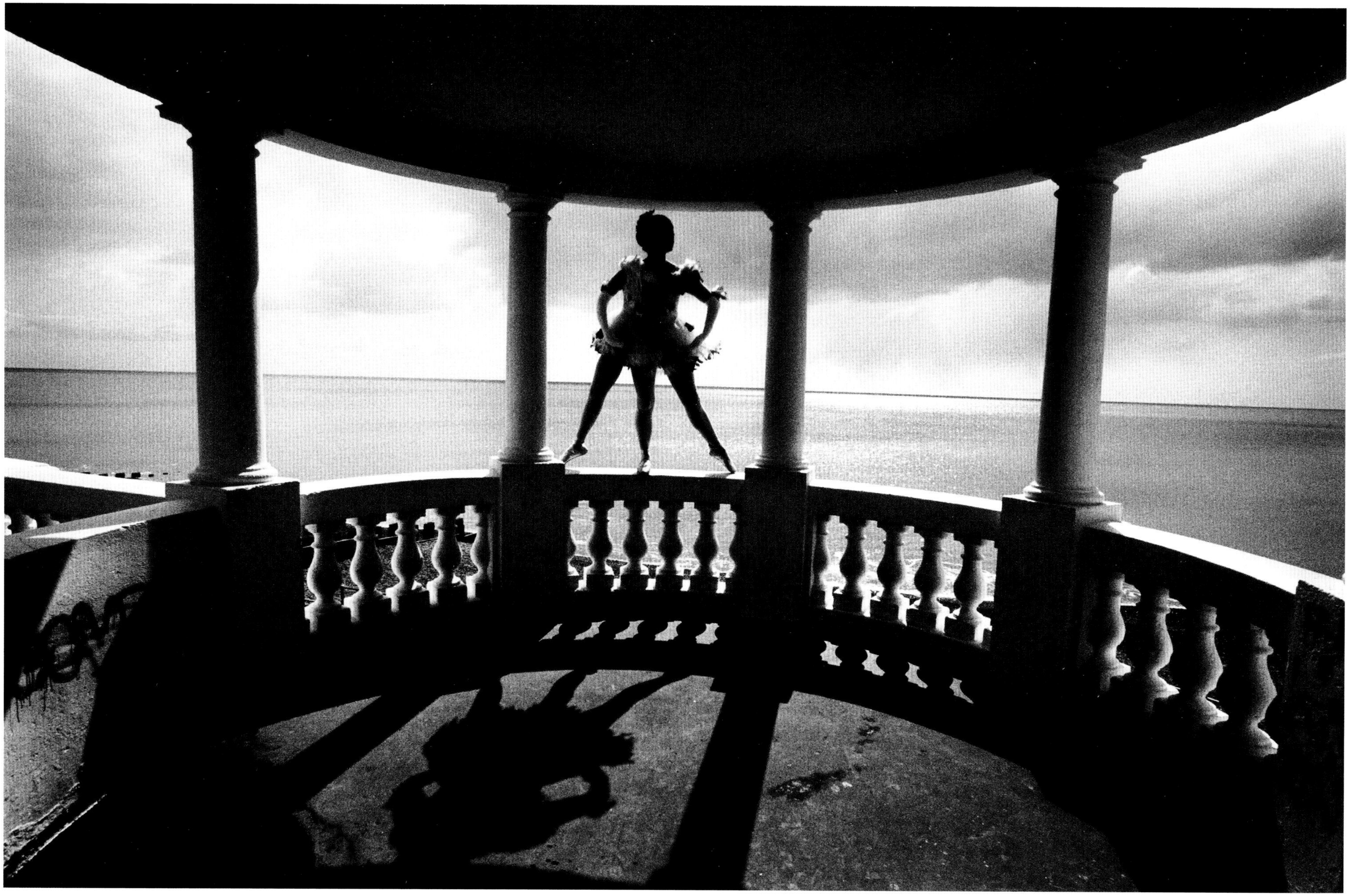

Dame Anna Peglova

The Guardian, 1996

I've been lucky to work with some wonderful people who seem to be able to change shape at will. Three-legged ballerina Dame Anna Peglova, alias dancer and actress Jane Bassett, was one. She displayed incredible sangfroid on the balustrade of the Colonnade by Bexhill's De La Warr Pavilion in a howling gale, balancing calmly on just one of her three legs as the wind buffeted her.

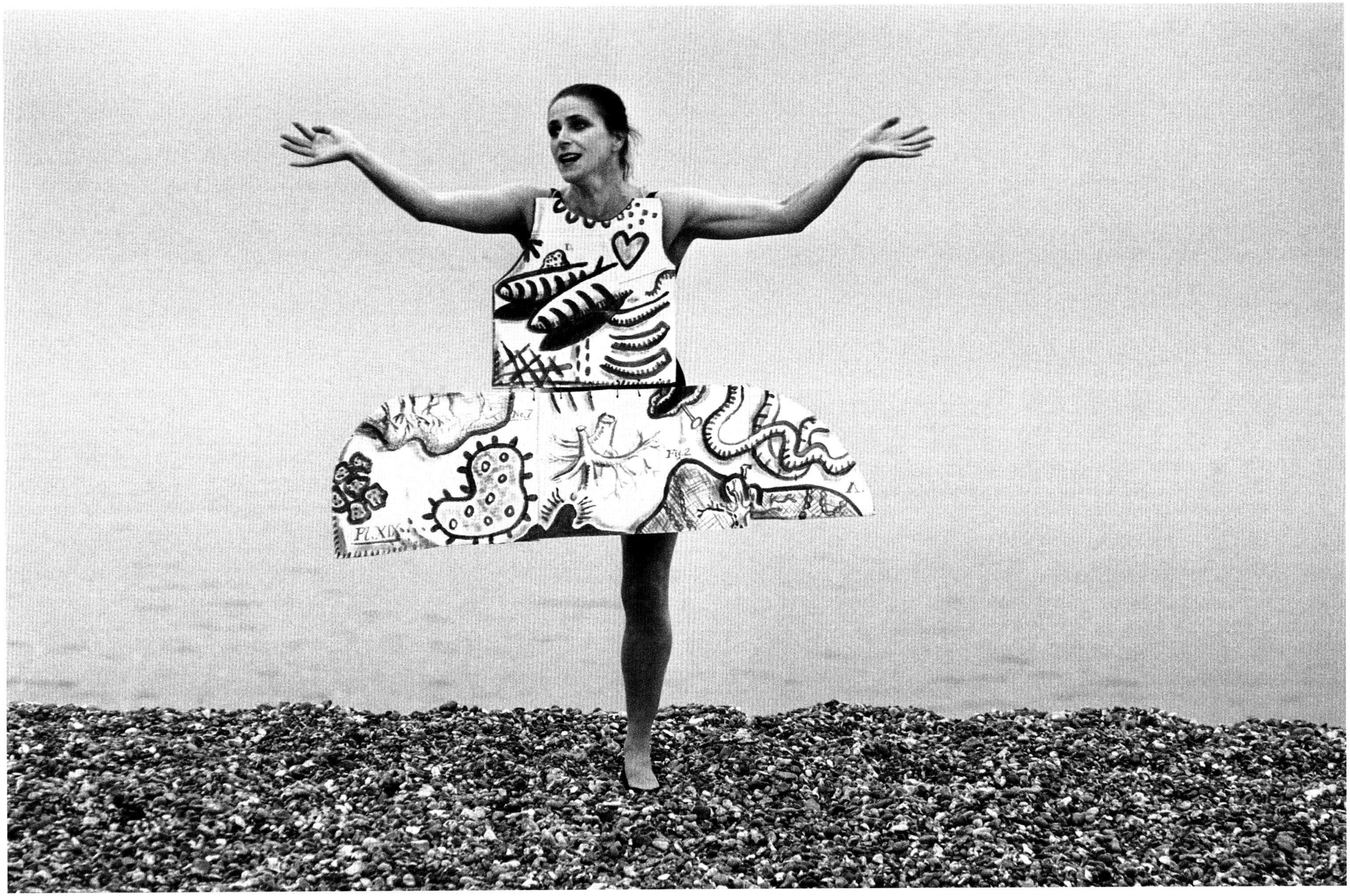

Flat Frock

The Guardian, 1993

Performance artist Liz Aggiss is the grand dame of anarchic dance and a surreal dream to photograph. For this picture on Brighton's pebble beach she wore her striking cardboard 'paper doll' dress with drawings of her heart, her breasts (as French bread sticks) her intestines and other bodily organs. Being a very talented and agile dancer, she tucked her right leg comfortably behind her skirt to become an unforgettable mono-legged, two-dimensional ballerina. She is now Emeritus Professor in Visual Performance at the University of Brighton.

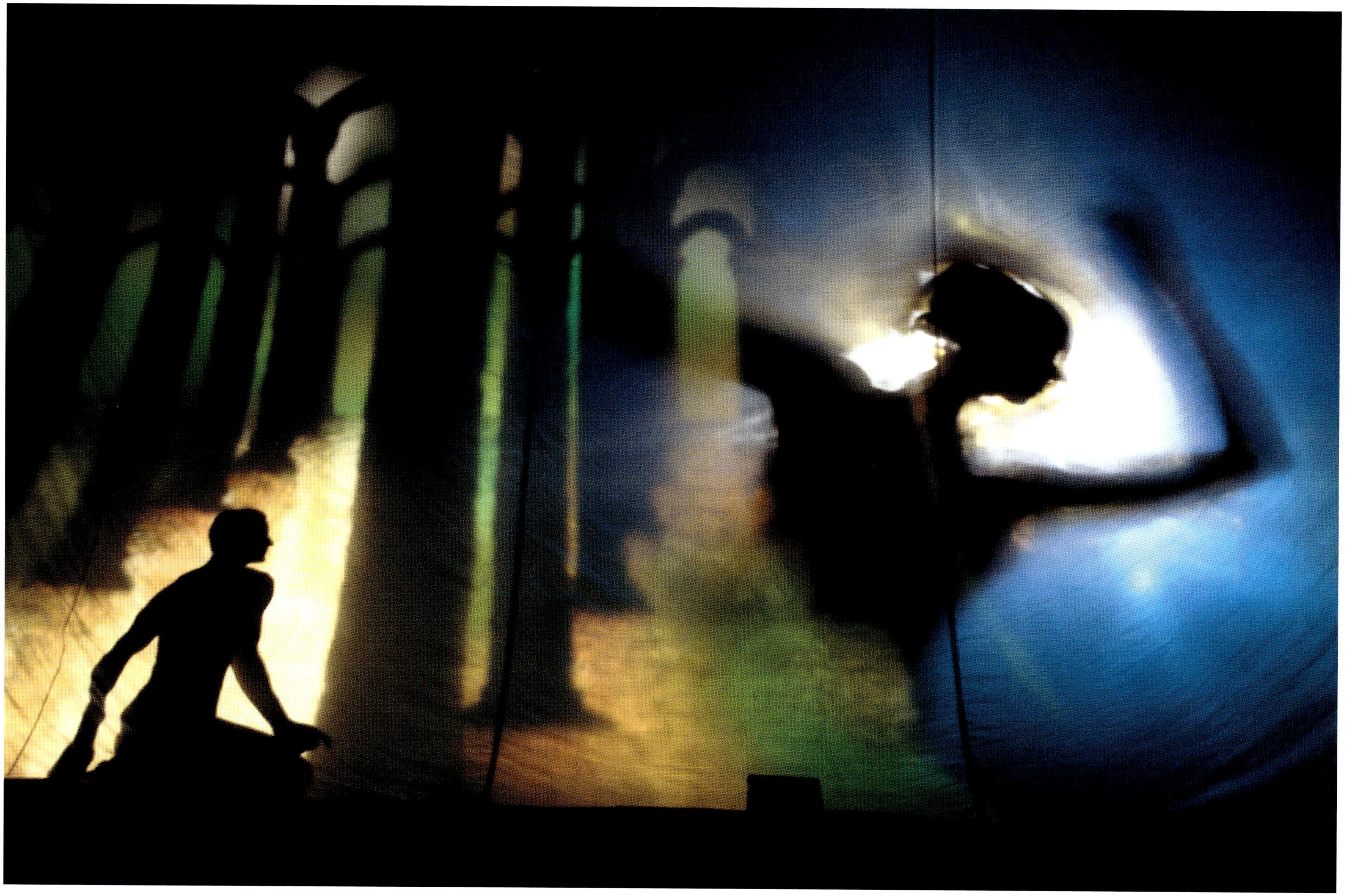

Shadows of our Former Selves

The Guardian, 2004

Actors Massimo Arbarello as Orpheus and Paola Bianchi as Eurydice, performing Canto a Orfeo, a passionate myth of Orpheus and the Underworld. They were projected as shadow figures on a screen of trees and skies. It was all very beautiful and very dark. I had to use a chair back as a tripod for a long exposure but the images were gorgeous.
It was part of the Visions Festival, at the Sallis Benney Theatre of the University of Brighton.

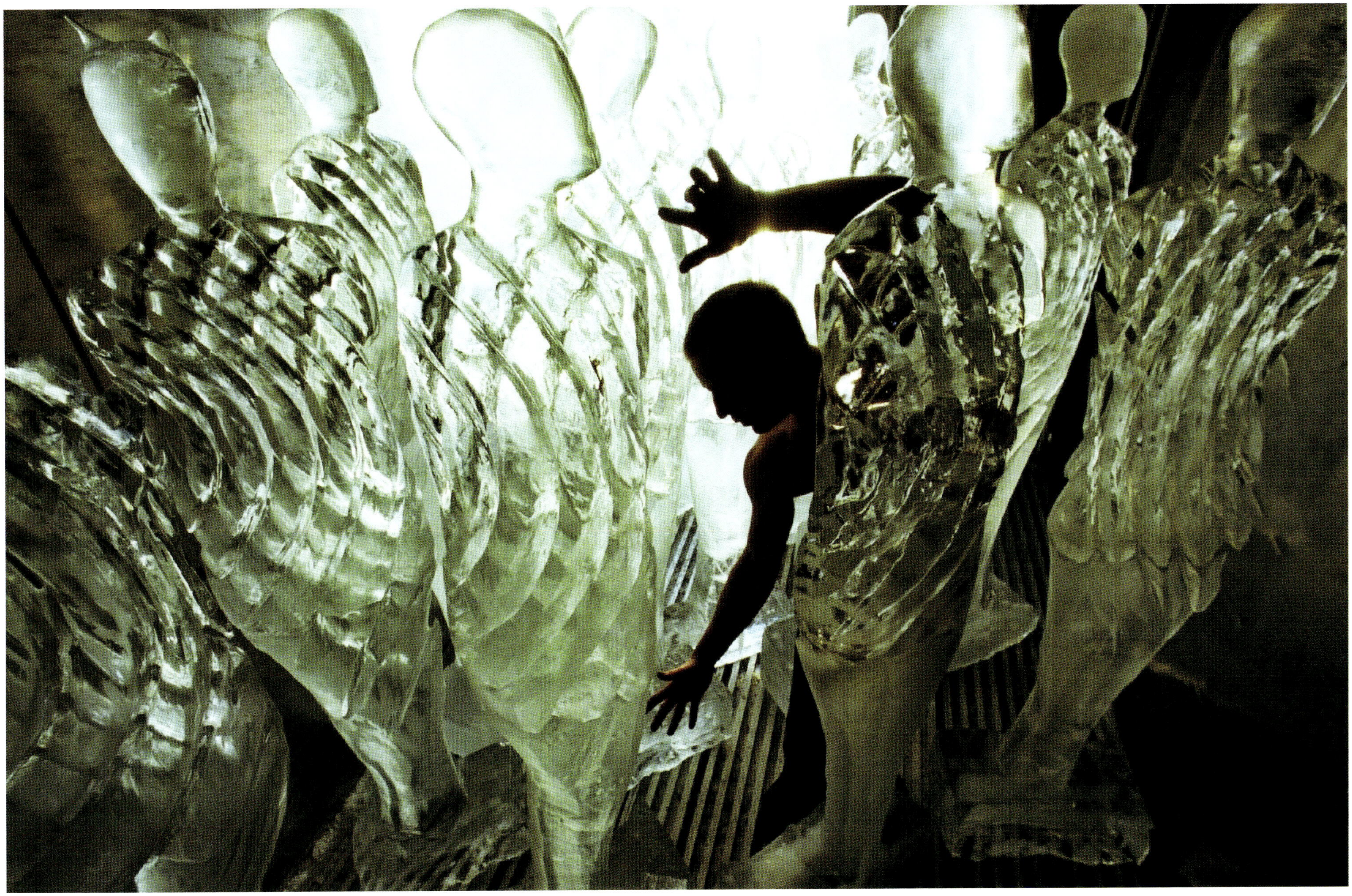

Chilling Out

The Guardian, 2007

Choreographer/dancer Charlie Morrissey rehearsing with thirty vast ice sculptures, carved with chainsaws, for the premiere of his show *Absolute Zero* at the Brighton Dome.
Refrigerated freightliner lorries had to stand by at all times so the fragile ice could be loaded into freezers whenever the curtain fell, to keep the sculptures from melting between performances.

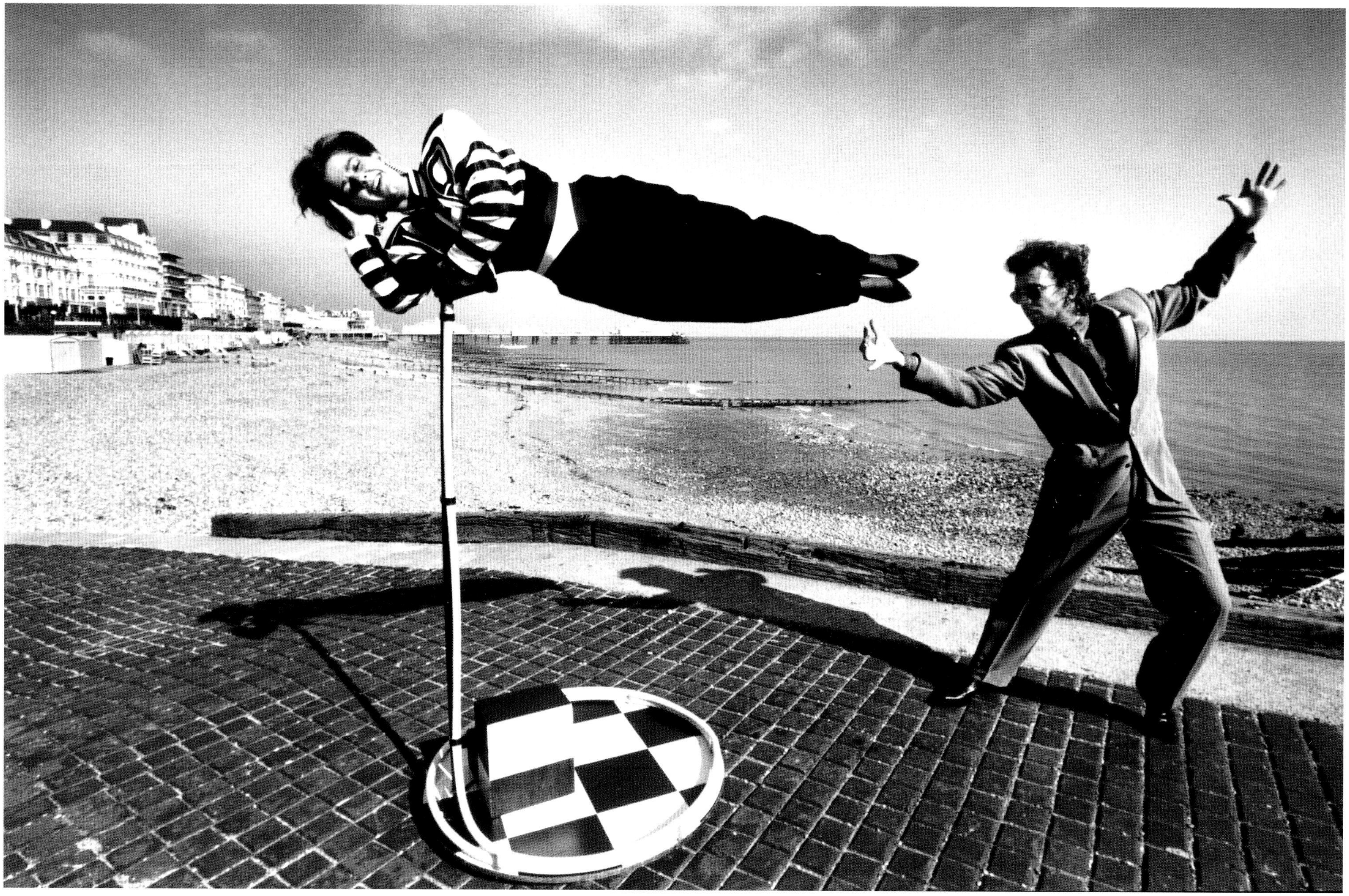

The Illusionists

The Guardian, 1994

The International Brotherhood of Magicians held their British Annual Convention at the Congress Theatre in Eastbourne in 1994. I went along to find hundreds of acts from all over the world, from card tricks to women being sawn in half, but not one that made a picture. Magic skills inside the gloomy theatre just didn't work.

A couple of brave illusionists agreed to come and perform outside in broad daylight. We carried the simple props, a pole set into a circular base and a Hula Hoop, over the road to the seafront. The pole was plonked on the walkway and the magician's assistant was lifted up so her shoulder rested on the top of the pole and her partner was holding her horizontally... He stepped away and there she was ... seemingly balanced on her shoulder. The Hula Hoop was swooped all round her body and up and down the pole, to show there was no support, no wires ... incredible ... great image. Job done, it went straight in the paper.

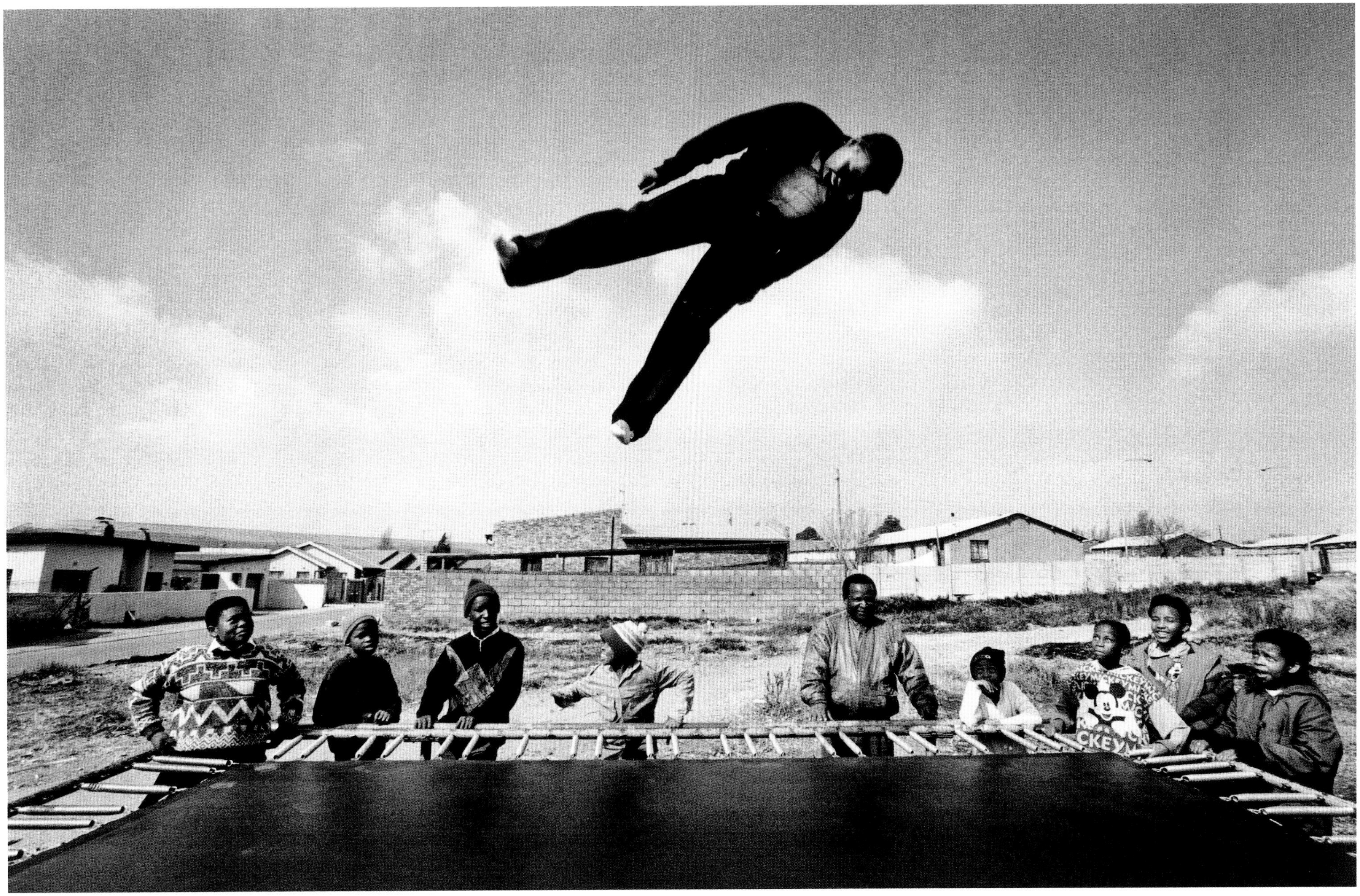

Keeping Afloat

The University of Brighton's Scholarship Project, 1996

This schoolgirl floating high above a communal trampoline in a square in a Soweto township near Johannesburg, South Africa has only a few minutes alone on one of her home's few leisure facilities. The springboard's owner, standing facing the camera, will soon slap the trampoline membrane to tell the girl her time is up and someone else is waiting to take to the air. The picture was part of the project's work to create links in education and health between townships and British schools and universities.

Street Stomp

The Guardian, 2002

Luke Cresswell, leader and co-founder of Brighton-based percussion group Stomp and two of his performers tested their rhythm march to the limit by wearing and playing oil drums as they advanced up a cruelly steep hill. Ski boots were welded to the top of the heavy drums so they could all stomp in step while beating out rhythms with these extra-long drumsticks. In the street it was very, very noisy; on a stage, deafening.
At the time, three Stomp companies were touring the USA and two more touring Europe, all with casts blasting out rhythms using anything that made a satisfying noise – including oil drums, dustbins, brooms, paper bags, Zippo lighters and even steel kitchen sinks.

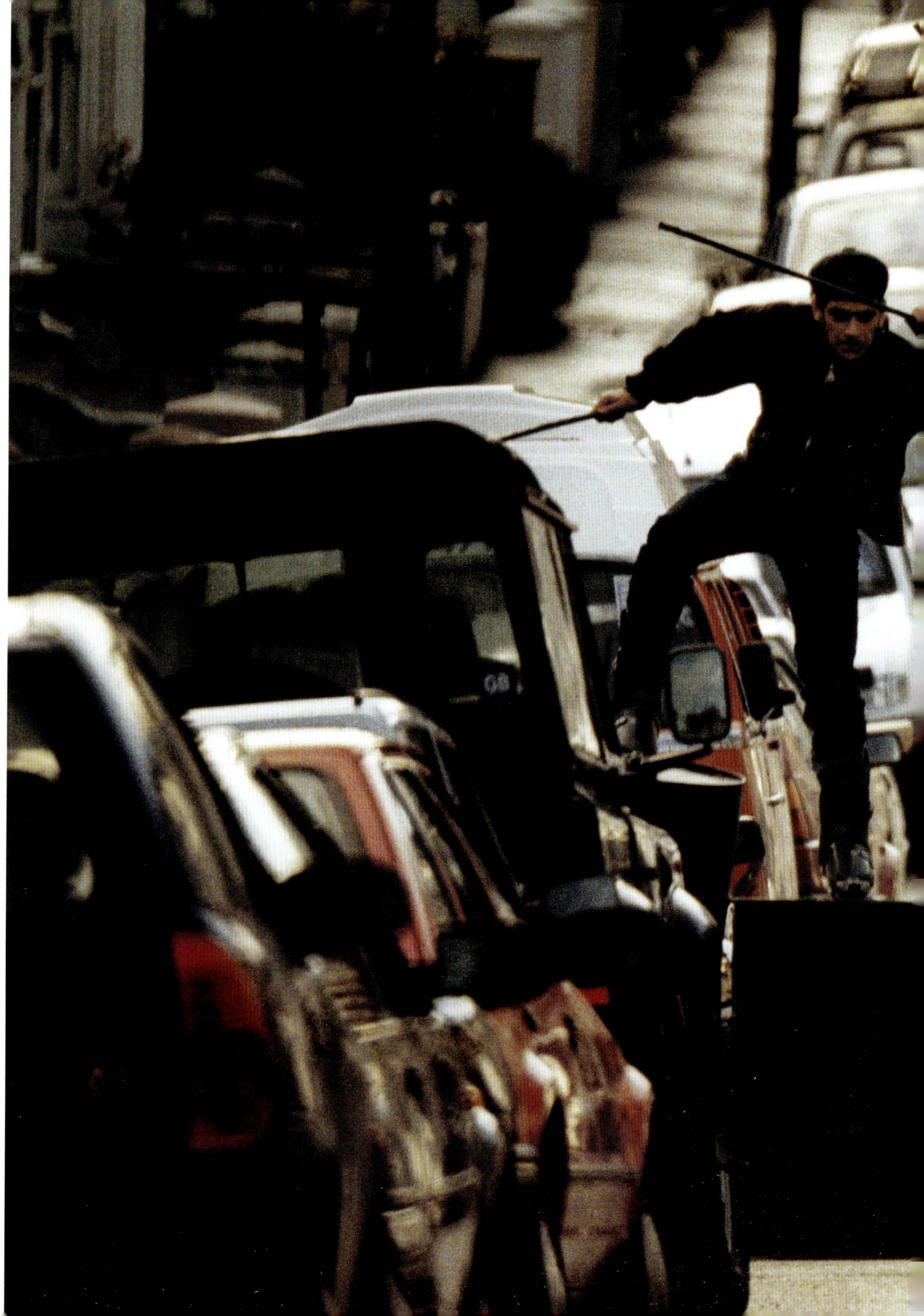

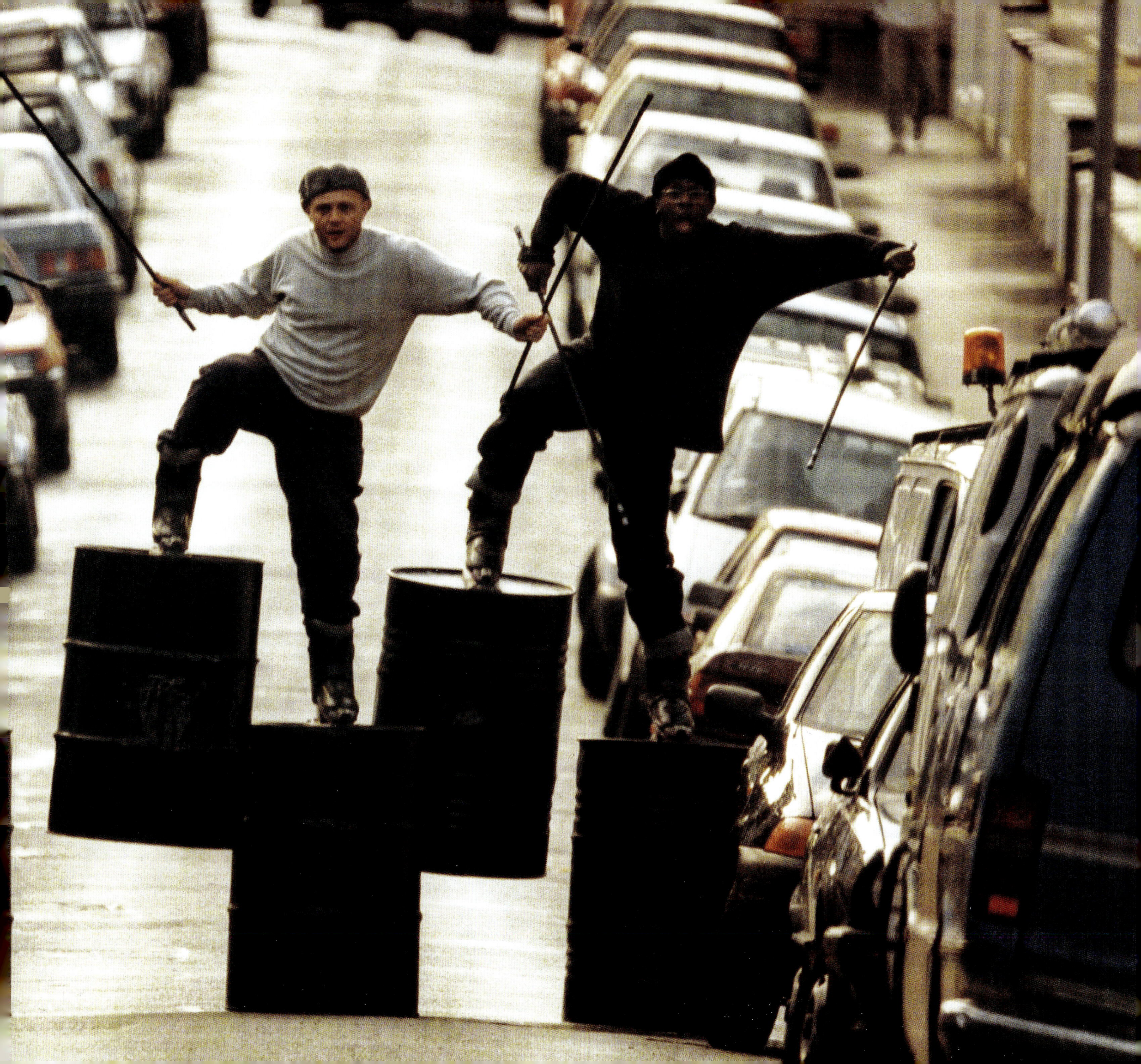

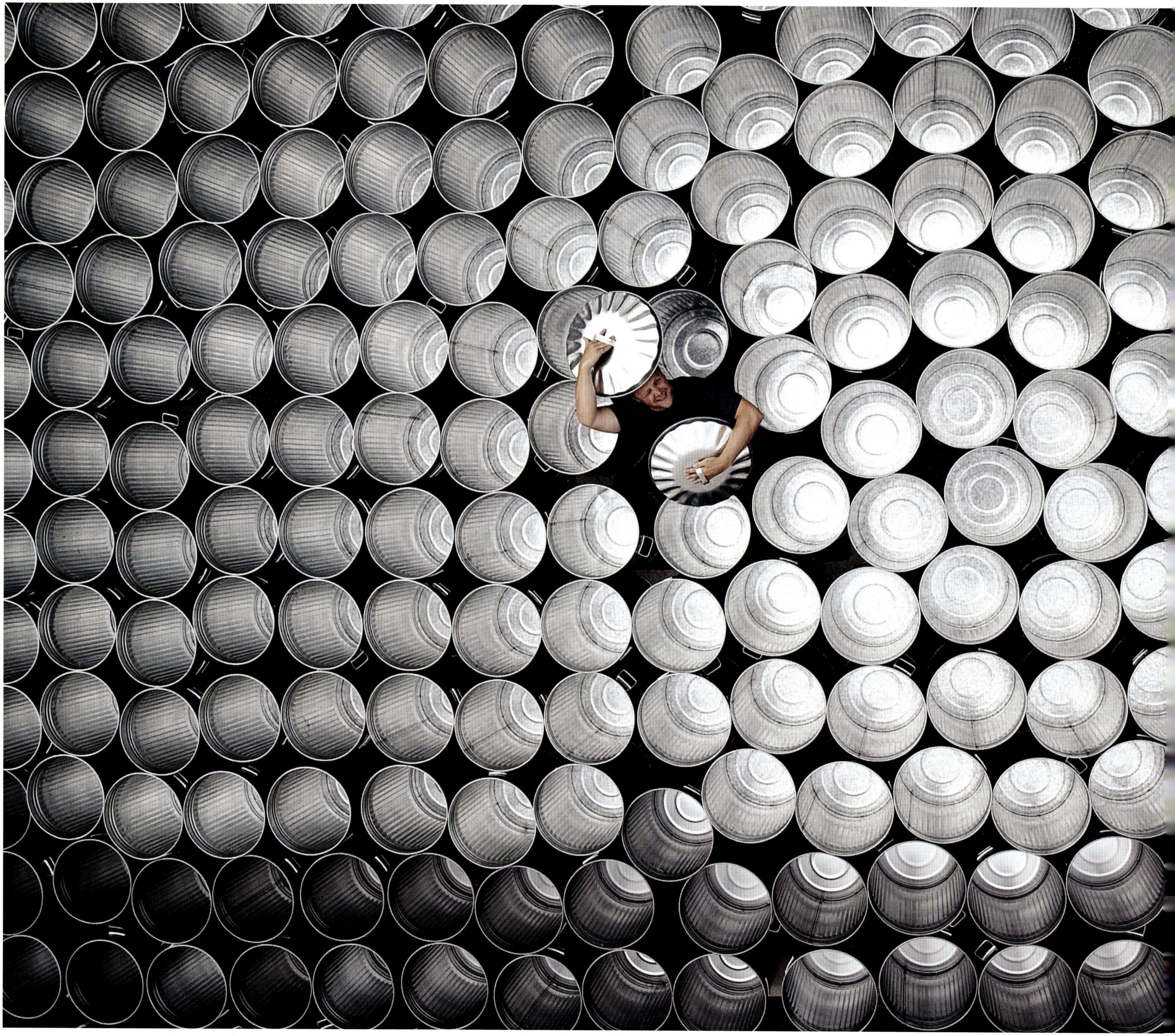

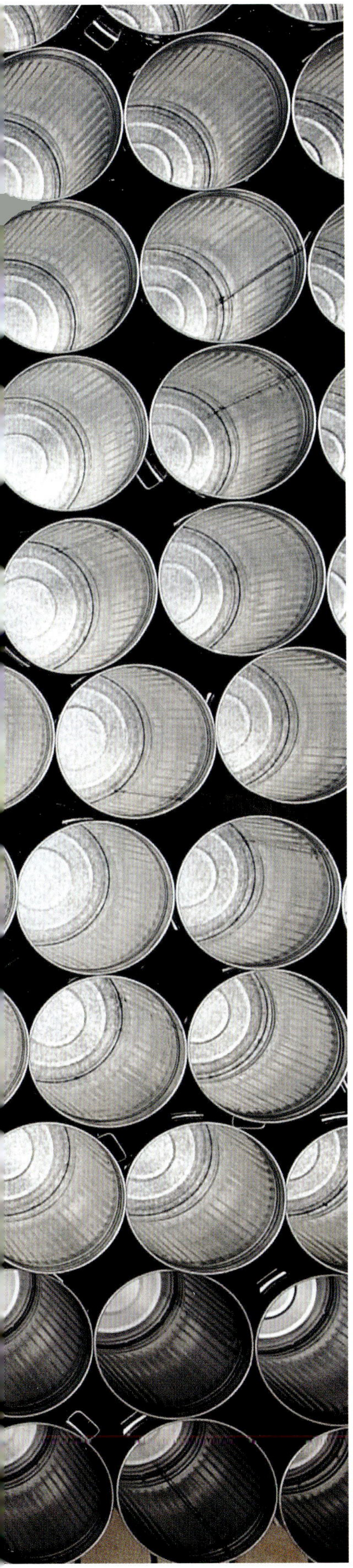

In the Bin

The Independent, 2002

Performances by Luke Cresswell and Stomp were always fun to photograph but I became curious about the sheer quantity of weird props the five touring companies were getting through. Luke mentioned casually that 1,110 galvanised dustbins were being shipped out with the performers every year because they were in no fit shape to be used after a season of being whacked twice daily by the drummers. We agreed I could come and photograph the next shipment.
Early on the day, Garrods of Barking, Luke's favoured dustbin suppliers, delivered 300 bins to the Stomp lockup, ready for a flight that afternoon. I had to make the picture work before they vanished into the hold of a plane. Unfortunately nobody else was there to help unload them, so it was down to me and one very grumpy lorry driver to hump clattering stacks of bins about for what felt like hours to assemble this display ready for Luke to step into.

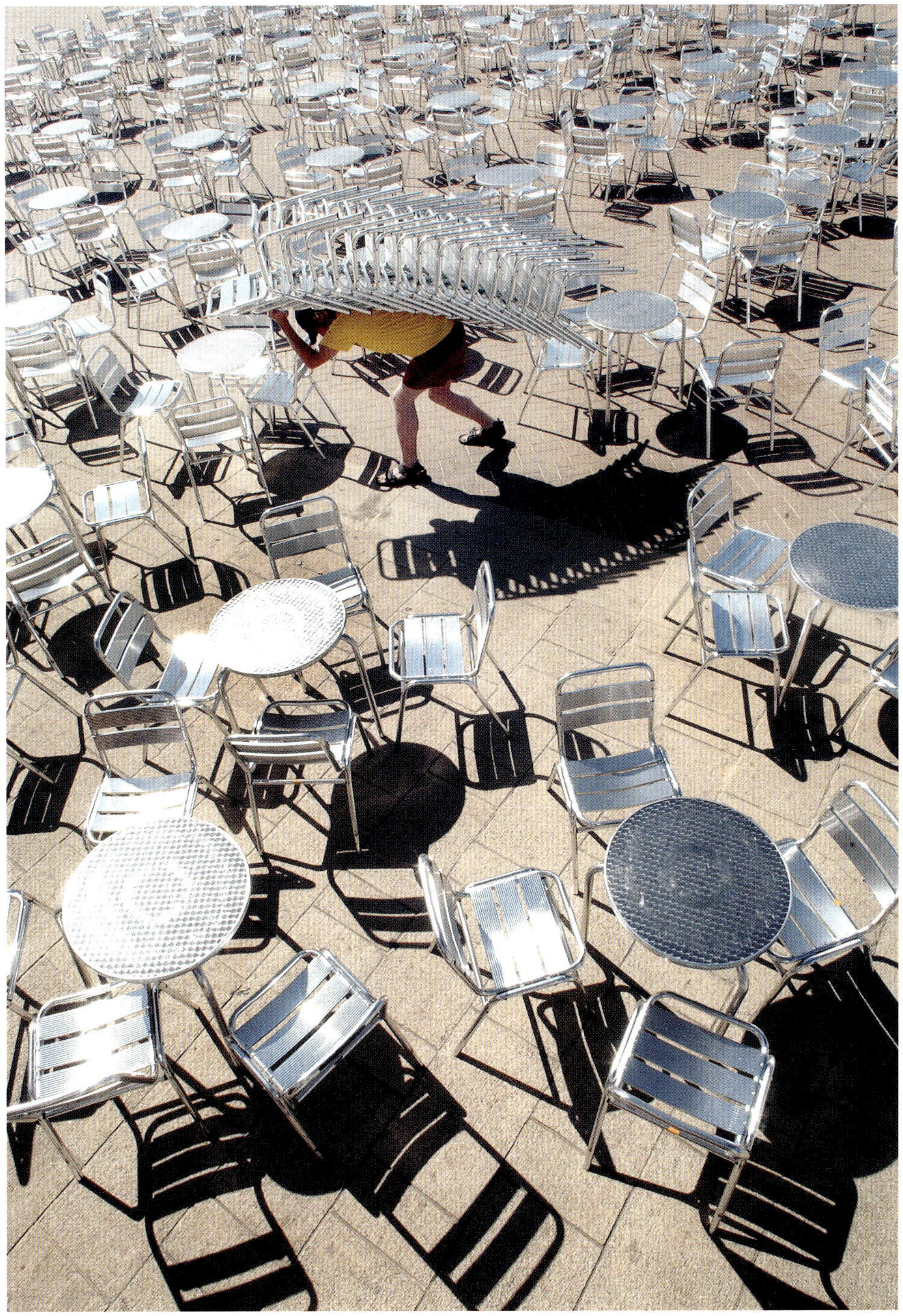

Stacking Up

The Guardian, 2003

A bar worker heaving stacks of aluminium chairs across a terrace caught my eye. He was preparing for a rush of tourists to Brighton seafront on a hot sunny day and his normal load seemed to be eight chairs, which made an interesting shape. With a little bit of gentle persuasion, this kind and very fit young man doubled his load for me, and made himself look like a human caterpillar.

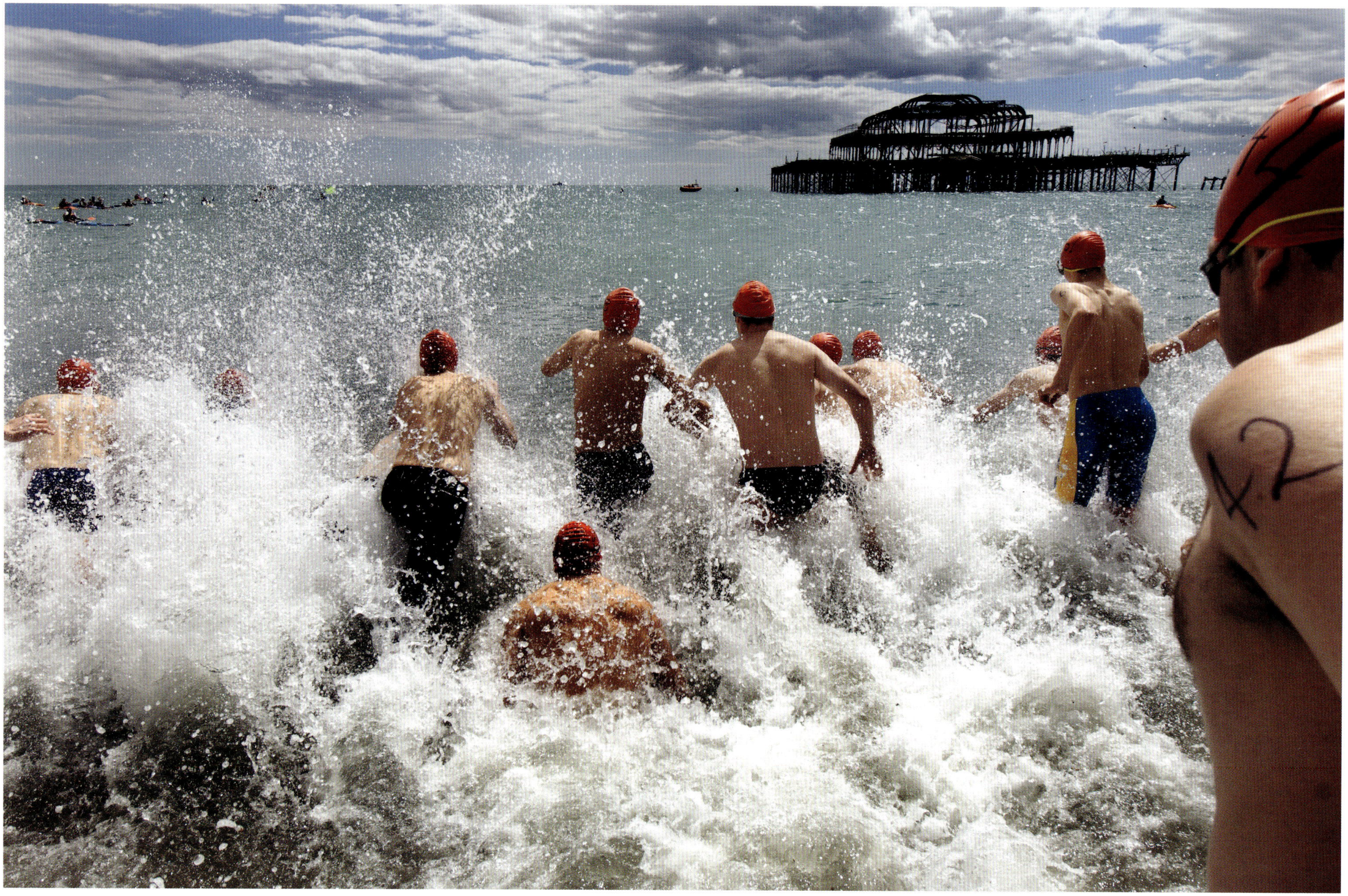

Come in Number 42

The Guardian, 2008

Swimmers always make an enormous splash as they dash into the sea at Brighton for the annual Pier to Pier Race. I wanted to catch that and positioned myself in front of the mass of sixty or so eager contestants, ready for the stampede. Then came entrant Number 42, a rather large man whose bare feet were really feeling the pain of the pebbly beach. He struggled slowly past me to get into the water. I only got three or four usable images before his bulk completely blocked my view for the rest of the big plunge. By the time he passed me, most of the swimmers were on their way. But in just this one shot his body and swimming hat made a perfectly framed picture.

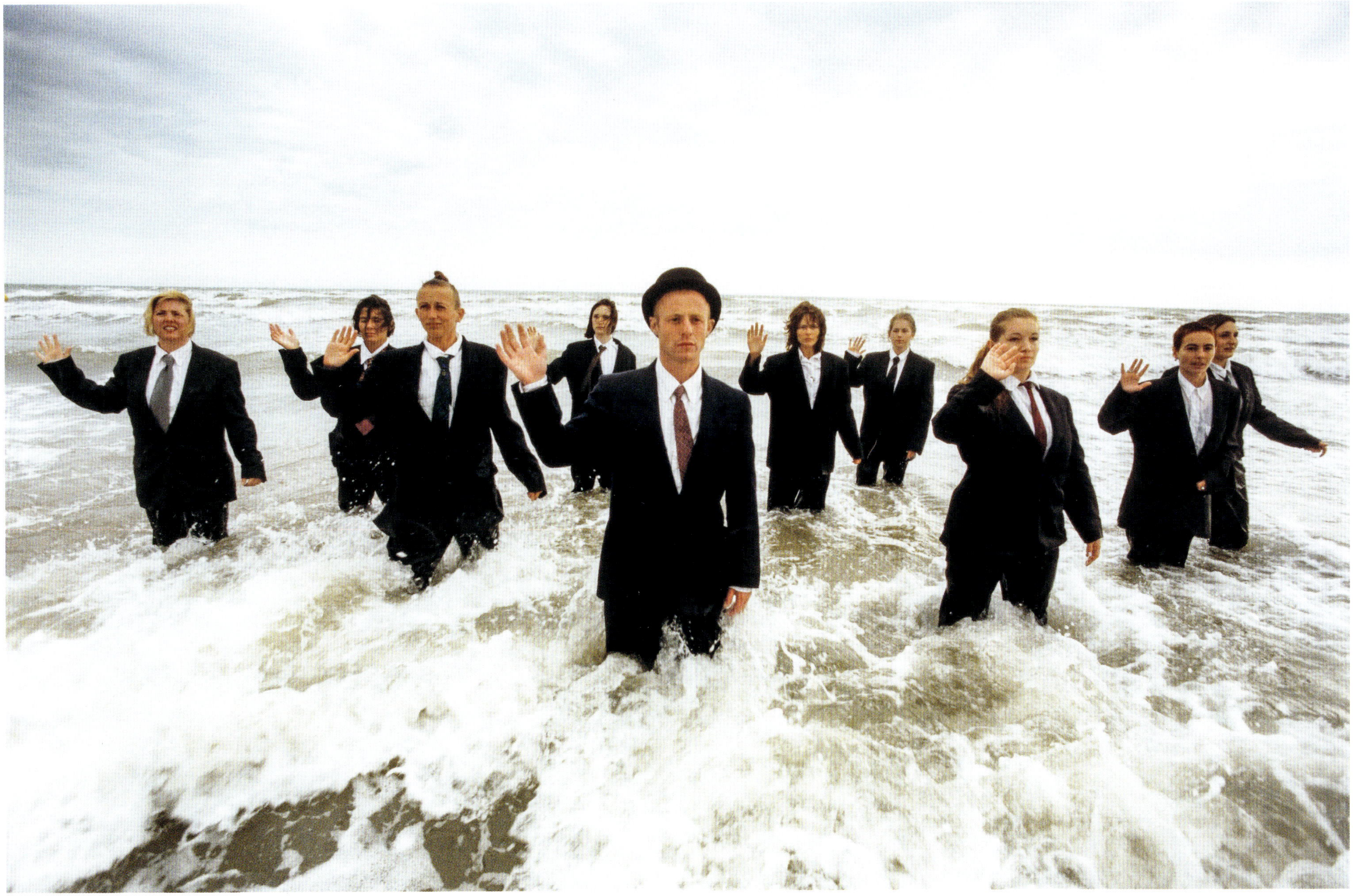

Wet Suits

The Guardian, 1996

Performer and choreographer Charlie Morrisey, the man in the bowler hat, with his dance troupe all in business suits, in the sea at Brighton. They had been rehearsing a performance of a show called *Knee High, Skin Deep,* due to be shown at low tide to an audience sitting on the beach. They hadn't actually planned to stand in the waves until I said that I was 100 per cent certain they'd make the paper if they did it. To a man and a woman, they waded in cheerfully.

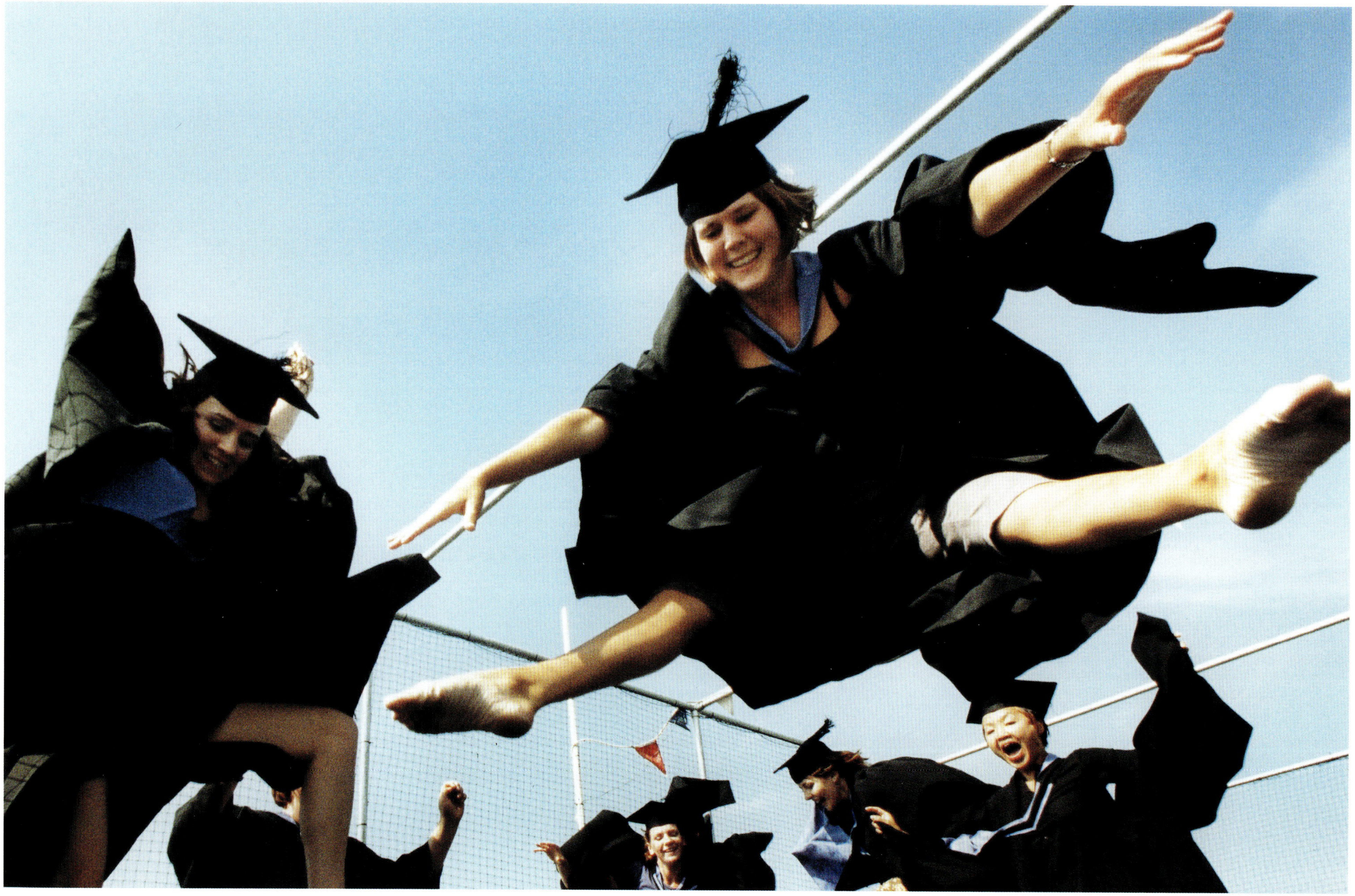

Jumping for Joy

The Guardian, 1998

Brighton has two universities, so every year there were two degree shows, with two chances to try to find something special as the graduates celebrated their degrees. This was the year I had an energetic group of performing arts graduates who were wonderful at bouncing around on a trampoline at Peter Pan's Playground on the seafront. The image was later picked to become a postcard as part of the World Press Photo Awards and the cards were then used to congratulate many more new graduates all over the world.

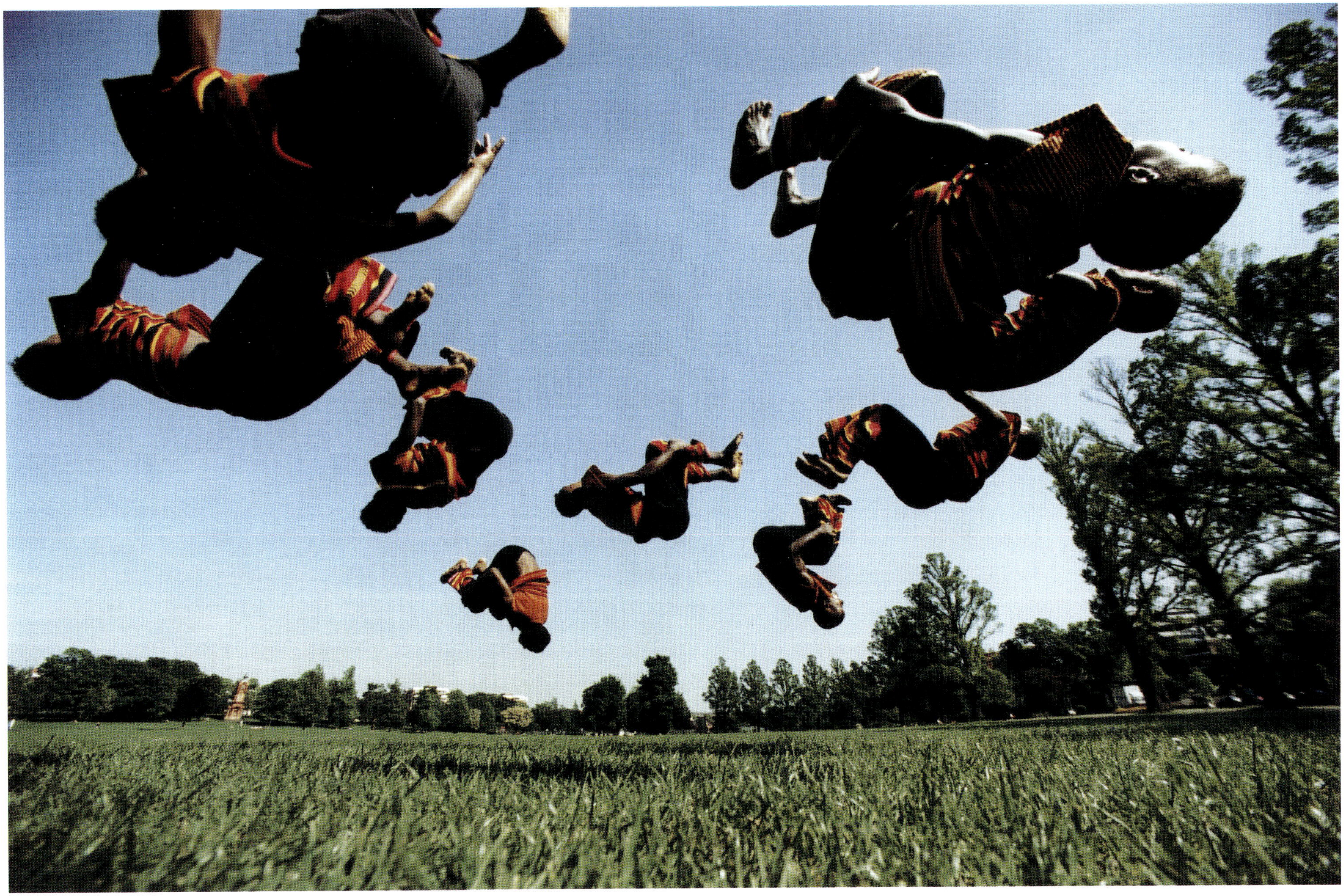

Spring in the Air

The Guardian, 1998

A flier dropped through my letterbox, advertising a circus from Ethiopia performing in town during the Brighton Festival. The cover showed a boy in mid-air, somersaulting as one of the circus acts. I went to the park and asked how many of the troupe could do such a spectacular leap. 'All of them,' he said. I arranged to go back the next morning, and was greeted by nine smiling ten year olds. Taking the pentaprism off my Nikon F4 camera, I put it down on the grass, and arranged the youngsters so nobody was hiding anyone else. Then I was ready for the word to be given for them to jump. Like magic, all nine took off as if they were on springs. We did this half a dozen times, resulting in six great usable pictures but this was my favourite.

Best Foot Forward

The Sun, 1985

After his release from Ford Prison, where he had served a sentence for drink-driving, George Best went on holiday to Mauritius with his Swedish girlfriend, former Miss World Mary Stavin. I went with them – a feature was planned on the soccer legend enjoying his freedom. But on the first day a cyclone struck and then it rained torrents. Best and his Miss World retired to their hotel room for five long days, emerging only for meals. I didn't blame them but I hadn't taken a single frame and time was running out. On the sixth and final day the sun shone in the nick of time, luring Best down to the beach where he had a kickabout with the football-mad local children.

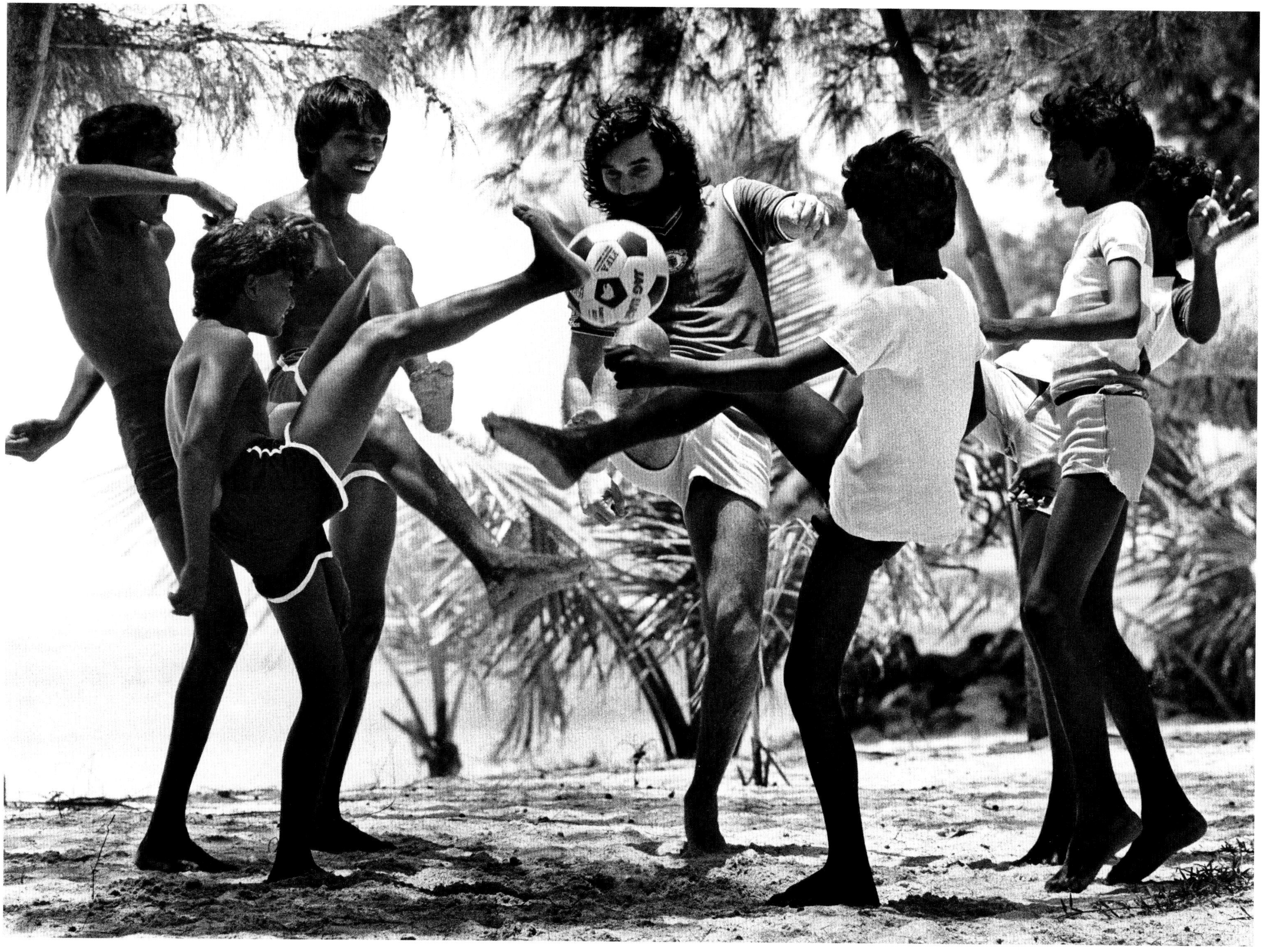

Goalmouth Scramble

The University of Brighton's Scholarship Project, 1996

Children on a dirt road in Alexandra Township in a suburb of Johannesburg, South Africa were playing an energetic sort of mass keepy-uppy with a rubber ball. As usual, none of boys or girls were wearing shoes. This was taken as part of a series commissioned to illustrate the need for podiatry (footcare) clinics in townships, as universities in Brighton and Johannesburg joined forces to work on the problem.

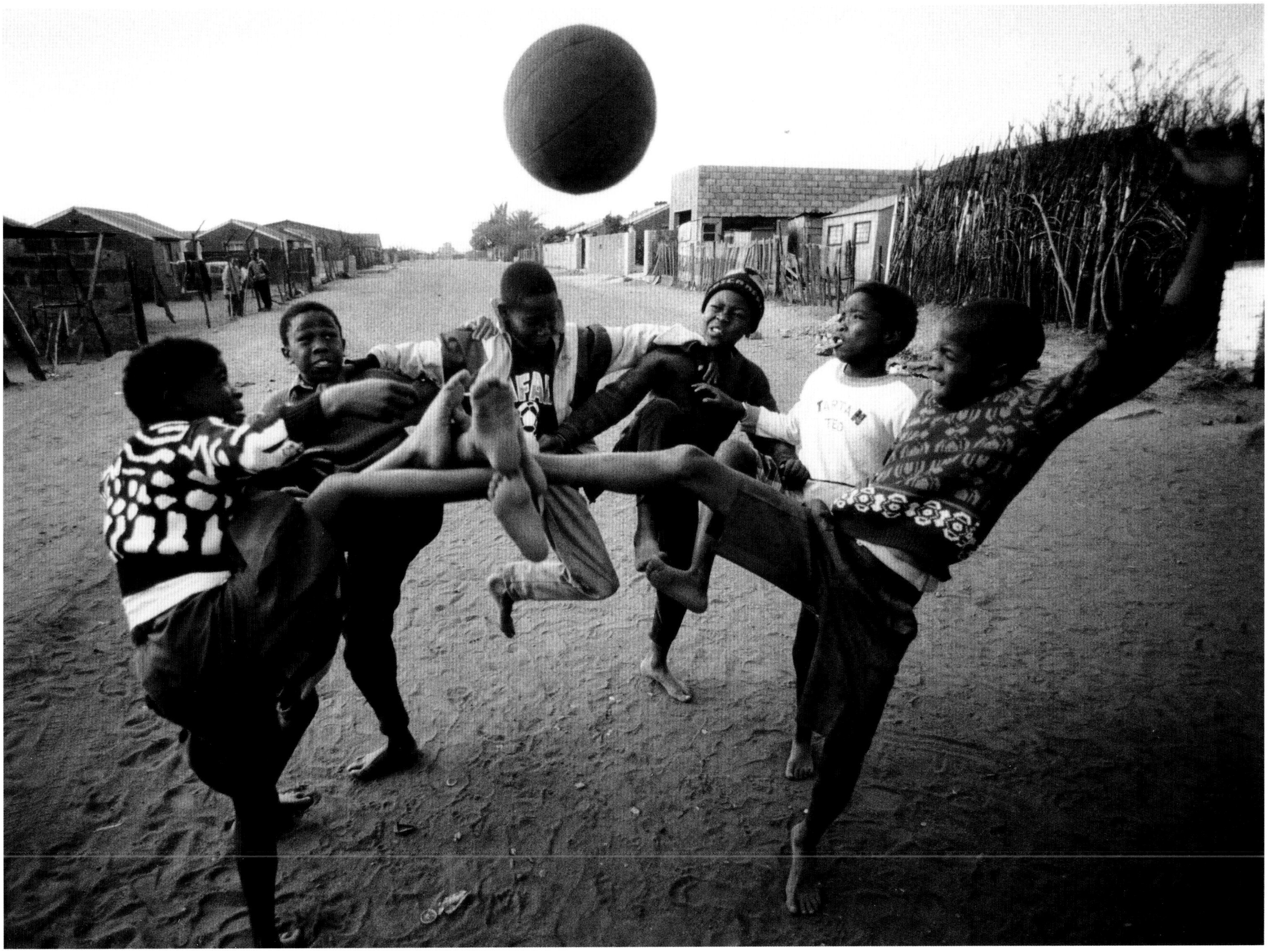

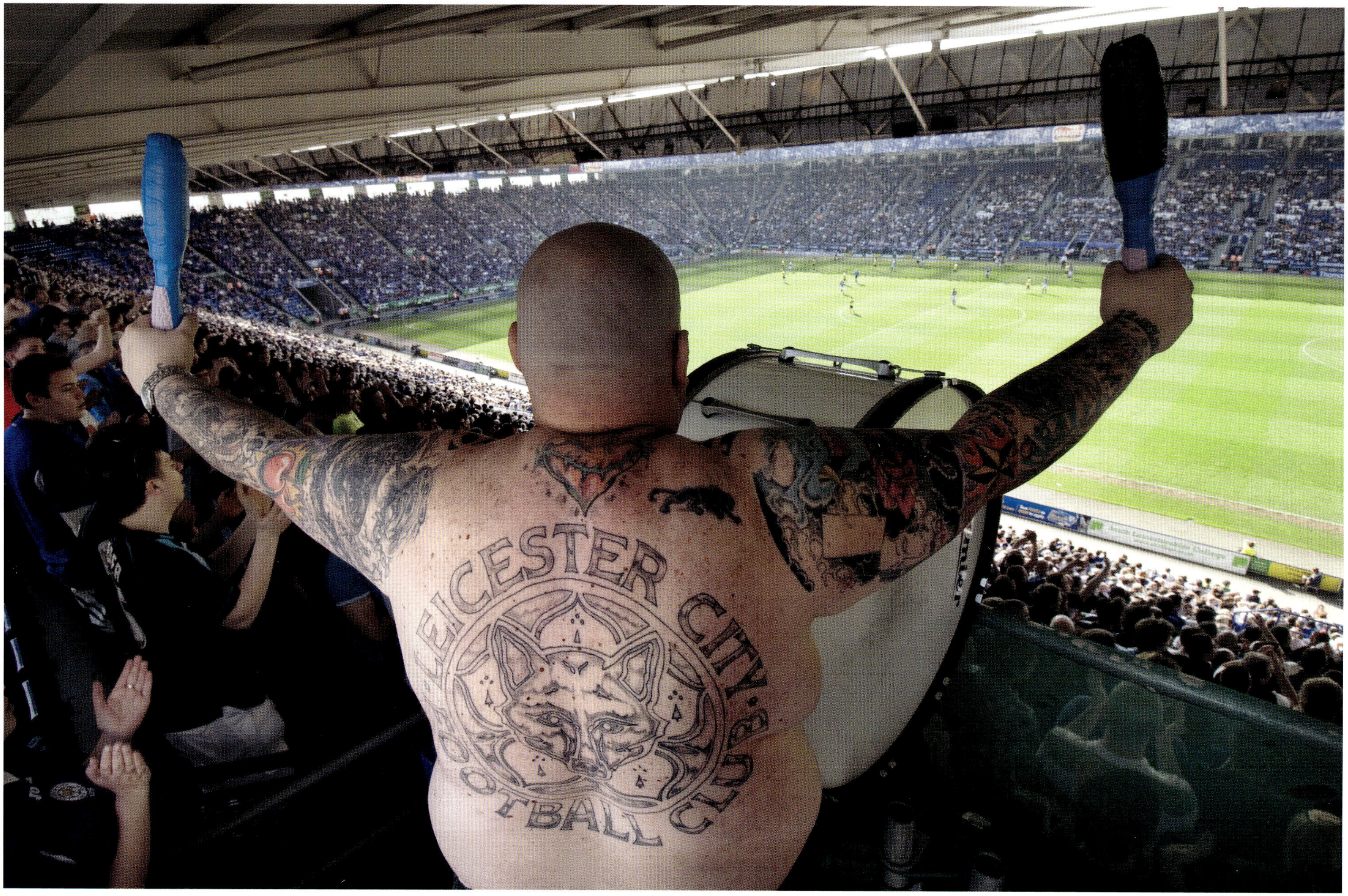

Drumming up Support

The Guardian, 2010

Lee Jobber, the chant drummer for fans and supporters at Leicester City football club, beats his Premier bass drum at Leicester's King Power Stadium through good times and bad. This was a good day, Leicester City beat Watford 4 – 1. Lee, a special needs teacher, is bare chested at every game, summer and winter, and has the club's badge and logo complete with a fox's head, (the club is nicknamed the Foxes), tattooed on his back just to underline his devotion to his, and my, team. It took Leicester another six years to win the Premiership for the first time, in 2016/2017 season, after 132 years of dashed hopes and at starting odds of 5,000-1. Lee was there to drum them on as the city went crazy.

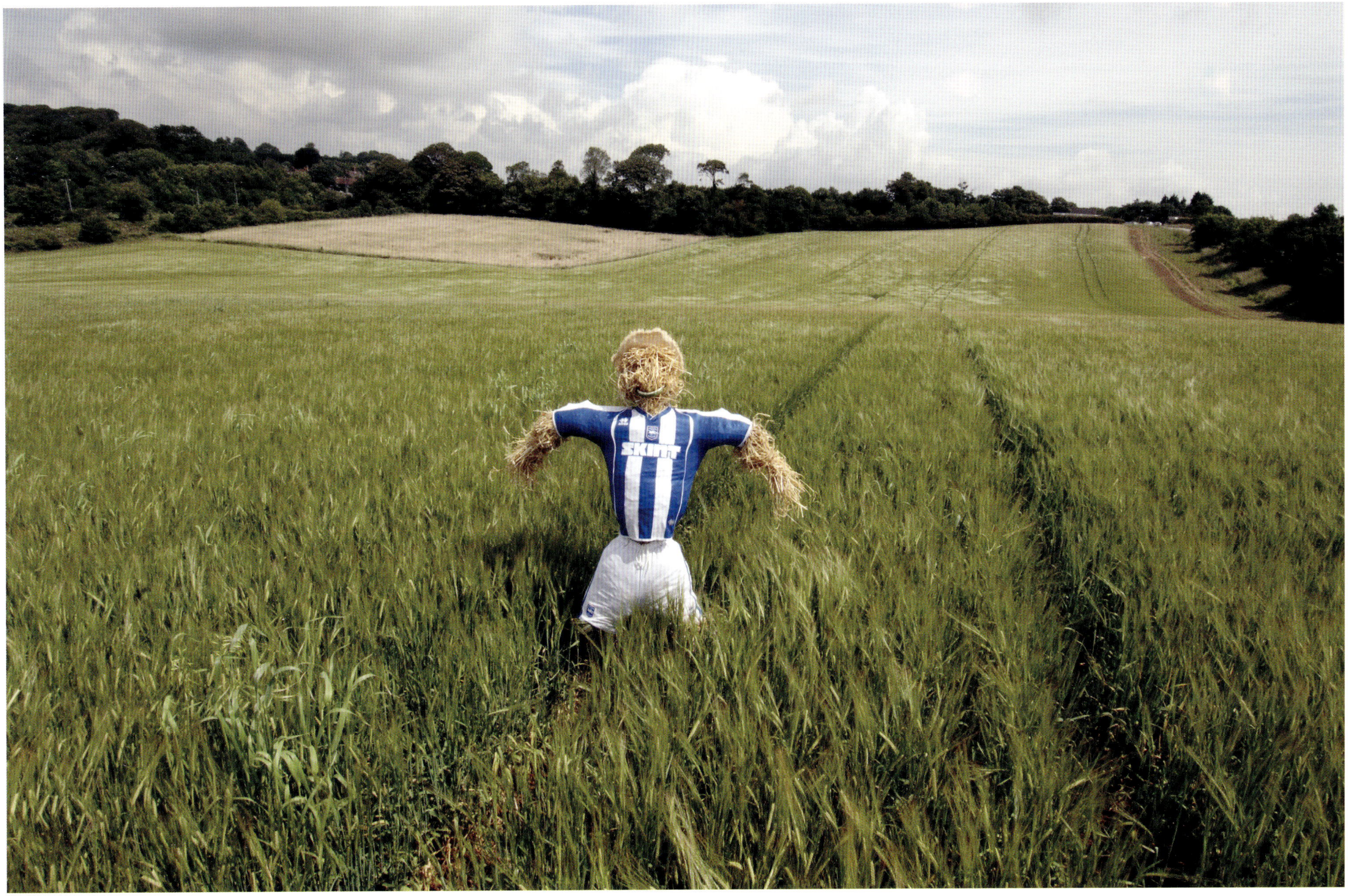

Field of Dreams

The Guardian, 2007

I was asked to photograph the proposed new site for a stadium for Brighton & Hove Albion football club. It was an unremarkable field in a small village called Falmer, just east of Brighton, but building a stadium there was very controversial. Not just because appalled Falmer residents believed they would be invaded by mobs of soccer hooligans but because seven-eighths of the land was owned by Brighton Council while the other eighth was owned by Lewes Council.

There was an awful lot of deal-making going on behind the scenes while Albion fans prayed for a miracle to save them from more seasons in their old cramped and inadequate quarters.

A picture of a field of barley didn't stand a chance of making the paper, but after putting my thinking cap on I had a word with a friendly farmer who helped me make a scarecrow in the Brighton & Hove Albion football kit. The picture made the paper and the dreams were realised – a beautiful stadium did get built in the end.

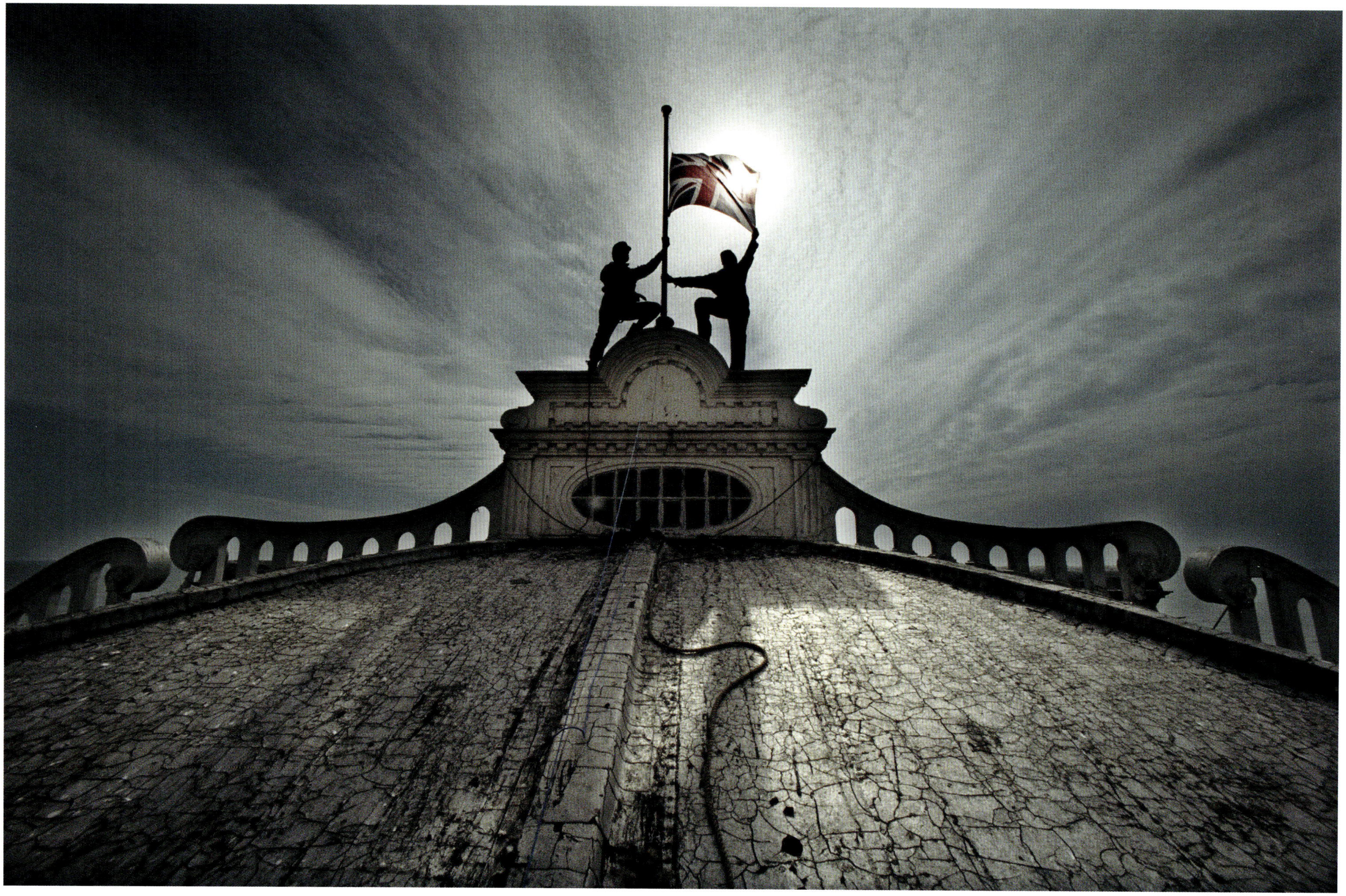

Flying the Flag

The Guardian, 1998

Two campaigning members of the West Pier Trust, hoisting a Union Jack up the flagpole on Brighton's near derelict Grade I listed West Pier to try to draw attention to the plight of the beautiful old Victorian landmark. I documented the decline of the pier with growing despair – it was such an elegant structure, it was easy to get its picture in the paper – but still no saviour came forward to fund its restoration.

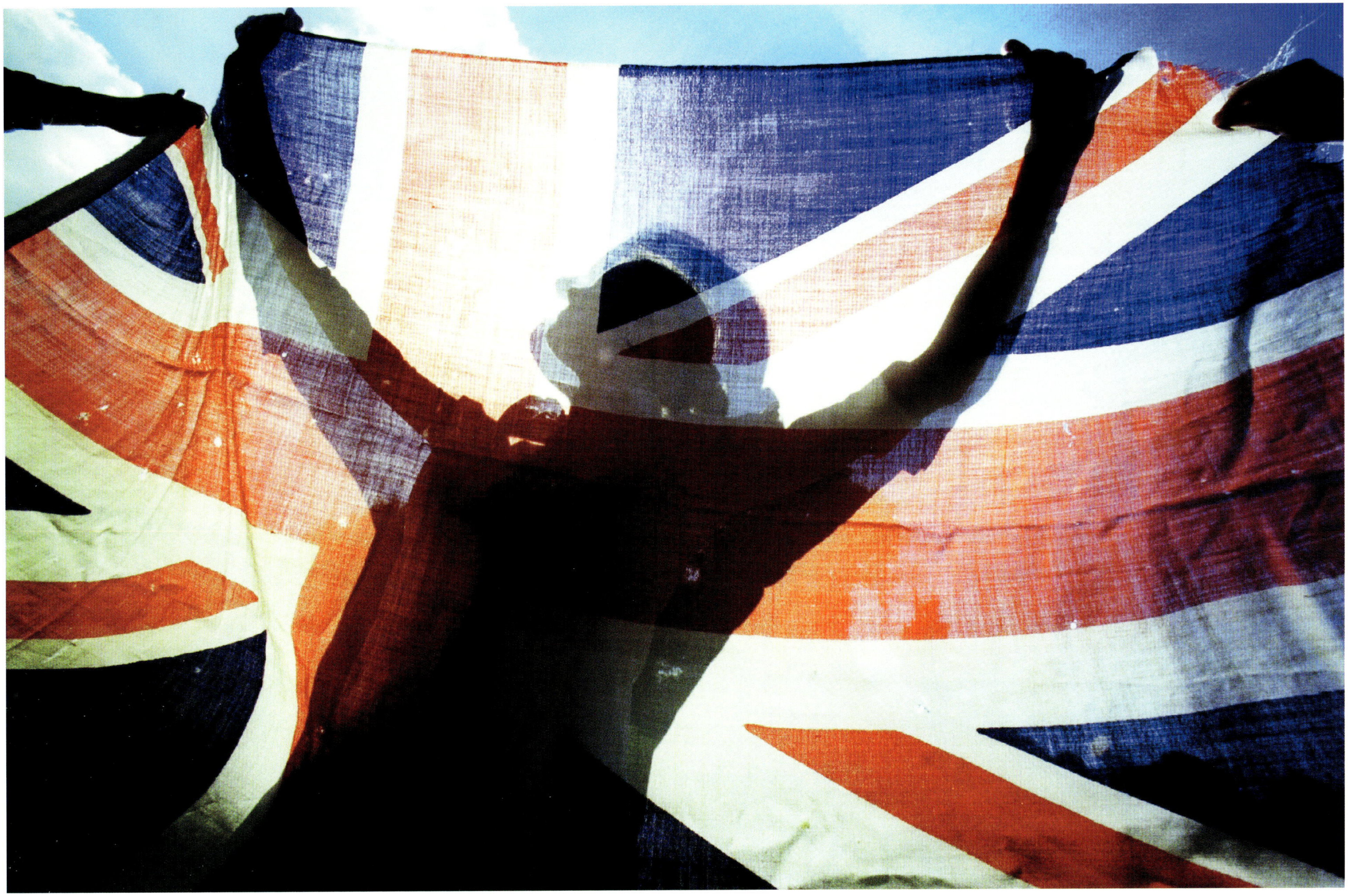

War Veteran

The Guardian, 1999

This Union flag was flying from the British Agency in Pretoria, South Africa when the Boer War broke out on 11 October 1899. Pretoria was Boer territory and Her Majesty's Agent, Sir William Conyngham Greene, took the sensible decision to haul down the flag and decamp immediately, to British-held Cape Town. Exactly one hundred years later, on the date of its hasty exit from Pretoria, the old flag was being auctioned by Sotheby's. It was incredibly fragile. One of the auction assistants unfolded it gently and held it against the light for me, to show off its battle scars.

Red Hot

The Guardian and Country Life, 2009

A heatwave in June 2009 made the wheatfields at Saddlescombe Farm on the South Downs blossom with a dazzling carpet of poppies. It was part of the biggest mass flowering of poppies on the downlands in many years and Charlie Cain, the National Trust warden for Devil's Dyke and Saddlescombe, found it warm work as he led me into the heart of the crop.

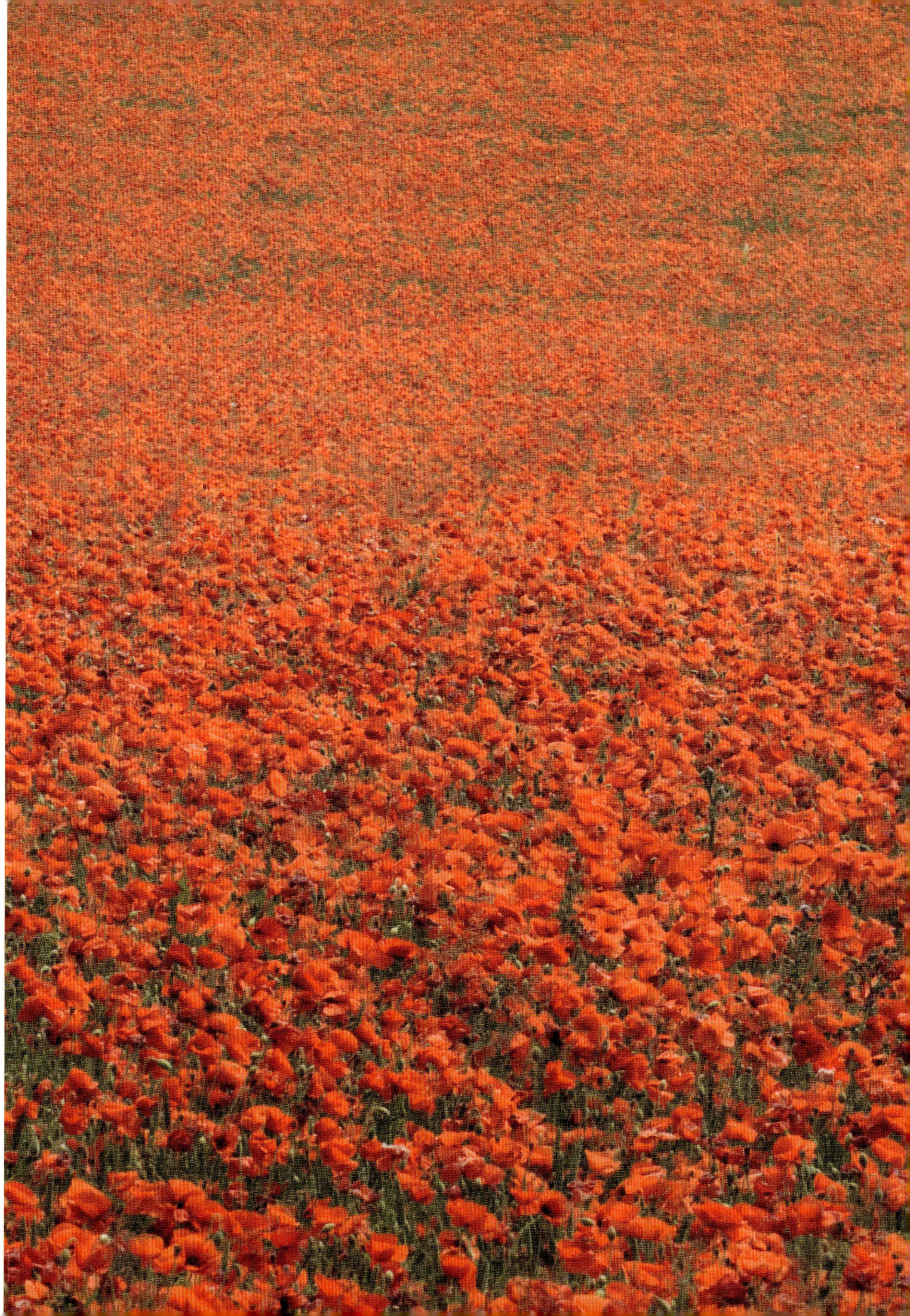

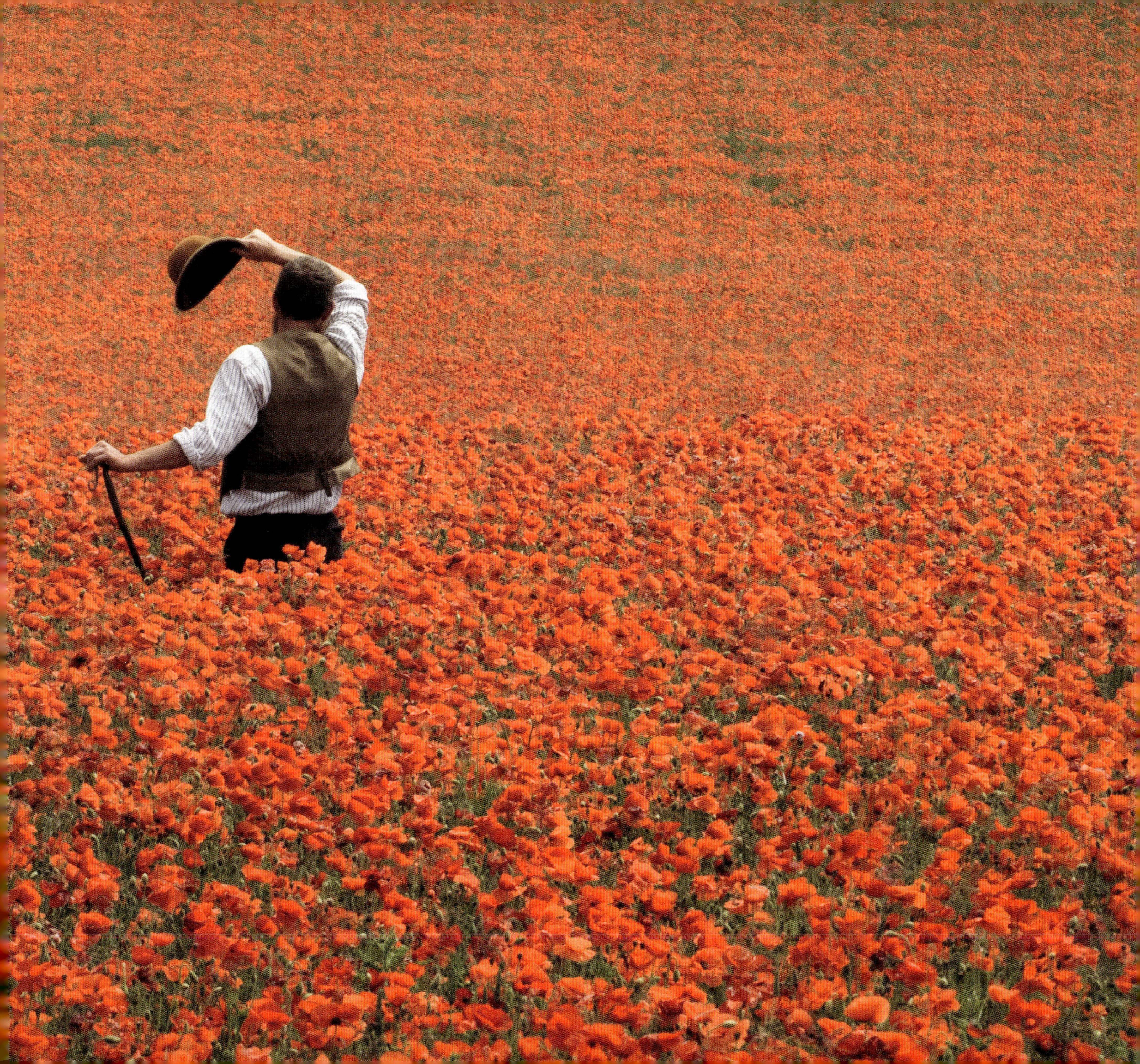

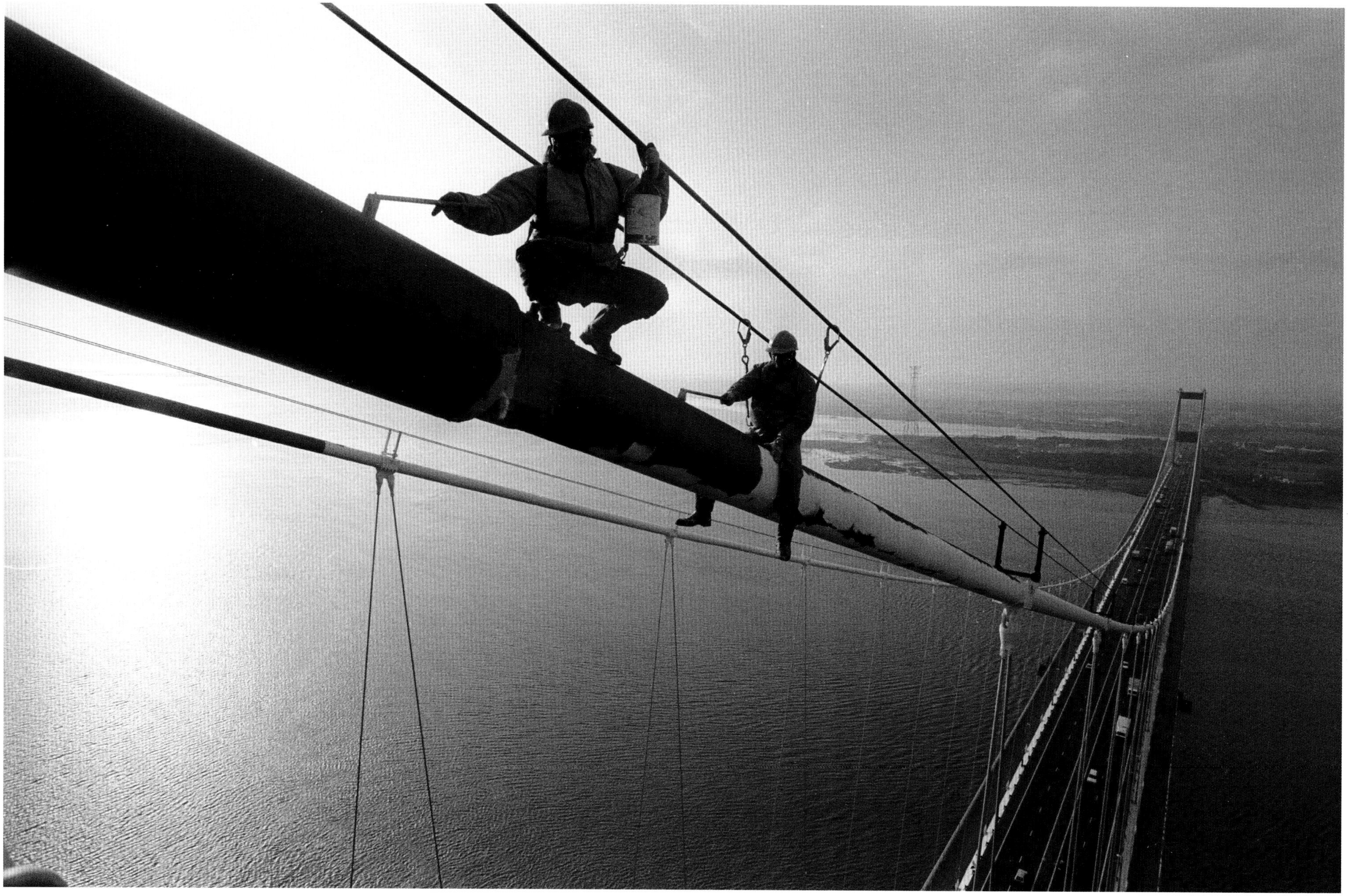

A Fine Balance

The Guardian, 1995

Two intrepid painters calmly work their way towards Wales, scraping down and painting the chains of the Severn Bridge. A long, long way below is the M4 motorway. I always admired workers like these. Not only did they have to cover both the mile-long chains with the red oxide rustproof paint they are applying here, they then had to do the whole thing all over again, to repaint the bridge the original light blue.

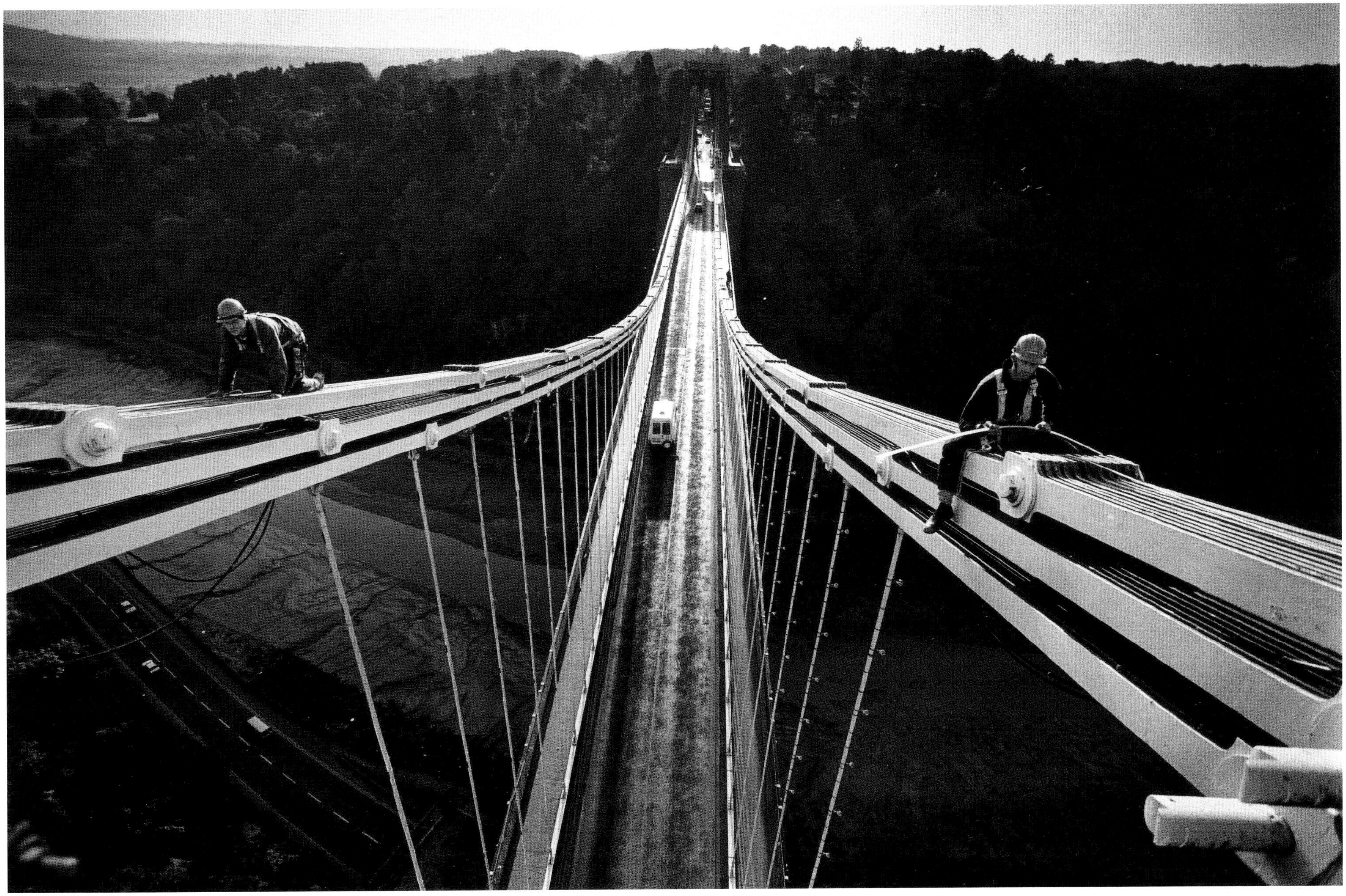

High Tension

The Guardian, 1992

Electrical engineers with very good heads for heights, Paul Tilley and Roger Taylor had to balance precariously on the chains of the Clifton Suspension Bridge in Bristol while fitting the latest innovative cost-saving, low-voltage, strip-lighting system.

It was supposed to replace conventional bulbs and save an estimated £4,000 a year.
Although all three of us were wearing safety harnesses, the drop to the gorge below made glancing down really daunting.

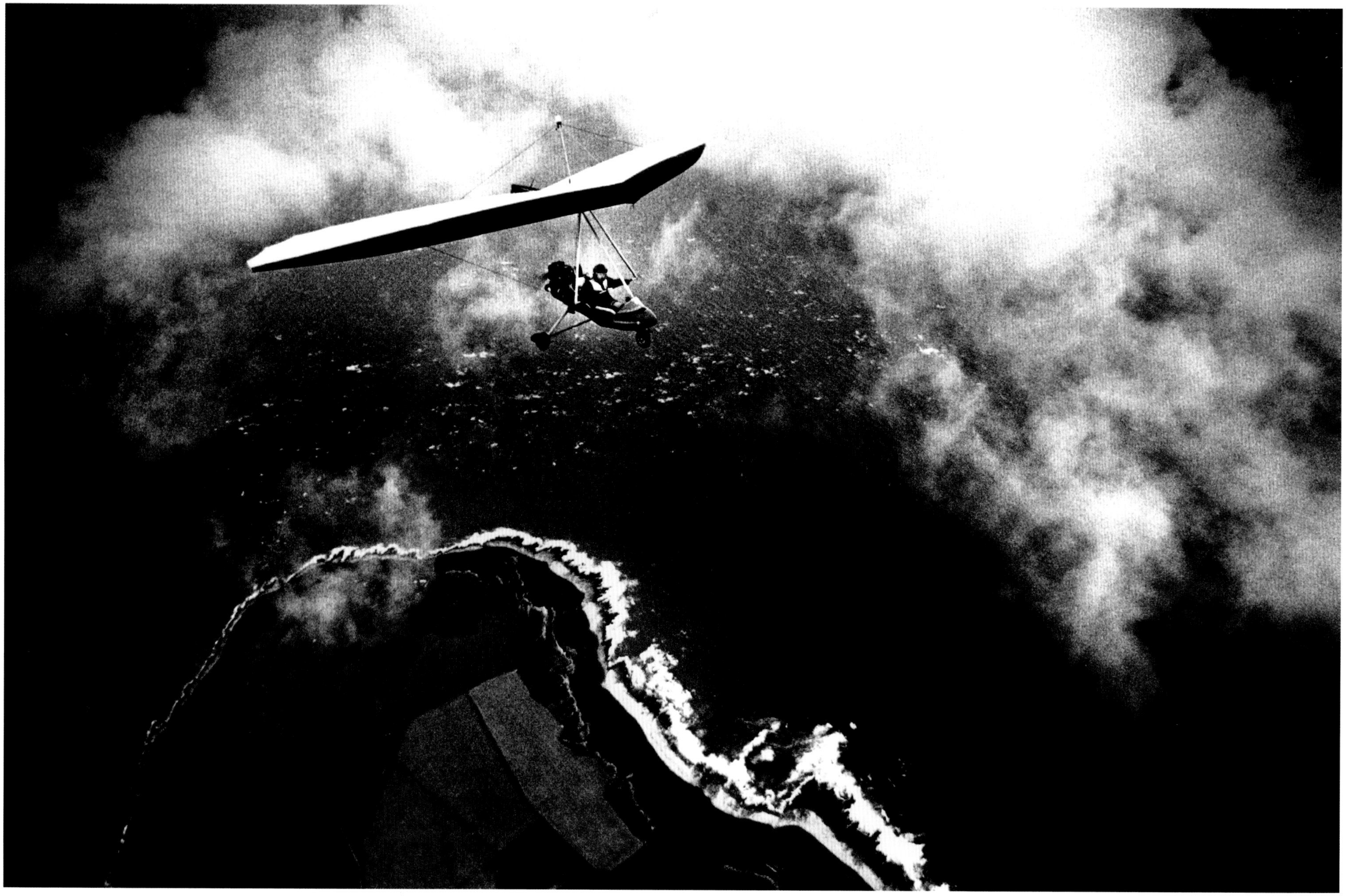

High as a Kite

The Guardian, 1989

Microlite enthusiast Rod Jenkins was making an attempt at an altitude record and planned to take to the skies over the Gower Peninsula in South Wales. I thought this would make an unmissable picture, made a few phone calls to arrange to photograph it and set off on a 250-mile journey in fine weather. By the time I made it to a little airfield in Wales, there was a gale blowing.
I found a pub with a room to let and spent the night worrying that this might not be such a great idea after all. In the morning, the gale had dropped to a stiff breeze and Rod introduced me to the pilot of the two-seater Microlite he had organised for me (I privately thought it looked like a lawnmower with a kite on top) and we all bounced across the bumpy field and soared into the sky. Up through the clouds we went, me taking snaps while hanging on for dear life. When I tried to change the film, the wind grabbed the roll and unreeled it all, leaving all thirty-six frames exposed and fluttering in the slipstream. As I looked down on the shrinking coastline below I suddenly realised that we were actually above the brave, death-defying would-be altitude record breaker. I did not feel brave at all.
We came in to land sideways. By this time I was just thankful to have survived. Back in my Land Rover for the long journey back to Brighton, all I cared about was that it had all four wheels firmly on solid ground.
The picture really was worth it in the end. It got a huge show on the front page of the *Guardian* and has been published many times since. But I still get nightmares about the flying lawnmower.

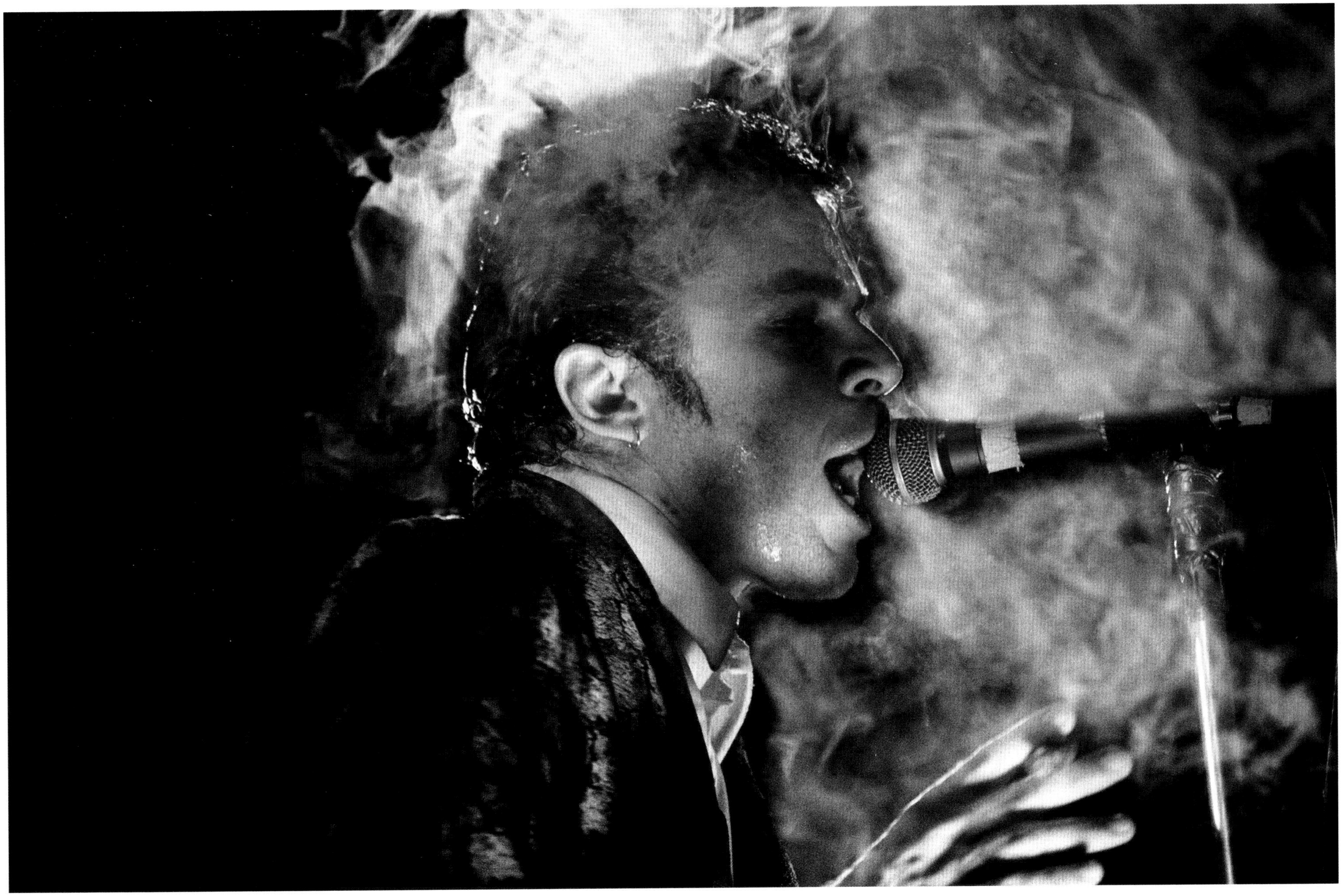

Ian Dury

The Sun, 1979

Punk rock star Ian Dury, of Ian Dury and the Blockheads, did a tremendous show at the Brighton Centre in 1979. He wound down towards the end by smoking a cigar while he sang.
As you did in the '70s.

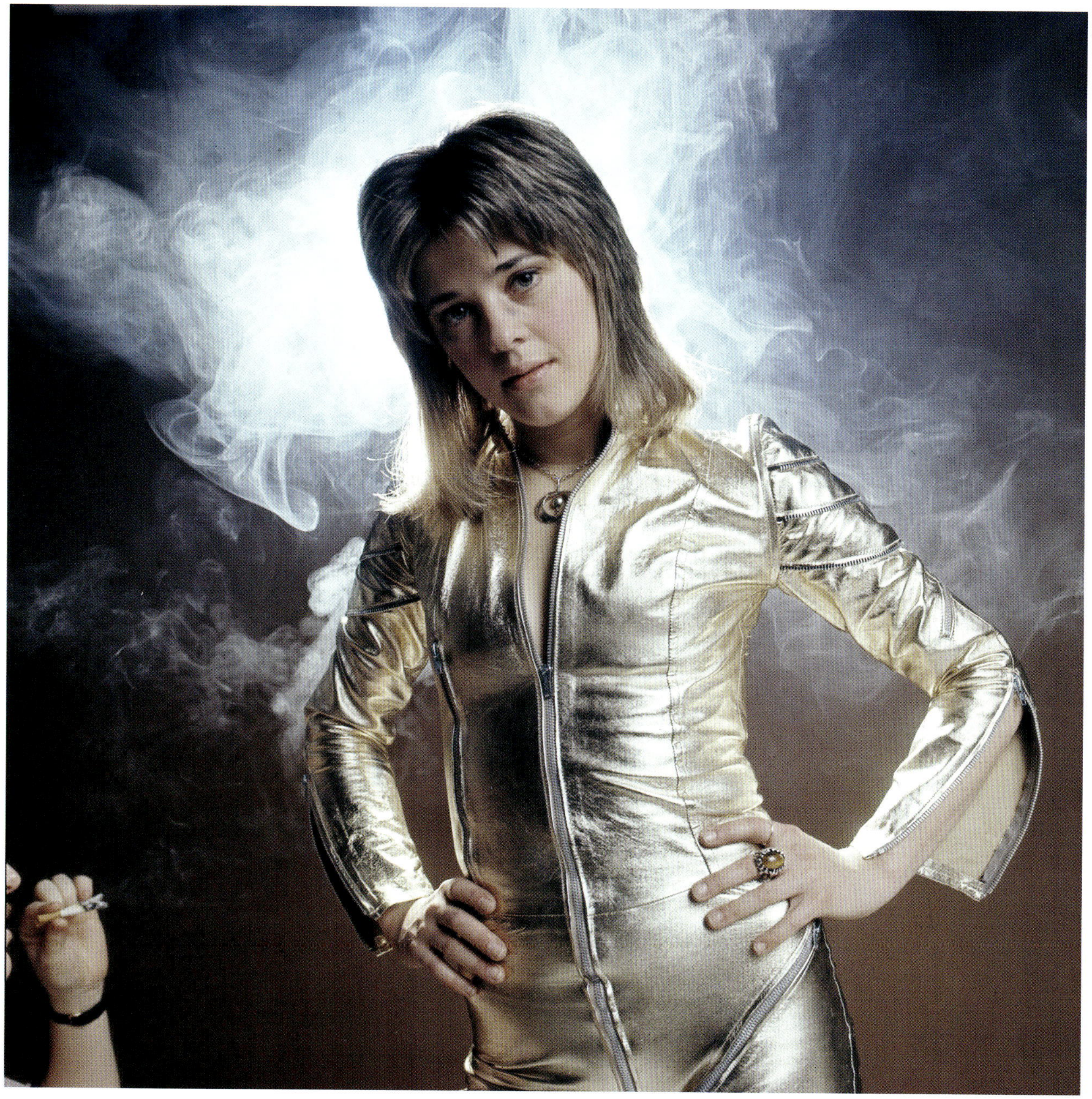

Smokescreen

The Sun, 1975

American singer-songwriter Suzi Quatro came to be photographed in the studio. She was hot property after a string of hits like 'Can the Can' and 'Devil Gate Drive'. In the '70s, smoky backgrounds were what every star wanted but I hadn't got a smoke machine. This uncropped image shows the low-tech solution. I used a couple of heavy smokers from her road crew to help us out by puffing away furiously at several cigarettes at a time to work up a moody fug.

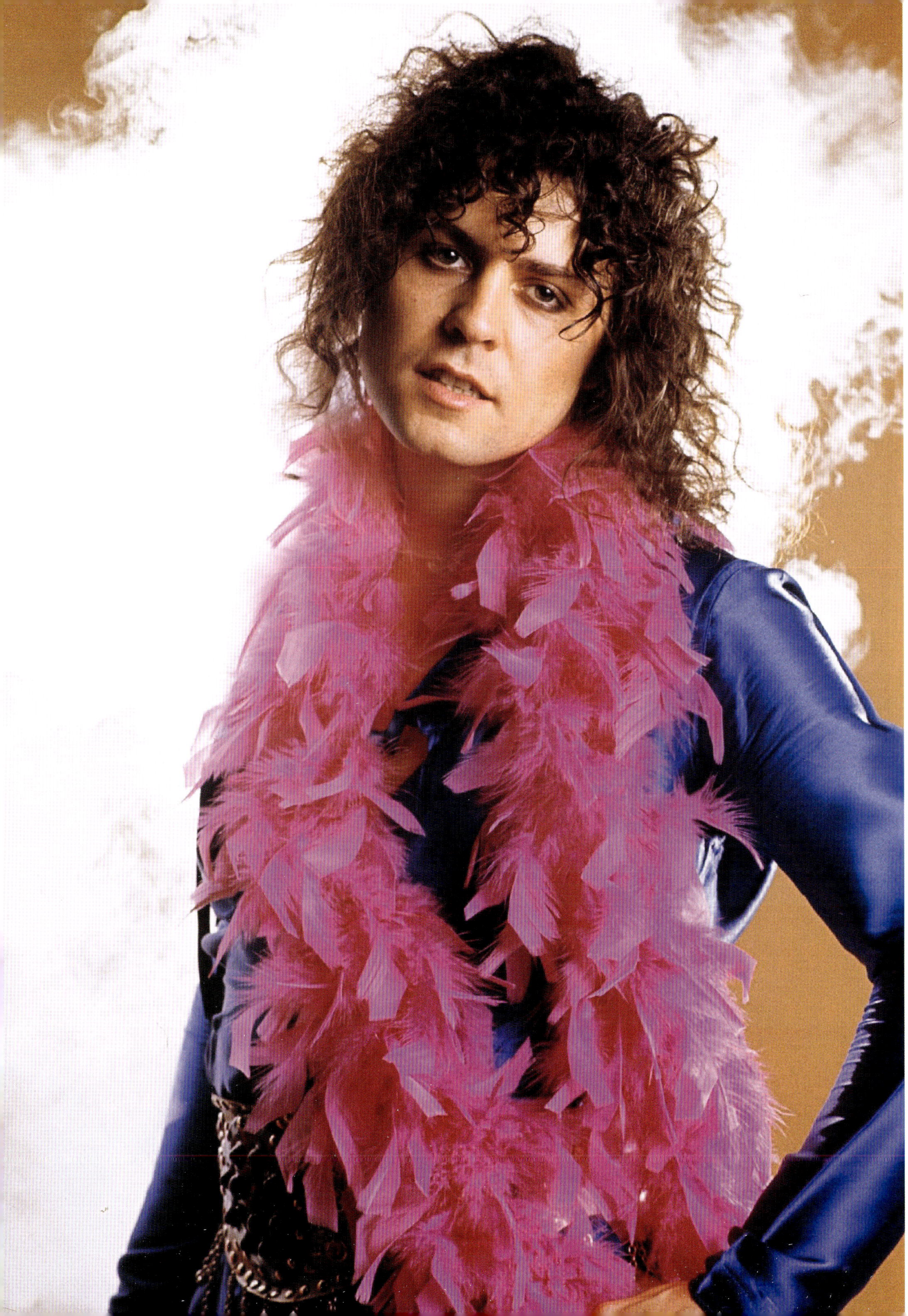

Glam Rocker

The Sun, 1973

Singer, songwriter, poet and glam rock pioneer Marc Bolan, the lead singer and front man of T. Rex, was a really sweet and good-natured soul I photographed several times in the 1970s. But this picture from 1973, where he's effortlessly out-glamming his own feather boa, is my favourite. His death at the age of twenty-nine was a terrible shock. He was killed when a car driven by his girlfriend Gloria Jones hit a tree in Barnes, London in September 1977.

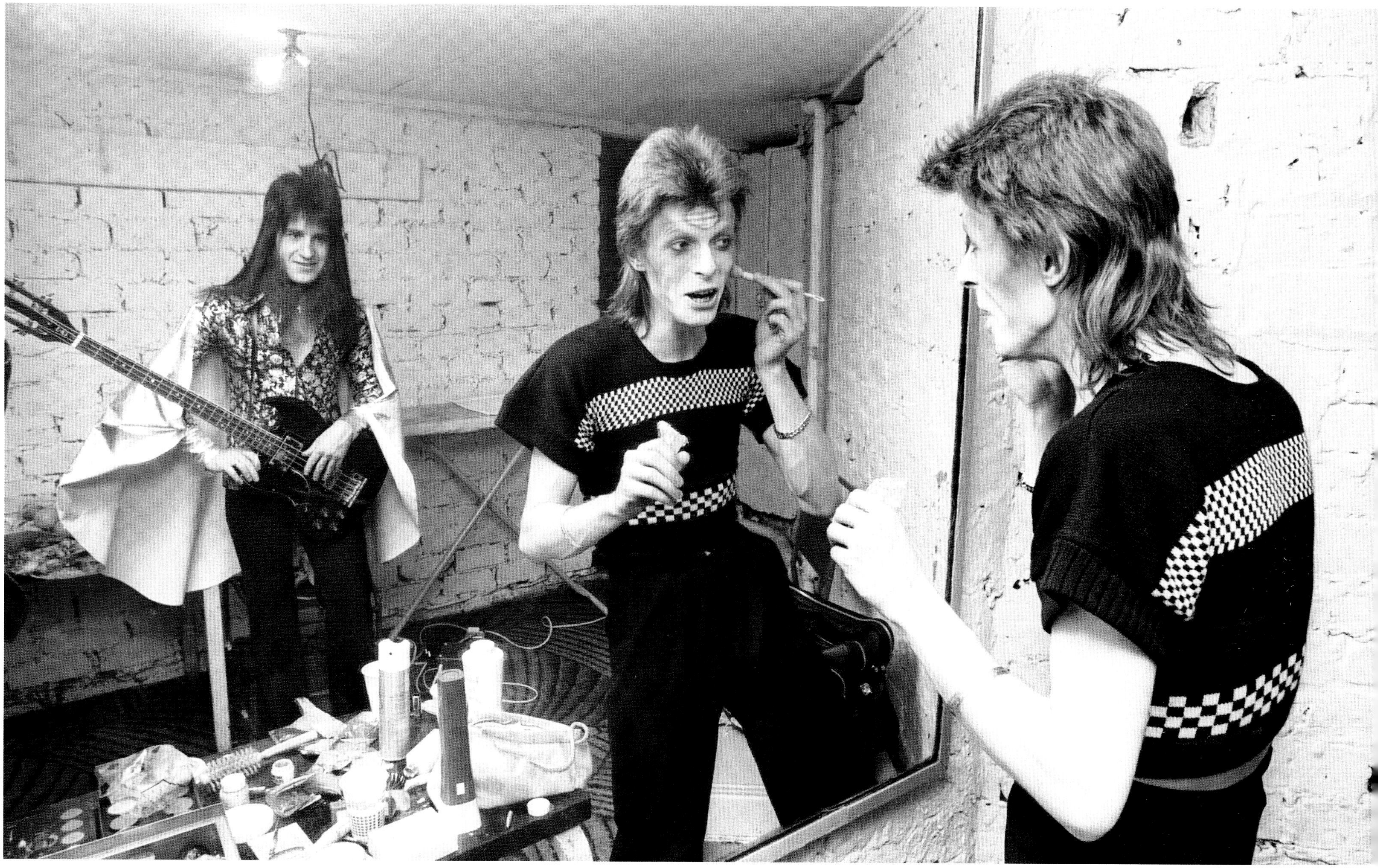

Stardust

The Sun, 1973

Rock icon David Bowie, let me hang about in the shabby dressing room of the Lewisham Odeon in South London to watch him applying his Ziggy Stardust make-up. Reflected in the mirror is his bass guitarist Trevor Bolder, who was waiting for the hairdresser to tidy his sideburns.
Bowie was always friendly and treated me as part of his team when I worked with them, so he tried to help when my prized Lotus Cortina was nicked that night, during the concert. He and his guitarist, Mick Ronson, put me in their tour bus and we drove around all the back streets of Lewisham, looking for the car. We couldn't find it so in the end, in the early hours of the morning, they drove me all the way home to my flat in West London.

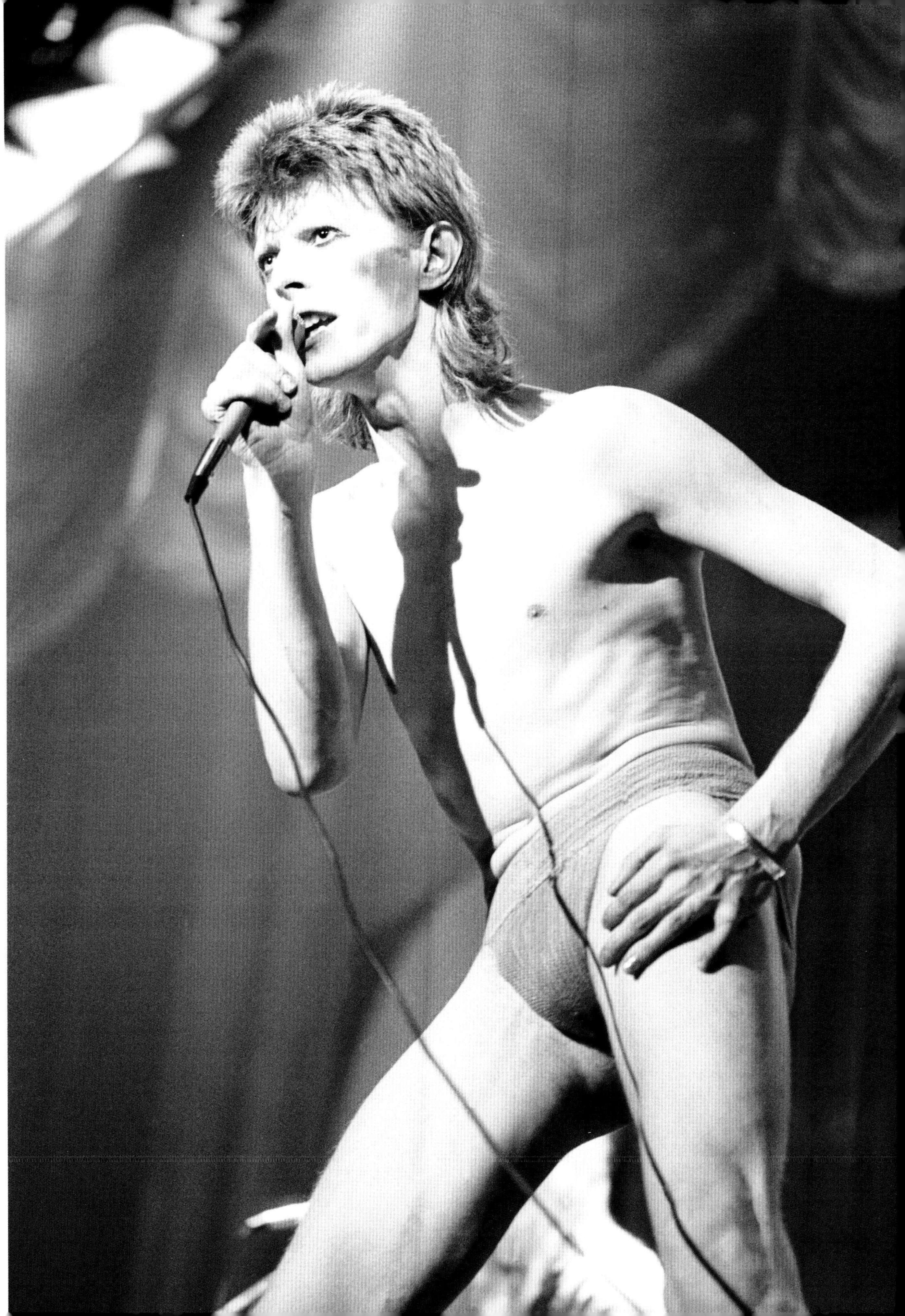

Rock Star in his Underpants

The Sun, 1973

Touring meant endless setting up and sound checks before performances. Bowie wasn't worried about dressing up as he ran through the set. When the crew called, he just strolled onstage. In his pants, on this occasion.

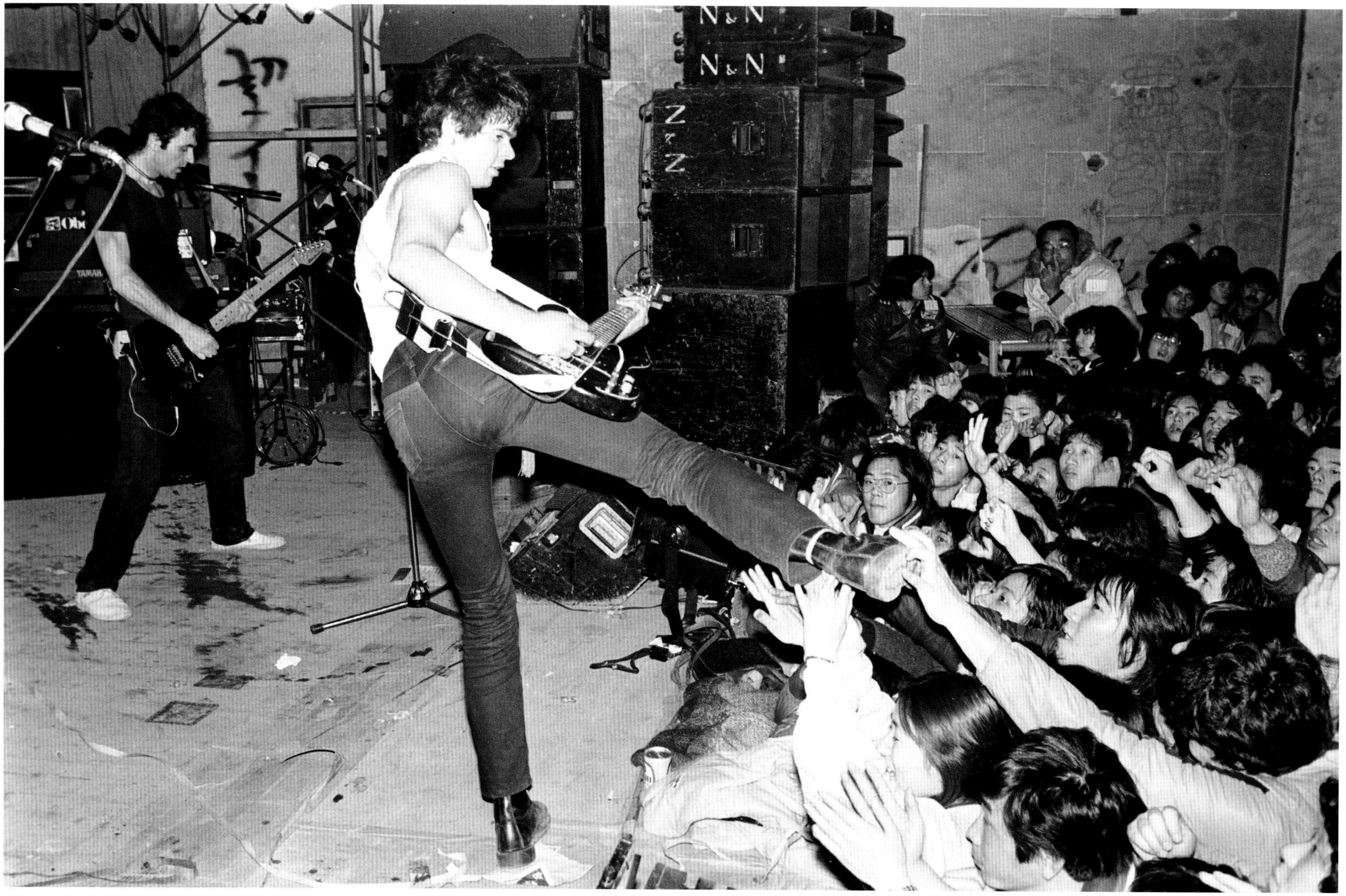

Strangled

The Sun, 1979

At the height of the punk explosion of the 1970s, the paper sent me to the Far East to cover a tour of Japan with the Stranglers, a rather more melodic outfit than the Sex Pistols and at that time topping the charts with 'Golden Brown' and 'Peaches'. Venues in Tokyo, Kyoto and Osaka were packed with adoring audiences, and the four band members were all great guys. This picture was taken in Osaka. I loved every minute of it. It must have been memorable for them too, because when they played Brighton in 2011 and I went backstage to say hi I was greeted by bass player Jean-Jacques Burnel with, 'Hello Roger, I haven't seen you for a while.' It had been thirty-two years.

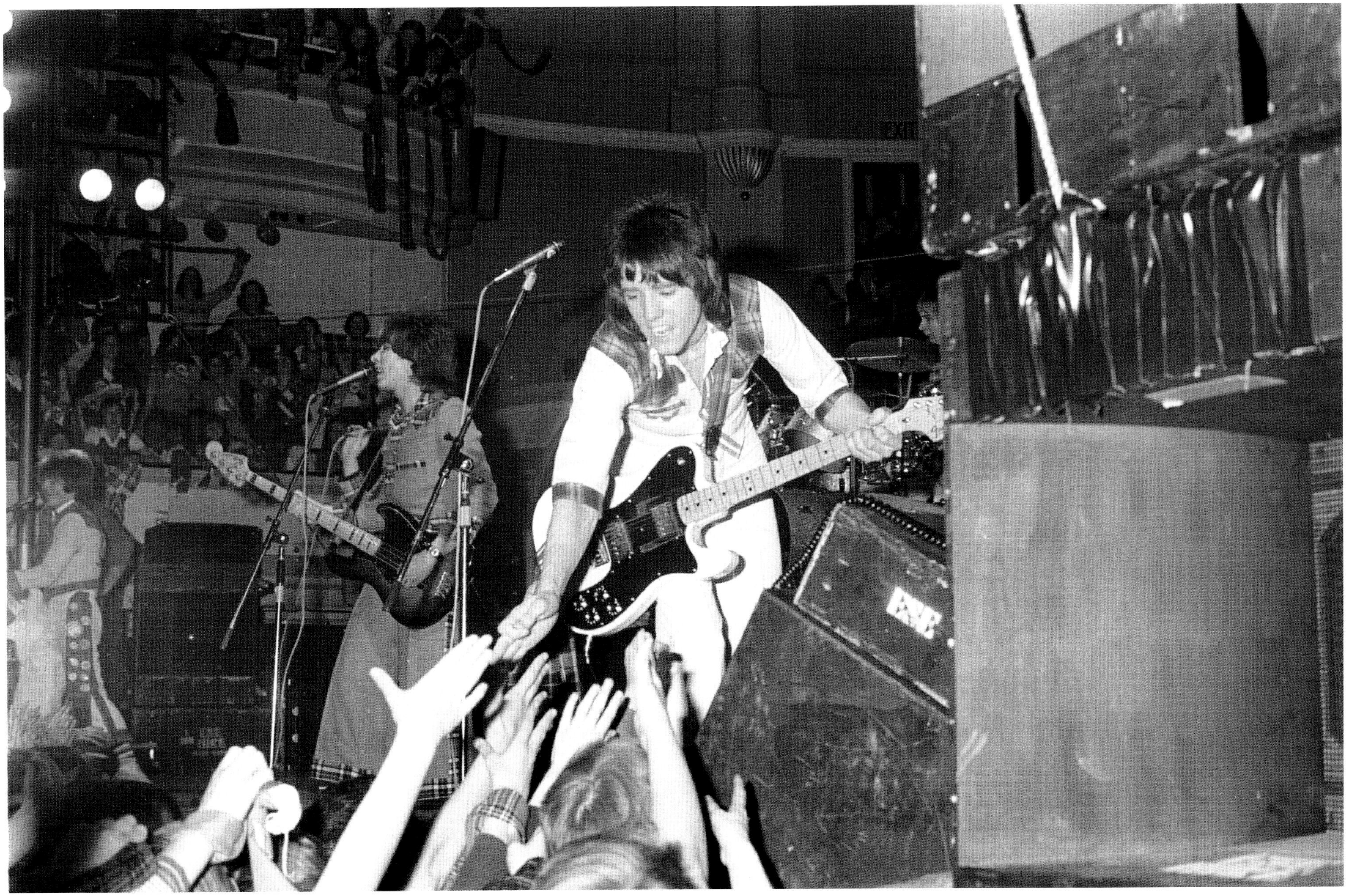

Bye Bye Rollers

The Sun, 1975

I used to enjoy photographing pop and rock musicians until this band entered my life. The Bay City Rollers were up-and-coming, so I contacted Tony Barrow, a press officer working with Arista Records to arrange to photograph them for the *Sun*. The answer was yes, but on one condition. Their manager, Tam Paton, insisted that I not only did one of their concerts, but I would then continue to photograph the whole tour, giving him the pictures after the *Sun* had used them.

The paper agreed, so off I set, doing concert after concert, photographing the same five Scottish guys in short trousers with tartan bottoms being screamed at by little girls night after night and staying in cheap motels.

Then came Oxford. This turned out to be my escape gig. During a particularly exuberant number the fans went a bit wild, which resulted in lead singer and front man Les McKeown whacking a fan with a microphone stand. The paper used it and my involvement with the Bay City Rollers was over. No more 'Keep on Dancing', no more 'Shang-a-Lang', no more 'Bye Bye Baby'. I got fired. Thank God.

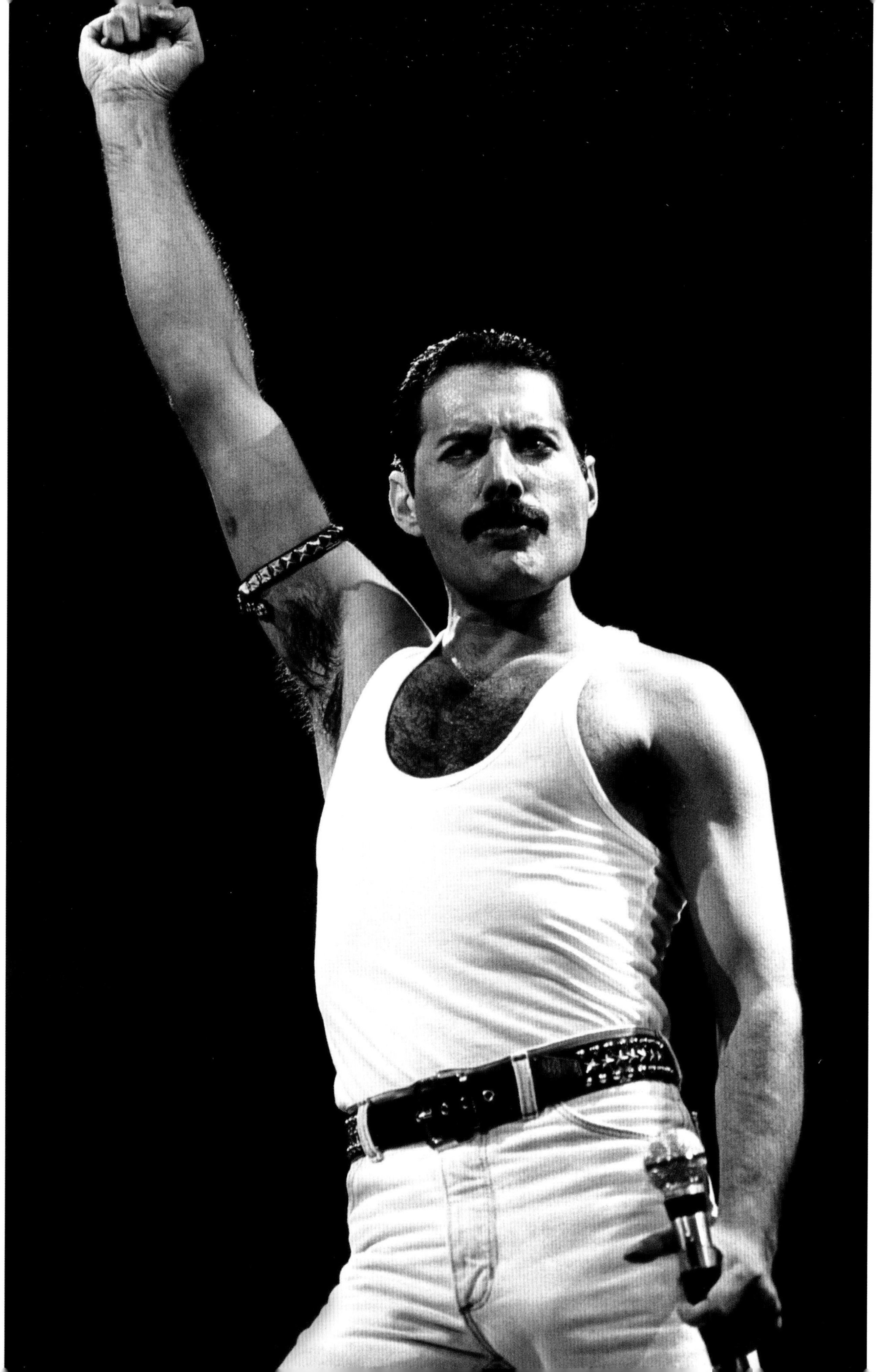

Live Aiding

The Sun, 1985

Fabulously flamboyant Freddie Mercury, frontman of Queen, salutes the crowd during the band's showstopping performance for Live Aid at Wembley Stadium in 1985. The twenty-four-hour-long fundraiser for famine relief in Ethiopia had been pulled together by Bob Geldof and Midge Ure. It became the show of the decade. The *Sun* sent only two photographers. Me to cover front of stage and the great Dave Hogan backstage. The *Daily Mirror* had fifteen snappers ... but we liked to think our coverage matched theirs.

Waste Man

The Guardian, 2006

Sculptor Antony Gormley is perhaps best known for his giant *Angel of the North* in Gateshead, but he built another vast figure on the site of the Dreamland funfair in the seaside resort in Margate, Kent. It was called *The Wasteman* and was designed to be destroyed only weeks after it was finished. Here assembler Will Shannon is abseiling down the 75-ft sculpture after adding to the hundreds of old discarded chairs, tables, beds, bookcases, and other household items (including a toilet seat for his nose) that were used in its construction. It was the centrepiece of the Margate Exodus project, which ended with *The Wasteman* being ceremonially torched and turned into a massive bonfire.

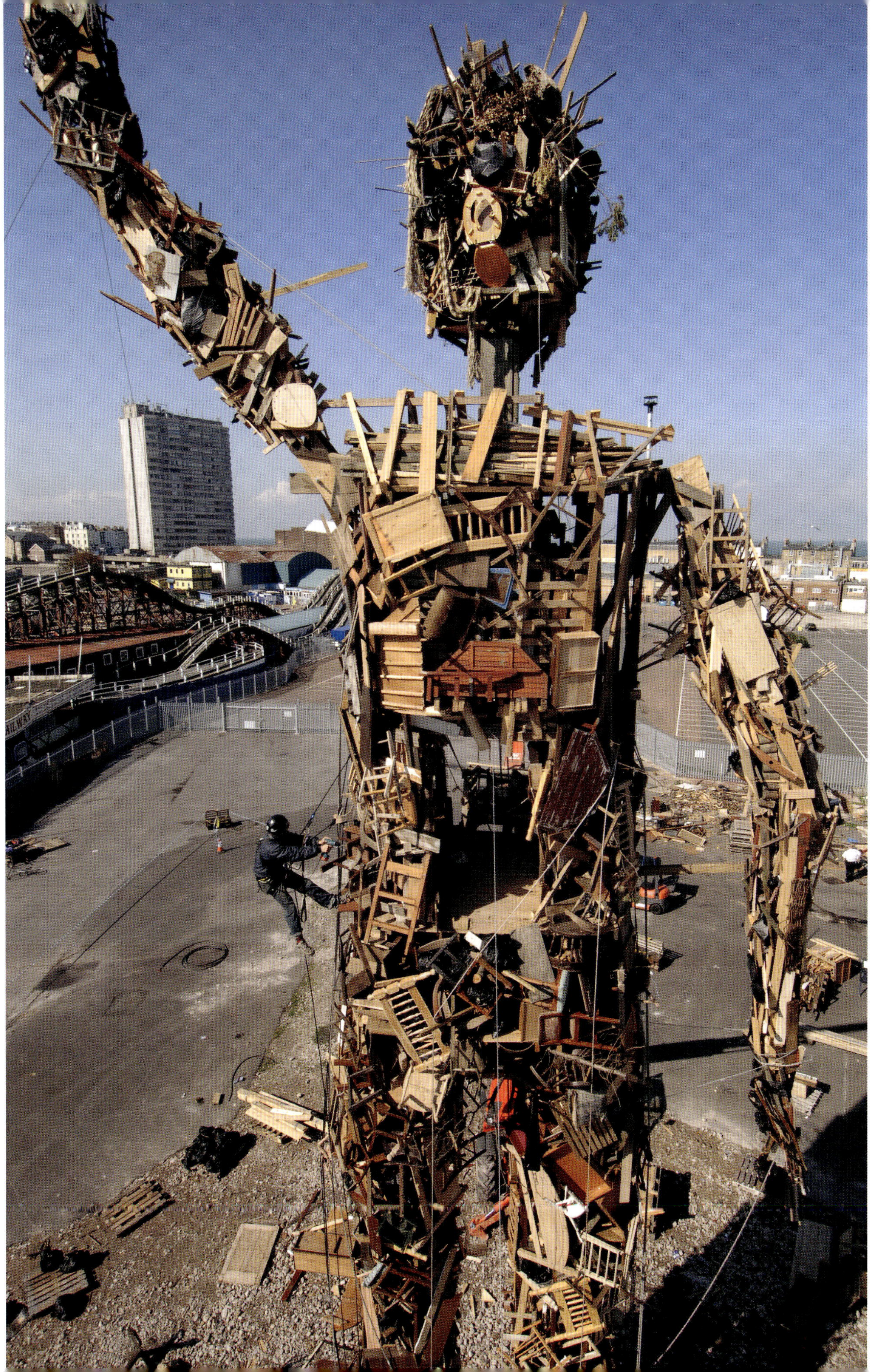

Satisfaction

The Sun, 1983

Jerry Hall was expecting her first child by Mick Jagger and the couple were rumoured to be on holiday somewhere in Barbados. I was sent off to the Caribbean to find them, the only small problem being that I didn't have the first clue where they were. A slice of luck came my way when I tried to hire a car. The Barbados police had to issue every driver with a Barbadan driving licence before the hire could go through, which meant that every applicant had to fill in a form saying where they were staying. If I had to give my address, then so did Mick Jagger. When I went to the licence office to fill in the application form, there was a pile of earlier applications on the desk. I had a quick look and, bingo, there was Mr Jagger.

So armed with my new driving licence, and a hired Mini Moke, I set off back to my hotel, to compose a 'congratulations on the baby-to-be' note and send it along with a gigantic bunch of flowers and a bottle of fizz to Mick and Jerry at their at their holiday hideaway.

Jagger responded quickly, coming down to my hotel for a drink and agreeing to meet the next morning on a local beach.

The result was this picture, where Mick is clowning about with a guitar on the shoreline, pretending to serenade Jerry – but he isn't singing. He's laughing at the daft, fully dressed photographer and all his equipment getting thoroughly soaked by a huge wave.

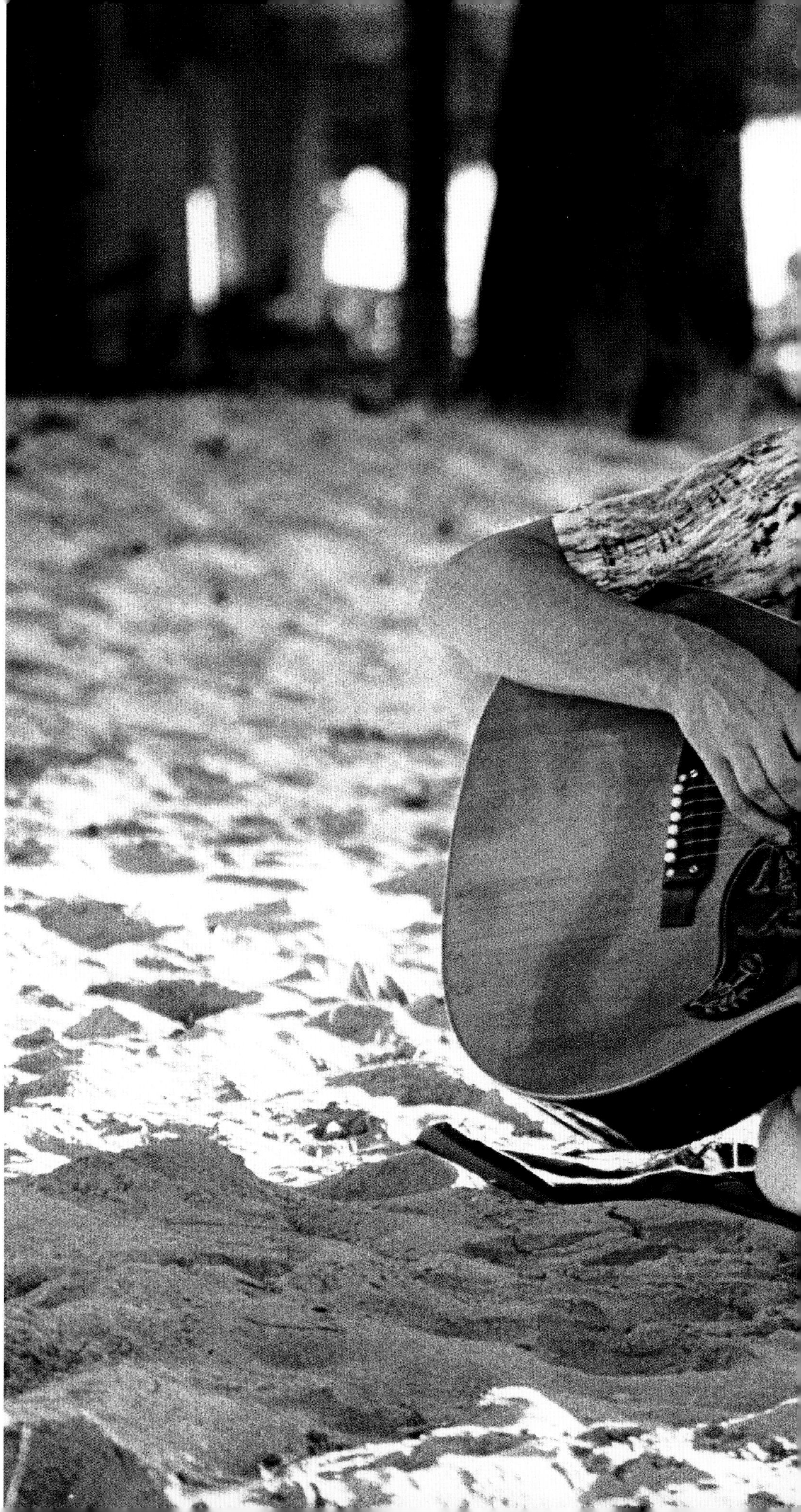

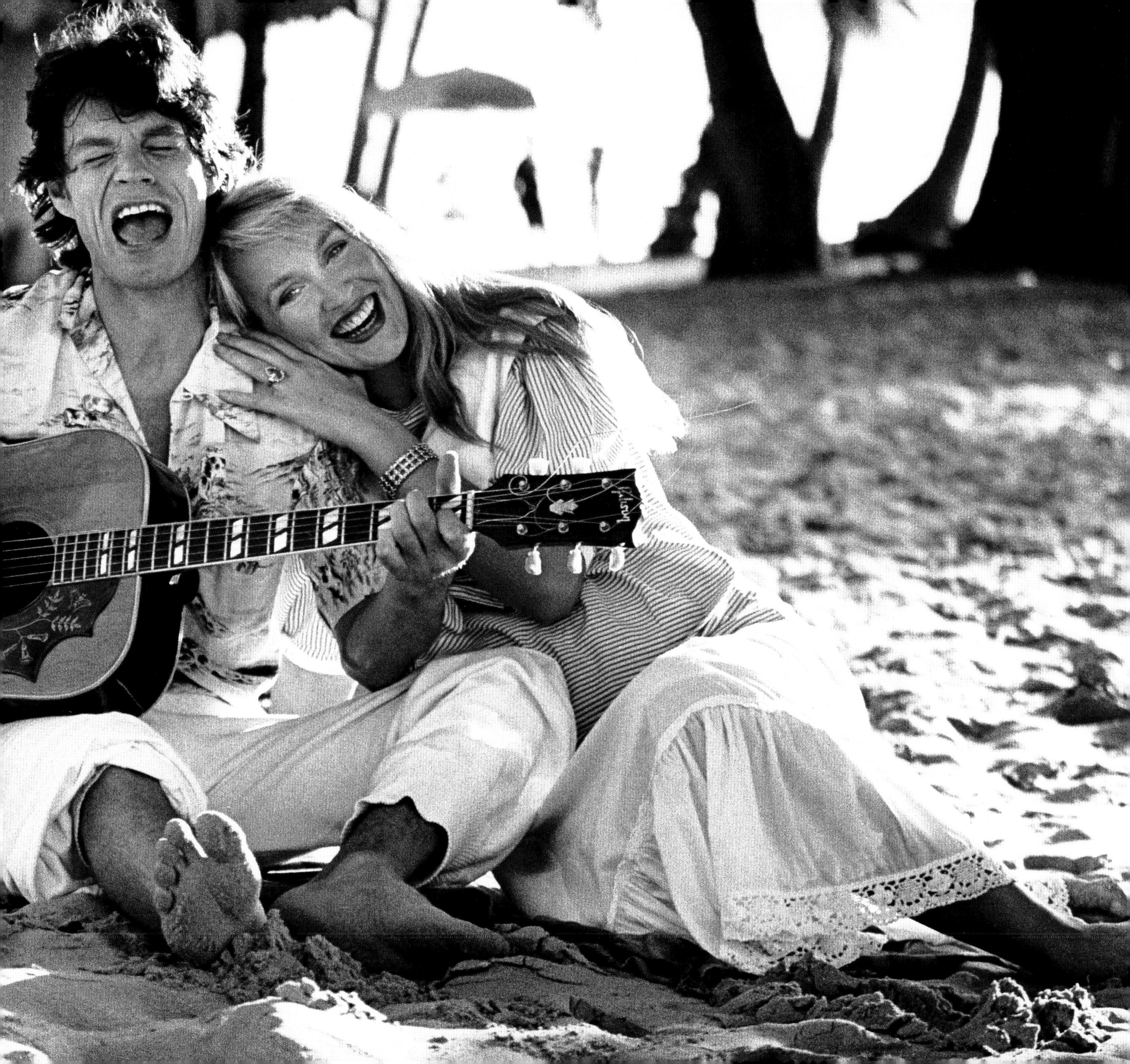
Gibson

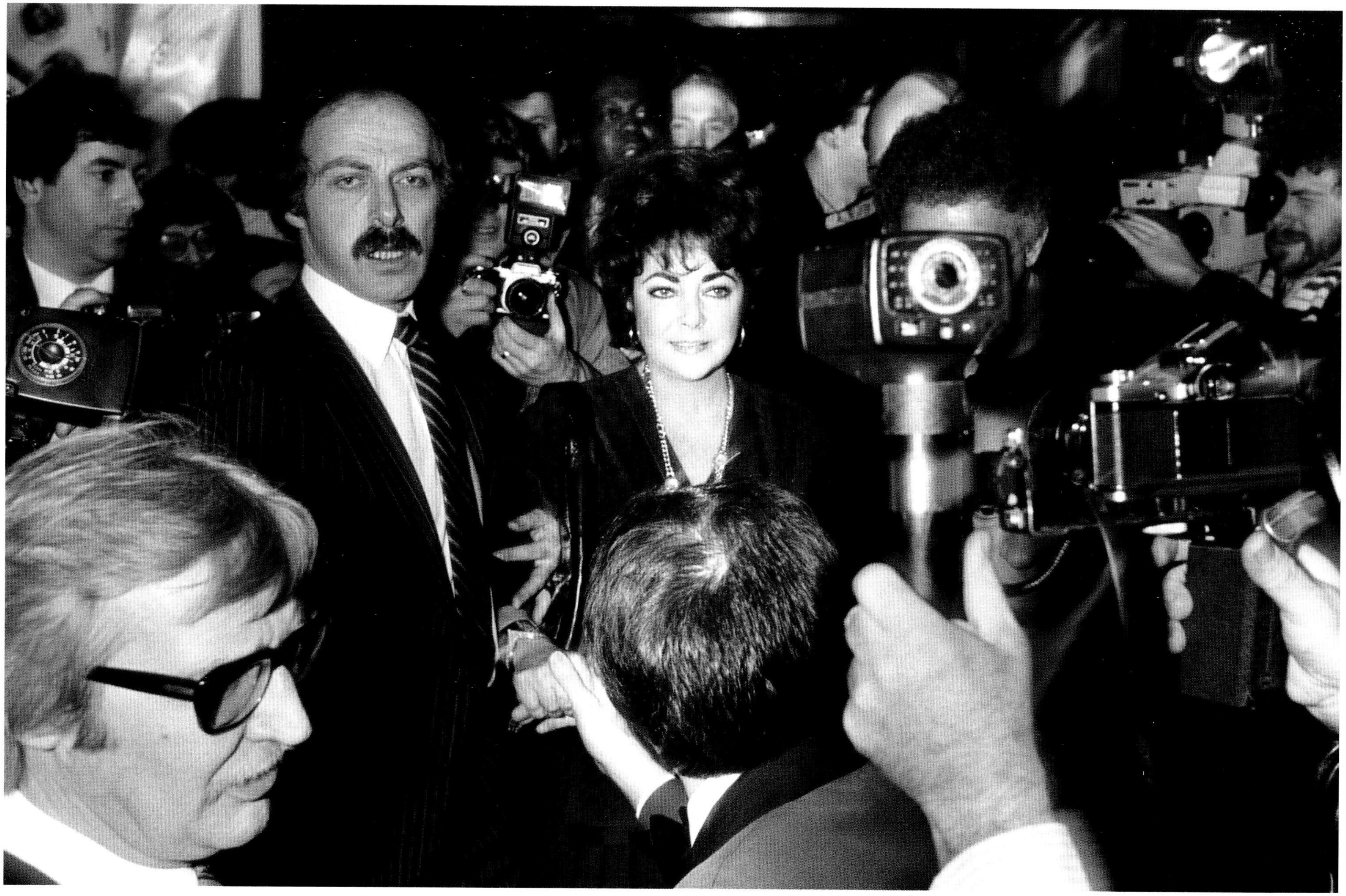

Lady of Quality

The Sun, 1982

Actress Elizabeth Taylor engulfed by a mass of journalists and photographers as she leaves the theatre at the London Palladium flanked by her security guards after publicising her play *Little Foxes*, her first British stage debut. I'd known her since meeting her with her then-husband, Richard Burton, in Gstaad, Switzerland when I was working for the *Daily Mail* back in 1967. Every time I saw her I felt there was something very special about her. You always knew you were in the presence of a real star.

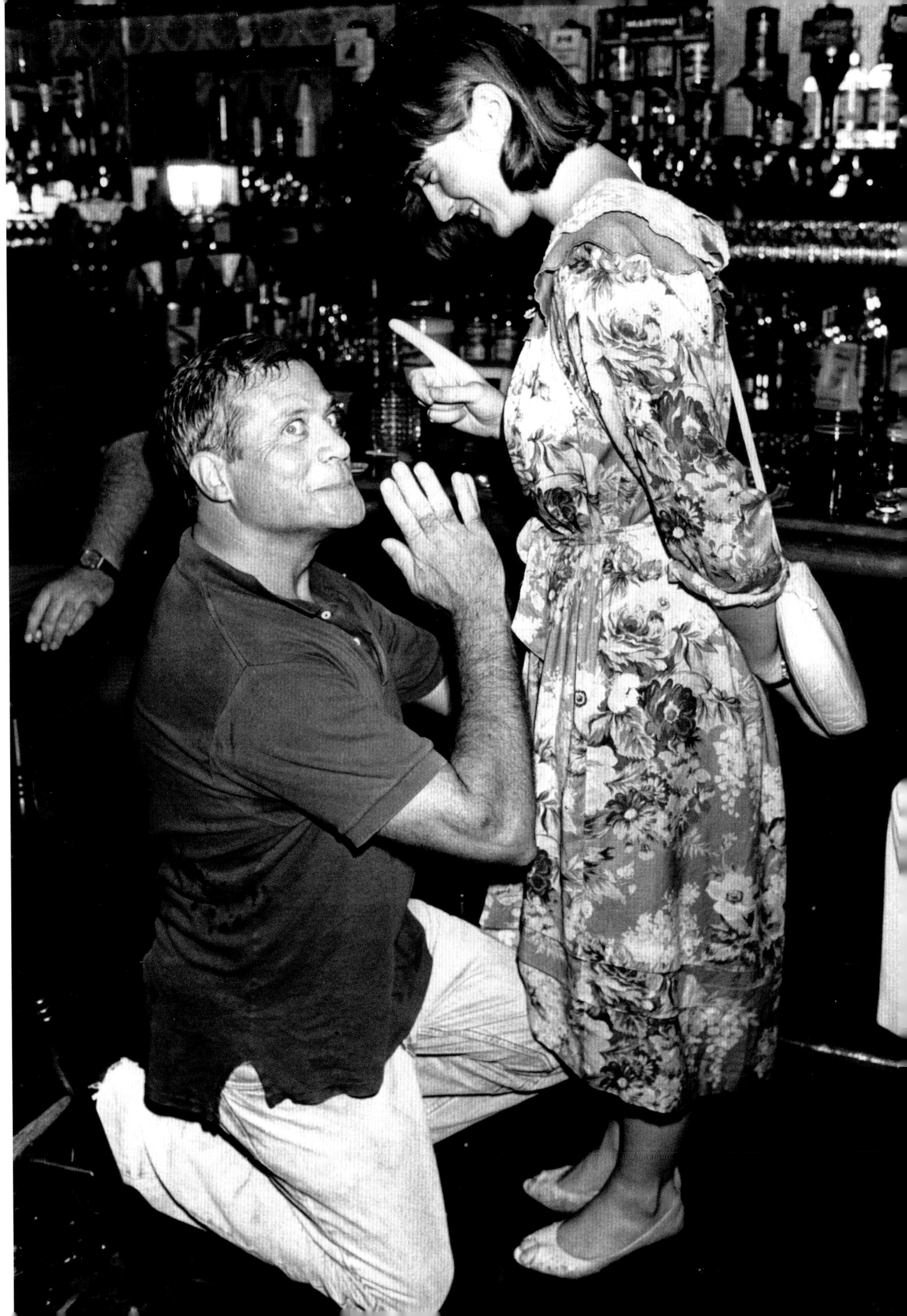

Sorry

The Sun, 1984

Actor and professional hellraiser Ollie Reed gets down on his knees to apologise to his girlfriend Josephine Burge in a pub in Guernsey. He had just spent a weekend in the island's jail after being arrested for wrestling naked with visiting Norwegian sailors in the streets. Josephine, thirty years his junior, not only forgave him, she actually married him a year later.
To the surprise of many, the marriage proved a success, although in 1986 Ollie was forced to dig up 9 acres of his back garden after forgetting where he had buried Josephine's jewellery when drunk.

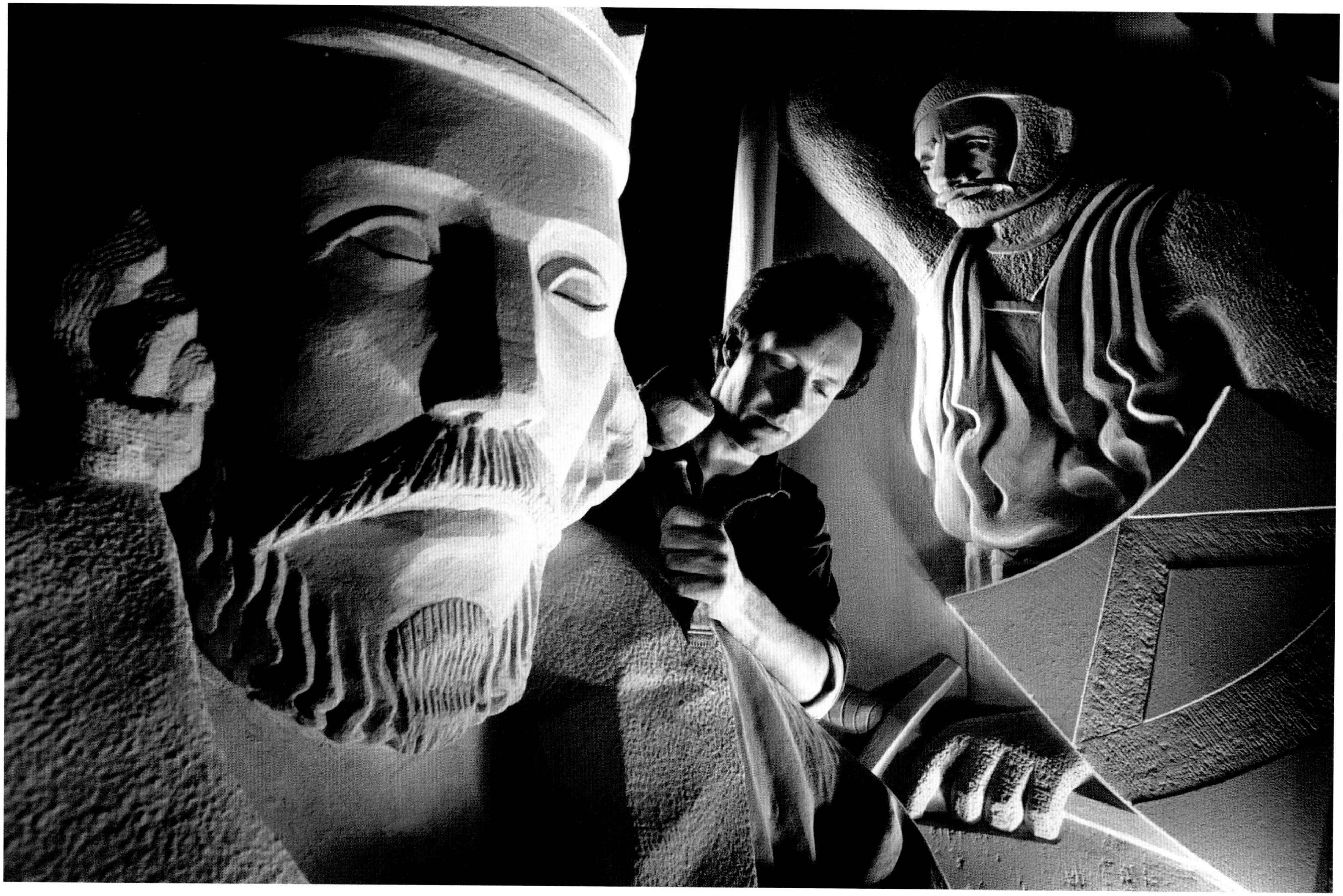

Chip off the Old Block

The Guardian, 1994

Sculptor and stonemason David Parfitt is finishing a Portland stone statue of King John for a Magna Carta memorial. It is now in situ in Egham, Surrey in the borough of Runnymede, close to the site of the sealing of the Magna Carta, a charter of rights, limiting the power of the monarchy. The knight in the background is Baron FitzWalter, one of the barons who persuaded the reluctant king to sign. I had to use builders' halogen lights to make the tiny, cramped studio where the statue was made look dramatic.

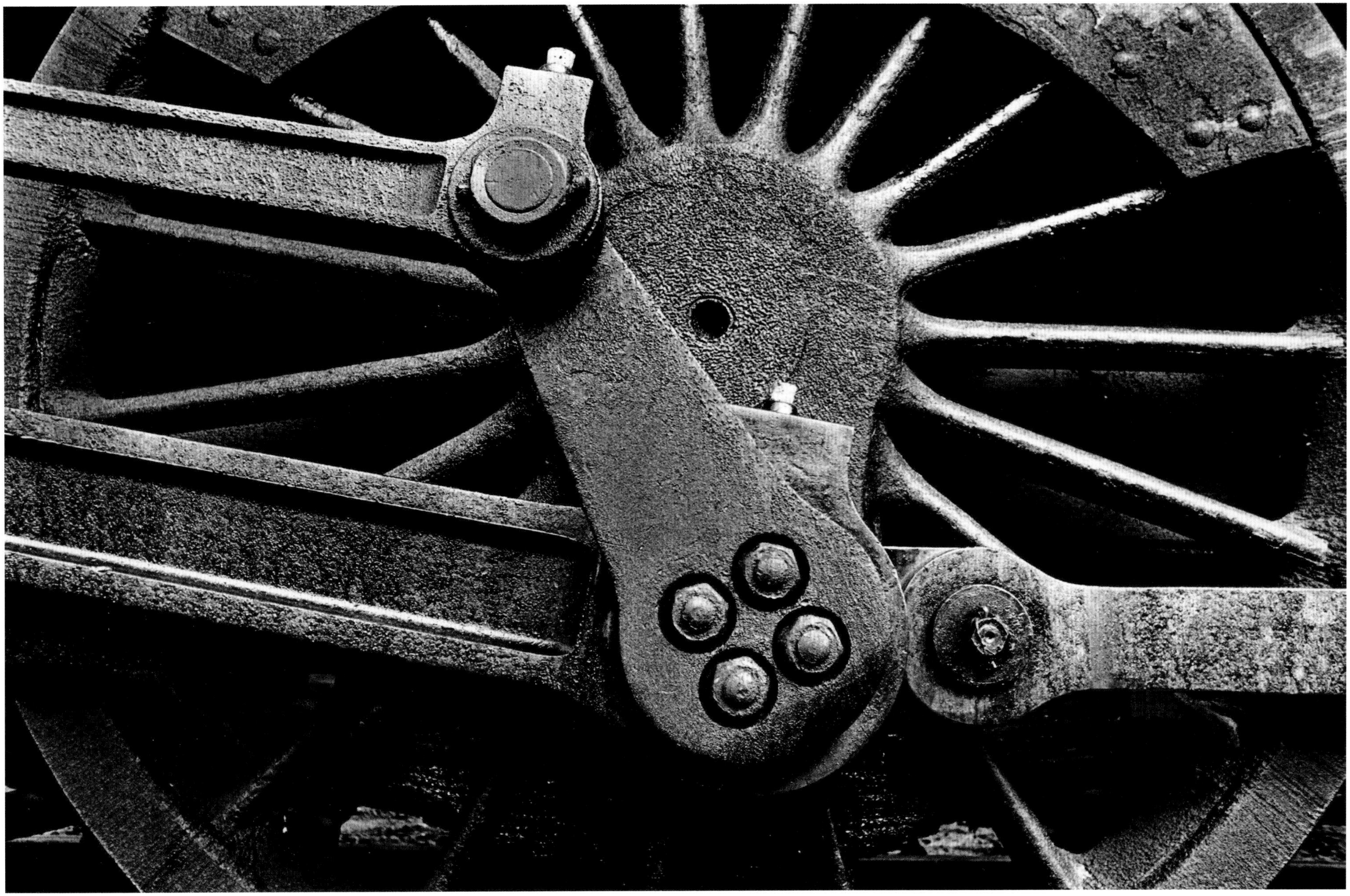

Driving Force

The Illustrated London News, 1968

Trackside dirt sticks to the central driving wheel and connecting rods of Stanier Black Five No 45346 as it waits in Leeds for its next journey. The wheel looks as if it's been pebbledashed – the result of dirty grease being blown about as the engine thunders along at speeds up to 70mph.

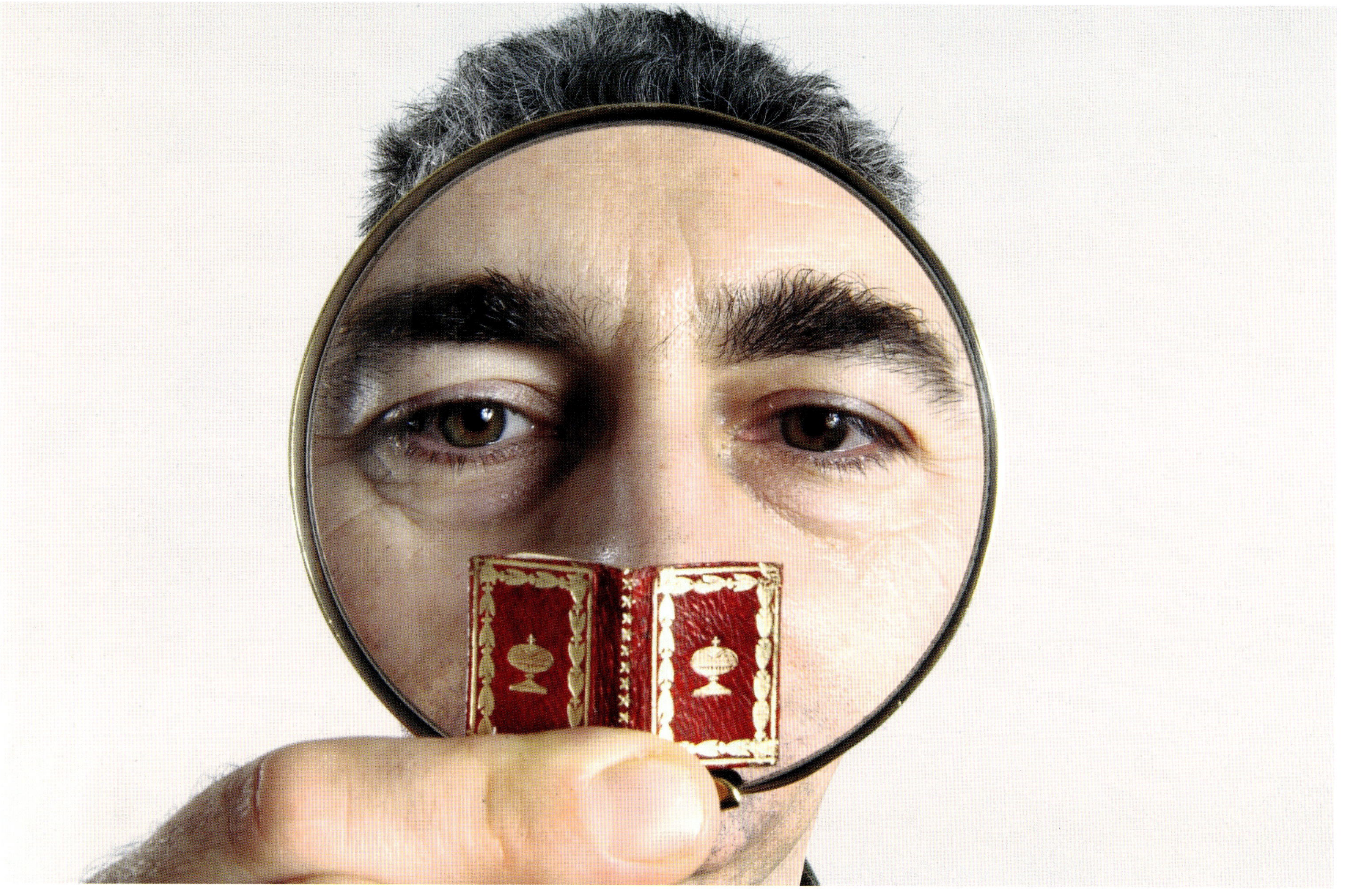

Thinking Big

The Guardian, 2005

At Brighton's Jubilee Library, collections specialist Nigel Imi uses a magnifying glass to examine a miniature Prayer Book, *Le Petit Paroissien* from the rare book section. The picture isn't photoshopped. We spent a long time tweaking the position of the magnifying glass until I managed to remove the sides of his face, leaving just his hair on the top.

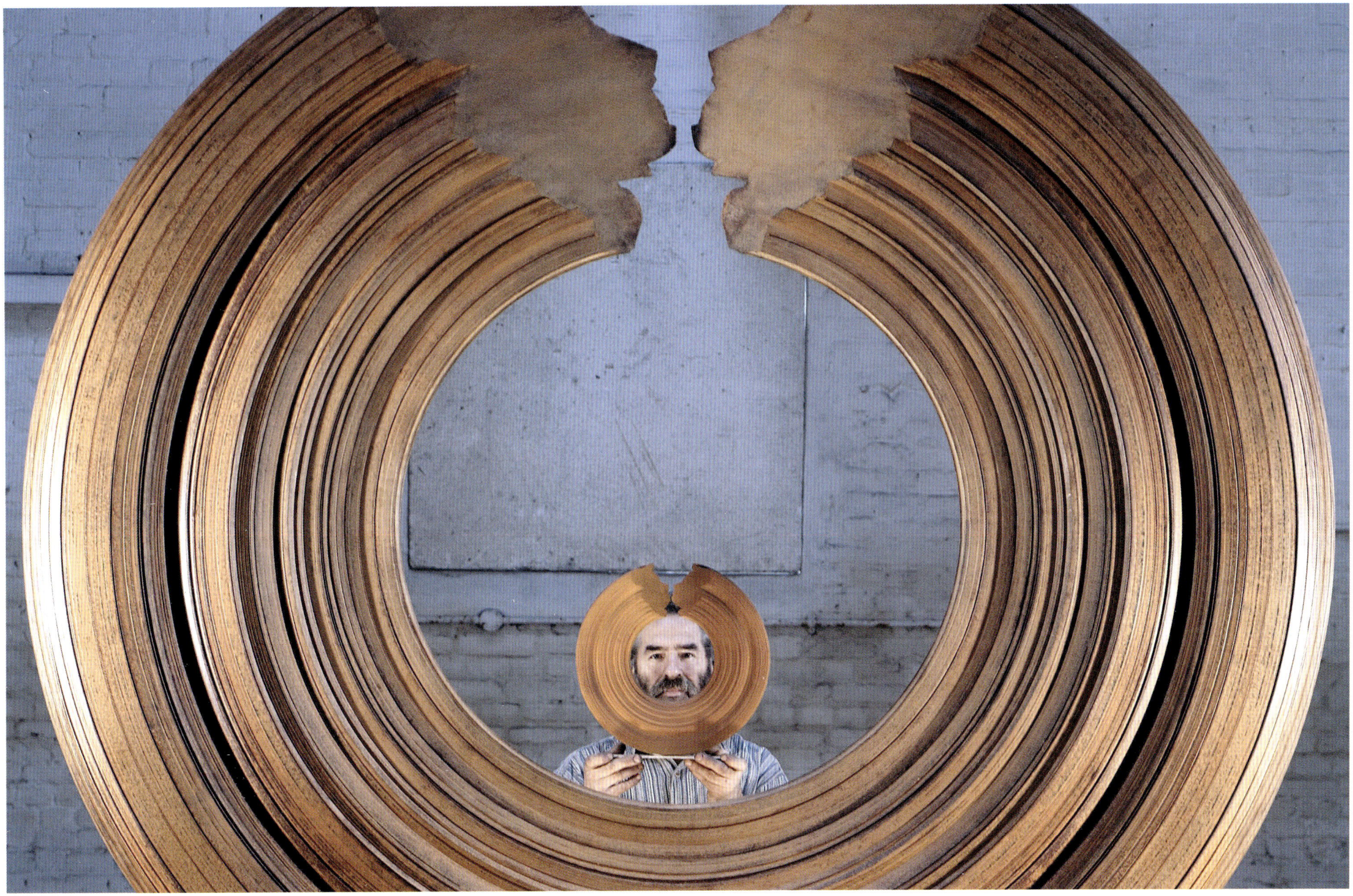

Inner Circle

The Guardian and the Independent, 2004

Sculptor Hamish Black with his maquette and finished work, *Westminster Double.* The 2.5-tonne sculpture of waxed, rusted steel, and its maquette, were commissioned by Jarvis Construction for the Hampden Gurney project, a city centre school and housing project in Marylebone, London. The oblique cut at the top mirrors a map of the London borough.

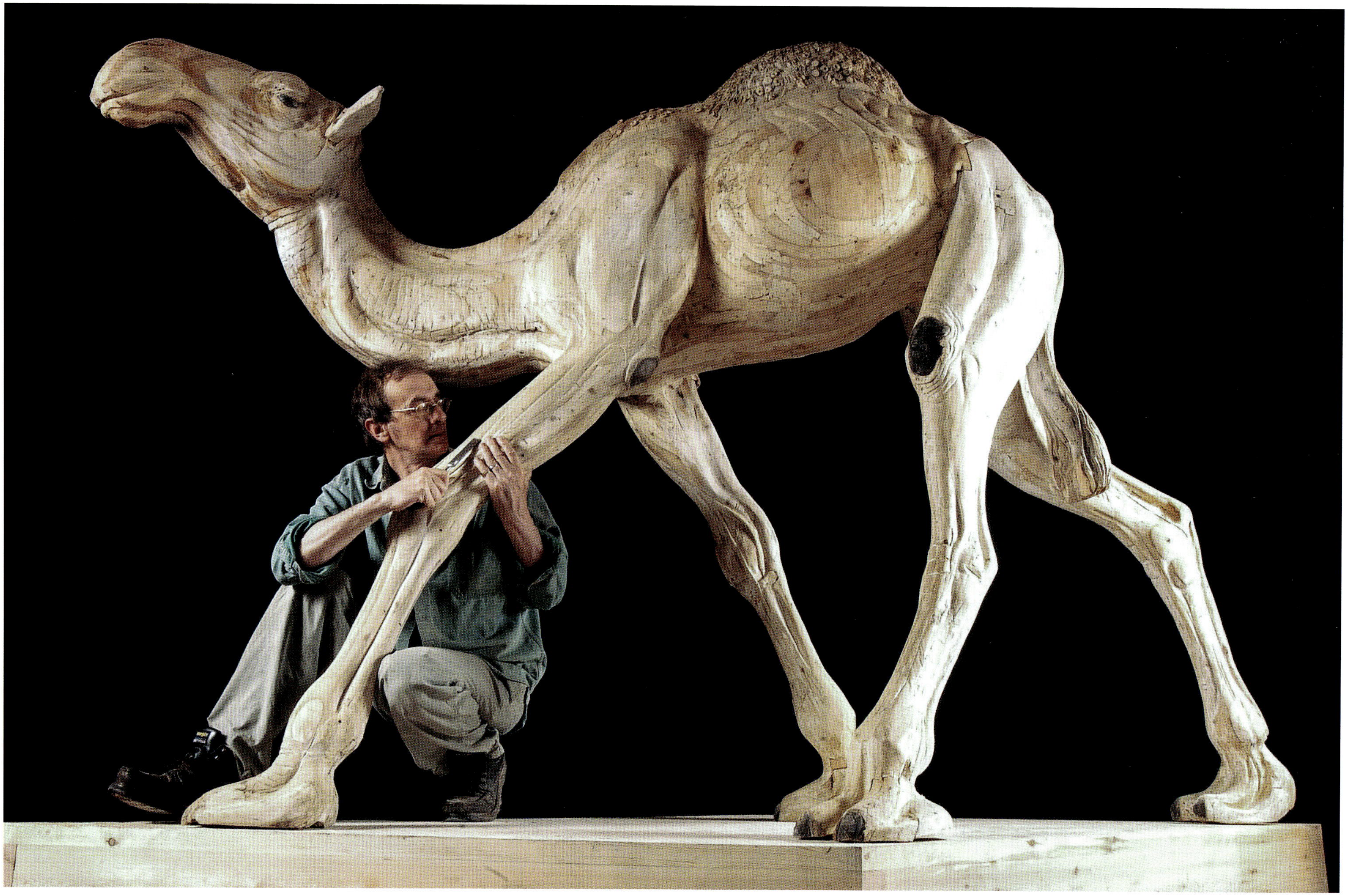

Boarding Up

The Guardian and the Daily Telegraph, 2002

Sculptor Nick Johnson carves animals and birds from recycled floorboards. This life-size dromedary, along with a rhinoceros, flamingoes, a cheetah, march hares, a cockerel, a hen and a lurcher, was made for an exhibition in the Browse & Darby Gallery in London. It all took him two years of painstaking work in his studio in Lewes, East Sussex.

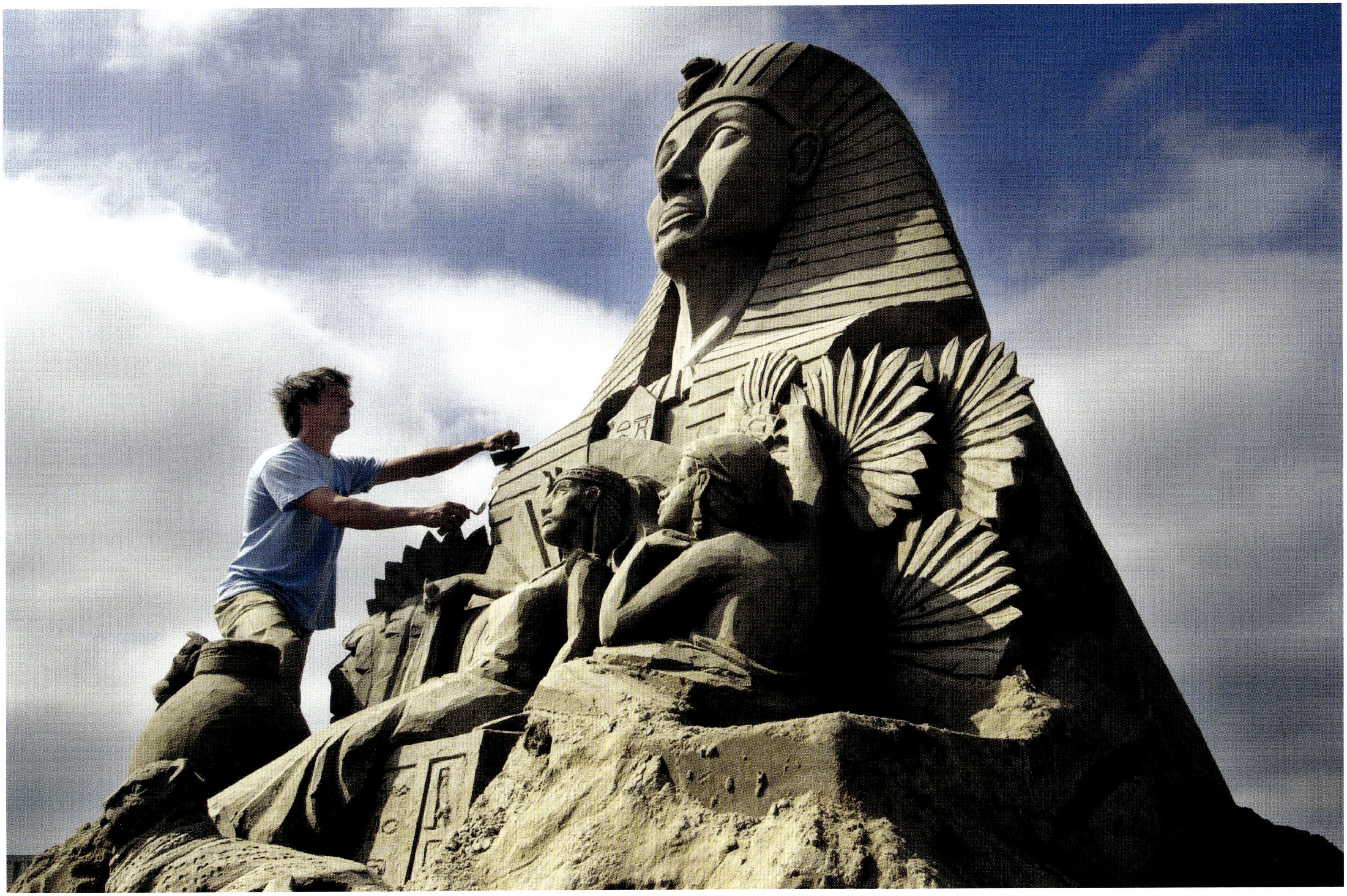

Carry On Cleo

The Guardian, 2005

Sand animation artist Martijn Rijerse models a portrait of Egyptian Queen Cleopatra at Black Rock on Brighton Beach as part of a giant sand sculpture exhibition. The display of sixty sculptures by sixty different modellers had an Egyptian theme, with pyramids, a sphinx, Cleopatra, slaves, camels and mythical beasts rising from the beach.
The project cost £1 million and used 13,000 tonnes of special sand which had to be shipped in. Brighton's beaches are mostly pebbles.

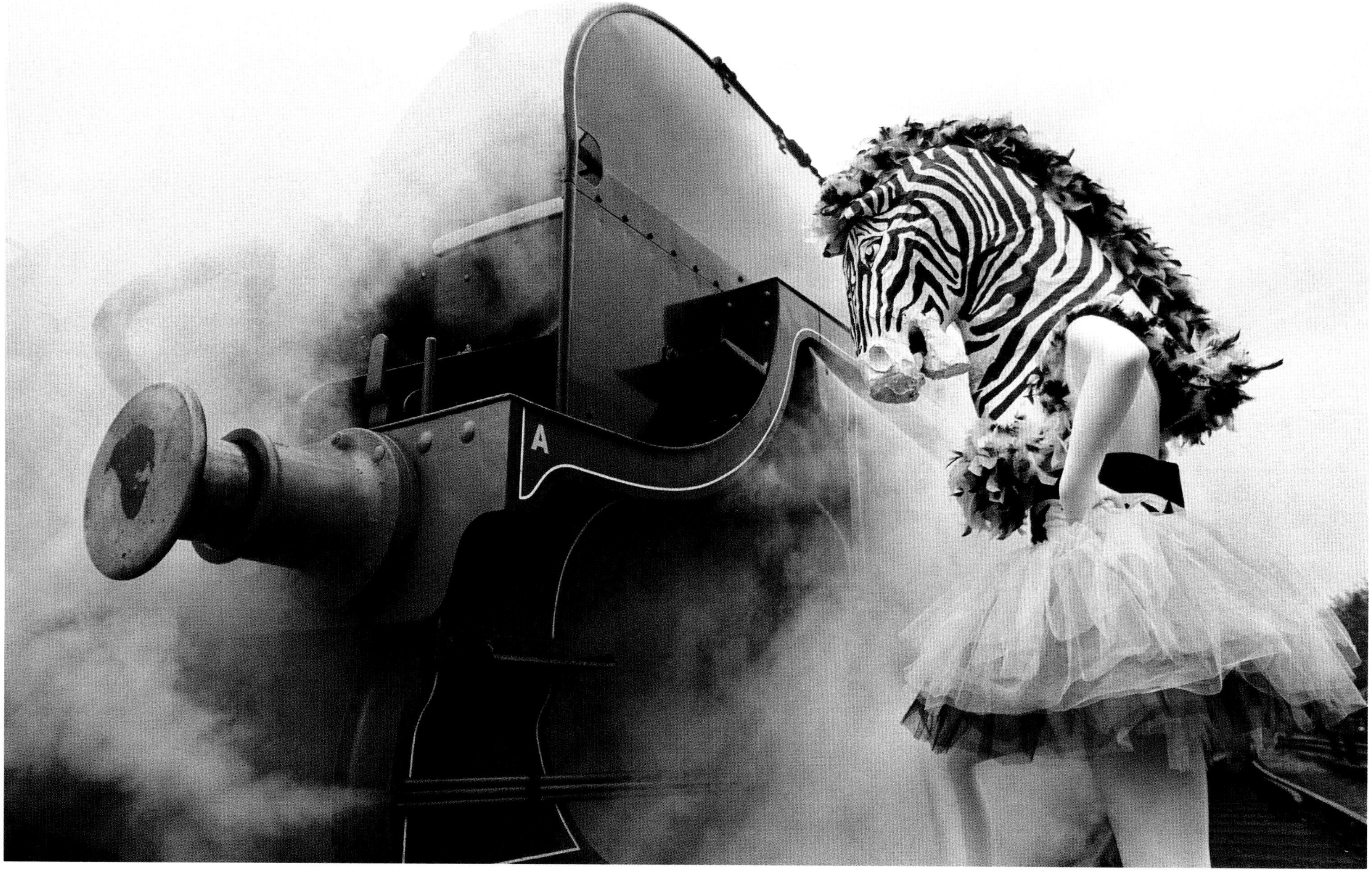

Brief Encounter

The Guardian, 1993

An unlikely but very happy combination of a troupe of actors and a steam train crew teamed up to make a station into a makeshift theatre for Brighton Festival in 1993. Eve Davies, the charming zebra here was one of the cast of Limn Gaza's surreal play, *The Joy of Return*, which was staged in the steam locomotive shed, on a train and on the platform of the Bluebell Railway at Sheffield Park, East Sussex. The play was billed as a journey of dance, speech, music and film. I never understood where the zebra fitted in but the audience loved it.

Artist and Muse

1963

Terence Cuneo was a great military painter, a dab hand at horses and the official artist for the coronation of Queen Elizabeth II in 1953, but his real love was railways. He adored them and is probably best known now for the classic posters he made for railway companies in Britain and France after the war. I was lucky enough to find him at work at Tyesley depot in Birmingham, sketching LNER class K4 No 3442 The Great Marquess. This picture was never published – I just wanted to capture the great man at work.

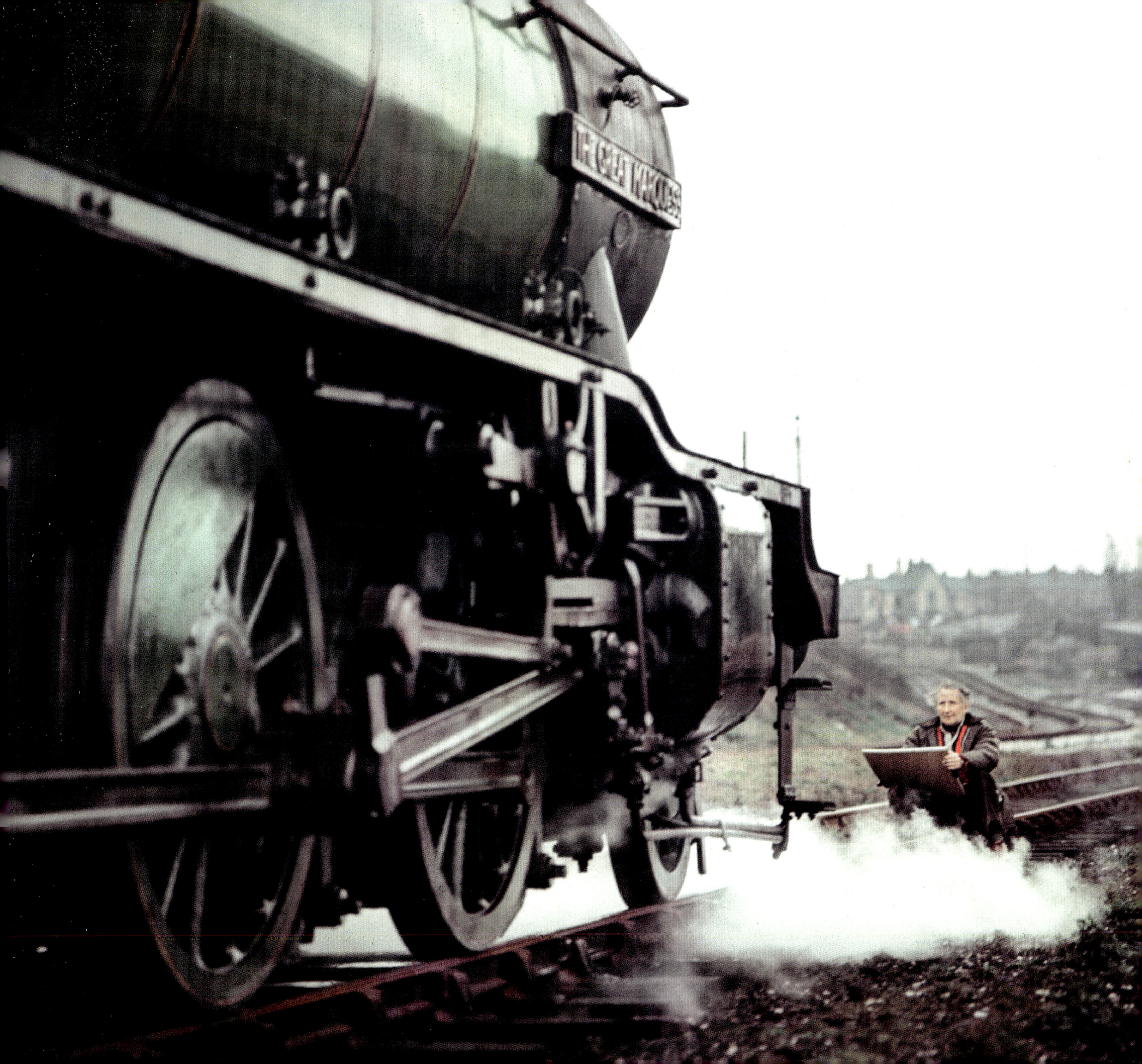
THE GREAT MARQUESS

Stepping Up

The Guardian, 2006

Leading British sculptor Sir Anthony Caro sits on his 120-ft-long creation, *Goodwood Steps*, at the time Britain's biggest sculpture. It had just been installed at the Sculpture at Goodwood sculpture park near Chichester, West Sussex and what neither the photographer nor the artist knew was that the park's staff had applied a coat of protective varnish to it the night before. Caro almost became a permanent display when he stuck to it.

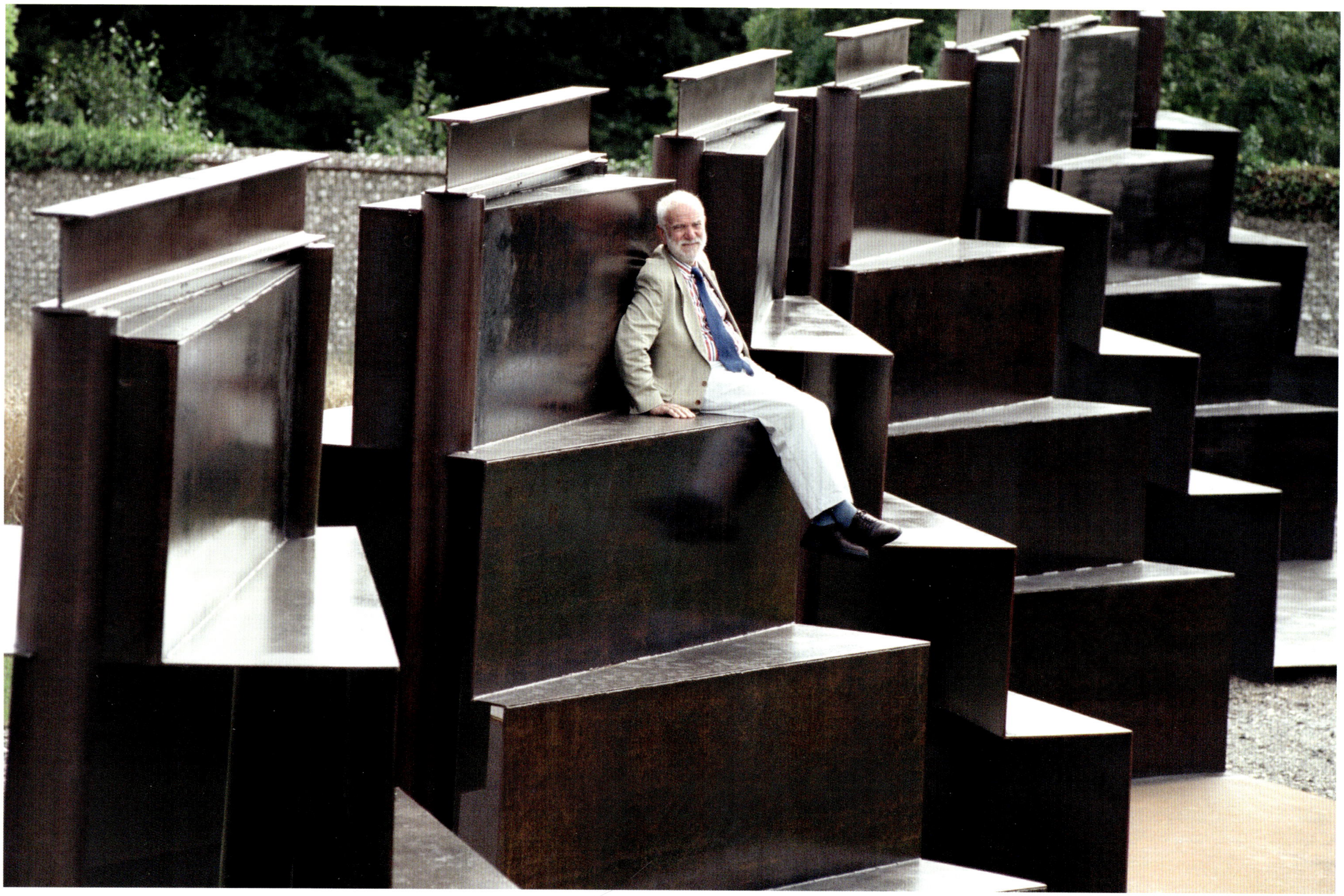

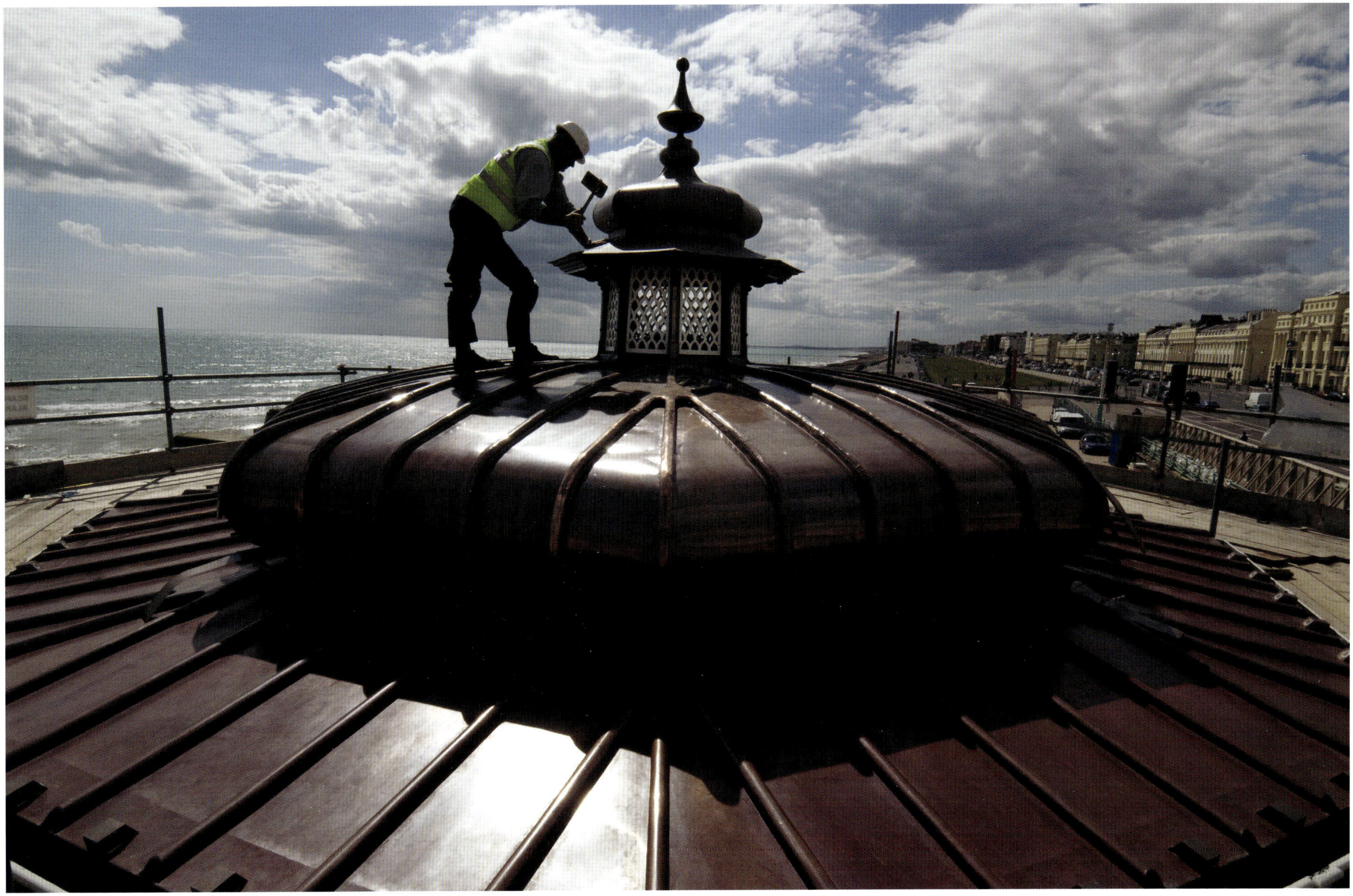

Copper Top

The Guardian, 2009

Coppersmith Tony Dines, hammering new copper sheeting into shape on to the cupola of the Victorian bandstand on Brighton seafront. It was undergoing a £1 million restoration programme after years of neglect. This was its first overhaul since the 1950s and I wanted to capture the copper with its raw, shiny, deep-red colour, before the sea air changed it to dull bronze and then to blue-green verdigris.

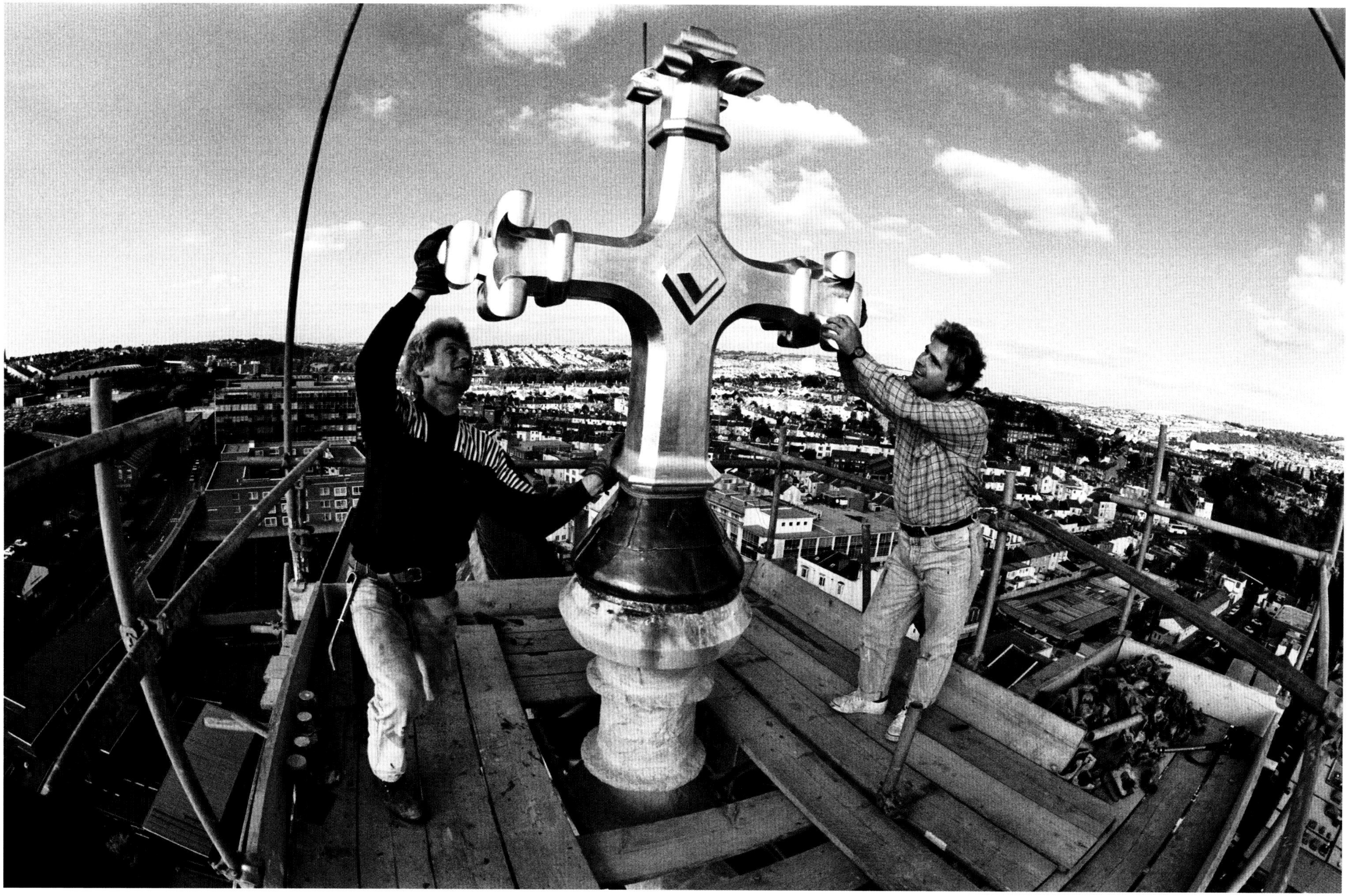

High Church

The Guardian, 1991

The view from the top of Britain's tallest parish church is dizzying but builders Leon Hazelgrove and Graham Buxton hardly gave it a glance.
They were perfectly happy 135-ft above the city streets, replacing the 9-ft gilt cross on the roof of St Bartholomew's Church, Brighton.
Below the roof is a church so lofty that John Betjeman once said it would be entirely in keeping if the priests made their entrance for Solemn High Mass riding on elephants.

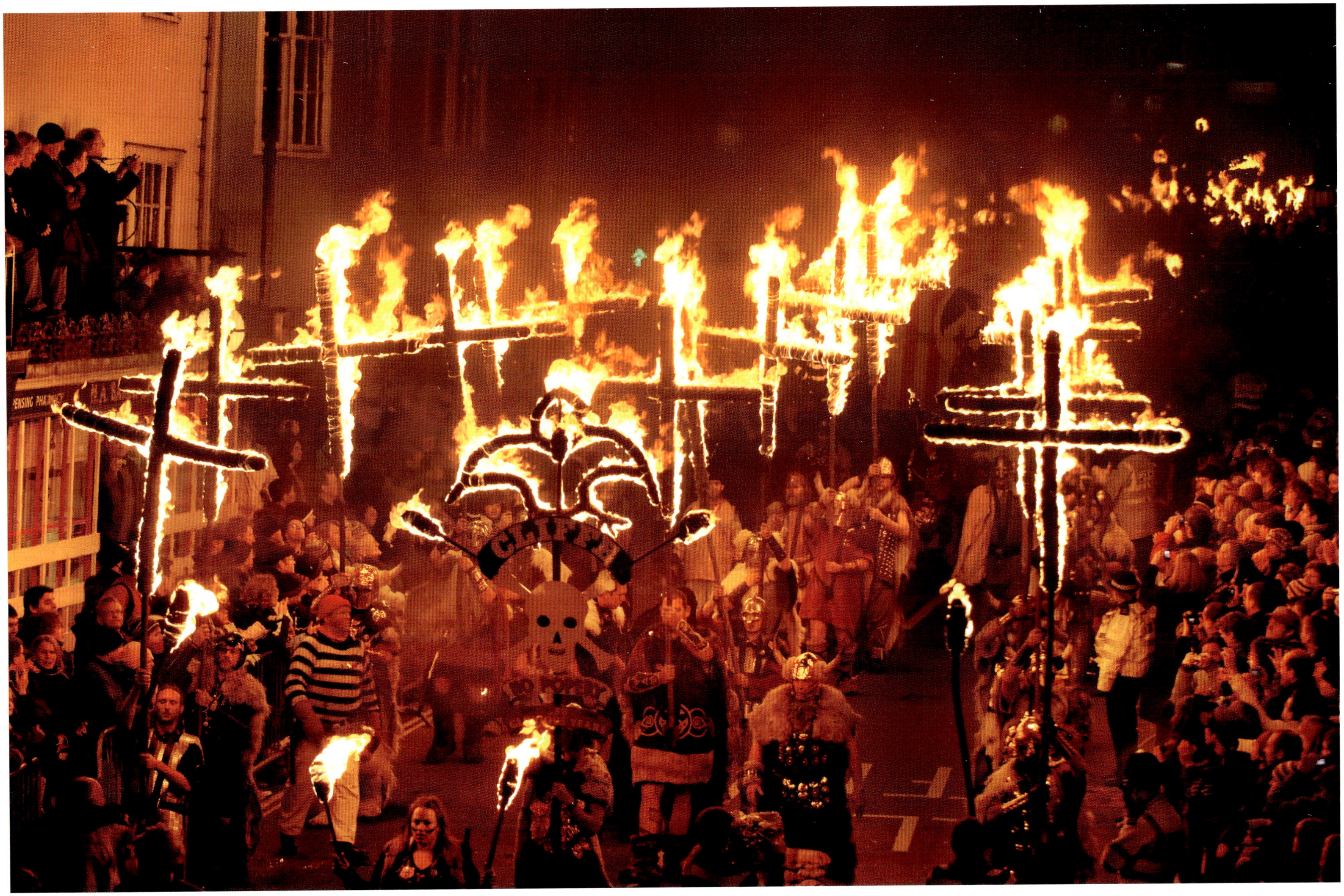

Bonfire Night in Lewes

The Guardian, 2006

Until this night I had never photographed the mammoth bonfire night celebrations in Lewes in the thirty-three years I'd lived in Sussex. The week before I met a broadcaster from local station, Rocket Radio, who couldn't believe I'd never done it and offered me a room above his studio in the heart of the town. It was an ideal viewpoint as the seven Bonfire Societies paraded through the town. Here is Cliffe Bonfire Society, carrying seventeen burning crosses to honour the seventeen Protestant martyrs, burnt at the stake in the town in the 1550s, for refusing to be Catholics.

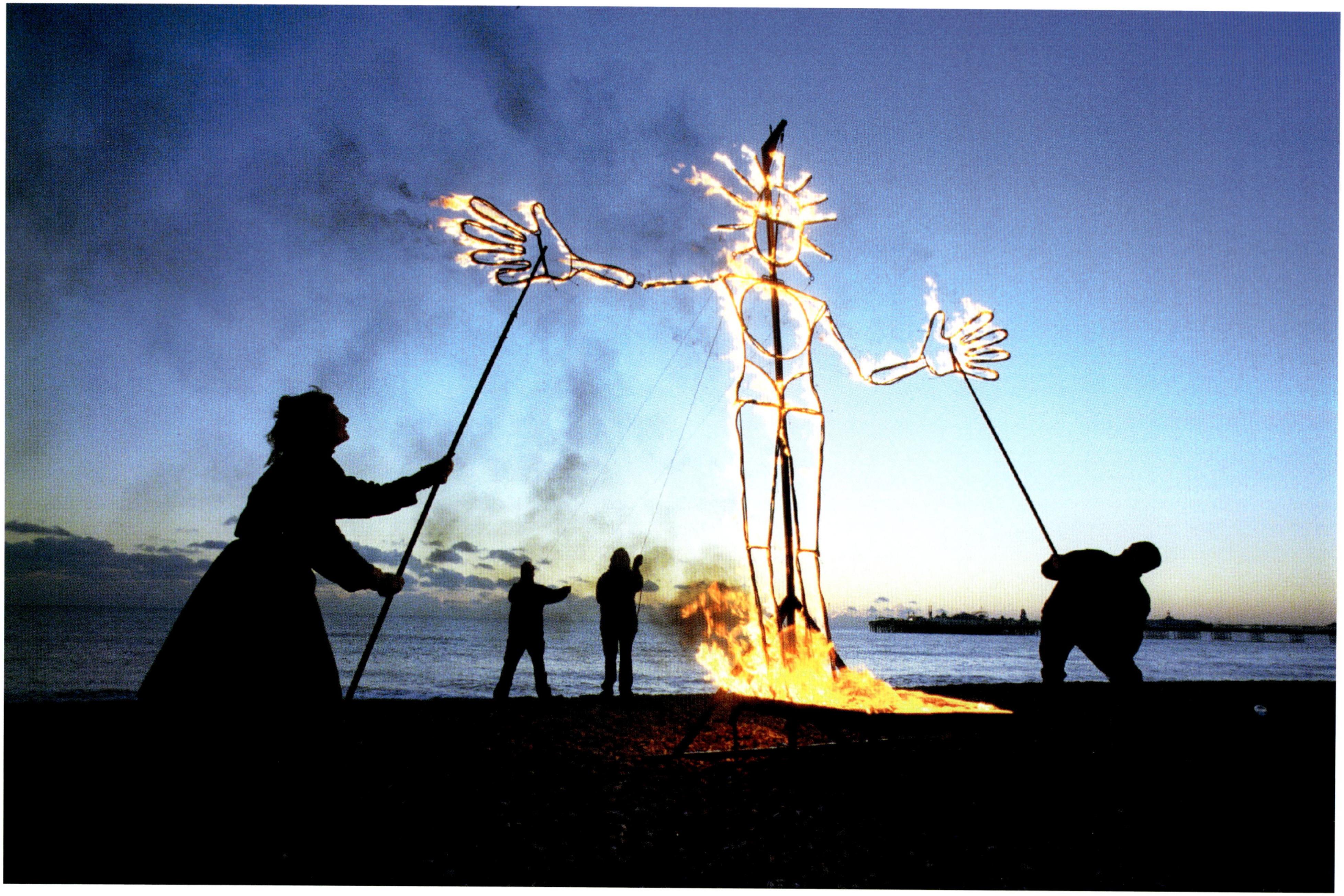

Winter Solstice

The Guardian, 1999

On the shortest night of the last year of the last century, this giant effigy of a sun god was burned in a river of fire on Brighton Beach. There was already local tradition of Winter Solstice celebrations called Burning the Clocks but there were special celebrations in 1999, on the eve of the millennium. More than 400 effigies and lanterns made of wicker and tissue paper were carried through the town to the beach at dusk, then set alight as a final farewell to the year.
Two decades later, community art group Same Sky still organises Burning The Clocks ceremonies every December. The end is always the same. The lanterns and effigies are burned, fireworks explode and everyone welcomes the return of the sun.

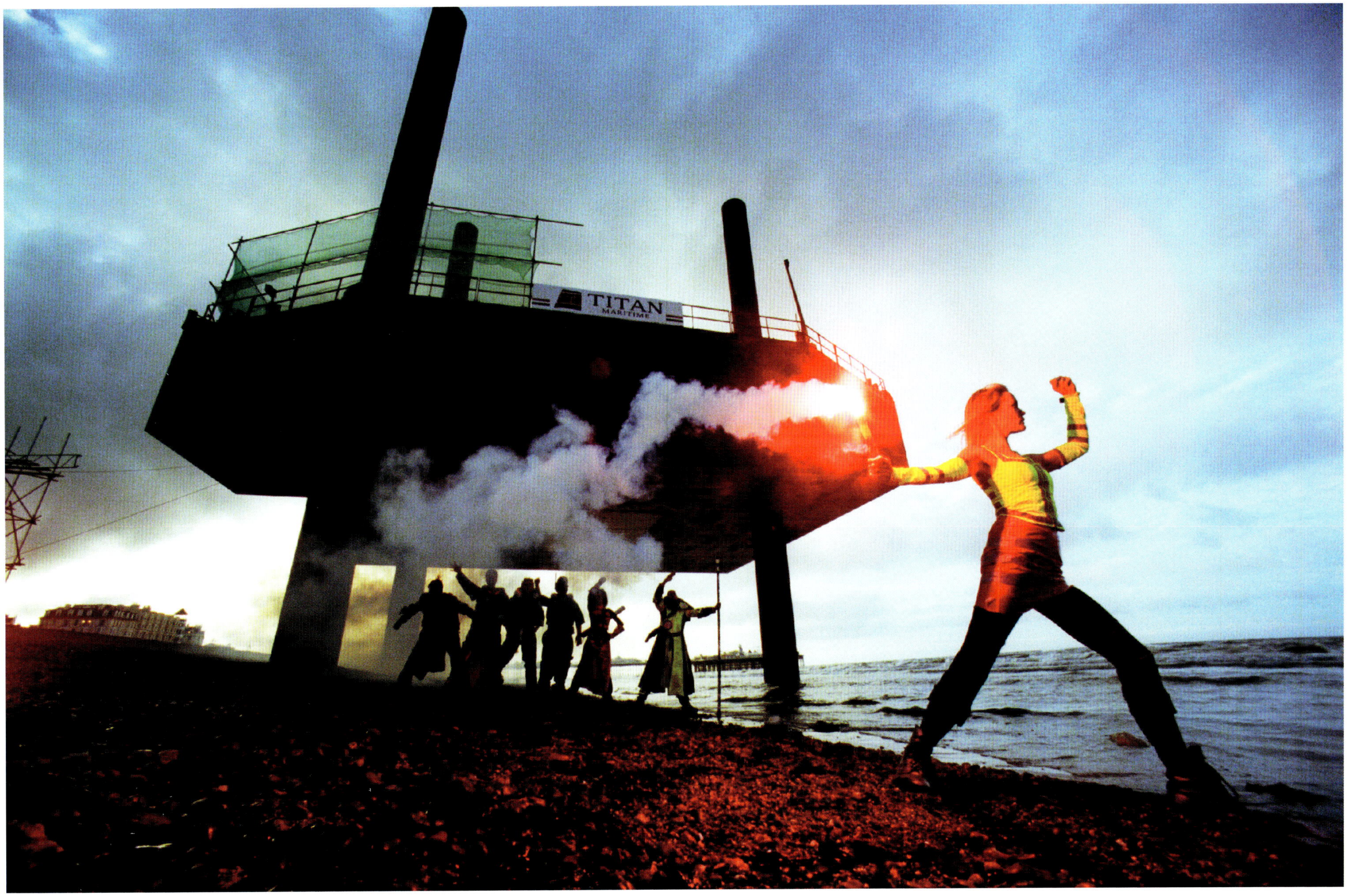

Flaring Up

The Guardian, 2000

Actress Polly Wiseman founded her Fireraisers drama company after realising 'most parts for women were rubbish and eighty percent of the population would never willingly set foot in a building called a theatre'. Here she is rehearsing her role as Miranda in *This Rough Magic*, a storming version of Shakespeare's *Tempest*, where women take centre stage and the magical island is an oil rig moored on Brighton Beach.

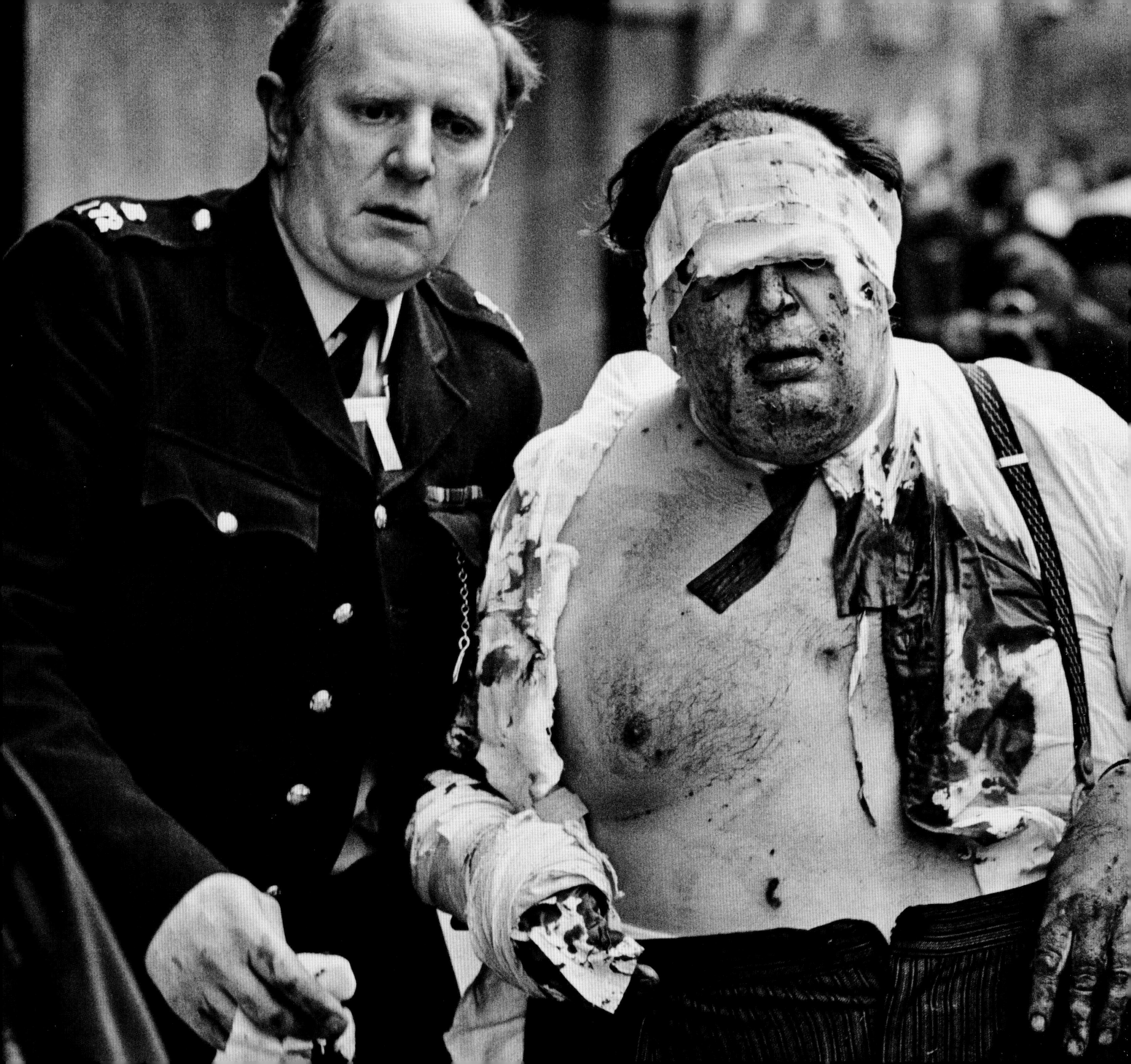

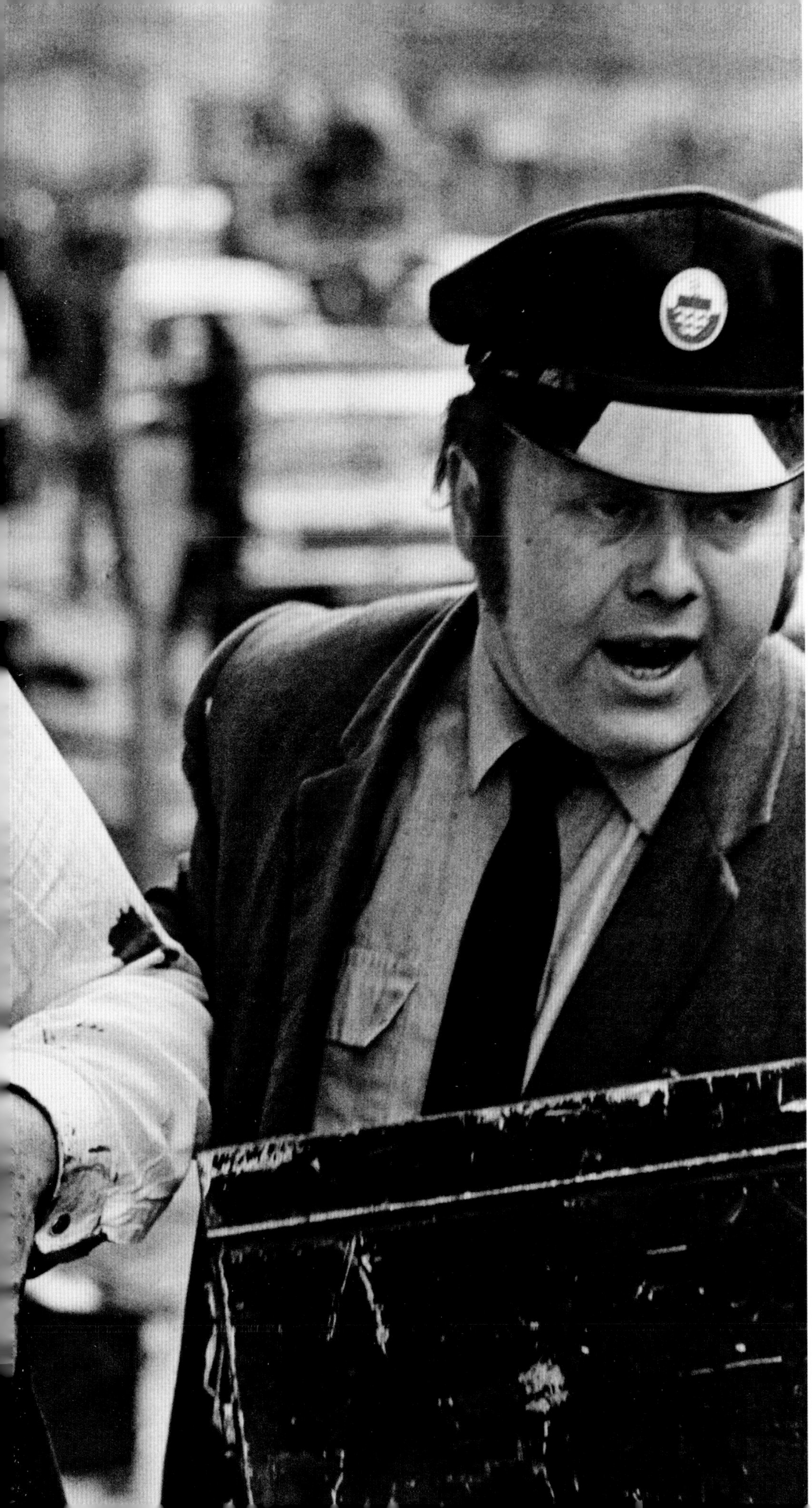

Old Bailey Bomb

The Sun, 1973

An IRA car bomb blew up the west front of the Old Bailey criminal court in the City of London on a terrible day of tension and bomb scares in 1973. I was just returning to the office in Fleet Street after a hoax bomb threat at the police HQ at Scotland Yard when there was a God Almighty bang. The noise echoed off all the buildings close by and you couldn't tell where the explosion was. I ran down Fleet Street in the direction of the City. I passed an office block with all its windows shattered. There were shards of glass everywhere and countless people being treated for cuts but there was a police cordon going up by the court and I realised the bomb had been in a car parked outside the Old Bailey itself. As I ducked past the police trying to rope off the area, I saw this portly barrister being rescued from the court by a policeman and an ambulanceman. His ripped shirt, blood-soaked wing collar, dazed gaze and bandaged head told the whole story in a frame. I was relieved to find he wasn't badly injured. This picture, taken in the split second after seeing him, later won News Photographer of the Year for 1973. But the icing on the cake was when a box from El Vino's, the legal watering hole of choice in Fleet Street, was delivered to me. It was full of wine and fine cheeses and there was a card from the barrister James Crespi on top: 'Dear Roger, thank you for the best portrait of me ever taken.'

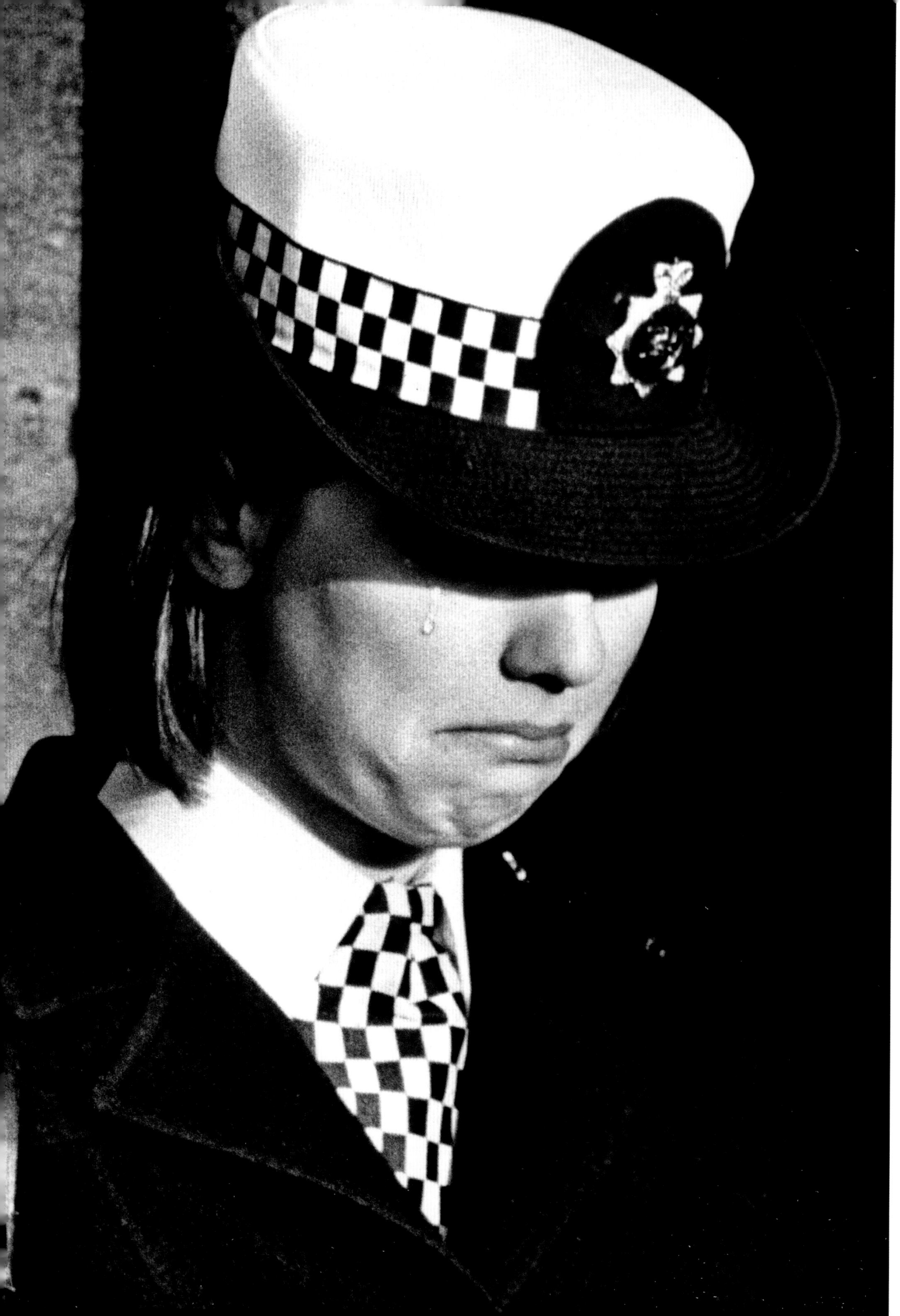

Shedding a Tear

The Sun, 1983

Ten years after the horrors of the Old Bailey bomb I covered the heartbreaking funeral of another IRA bombing victim, WPC Jane Arbuthnot.
She was only twenty-two and her death shocked even her toughest colleagues.
On the day of her funeral, photographers were asked to stay at an unobtrusive distance, 200ft away from the stony-faced mourning police officers who were forming a guard of honour for her at the church.
As her coffin was carried into the church I was looking down my long lens and spotted a lone WPC let a tear escape. It was caught on a single frame, before she hastily wiped it away.

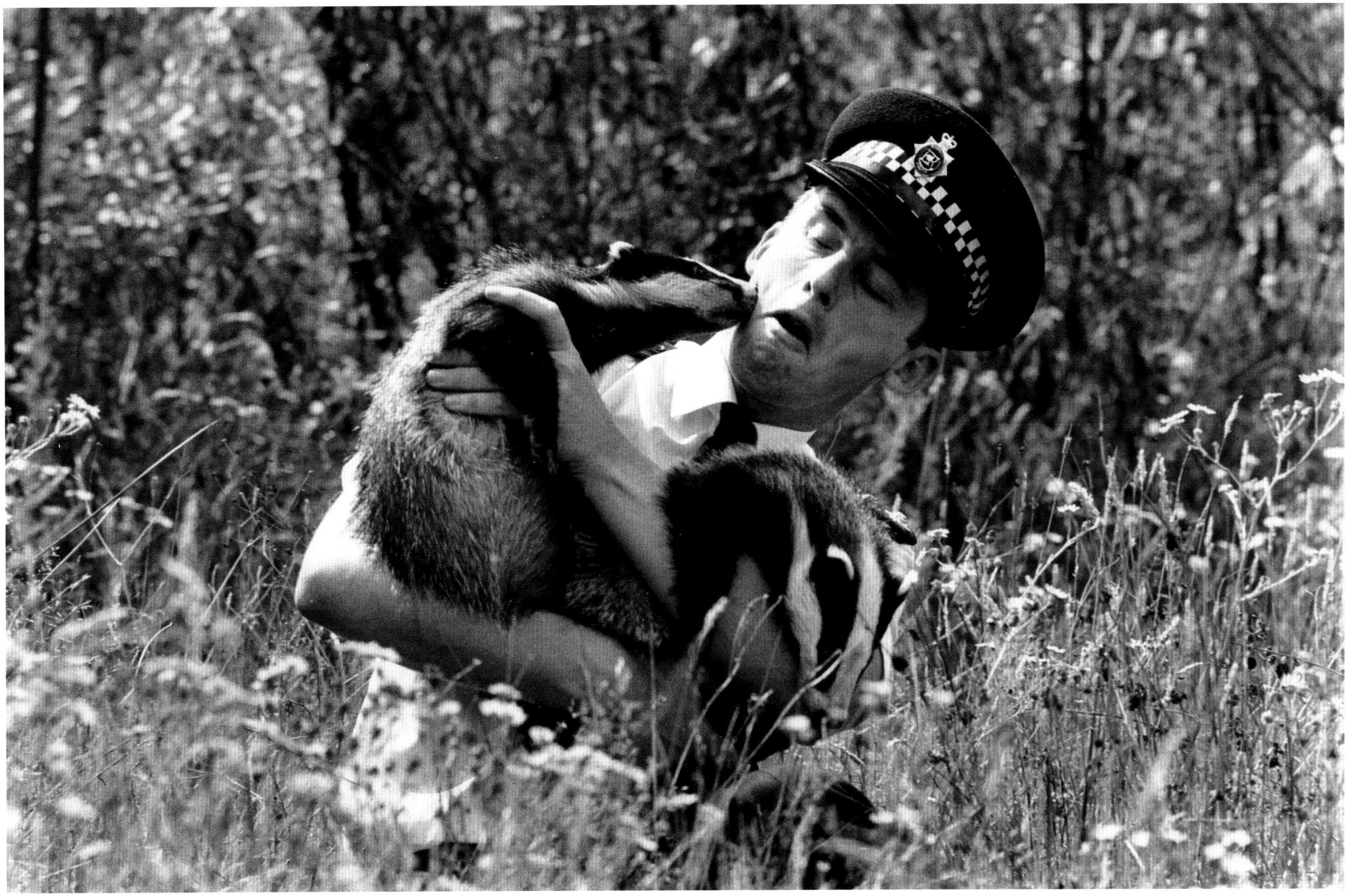

Being Badgered

The Guardian, 1993

Ten years on again, and a much happier police job – with a wildlife conservation officer. The inspector holding two squirming baby badgers in his arms was part of a team that rescued endangered animals in East Sussex in the early 1990s. One of the badgers appears to be kissing his rescuer, but moments later it bit clean through the peak of his cap.

Witness

The Mail on Sunday, 1989

Amish children living in the Conewango Valley, near Niagara Falls in New York State were being struck down by a whooping-cough epidemic.
The Amish, who shun modern drugs and vaccines, were treating the children with lemon juice and honey and three babies died, becoming the first whooping-cough fatalities in America for three years. It was big news, as this tragedy was happening only 300 miles north of New York City, where life was so different. It could have been on another planet. The Amish try not to use machines of any kind, including cameras, so although they welcome tourists, children are always told to not to pose for photographers ... but this little girl couldn't resist peeping at what was going on. The picture was a British Press Awards winner the following year.

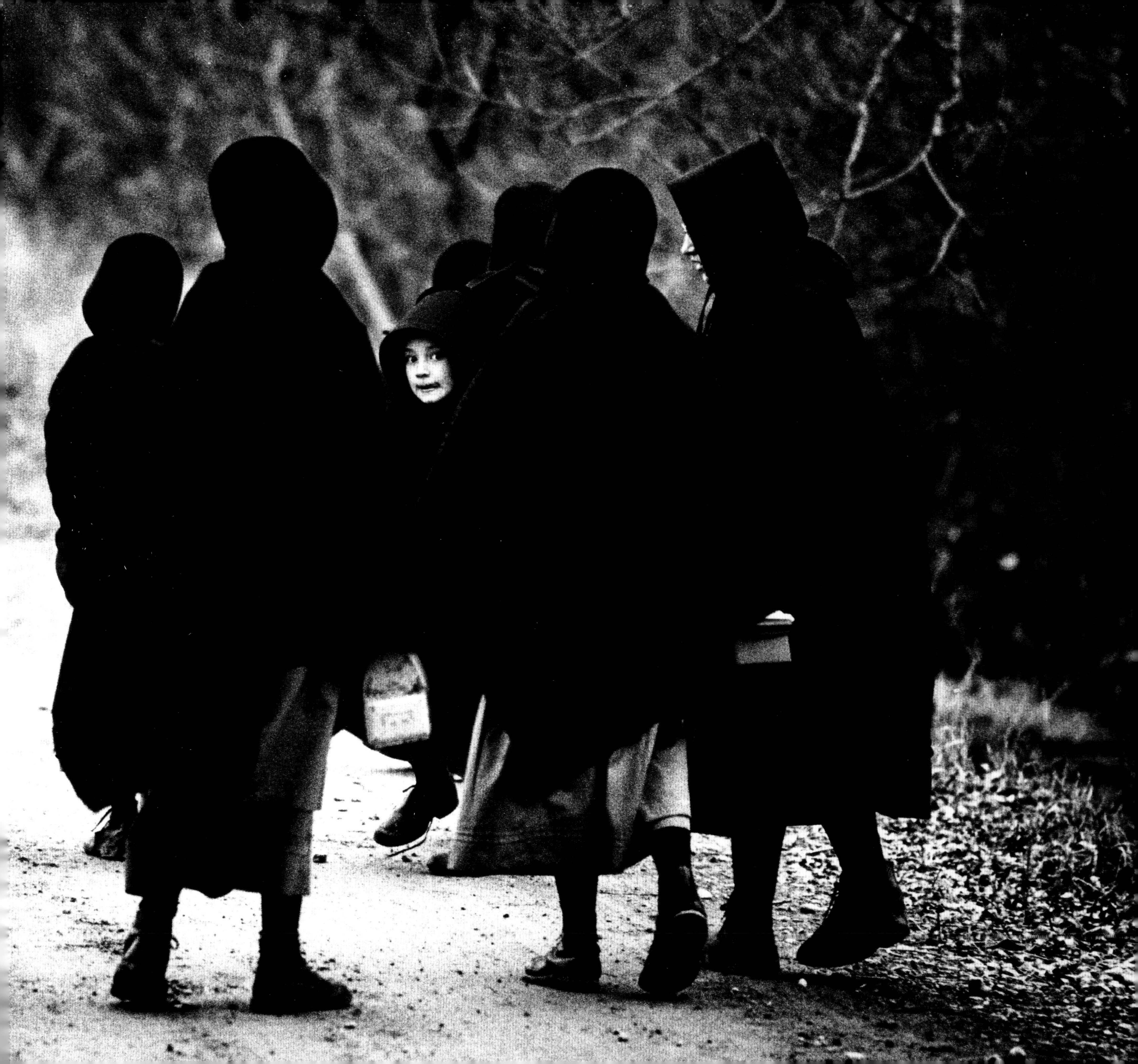

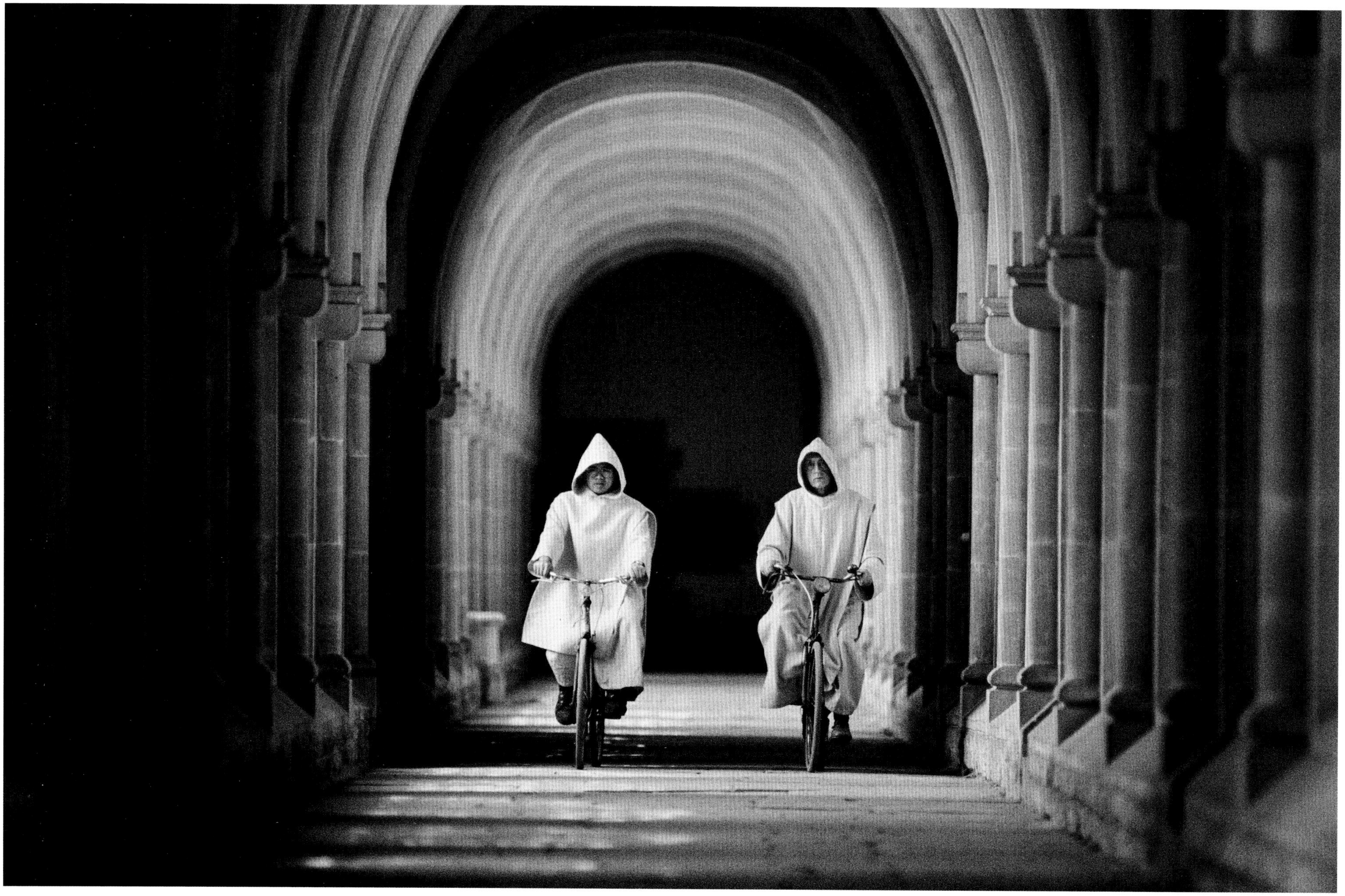

Prayer Wheels

The Guardian, 1995

The Carthusian monastery of St Hugh's Charterhouse in Cowfold, West Sussex, was originally built to house up to 250 brothers and staff. When I visited in 1995, there were only twenty-three monks in the religious community, although their numbers have risen a bit now. All of them, novices and the abbot alike, glide serenely along on bicycles for trips around the cloisters from their cells to prayer and work. The monastery is so vast, covering a 240-acre site, that bikes are the most practical way to get about.

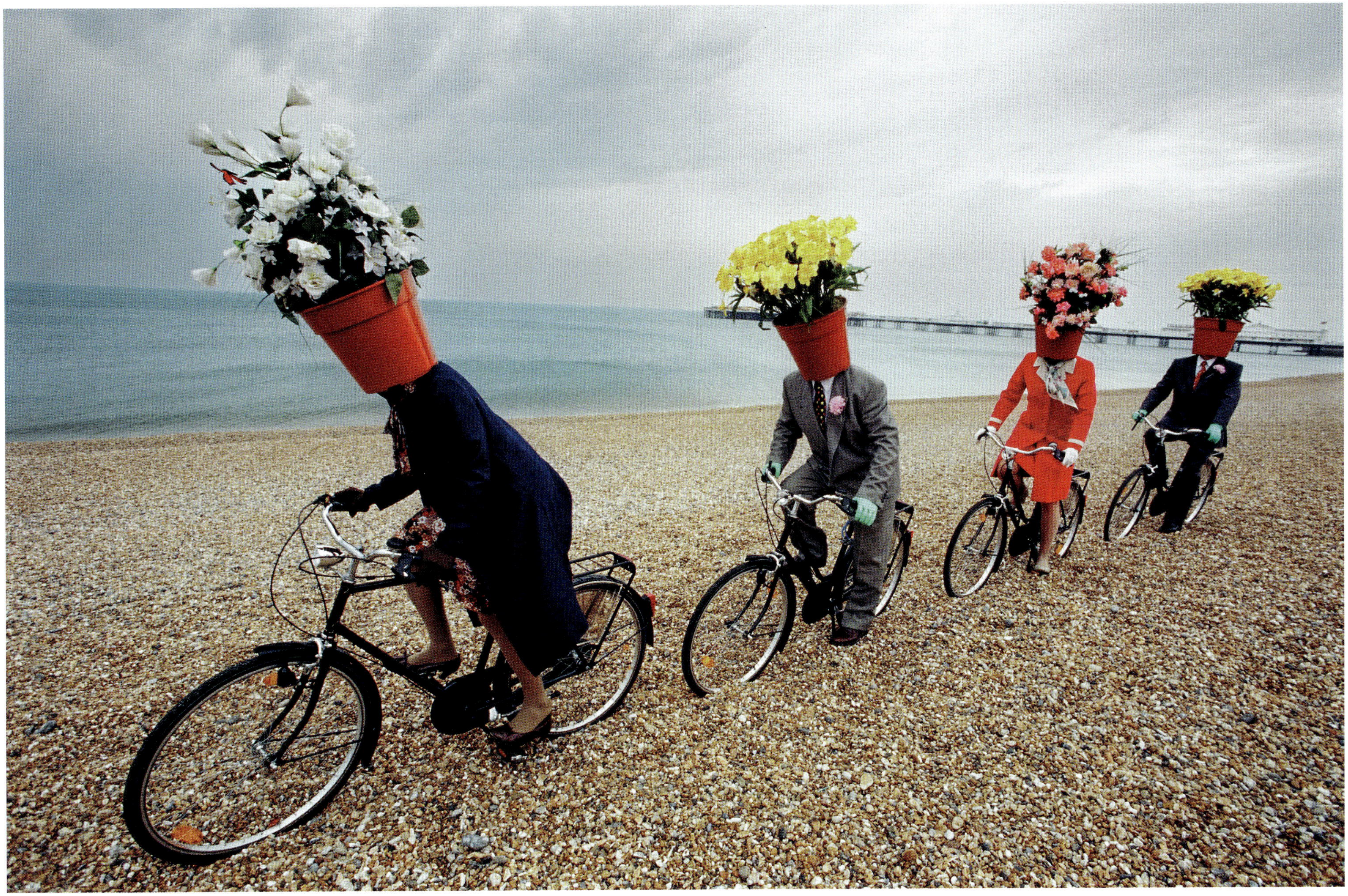

Flower Pot Heads

The Guardian, 2001

The Natural Theatre Company, one of Britain's first alternative street theatre groups, is based in Bath and has been making people laugh for more than forty years. It was a massive hit when it came to the seaside to appear at Brighton Festival in 2001. Here are the players in their Flower Pot Heads – everyday workwear for them – getting to grips the new terrain.

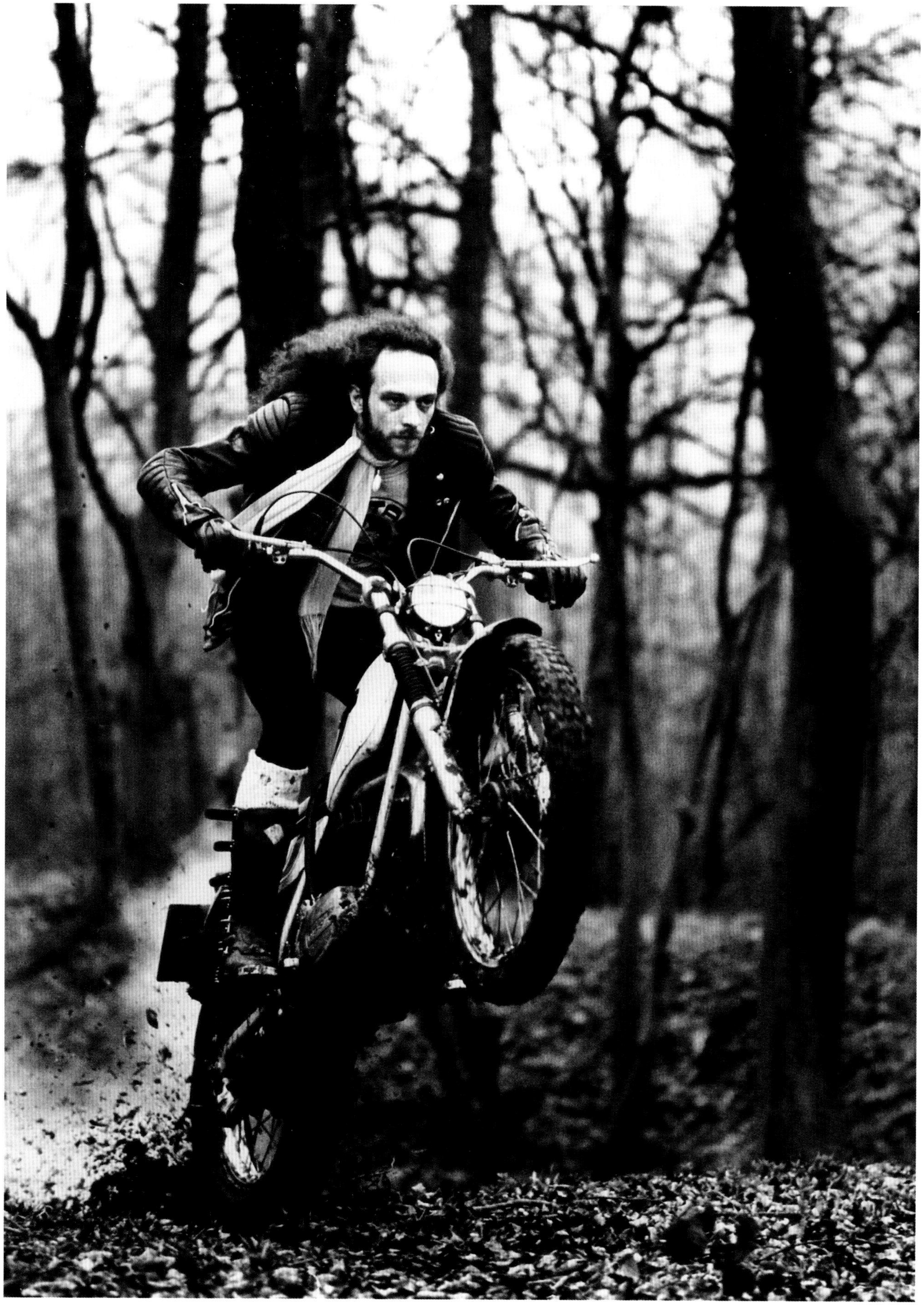

On Your Bike

The Sun, 1979

Flautist Ian Anderson, the lead singer and flute player with rock band Jethro Tull, was renowned for playing his flute while standing whimsically on one leg. But offstage he was completely different, a passionate biker and a massive fan of off-road riding. I went to his home in Berkshire and discovered he was so uninterested in cars he had never taken a driving test but was happy to show off his favourite trail bike in the woodland next to his home.

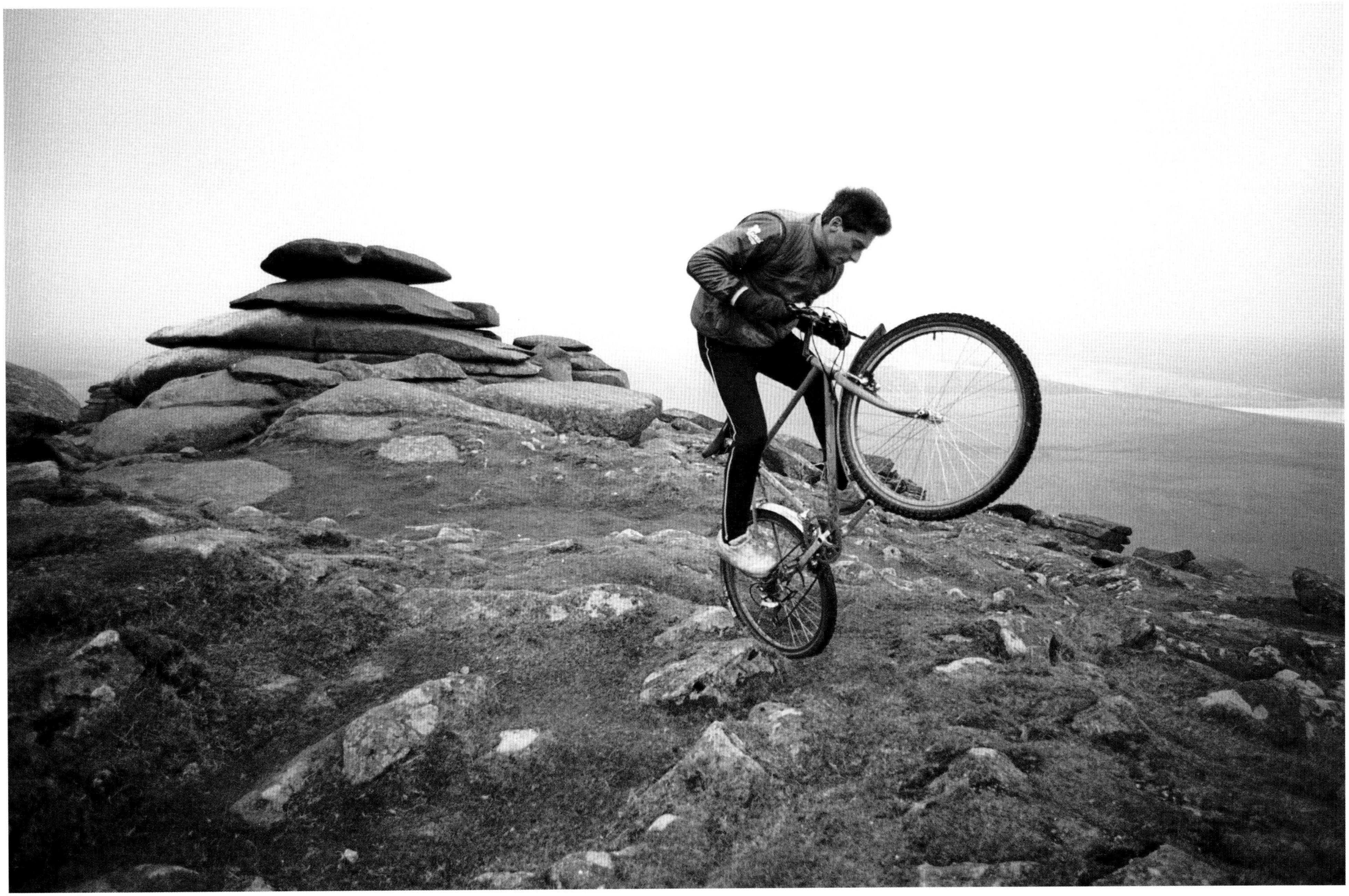

Rough Ride

The Observer, 1989

A junior mountain bike champion powering his way up the rock-strewn summit of Cornwall's highest landmark, Brown Willy, a Neolithic tor on Bodmin Moor. Walking up Brown Willy is a favourite outing for the Cornish branch of my family, but nobody else I know has managed to race a bike up there.

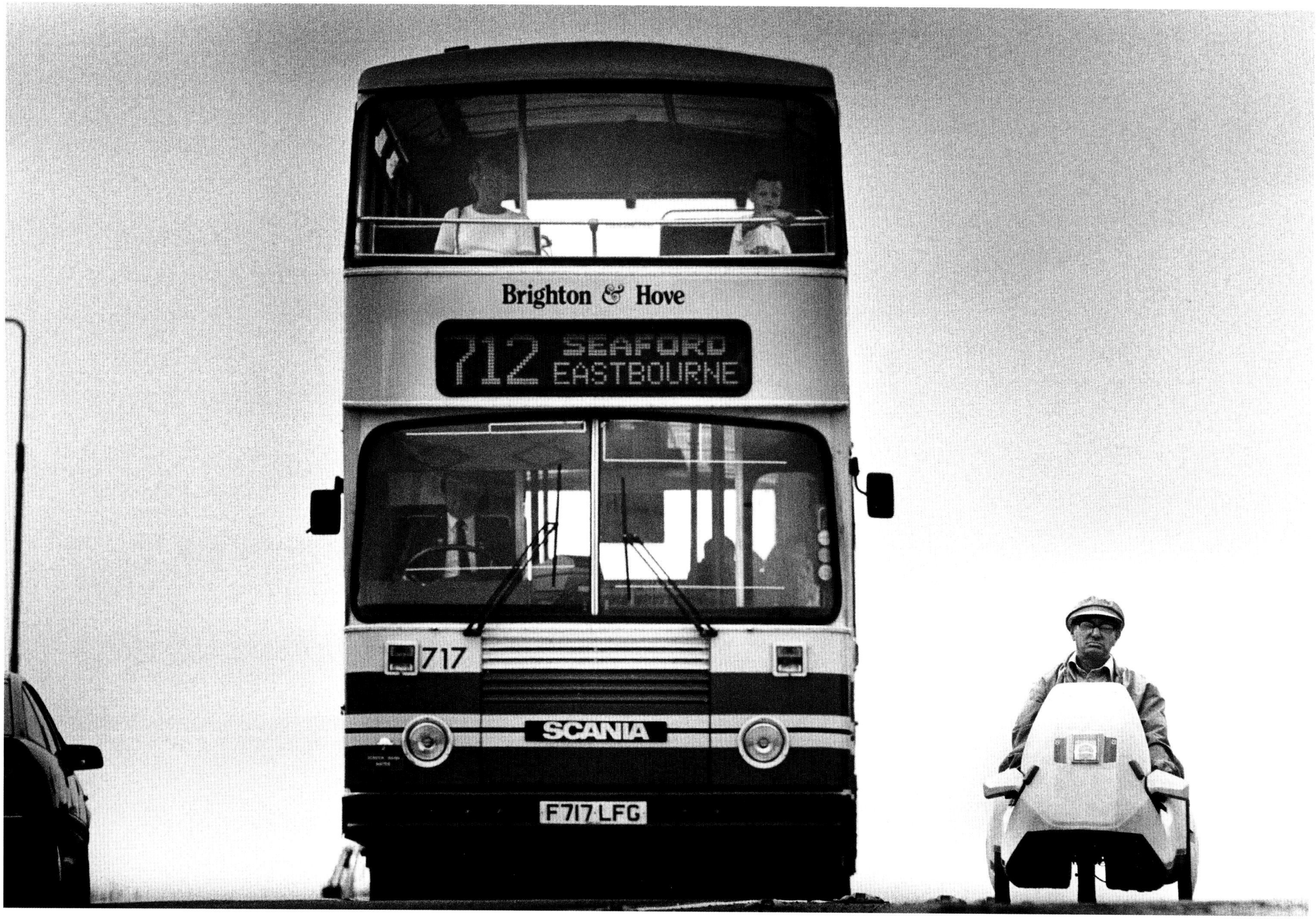

Over the Hill

The Guardian, 1990

Dick Kingshott, a man decades ahead of his time, commuted to work in Newhaven, East Sussex in a tiny Sinclair C5 electric car, one of the few on the road after the flop of its launch in 1985.
He shrugged off rude comments from passersby, smug in the knowledge that it cost him about 20p per week to charge the battery. Much cheaper than going by bus.

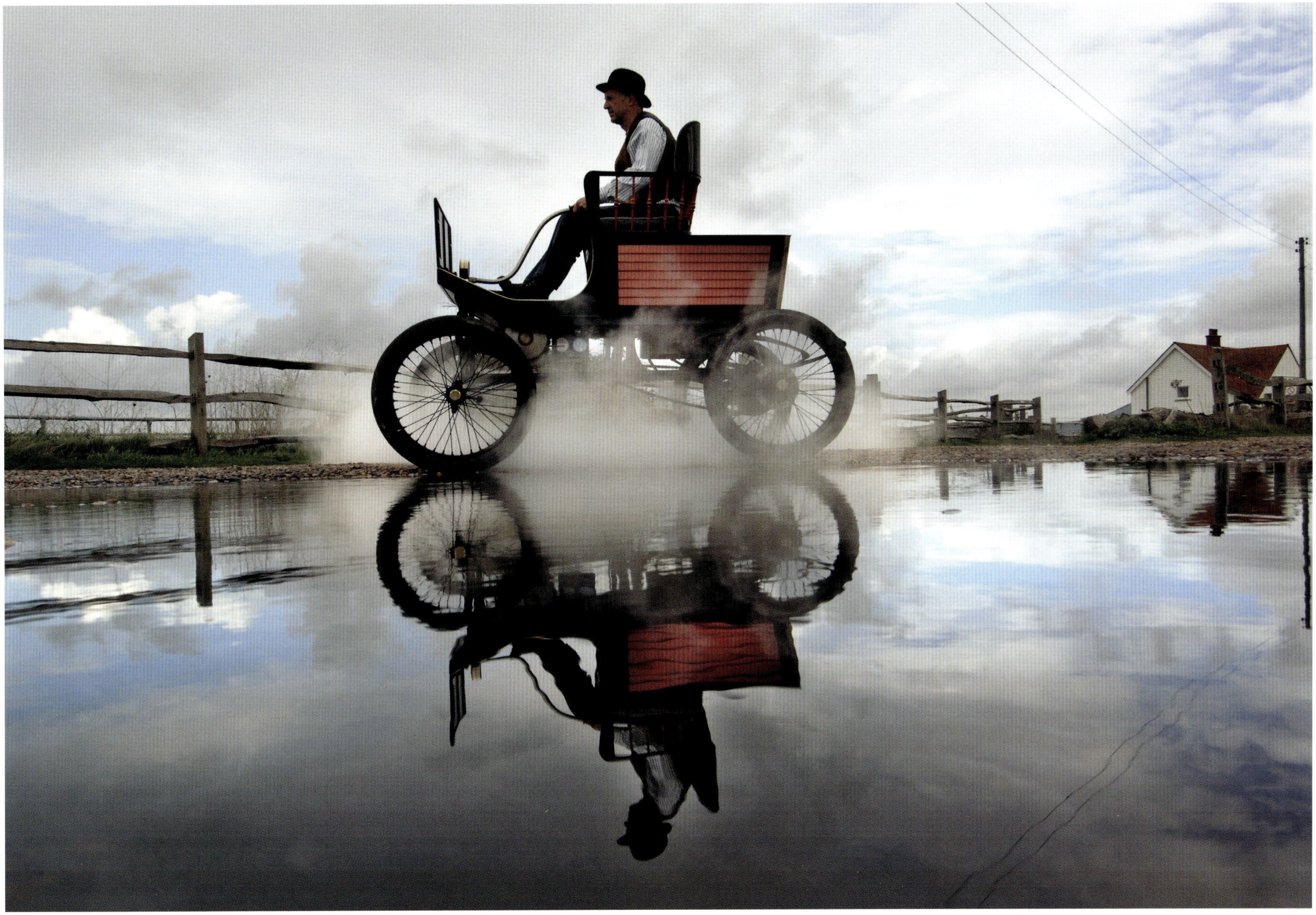

Building up Steam

The Guardian, 2006

Engineer Martin Nutter drives his perfect replica of a 1902 Stanley Twins Locomobile Spindle Seat Runabout steam car through Normans Bay, near Eastbourne, East Sussex. He had just spent six years painstakingly recreating the vehicle from scratch in every spare moment from his day job as a forklift truck engineer.

It was remarkably environmentally friendly, running on a tiny amount of diesel and regular top-ups of tap water, could cruise at 30mph and used a special monotube generator system which, he assured me, meant that there was no danger of the boiler exploding. It was insured for £20,000. He built it by hand in a workshop at his home, which is on an unadopted road prone to getting plenty of puddles. Very useful for reflection pictures.

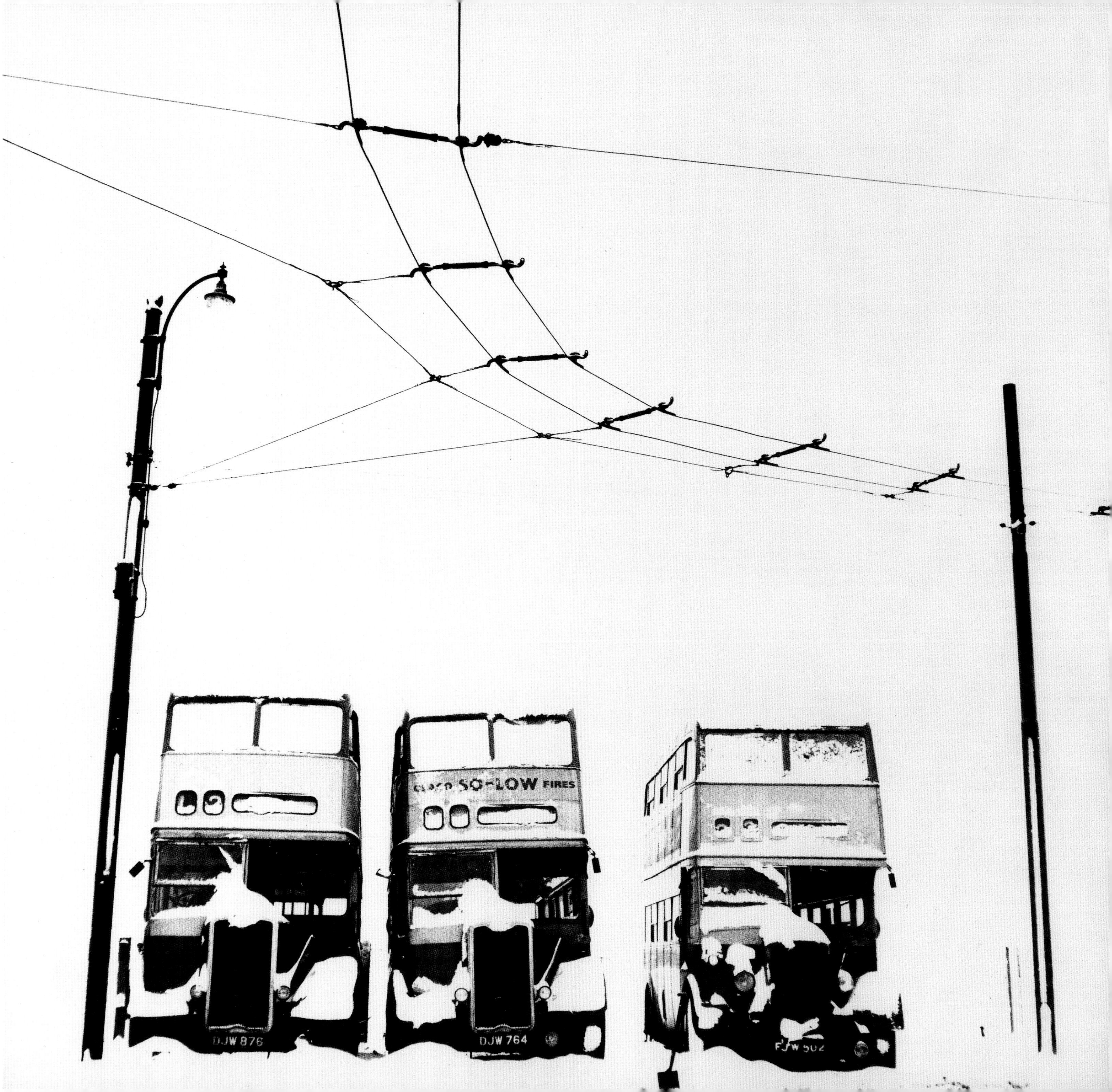
SO-LOW FIRES
DJW 876
DJW 764
FJW 502

Cold Comfort

Leicester College of Art, 1962

An advertisement for SO-LOW Fires, barely visible under drifting snow on the front of a double-decker bus caught my eye during the famously freezing winter of 1962. The buses were parked under electric trolley bus wires, at a bus garage in Wolverhampton.

Wired Up

The Guardian, 2013

Don't laugh at the weird-looking transport of years gone by; one day our own buses and trains will probably look equally quaint.
In 1904, Newcastle Corporation's tram 114 here, powered by newfangled electricity, would have cut a dash as one of the first of its kind to serve its home city. Now it makes tracks through the cobbled High Street of the old town of Beamish open air museum at Stanley, County Durham.

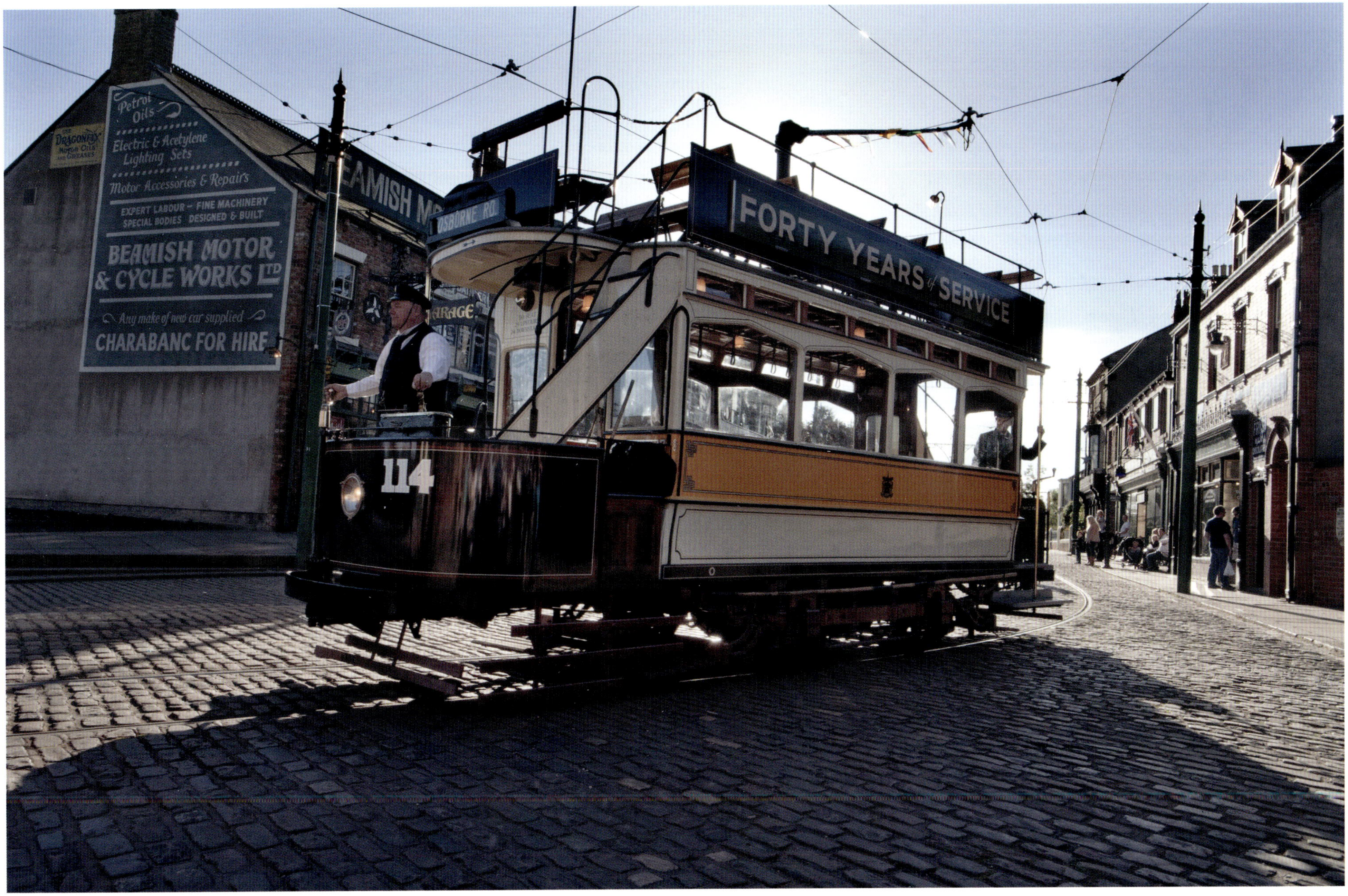

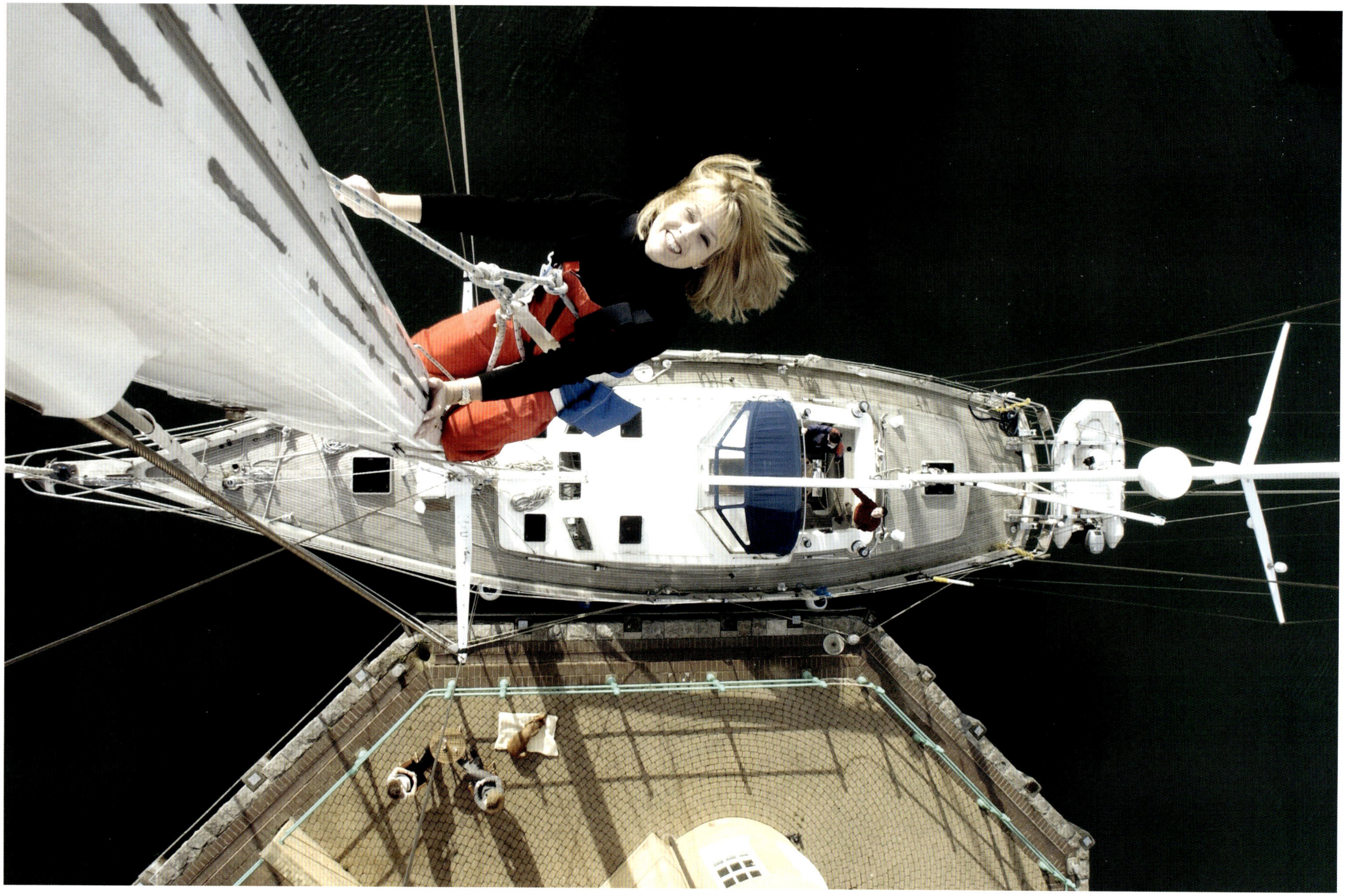

Chair Lift

Brighton City Council, February 2002

Yacht owner Sarah Bruce uses a bosun's chair to scale the 65-ft mast of her ketch *Indigo Drum*. It was moored at Brighton Marina just before she set off on a round the world voyage with her husband Nick (standing on deck) and their labrador (lying on a blanket on the quay).

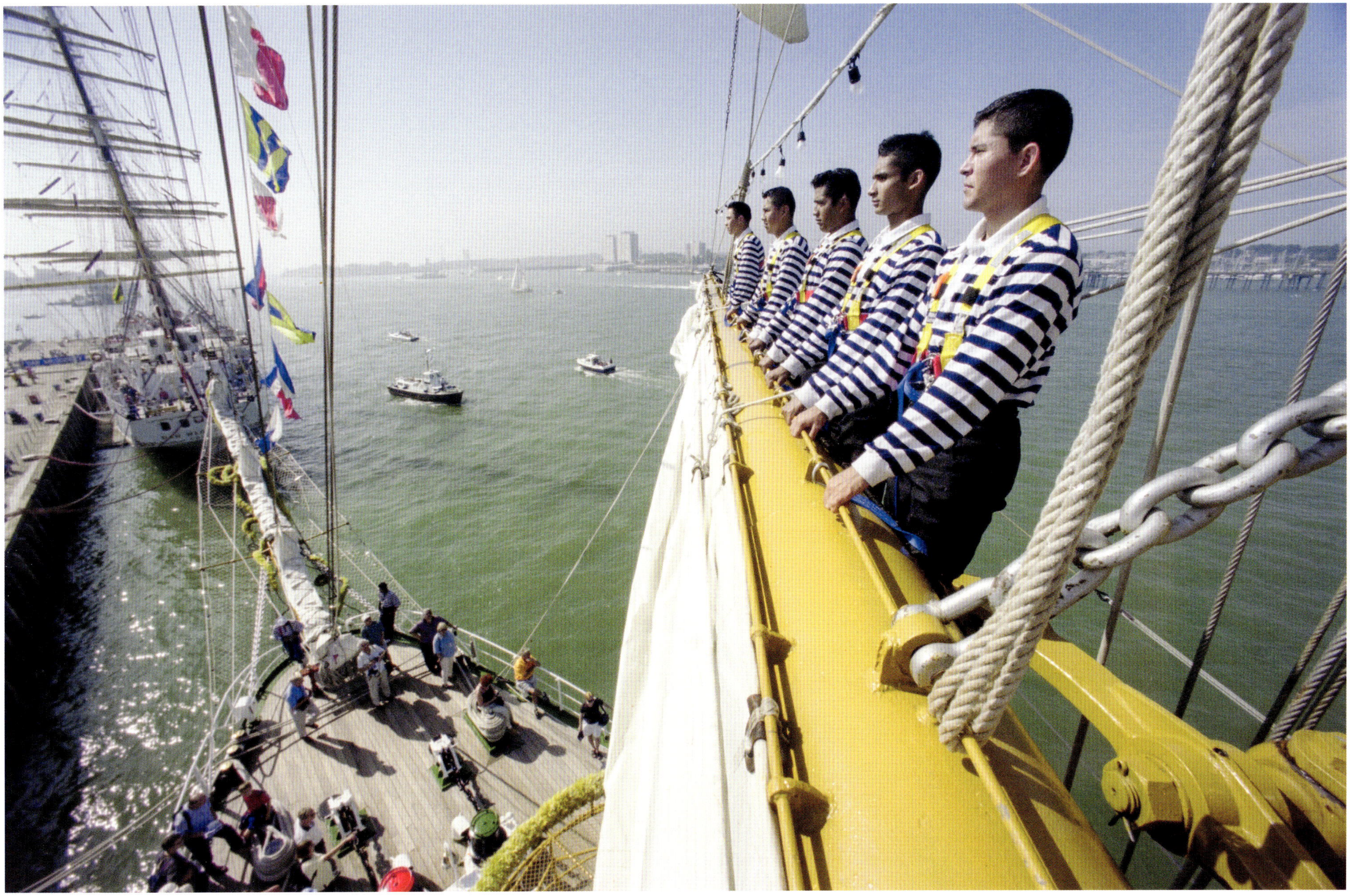

Tall Order

The Guardian, 2001

Mexican tall ship, the Cuauhteemoc, had a crew of trainee sailors who were learning the ropes by sailing her on the high seas. Five of the crew here were about to adjust the rigging high on the second mast as the ninety-year-old ship joined more than 1,000 other windpowered craft taking part in a Festival of the Sea at the Royal Naval Dockyard in Portsmouth. I had to climb even higher up the mast, with my cameras rattling around my neck, to get above the sailors as the ship rocked at anchor. Even thinking about it now makes me feel giddy.

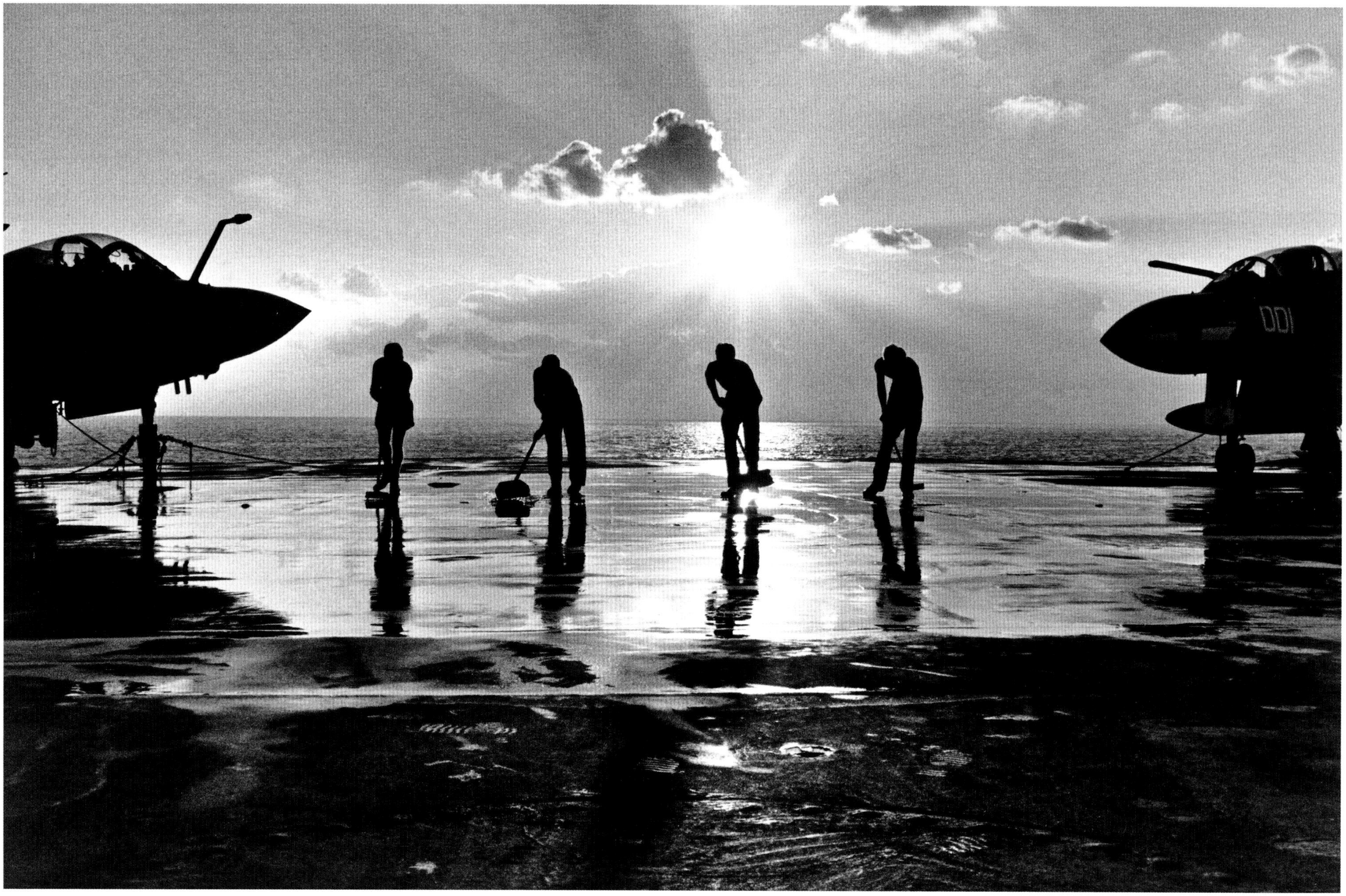

Plane Sailing

The Sun, 1978

Ratings on Britain's last fixed-wing aircraft carrier, HMS *Ark Royal*, clean the deck, flanked by a Buccaneer and a Phantom Jet. This was the ship's final voyage but right to the very end, the crew was cleaning, polishing and painting her so she looked her very best. After this final exercise in the Mediterranean, HMS *Ark Royal* returned to Plymouth to be scrapped.

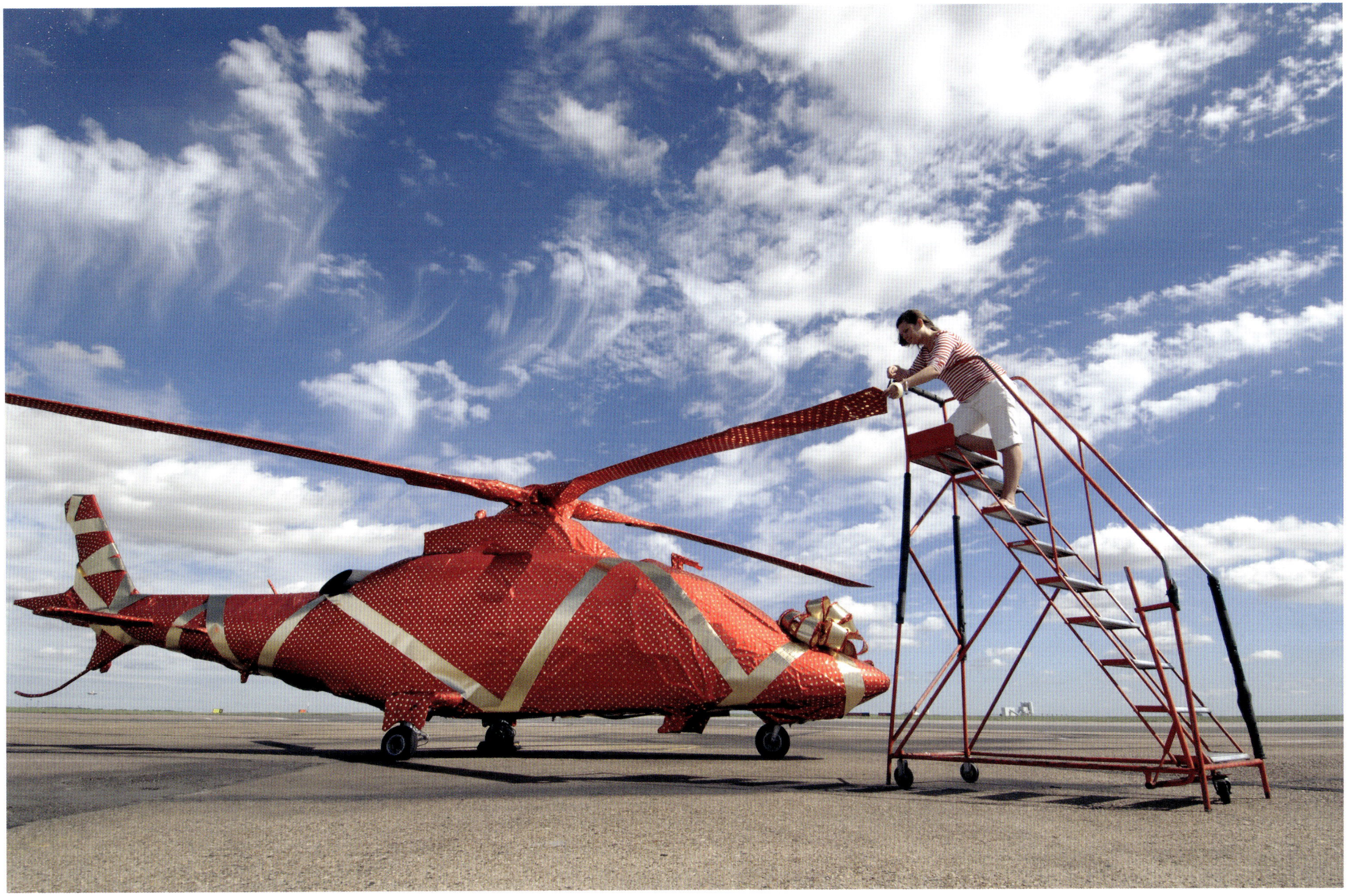

Guess What I've Bought You

The Guardian and seven other papers, 2006

The PR company handling publicity for Harrods, rang me to ask for my ideas on their 'We Can Wrap Anything' campaign. After a few minutes' thought, I rang them back and suggested that as the store was then owned by Mohamed Al-Fayed who also had a Boeing 737 plane and a couple of helicopters, why not get them to wrap one of those? It would make a very funny picture! They thought it was a great idea, but 'a bit difficult to do'.

They decided to ask the powers that be anyway, and rather to their surprise they got the go-ahead. The plane was a bit big, so I opted for Mr Al-Fayed's Agusta A109 chopper instead. I asked for red and gold paper (presents always look special in red and gold) which had to be specially printed so they had enough on hand for the job. I told them every inch apart from the wheels had to be wrapped.

After a very thorough weather check, at 7pm the Harrods team set to work in a hanger in Stansted Airport. They worked all night, using more than 600m of the red and gold paper and 150 rolls of industrial strength sellotape.

As a sunny day dawned the helicopter was dragged out to the apron for the chief wrapper Cora Kemp to inspect. Wingtip to wingtip it was perfect. The picture made almost every paper the next day.

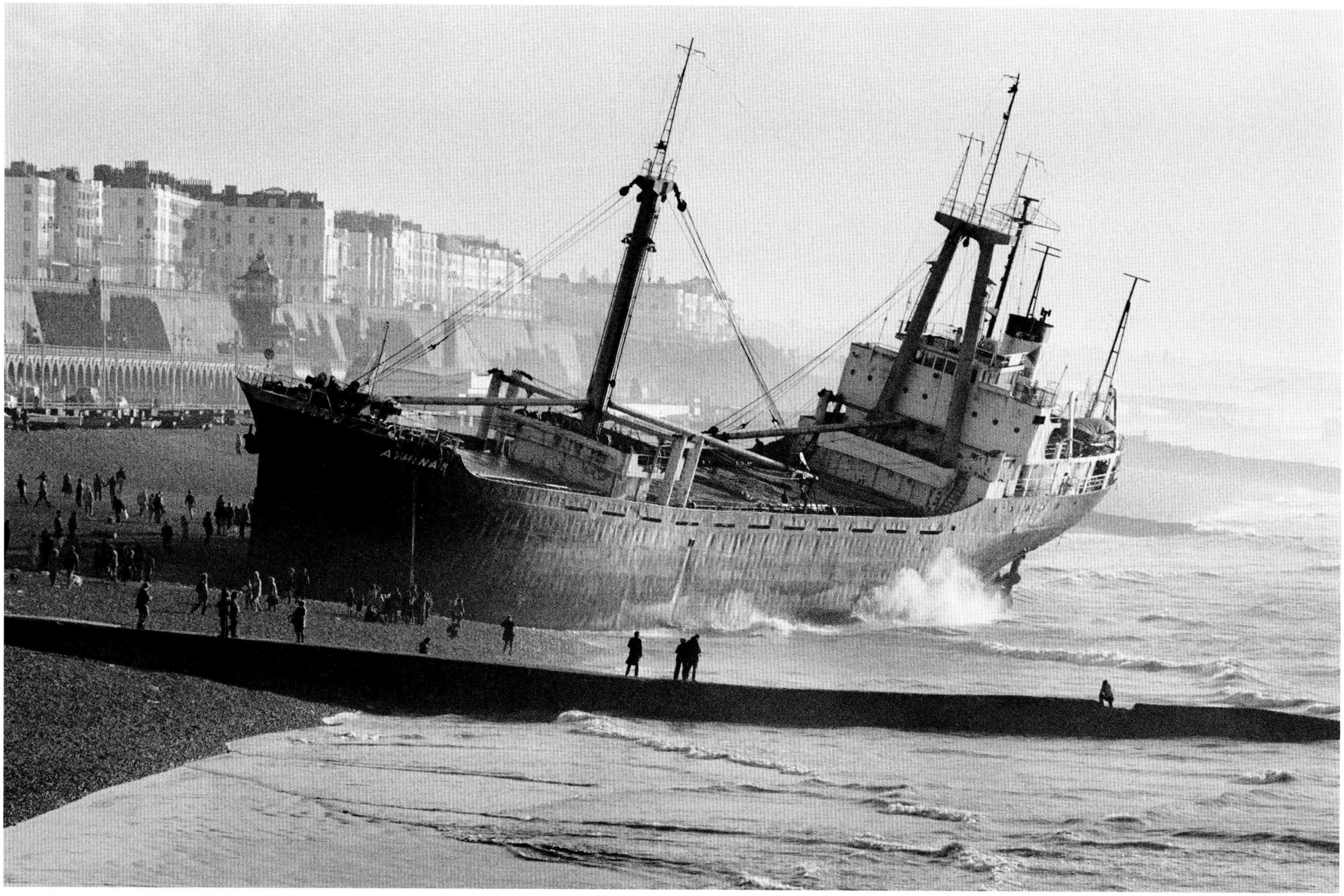

All Washed Up

The Sun, 1980

Shipwrecked merchant ship, MS *Athina B* sits forlornly beached on the shingle at Brighton after suffering engine failure during a storm, drifting, narrowly missing the Brighton Palace Pier and then ignominiously running aground and washing up on a beach where the largest craft seen are usually paddle boards.
The 90-m Greek cargo ship was grounded there for two months before being unceremoniously towed off by three tugs and taken to Scotland for scrapping. By then she had become a celebrity. Hundreds of people came to wave her farewell.

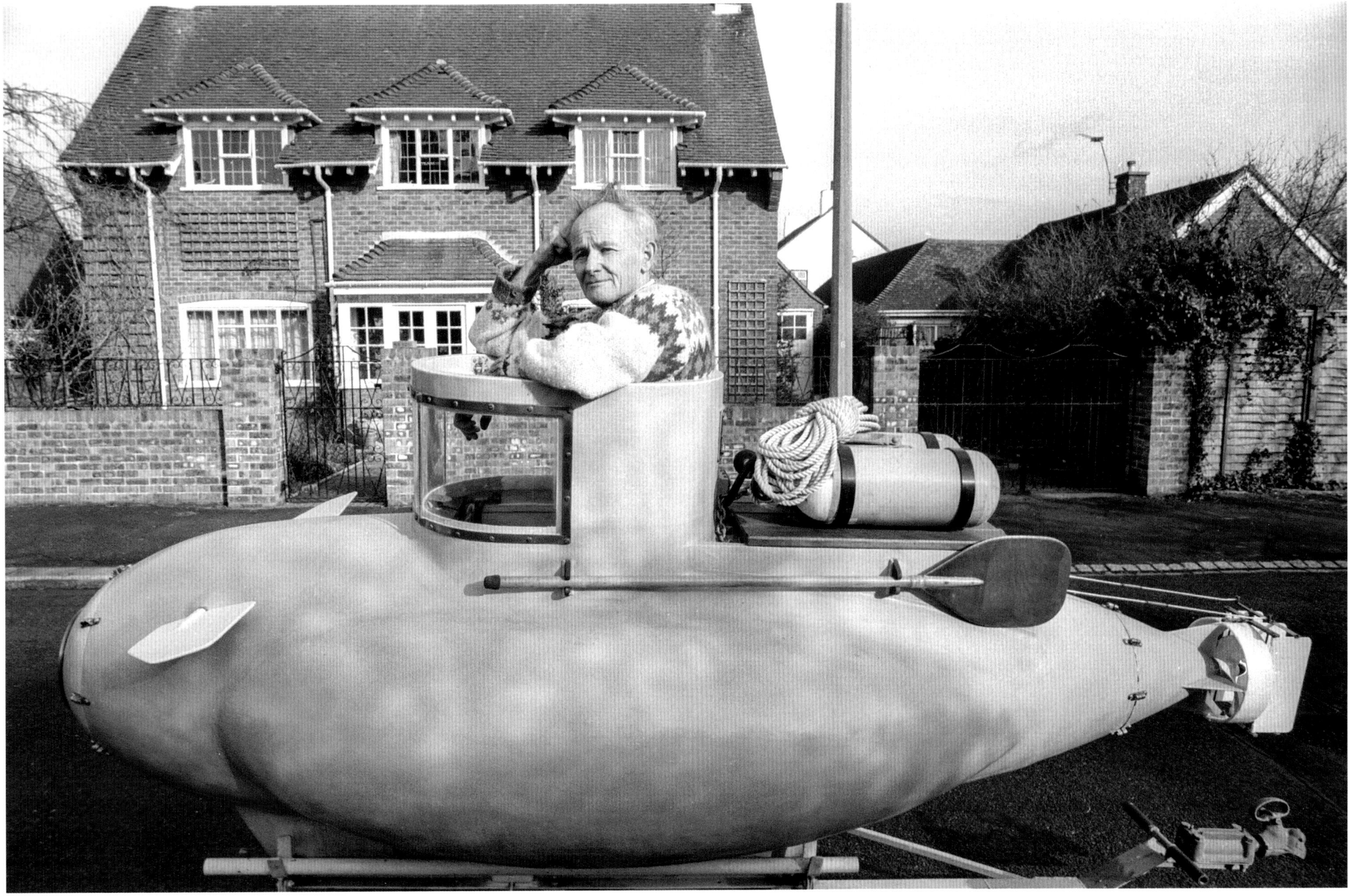

Sub-urbia

The Guardian, 1992

Retired Navy Officer Bill Smith fulfilled a lifetime ambition by building his own one-man submarine in the garage of his home in Bognor Regis, West Sussex. He originally only agreed to be photographed inside the garage, not outside, in case the neighbours thought he was 'silly'. I kept talking and gradually coaxed the craft out, down the 40-ft garden and – two hours later – into the road. The neighbours were agog.

End of the Road

The Guardian, 2007

In 2006 I went to the funeral of a close relative in Cornwall, who instead of a conventional coffin had a wonderful, decorated pea-pod shaped casket covered with Heath Robinson style drawings. The deceased was an inventor, forever designing crazy Heath Robinson-ish gadgets and I admired his fitting ending.
This led me to The Crazy Coffins Company, an offshoot of Vic Fearn coffin makers in the East Midlands. They agreed to let me loose in their workshop in Bulwell, Nottingham.
It was astounding. There was such diversity of themes. In the foreground is master craftsman George Spencer building a personalised coffin as a 1927 Rolls Royce Phantom car. Behind him is Wingrove Warner crafting a guitar. Look closely and you can see the acupuncture coffin, an Angel of the North, a canal narrowboat, a wicker man, a Sun Voyager motor yacht, a skateboard, a ballet shoe ... there was even a skip, but we couldn't get it through the door for the picture.

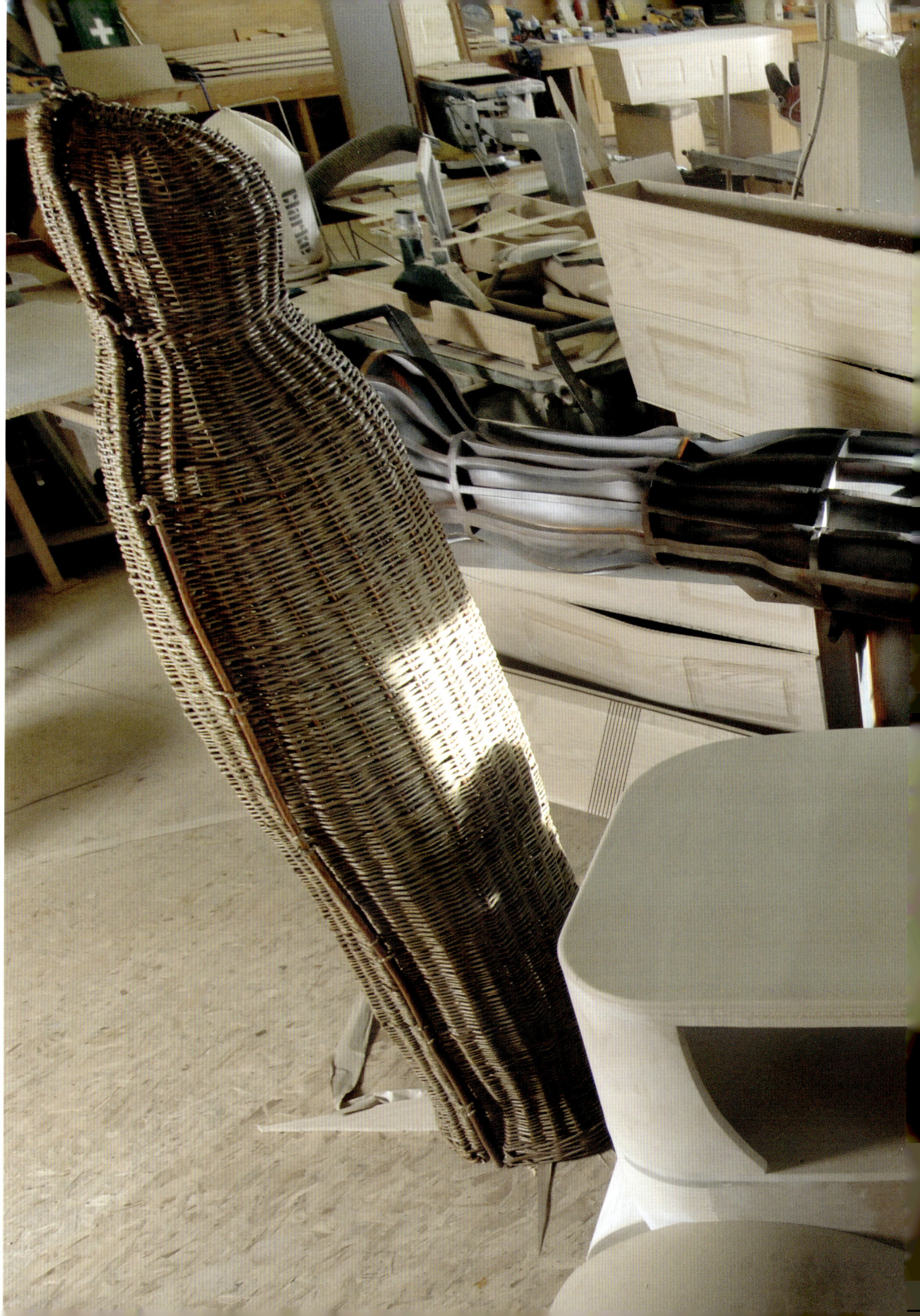

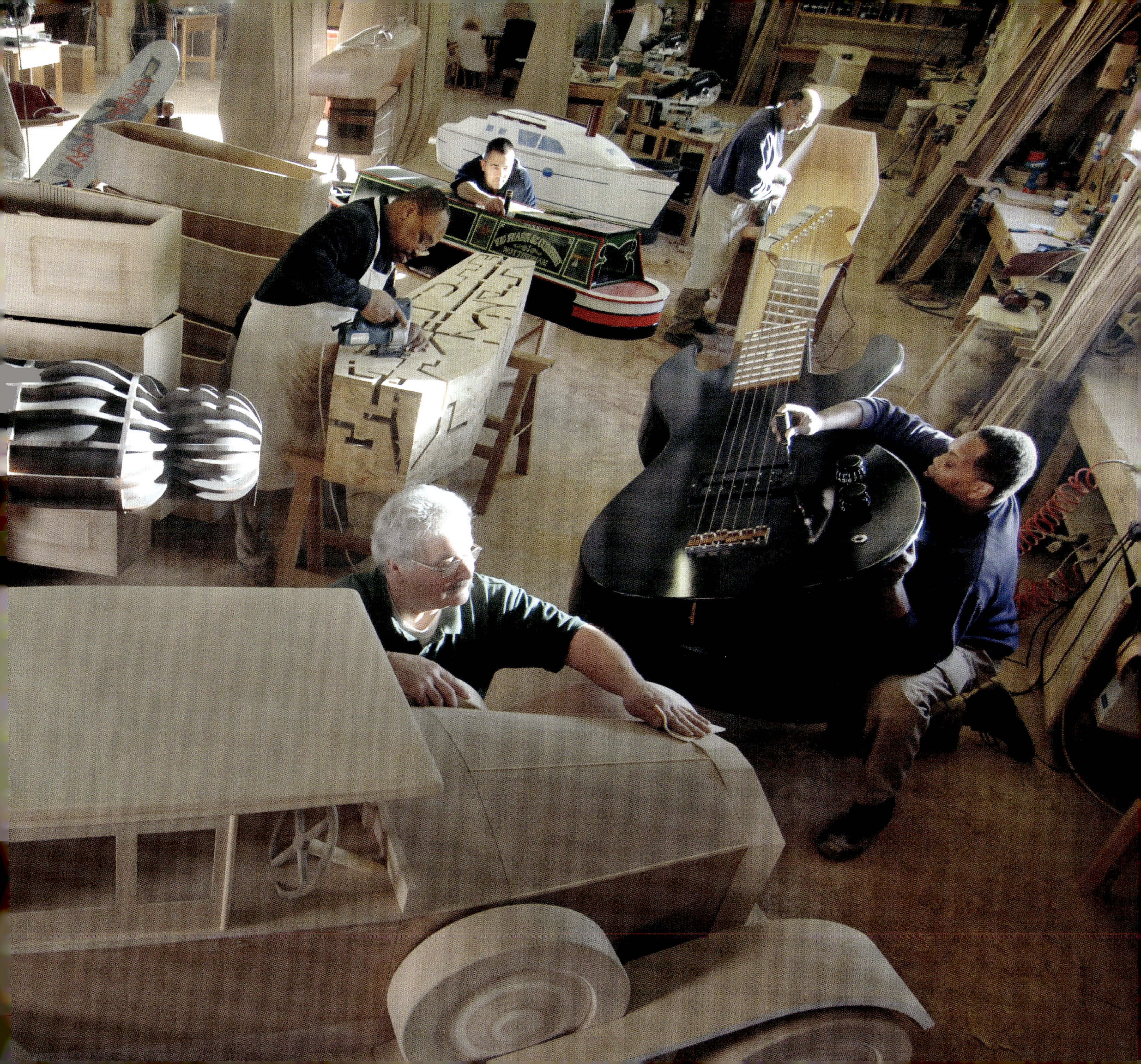

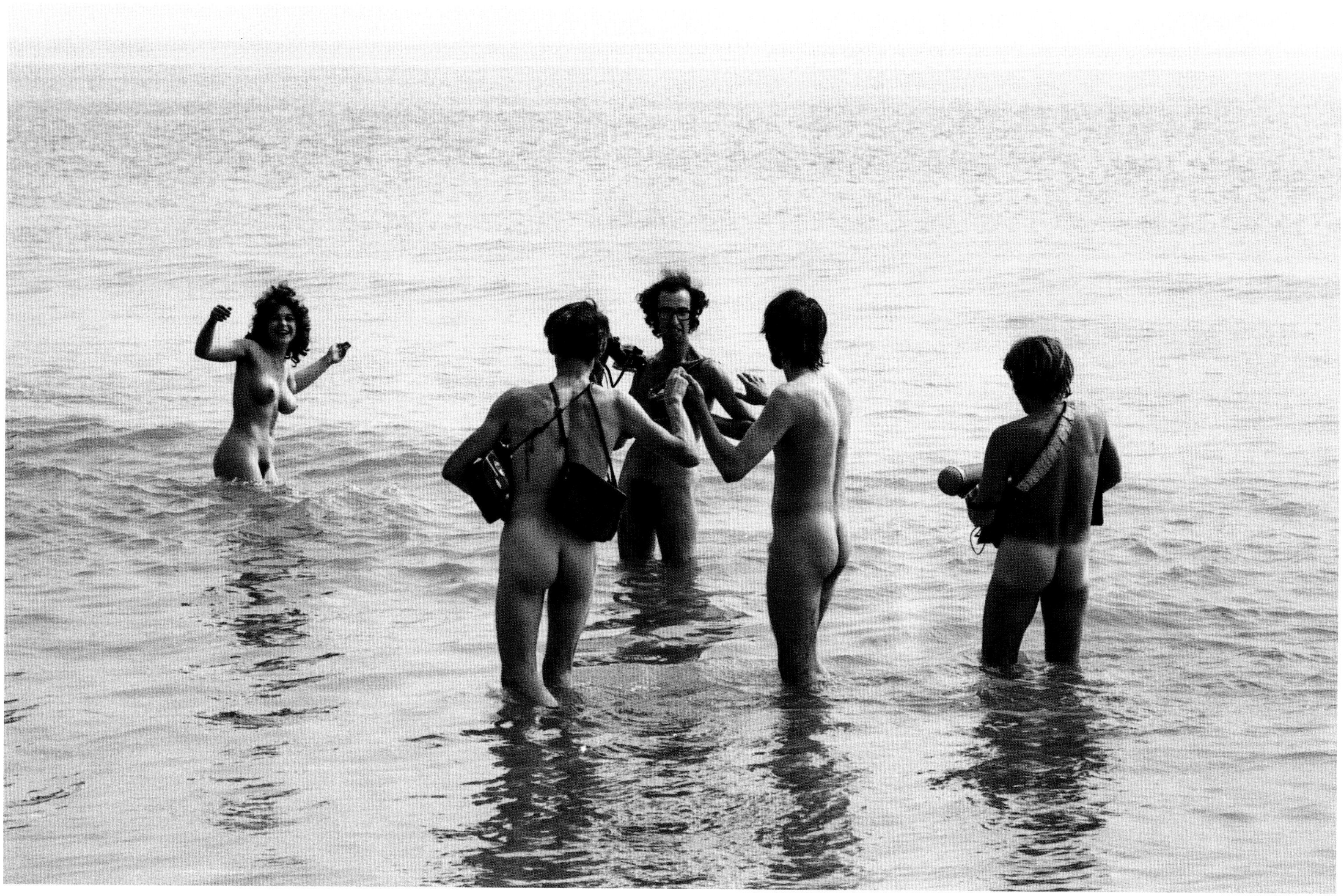

Just Part of the Job!

The Sun, 1970

The Isle of Wight Pop Festival at Freshwater in 1970 followed the massively successful American festival at Woodstock. The previous Isle of Wight festival in 1969, had been quite folky, with stars like Bob Dylan and Joan Baez headlining. The six-day 1970 festival was much wilder, headlining classic rock bands like the Doors, the Who and Jimi Hendrix. The crowds were still very groovy and hippy though, and there was a free love and anything goes sort of atmosphere.

I noticed a group of totally naked festival-goers taking a break from the music, happily swimming and basking in the sunshine. I photographed them, with their permission, and an image made the paper's festival coverage the next day.
I revisited the group the next morning to thank them and found them talking to a TV crew who had seen my picture and wanted to do their own story. They had approached the girl in this picture, who seemed to be the boss, and politely requested to film a news item. The girl agreed but this time, she said, after conferring with the rest of the group, only if they took their clothes off too.
The crew thought it was hilarious. They stripped off and cameraman, reporter, producer and soundman waded in, to get their shots. I kept my trousers on and took this picture from the beach as I left them to it.

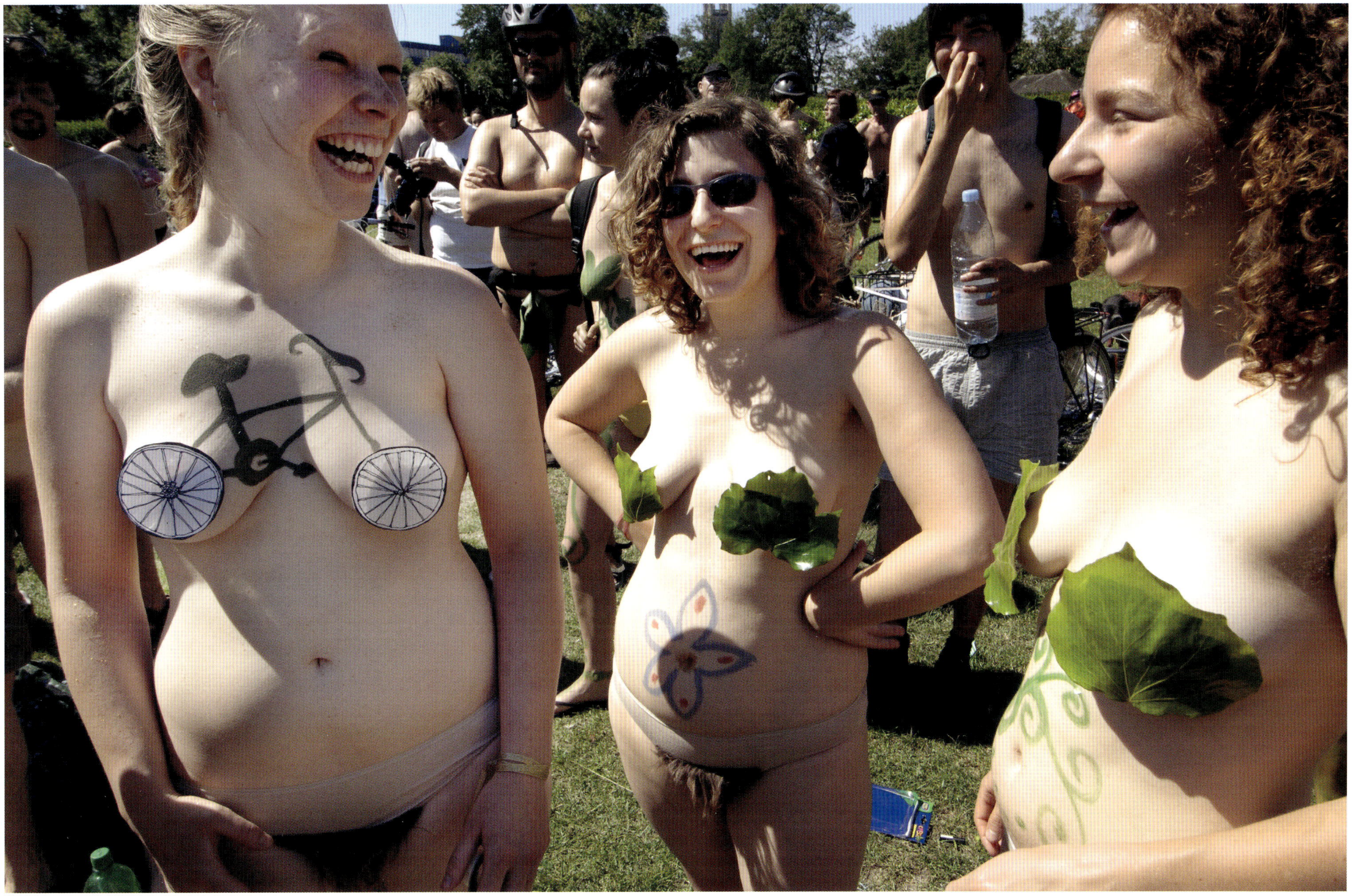

The World Nearly Naked Bike Ride

The Guardian, 2006

A global demonstration to protest against oil dependency, celebrate cycling and promote acceptance of the human body, the World Naked Bike Ride is now an annual event in cities all over the globe.
However, this was the first time it came to Brighton and the police were cautious about it. They told the riders gathering at the start that they could not go completely naked. Everyone got creative.
These three girls obeyed the police directive by using fig leaves and drawings of cycle wheels above some inventive homemade merkins. They passed the police checks without a hitch and I saw them set off around the city on a route which ended at the (legal) nudist beach.

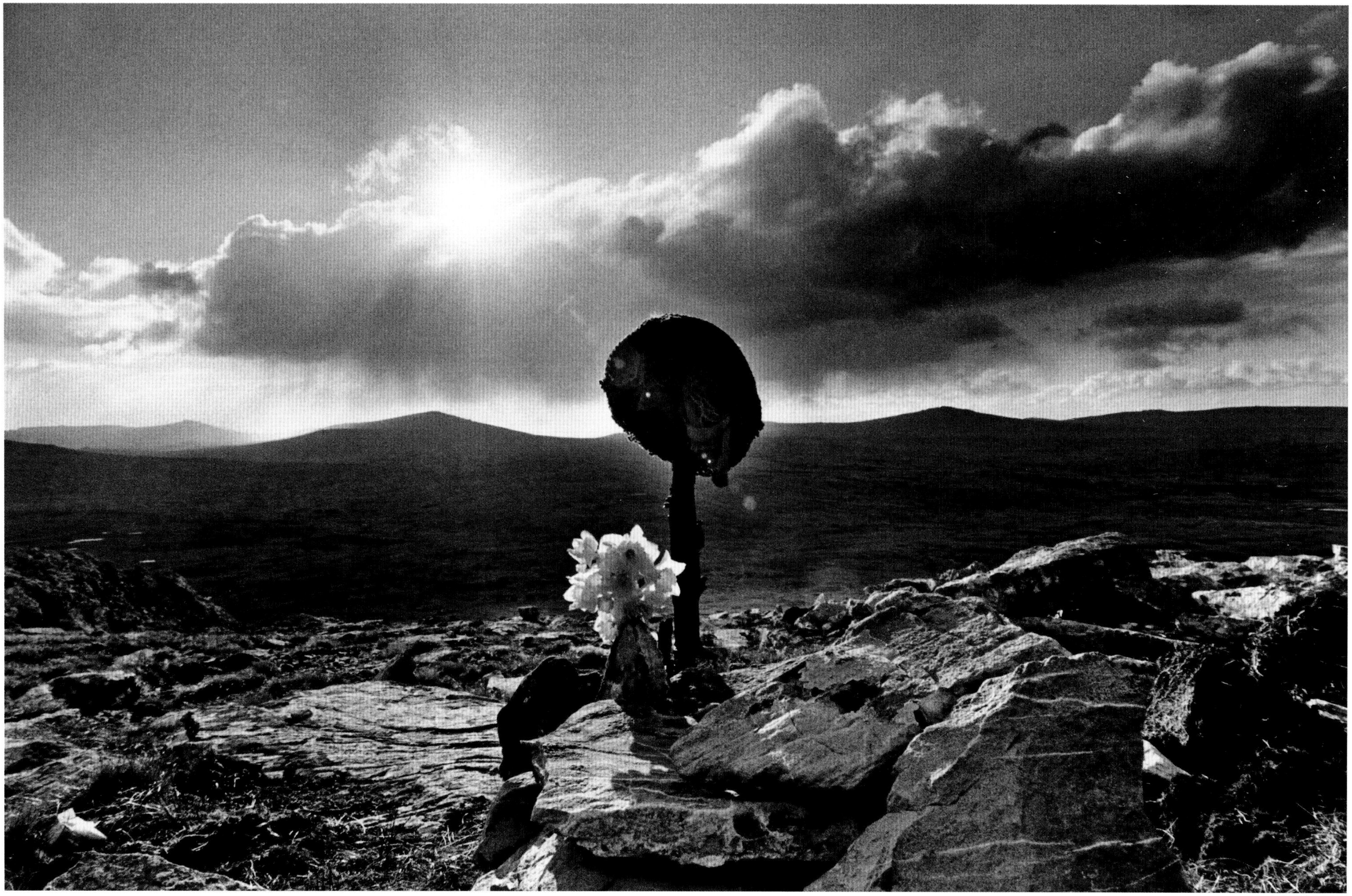

Gone but not Forgotten

The Sun, 1982

I took this picture two weeks after the reoccupation of the Falkland Islands, following the Falklands War. Two Victoria Cross medals, the highest award for valour, had been awarded to soldiers who had recently died in the battle for the Islands, but the media mainly wrote about just one, Colonel 'H' – Lieutenant Colonel Herbert Jones, who was shot at Goose Green on 28 May 1982 and buried at San Carlos Cemetery on the Islands.
There was far less attention paid to the other VC, Sergeant Ian McKay of the Parachute Regiment, who had died on Mount Longdon, on 12 June 1982. I wanted to know where he lay.
A bomb disposal officer told me that the Paras had buried him in a temporary grave close to where he fell and marked the place with a pile of rocks and his rifle with his helmet on top.
I picked some daffodils from the garden of the Upland Goose hotel and set off to find the grave. It was very moving to discover it on the bleak mountainside. I took some pictures, left the flowers and felt very glad I'd visited. A few months later Sergeant McKay was brought home and re-buried with full military honours in Aldershot.

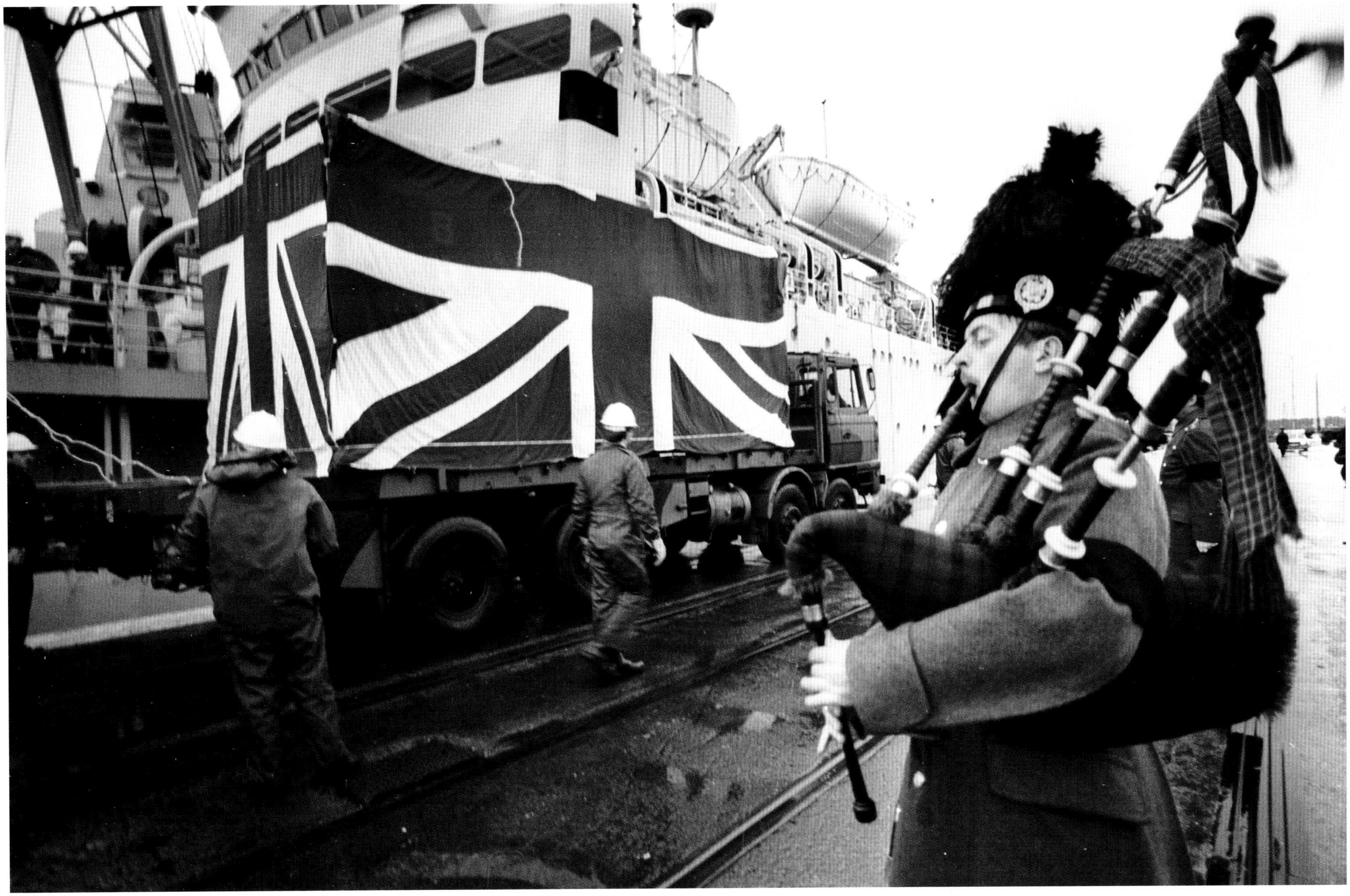

The Homecoming

The Sun, 1982

In the Portsmouth Royal Navy Dockyard, a ship has just returned from the Falklands Islands with the bodies of British servicemen killed in the war. I don't know if Sergeant McKay was among them but the simple ceremony was always the same. A military bandsman is on hand to salute the fallen and pipe the coffins ashore as they are transferred to a lorry, draped with a giant Union Jack flag

Moos Paper

The Guardian, 1990

Farmer Ray Boyer experimented with newspaper recycling on his farm at Castle Cary, Somerset by using papers as bedding for his herd of Charolais cattle. He was surprised when he discovered the cows were eating them.
Checks with a vet assured him that the newsprint would do the animals no harm and they actually had the same nutritional value as straw bran.
When I heard about it I absolutely knew it would make a great picture.
Meeting them face to face, I found that Charolais are bigger than you expect when you are close up. They were packed in their barn, contentedly browsing, and I had an arduous half hour, squeezing myself and the camera gear through the scrum until I found the right vantage point.
They had the most beautiful manners though, and never trod on me once.

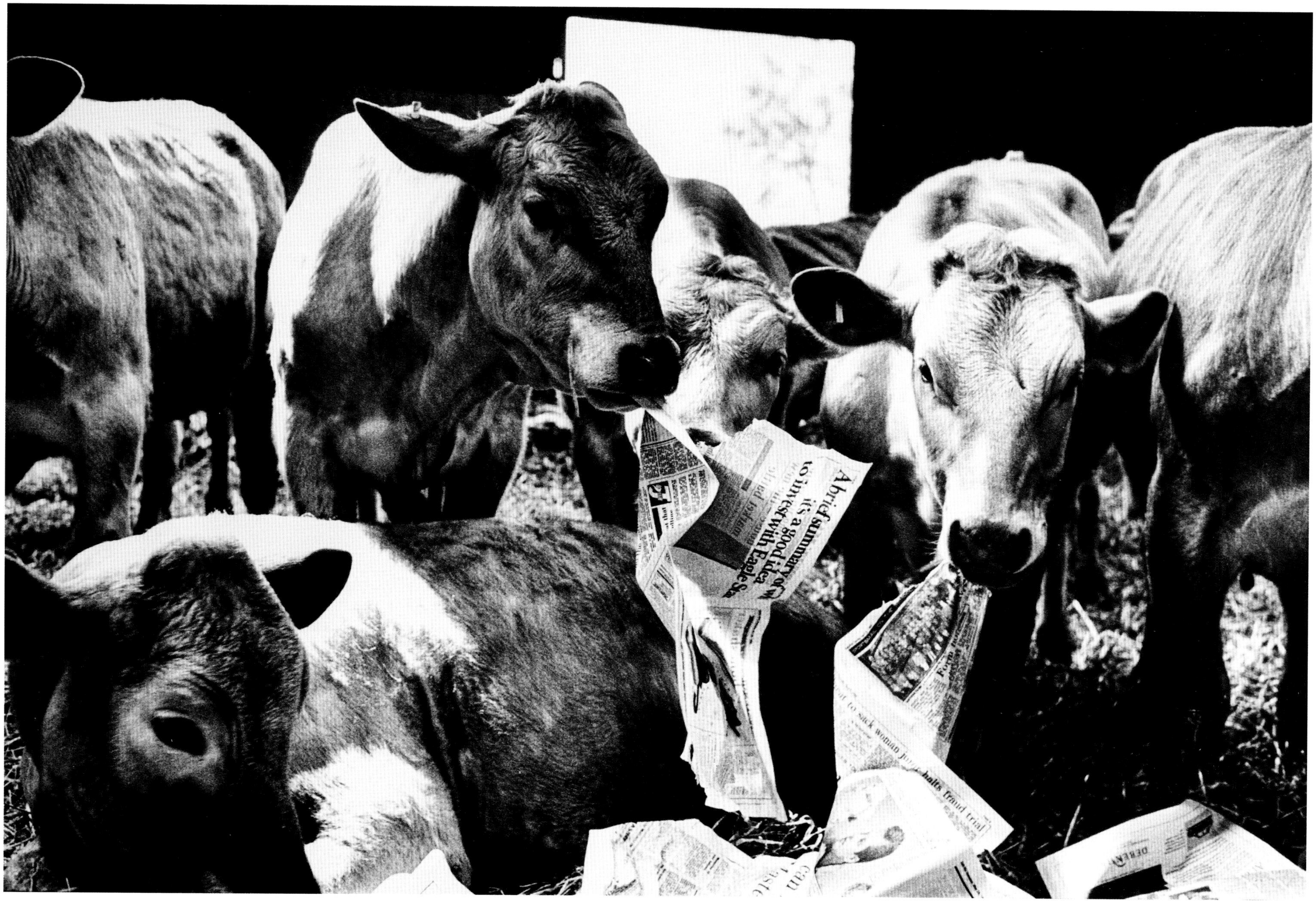

Maggie gets her Hands Dirty

The Sun, 1983

During her election campaigns Margaret Thatcher always provided her accredited press team with a daily photo opportunity. On this occasion in Cornwall she was visiting a farm and was about to turn to a TV crew with her hands full of lovely golden straw. She plunged her hands into a pile without finding out what was underneath. It proved to be a heap of manure the farmer had hastily camouflaged when she arrived. I'd been hanging about, focused on her just in case there was anything worth seeing. It paid off, as she pulled a disgusted face before quickly dumping it all and moving swiftly on.

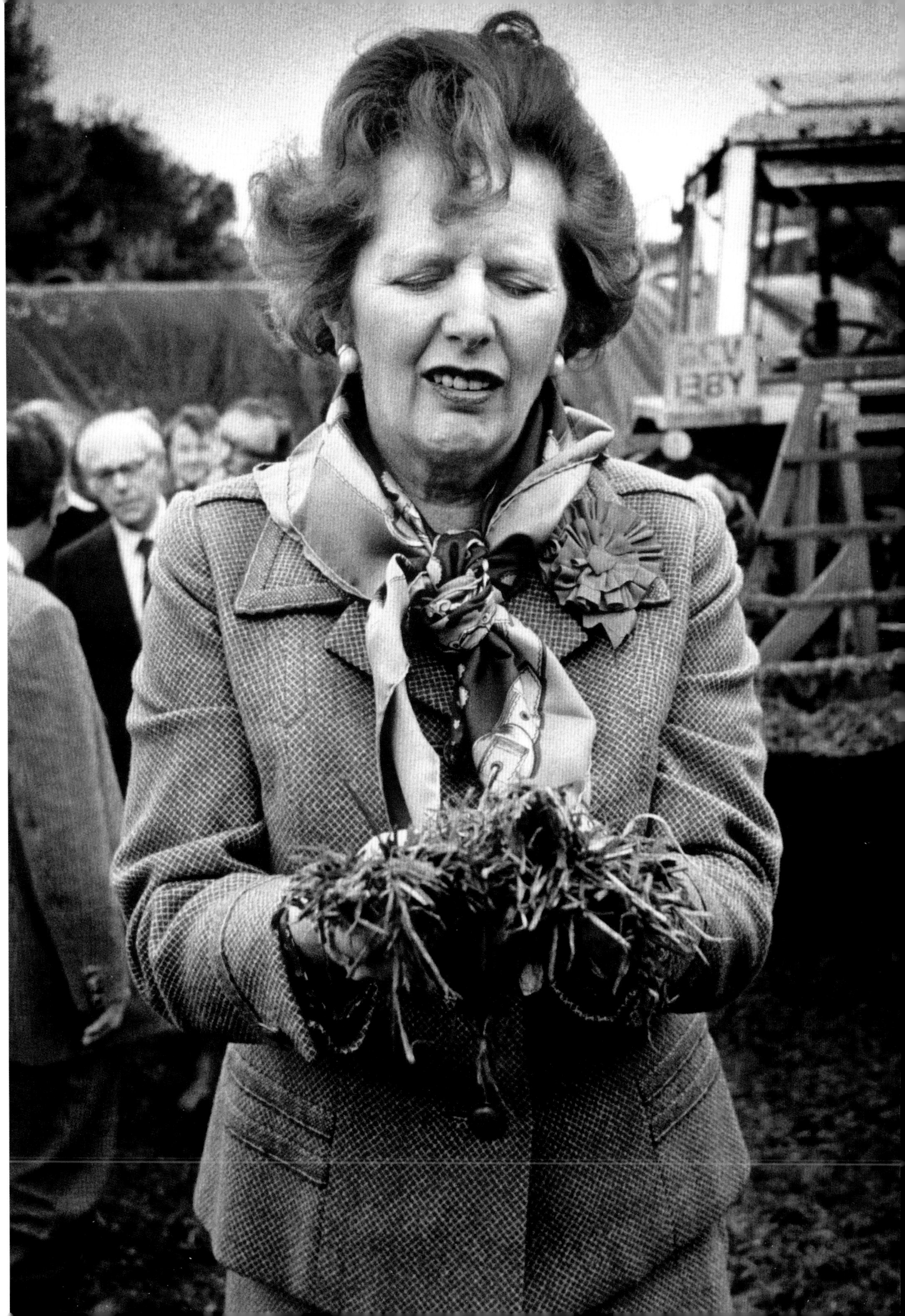

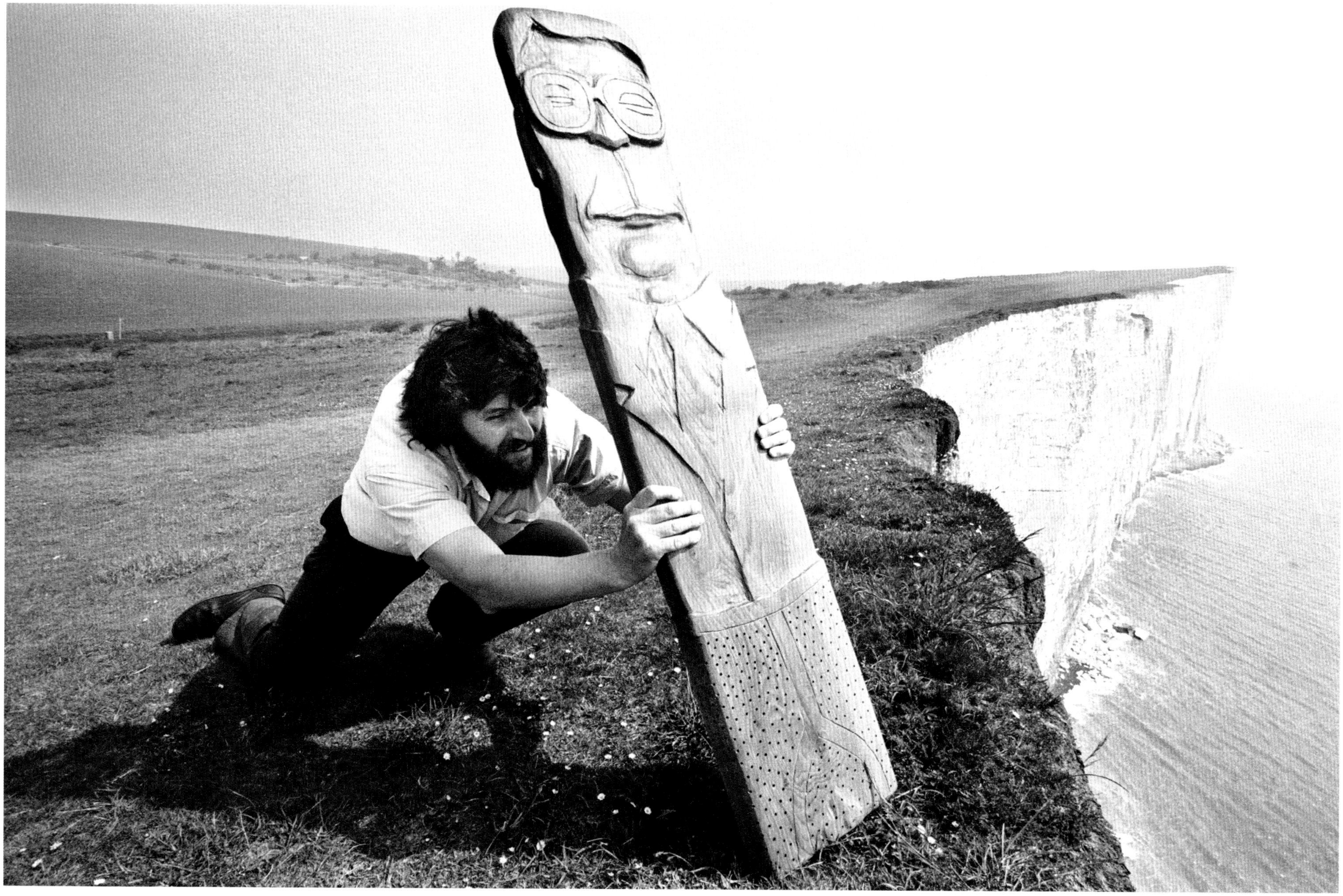

Major Problem

The Guardian, 1994

The *Guardian's* political cartoonist Steve Bell was renowned for his scathing caricatures of politicians. After Margaret Thatcher, the Tory leader was John Major, who was instantly labelled the Grey Man after Steve began drawing him as a completely grey but instantly recognisable character who for some reason always wore his Y-fronts outside his trousers. Steve's artist friend Hugh Card carved the caricature into 'Plank Man' for the cartoonist to throw over Beachy Head.

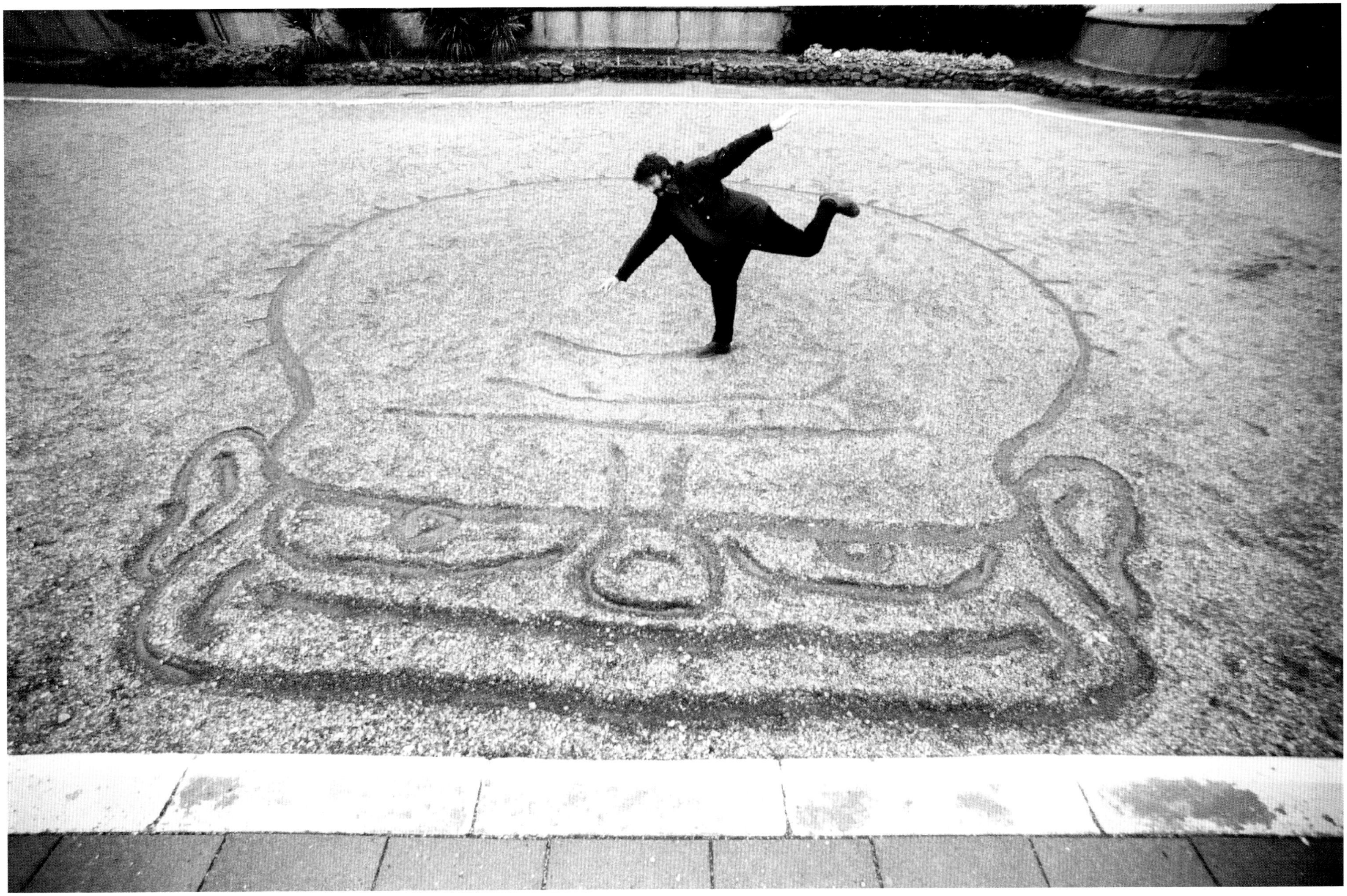

Laugh Lines

The Guardian, 2000

Steve Bell again, this time drawing yet another Tory leader, William Hague, with the heel of his shoe in the shale on Brighton seafront. He was taking part in The Big Draw, an event when thirty top cartoonists and comic strip artists assembled for A Fun Day Drawing, a nationwide celebration of the power of the pencil. Or the shoe in this case.

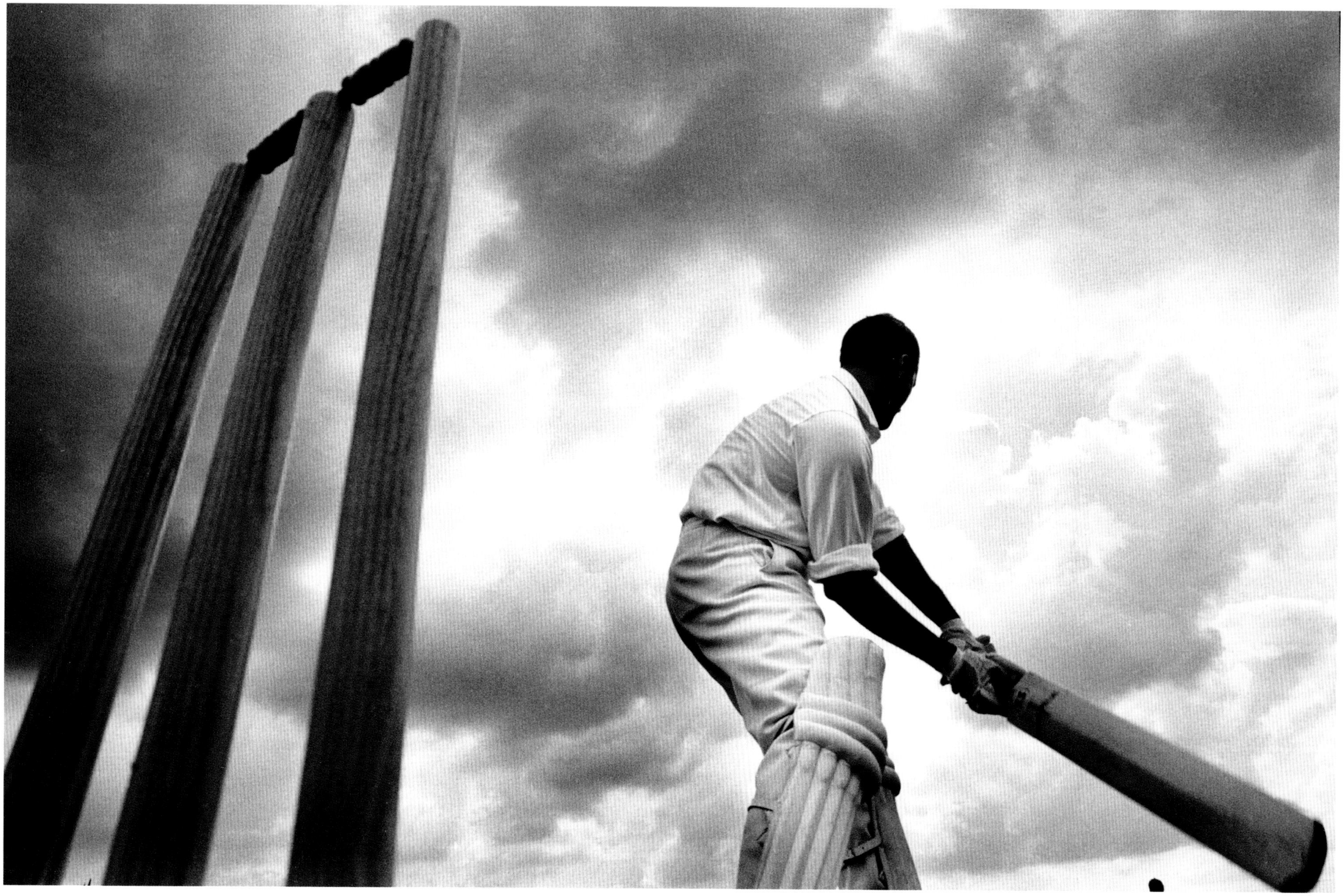

Fair Play

The Daily Mail, 1967

Worcestershire and England cricketer Basil D'Oliveira was a figurehead for anti-apartheid cricket campaigners in the 1960s. As a mixed race player he was denied the chance to play for his native country, South Africa, so he moved with his family to England to become a hugely popular county and Test player.
In 1967 he was named one of the five Wisden cricketers of the year and I went to photograph him at the Worcester ground where his young son Damian - later a county cricketer himself - was bowling to him. Basil was hoping to be able to return to South Africa with the England Test team and not long afterwards he was picked to be in the Test side for the 1968–9 tour of South Africa.
His hopes were dashed when the South African Government refused to allow him to play. England cancelled the whole tour in protest and South Africa was excluded from Test cricket for the next twenty-two years.

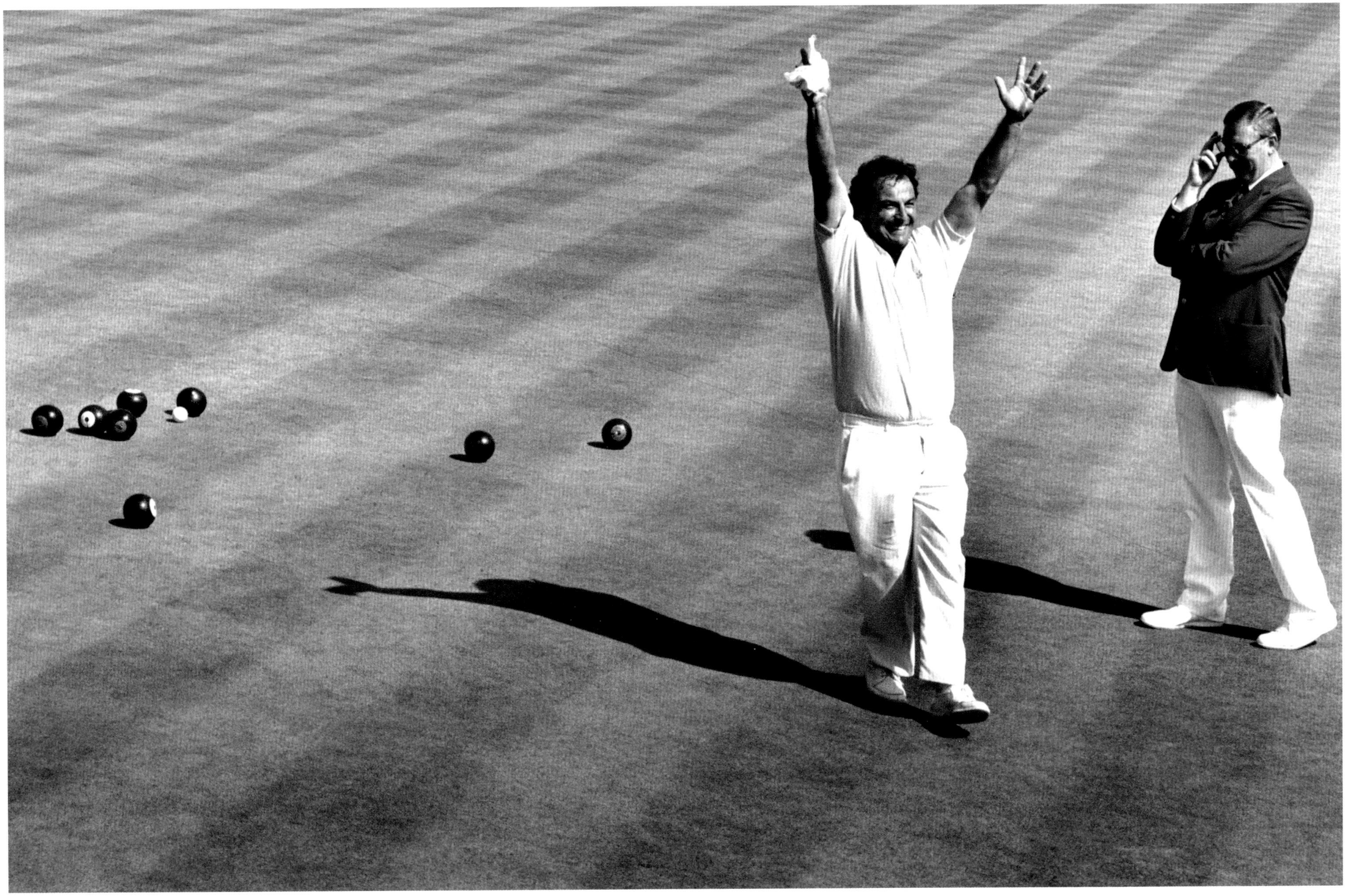

Jumping Jacks

The Guardian, 1992

Bowls is an intense, sedate, slow, yet skilful game that provides very little photographic action. Covering the World Bowls Championships in Worthing in 1992 was a bit of a challenge. Then Israeli Jeff Rabkin, the only player unbeaten but trailing ten ends down to his opponent Mark McMahon suddenly started to stage an enormous recovery. McMahon had only needed one more victory to win but Rabkin was winning end after end. I counted to see which end he would finish if he could win every game left, found the perfect position to see the result and crossed my fingers. The fans were starting to cheer. When he came back from 10 down to win he celebrated with such enthusiasm that even the usually inscrutable umpire had to smile.

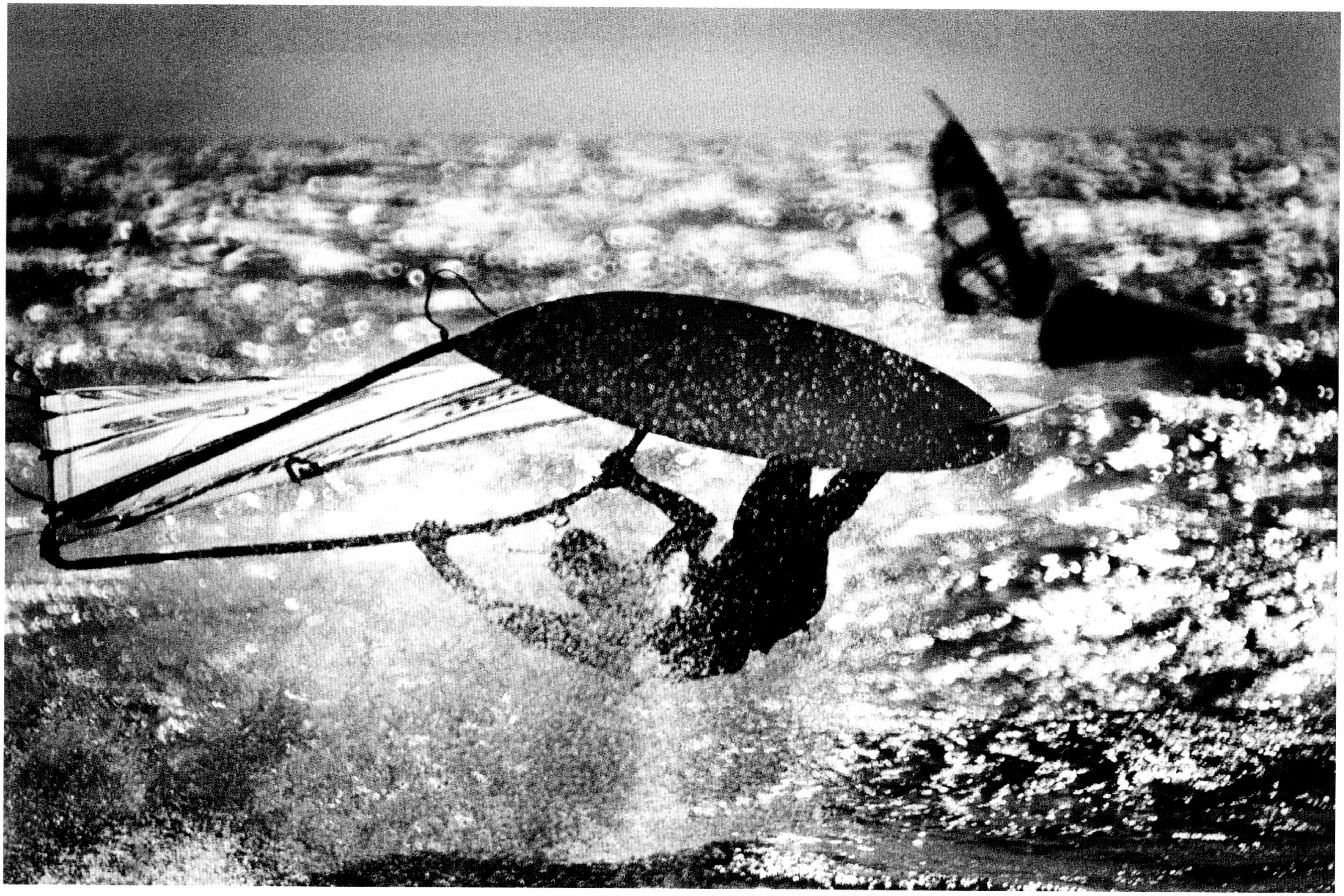

Surf's Up

The Guardian, 1994

Nik Baker, British Windsurfing champion and the best windsurfer Britain had ever produced, sailed into trouble during a World Windsurfing Association event at Brighton. The week-long championships had been becalmed until this last day, when the surf picked up and the top man took on the wind and waves. And promptly fell off. This dramatic upside-down image made a page 1 splash the next morning.

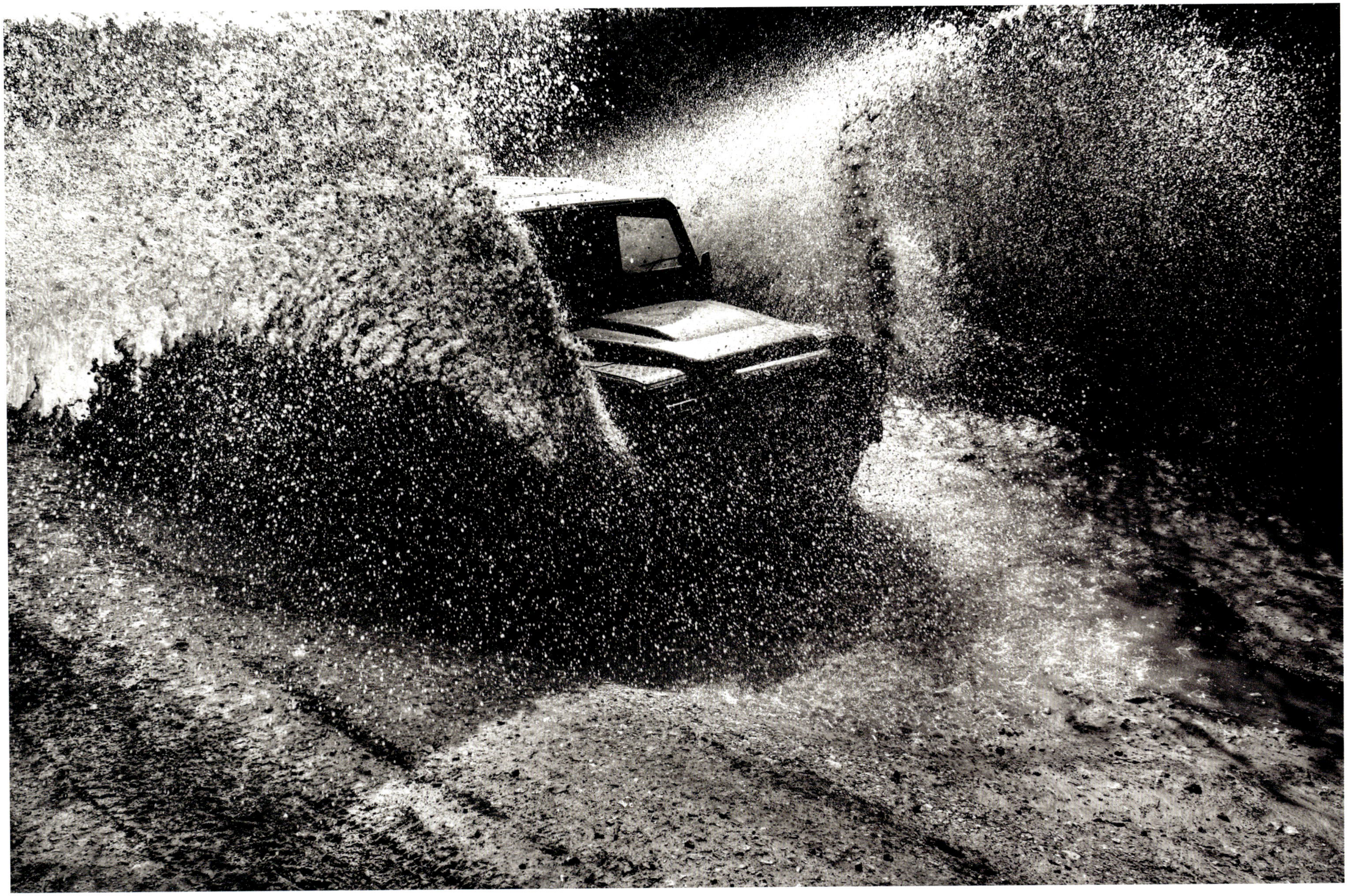

Mud Larking

The Guardian, 2009

I bought a Land Rover Defender in 2009. It was a new model with a huge bump in the bonnet to accommodate a larger engine size. Because the shape was so obvious I decided to photograph it – if anyone needed a Land Rover picture, I'd have something up-to-date to hand.
There was a perfect off-road course through woodland at Slindon, near Arundel, so I booked in and spruced the Landy up at a car wash beforehand, to look immaculate for its photo shoot. Which in retrospect was rather silly.
At Slindon, an off-road driving expert roared up hill and down dale for me, and then roared through the spectacular deep water splash.
The next day I returned to the car wash with my precious new vehicle. Eight men spent most of the morning trying to restore it to its former glory but it was never as shiny again.

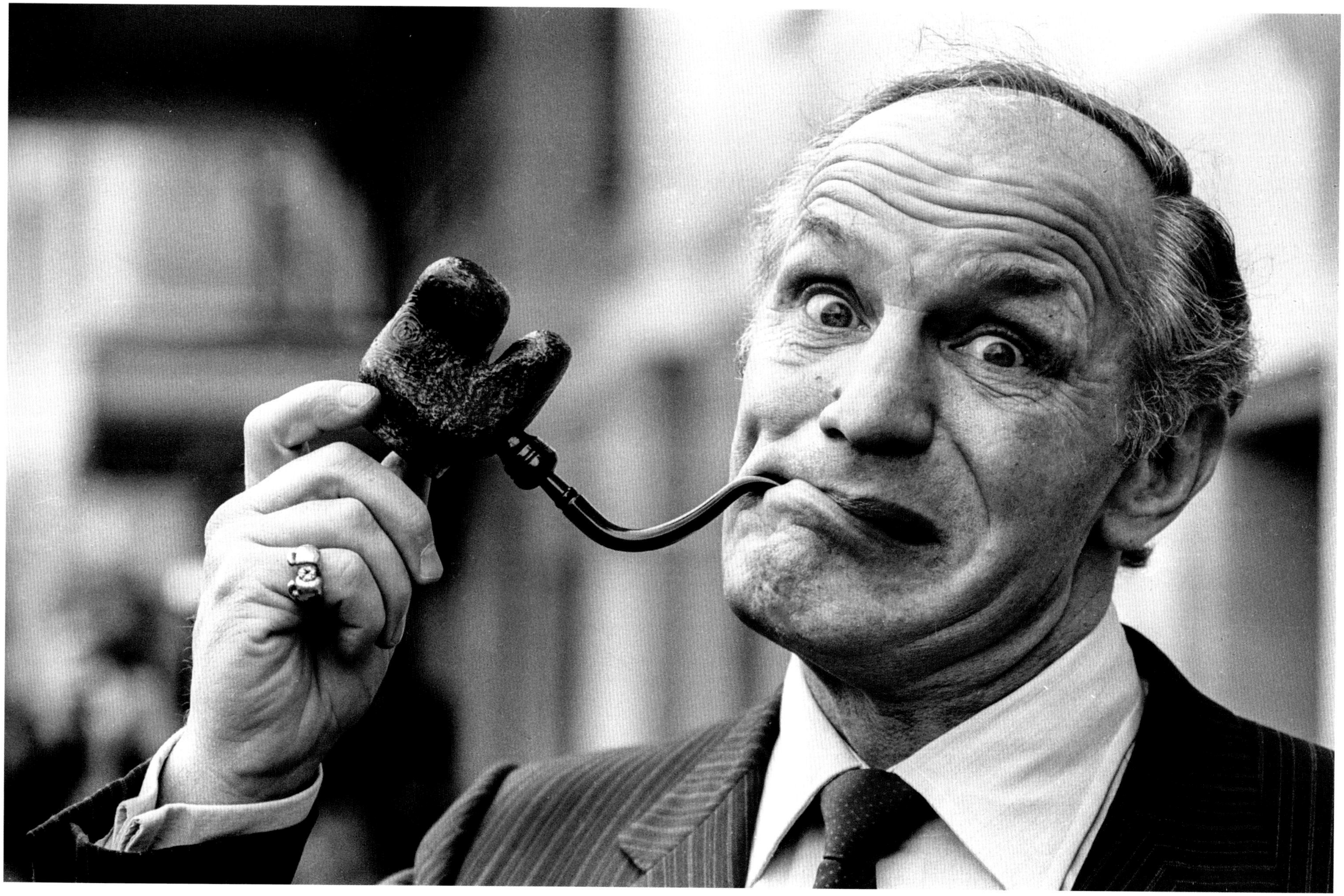

Packing a Punch

The Sun, 1984

Before health and safety got a grip, the annual Pipeman of the Year Awards celebrating high-profile smokers always made pictures for the papers. British heavyweight boxer Henry Cooper, who once famously knocked down Mohammed Ali during an epic fight, saw nothing to worry about and sportingly puffed away on a boxing glove pipe.

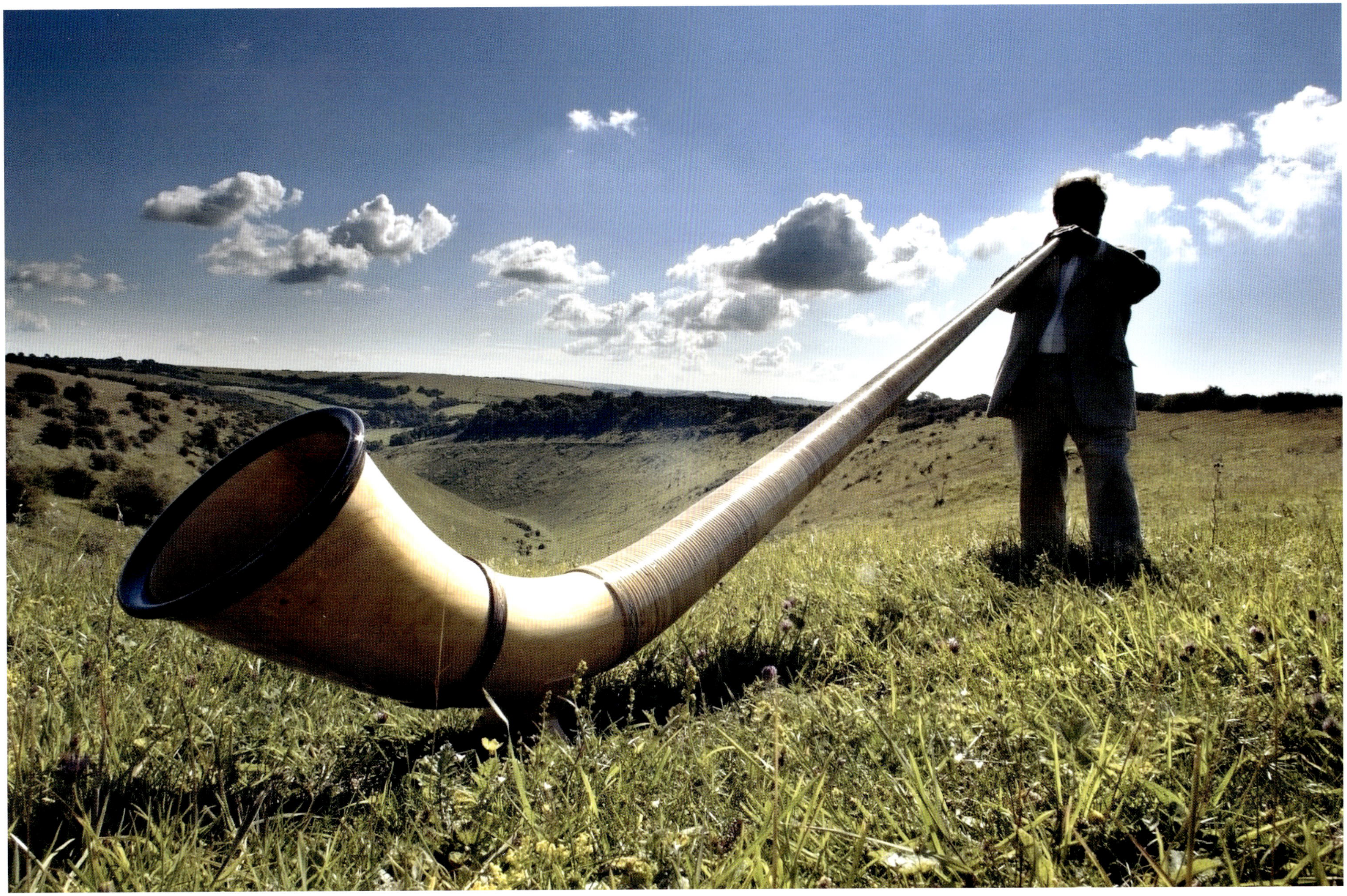

High Note

The Times, 2004

Gavin Henderson, artistic director of Dartington Summer School of Music, was an alphorn enthusiast. He had two of his own and had just commissioned composer Orlando Gough's new work 'Thin Air', for six alphorns, a brass orchestra, an ensemble of drummers and two yodelling choirs to be premièred at Dartington Festival in Devon. Of course, he planned to be part of the performance. An alphorn simply has to be seen in its natural hillside setting, so I persuaded Gavin to haul his instrument out into the South Downs National Park, for a practice session.

Seeing Eye to Eye

The Guardian, 2002

I was sent a new mobile phone by Vodafone with a CAMERA. Believe it or not, at the time this was an exciting innovation. I though it would be fun to play with this new toy, so I contacted a local supplier, borrowed two more of the mobiles and photographed the beautiful eyes of a neighbour over the road, the mouth of my next door neighbour and asked lovely barmaid Charlotte from the local pub to hold them up in front of her own face. Put together it made a striking image – just the start of all the fun people have with camera phones today.

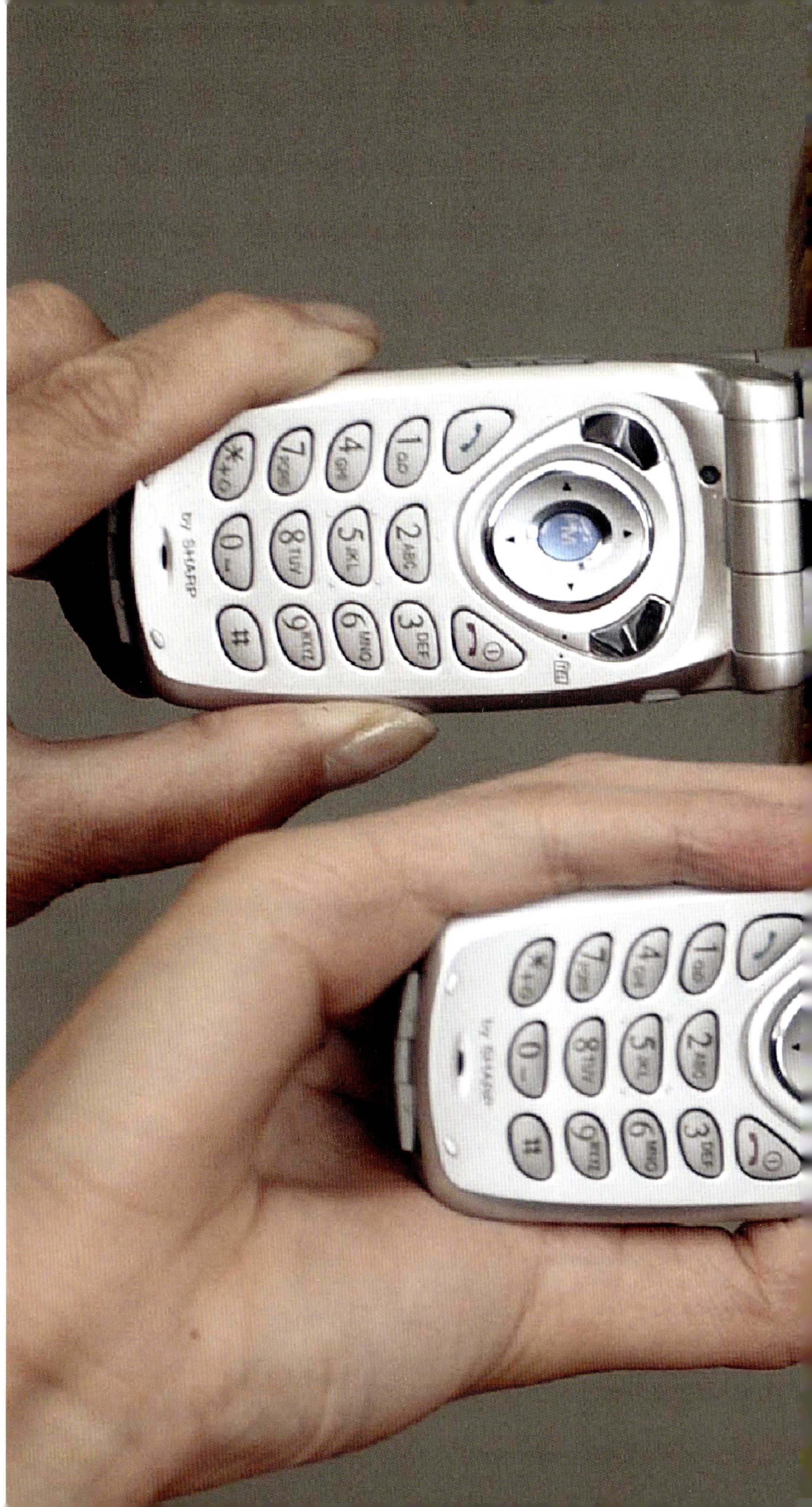

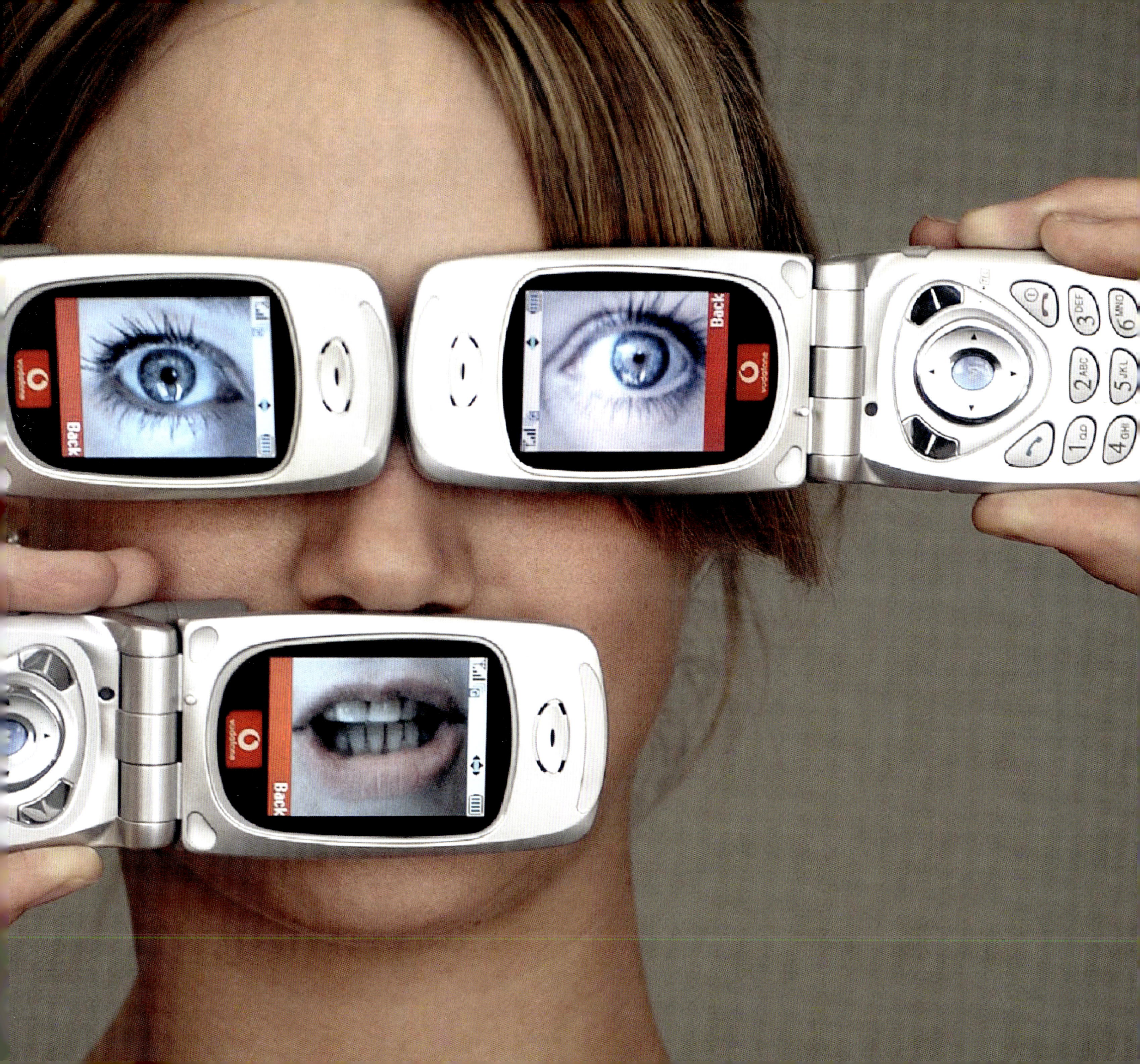
Back
Back
Back

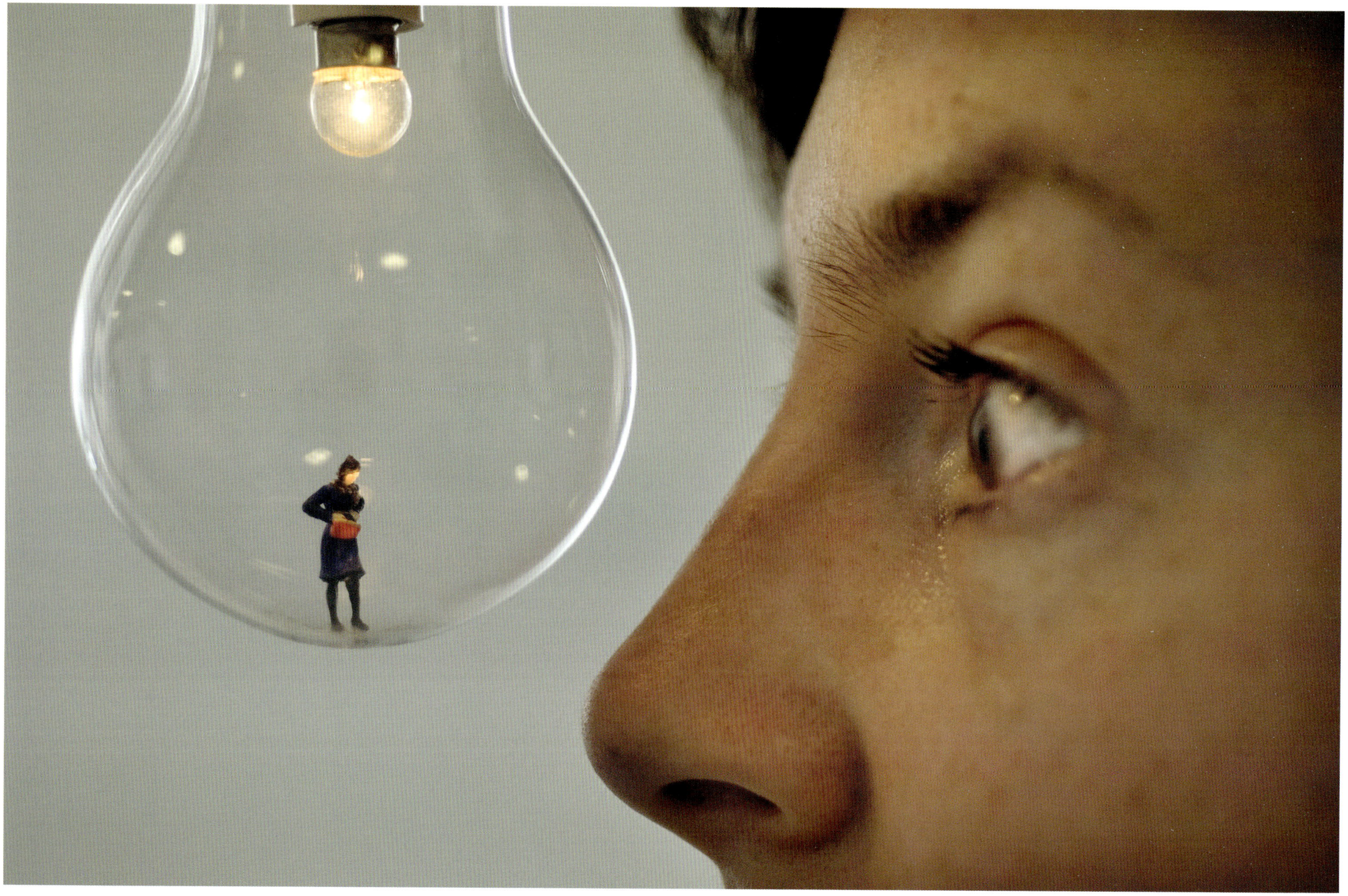

Making Light Work

The Guardian, 2008

Graduate sculpture student Bridget Caswell made a 1-cm-high self-portrait of herself standing inside a light bulb in a display called *Frustrating Search for that Moment of Clarity*.
The tiny effigy was part of her series 'Small Works' exhibited in the 2008 University of Brighton graduate degree show.

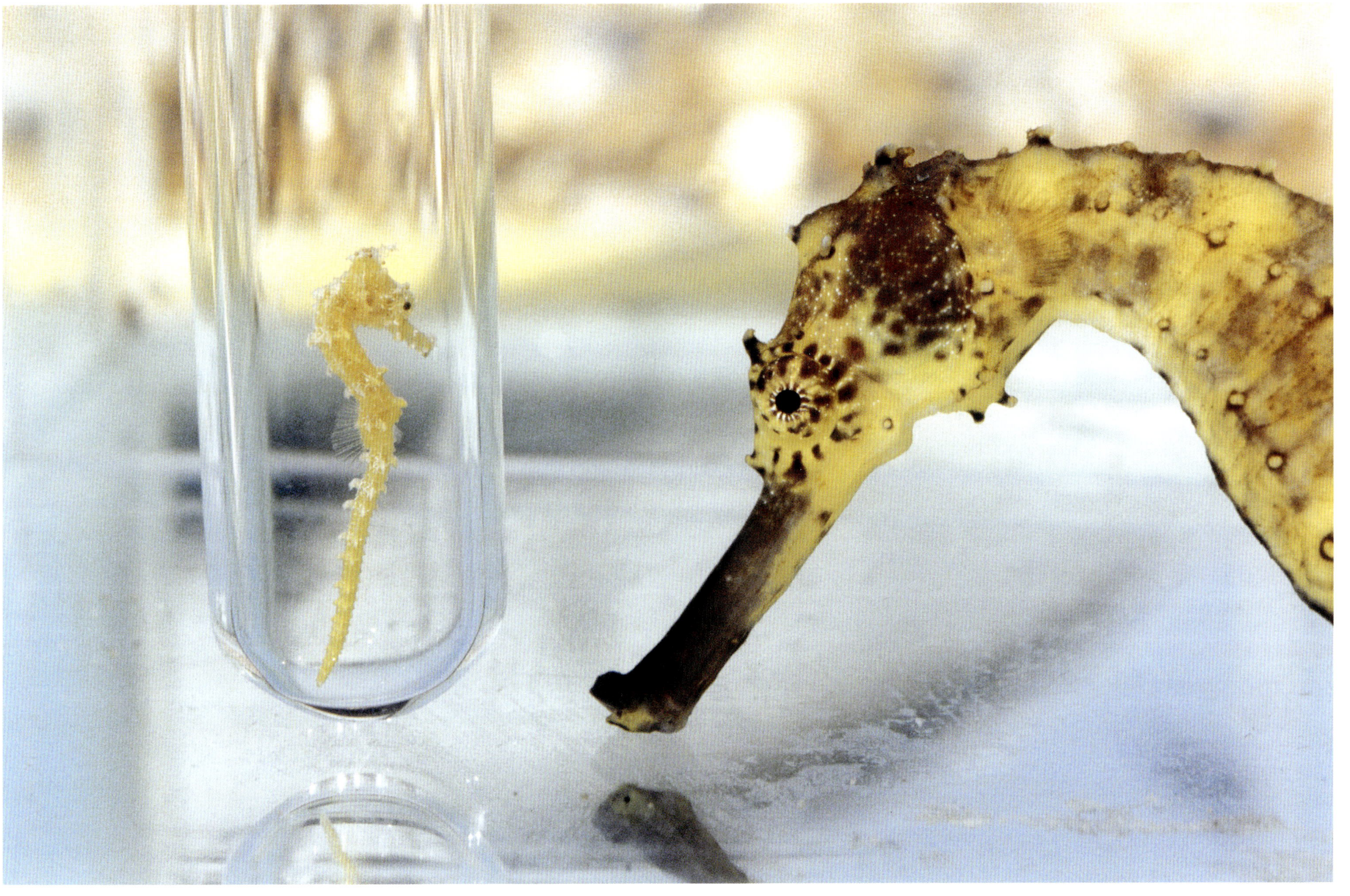

Father and Son

The Guardian, 1999

Sealife Centres are dotted all over the country, and each one tends to specialise in looking after different creatures. Brighton has a special seahorse nursery as part of its breeding programme for endangered seahorse species.
For this picture, taken to celebrate a particularly successful breeding programme, I asked the team to pop a baby tiger tail in a test tube so I could get a picture of it with its father. Only a few weeks earlier it had been incubating snugly in its father's pouch, alongside hundreds of brothers and sisters. More than 20 million tiger tails are killed each year for China and Japan to use in treatments for baldness and impotence. World stocks are dwindling. What an absolute waste of life for such a beautiful creature.

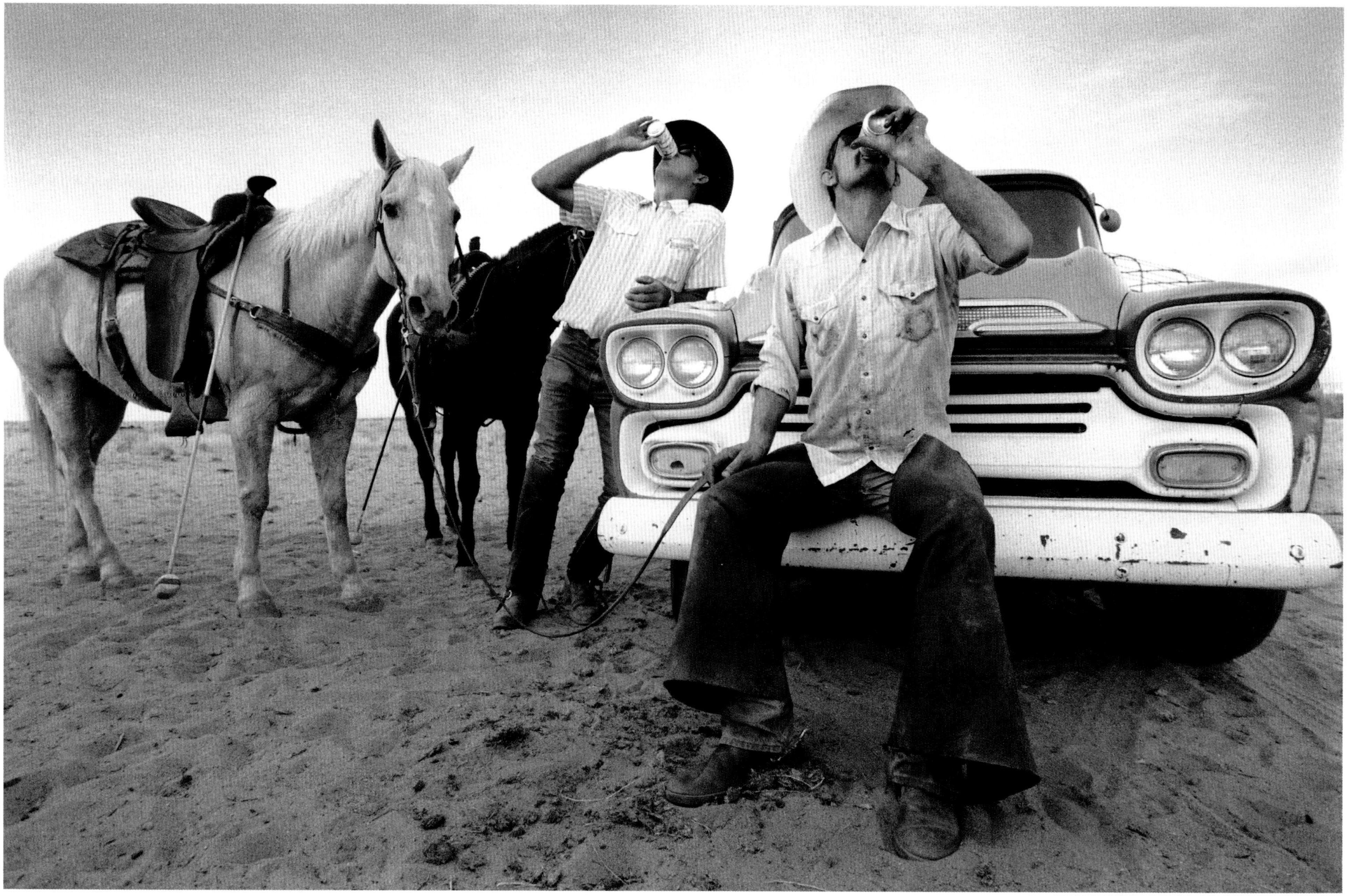

Cowboy Polo

FHM Magazine, 1992

When Prince Charles started courting Lady Diana Spencer, he took her to watch him play polo. Awareness of polo suddenly shot up. Everybody knew it was something like hockey on horseback and frightfully exclusive.
But they do things differently in the USA and I jumped at the chance to do a feature about polo as played by cowboys in Albuquerque, New Mexico.

There wasn't a blade of grass on the dusty clay pitch, no stadium, no seating, no refreshment tents. Everyone parked up and sat on their cars or trucks to yell for their team. These players were relaxing between chukkas by swigging beers. Their Quarter horses were casually tethered to their pickup truck. A sticker in the truck's rear window boasted 'Cowboy Polo Players have Rubber Balls'.

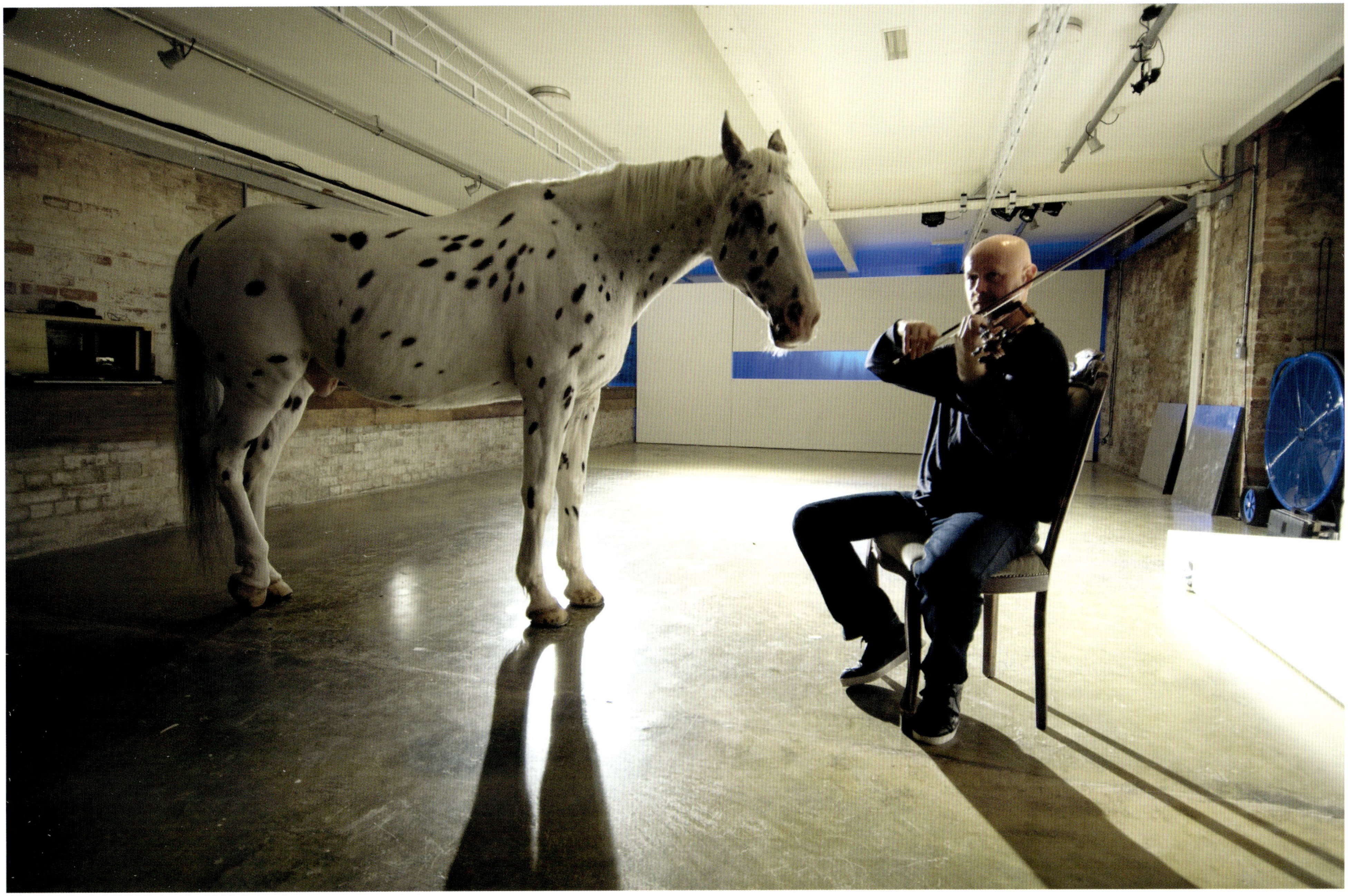

Serenade

The Guardian, 2008

Phoenix, a marble spotted Knabstrupper, was astonishingly relaxed about being led into a basement and faced with a man playing a violin. Man and horse were taking part in a play by a theatre company called *Fevered Sleep* at Brighton Festival, and violinist Jamie McCarthy's role was to serenade Phoenix while the rest of the cast crossed their fingers and held their breath.
It was fine. The gentle horse appeared to rather enjoy it.

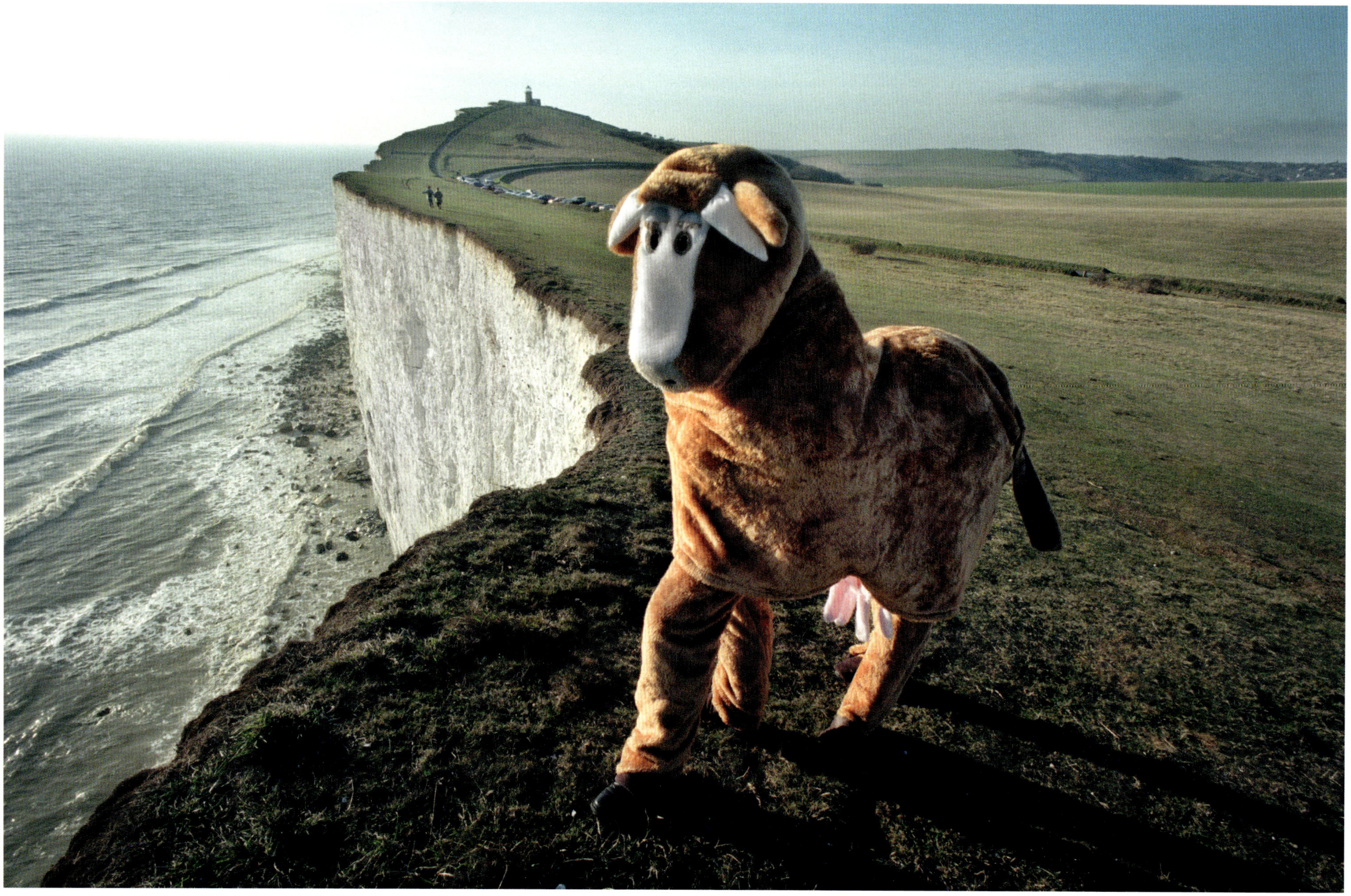

On the Brink

The Guardian, 1999

A pantomime cow on the cliffs at Beachy Head, near Eastbourne, East Sussex, was making a serious point – it was looking over the channel to France as part of a protest against the suffering of real-live cattle and sheep. The animals were being crammed into lorries and ferries for export to Europe and enduring terrible conditions on long journeys to foreign slaughterhouses.

The couple in the cow costume both needed a stiff drink after the picture session as neither could see where they were standing and had to rely on me saying 'left a bit' and 'stop!' as they got nearer and nearer the cliff edge.

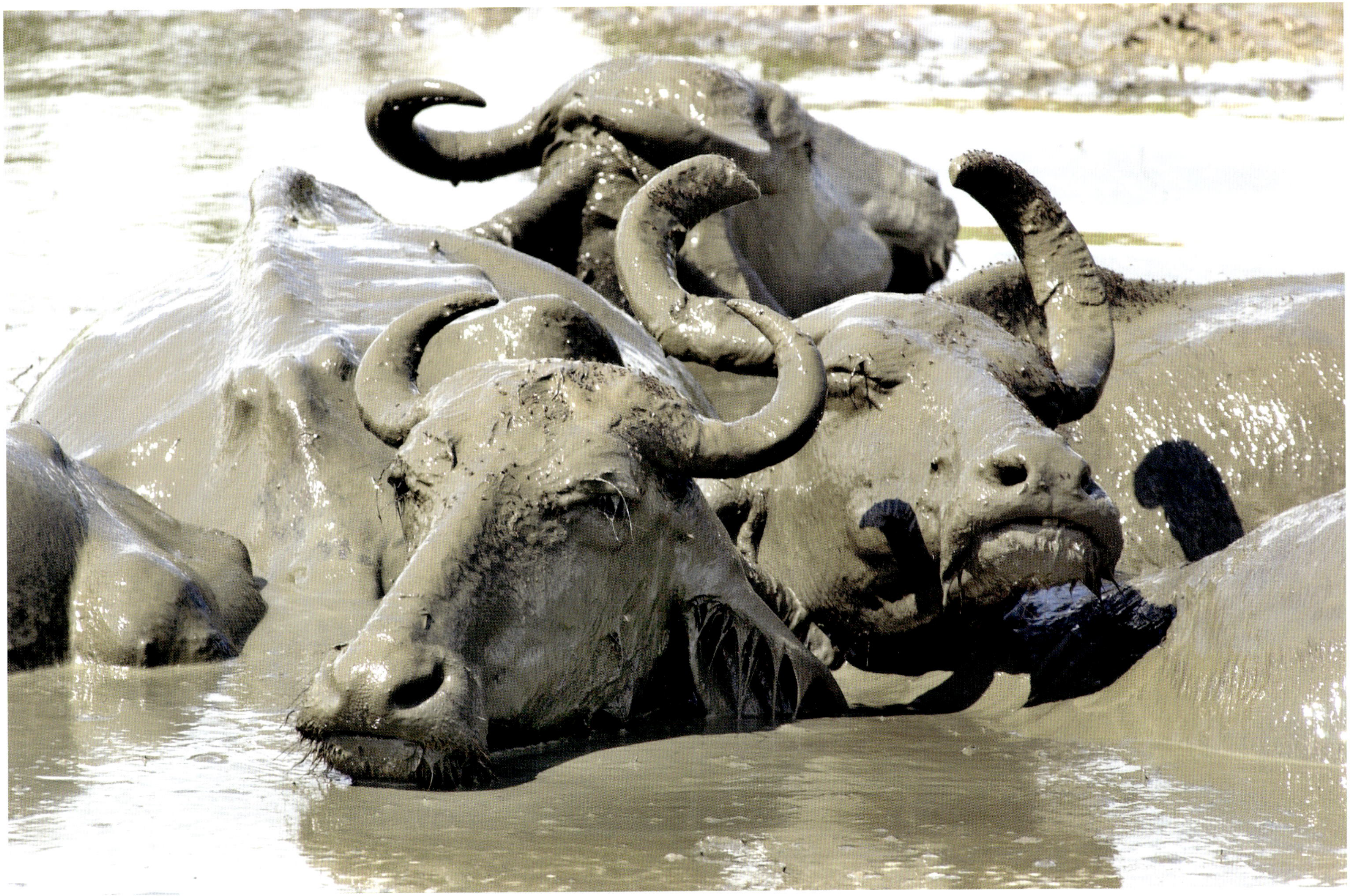

Glorious Mud

The Guardian, 2010

I was in Sri Lanka, and on the way to the temple city of Kandy I drove past a herd of water buffaloes cooling off in a water hole.
There were about twenty of the enormous creatures wallowing in a gigantic mudbath and they looked so extraordinary I did an immediate u-turn, temples forgotten. The next hour was spent getting very, very muddy on the edge of the pool, trying to capture the way they were all tangled up with each other in the slimy, slippery sludge.

Sundowner

The Observer, 1989

One of my first commissioned stories for the *Observer* was a feature about birdwatchers. I set up to watch the watchers at Dawlish Warren, on the River Exe in Devon, and heard them debating if they were watching a turnstone, a grey plover or a sanderling. All I could see was a tiny bird standing on one leg a very long way off on a mudflat.
The patient watchers waited as the tide rose and fell. As the sun began to set, one birder with a telescope was focusing on one little bird and I got my picture at last.

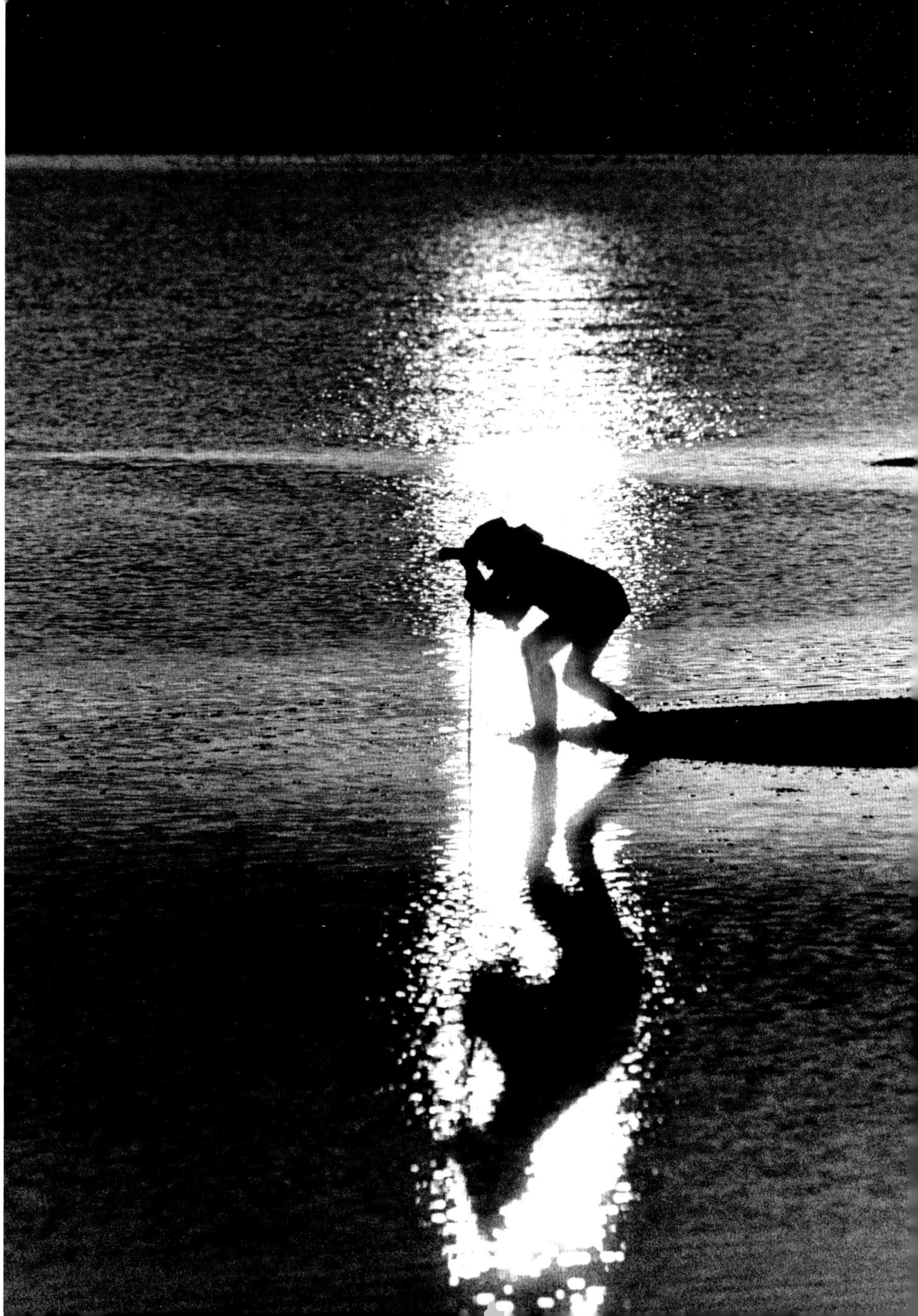

Mori Cat

Greetings card, 1985

I was adopted by a black cat called Mori, who had a huge personality and the profile of one of those inscrutable statues found in the pyramids of ancient Egypt. He was an elegant creature, photographed often, but this is the only picture that did him justice. I was passing a room where the door was just ajar and he was sitting in shaft of sunlight. I grabbed my camera and caught the moment. I used the picture on my Christmas cards that year and a greetings card after that. I've always got a stack of Mori cards somewhere.

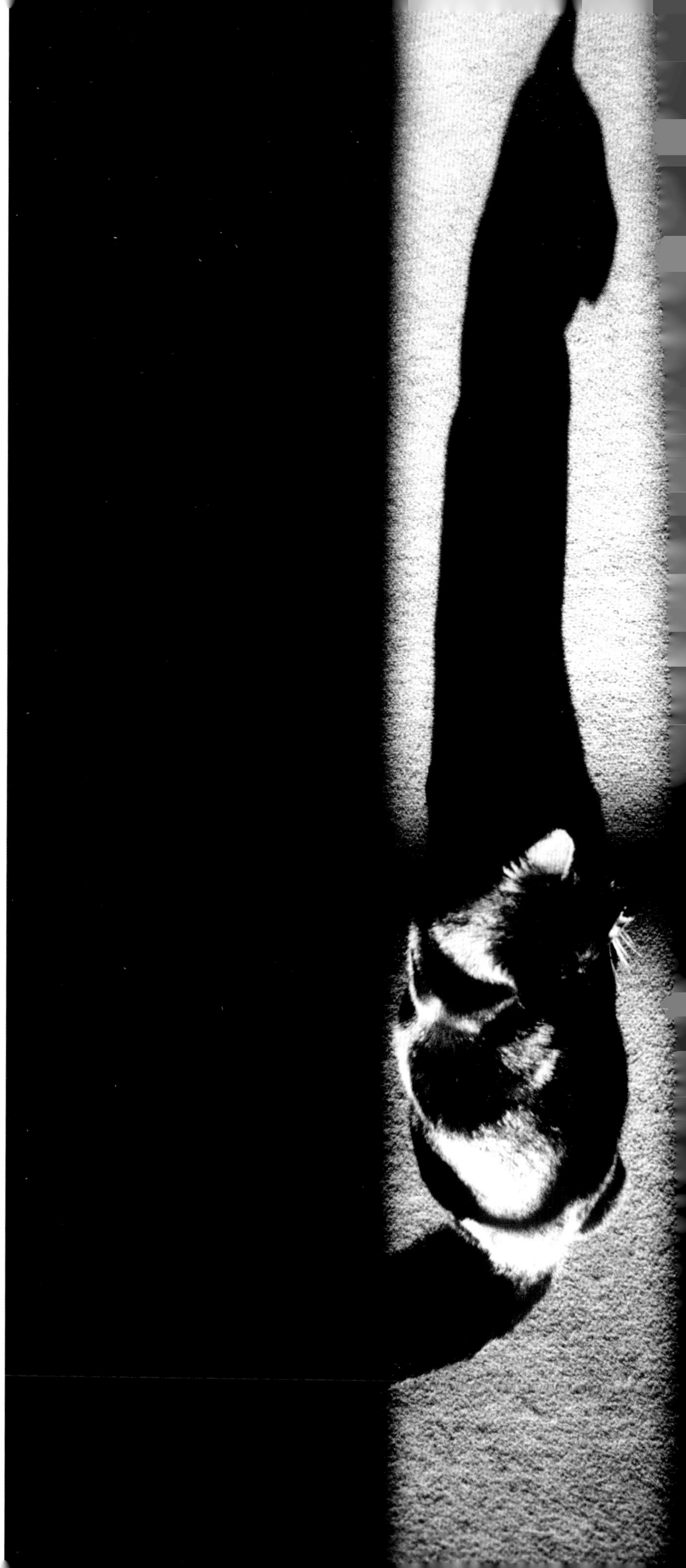

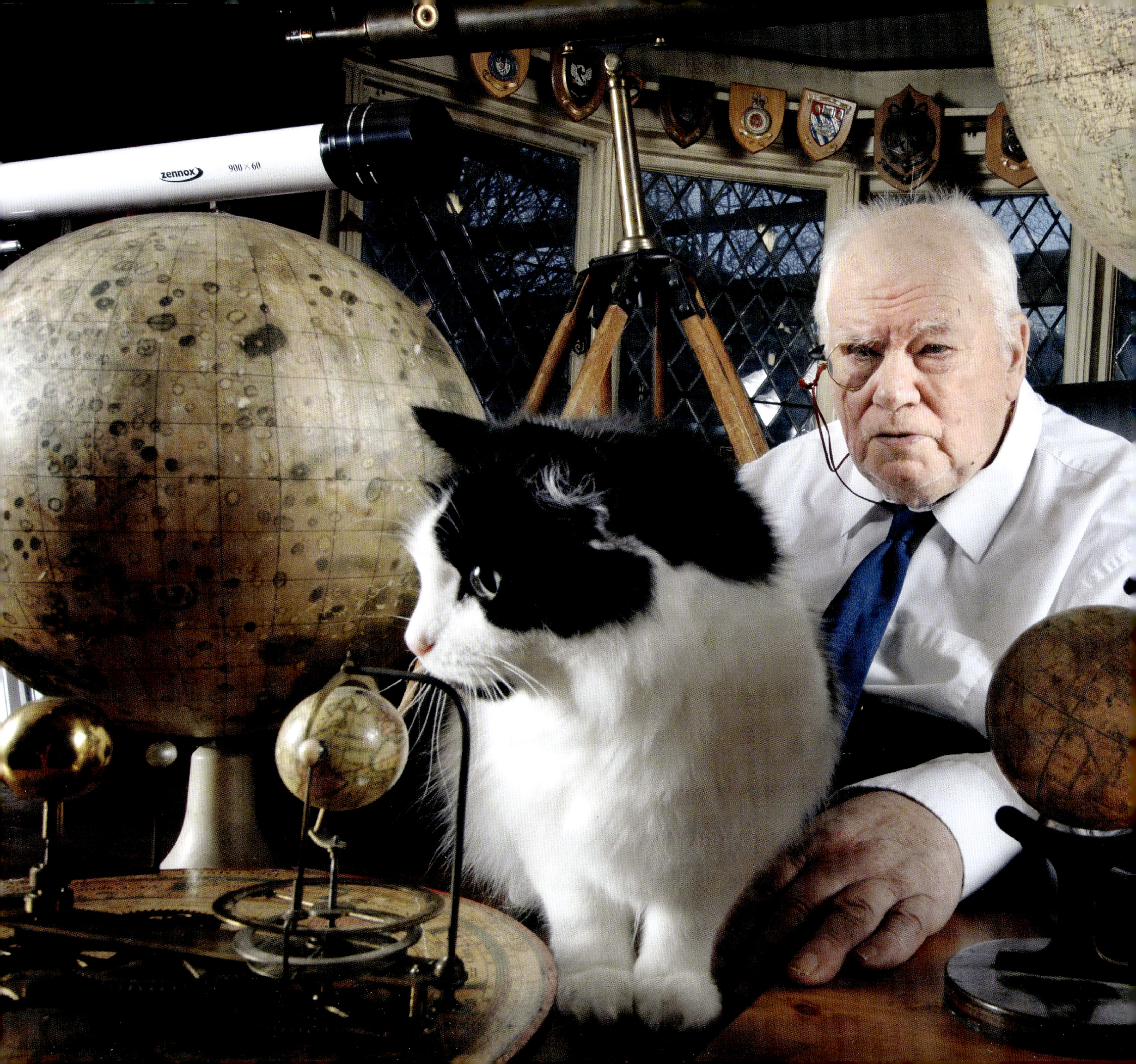
zennox
900 × 60

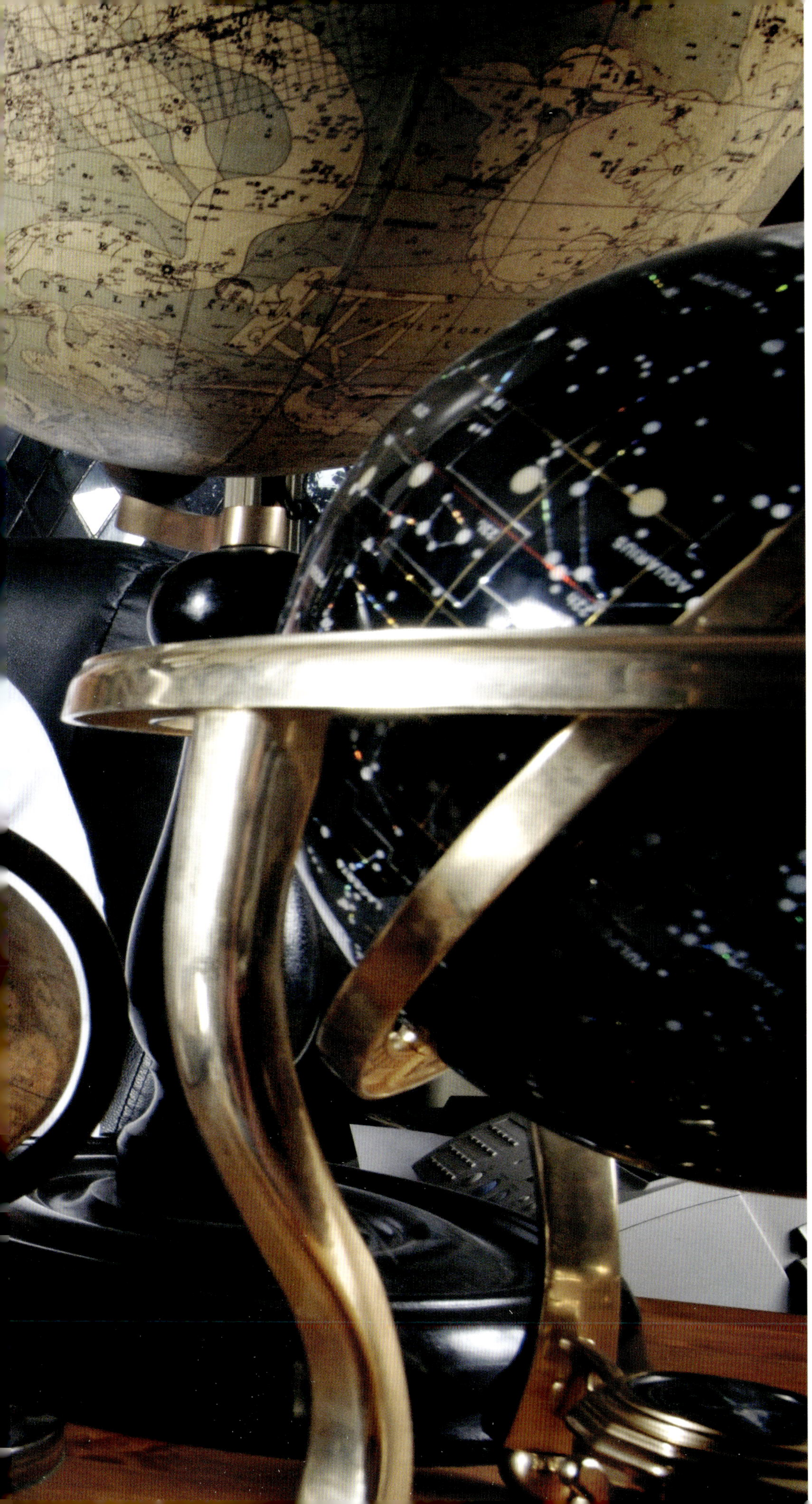

Worlds Within Worlds

The Guardian, 2006

Sir Patrick Moore, the distinguished astronomer, broadcaster, author, manic xylophone player and cat lover was about to record the 650th edition of *The Sky At Night,* the show he had presented with barely a break for fifty years.
The BBC crew had to come to him – at eighty-three he was no longer prepared to budge from his home in Selsey, West Sussex. His study was like a tiny universe with globes of moons and planets and star charts everywhere – and Jeannie his cat at the centre of it all.

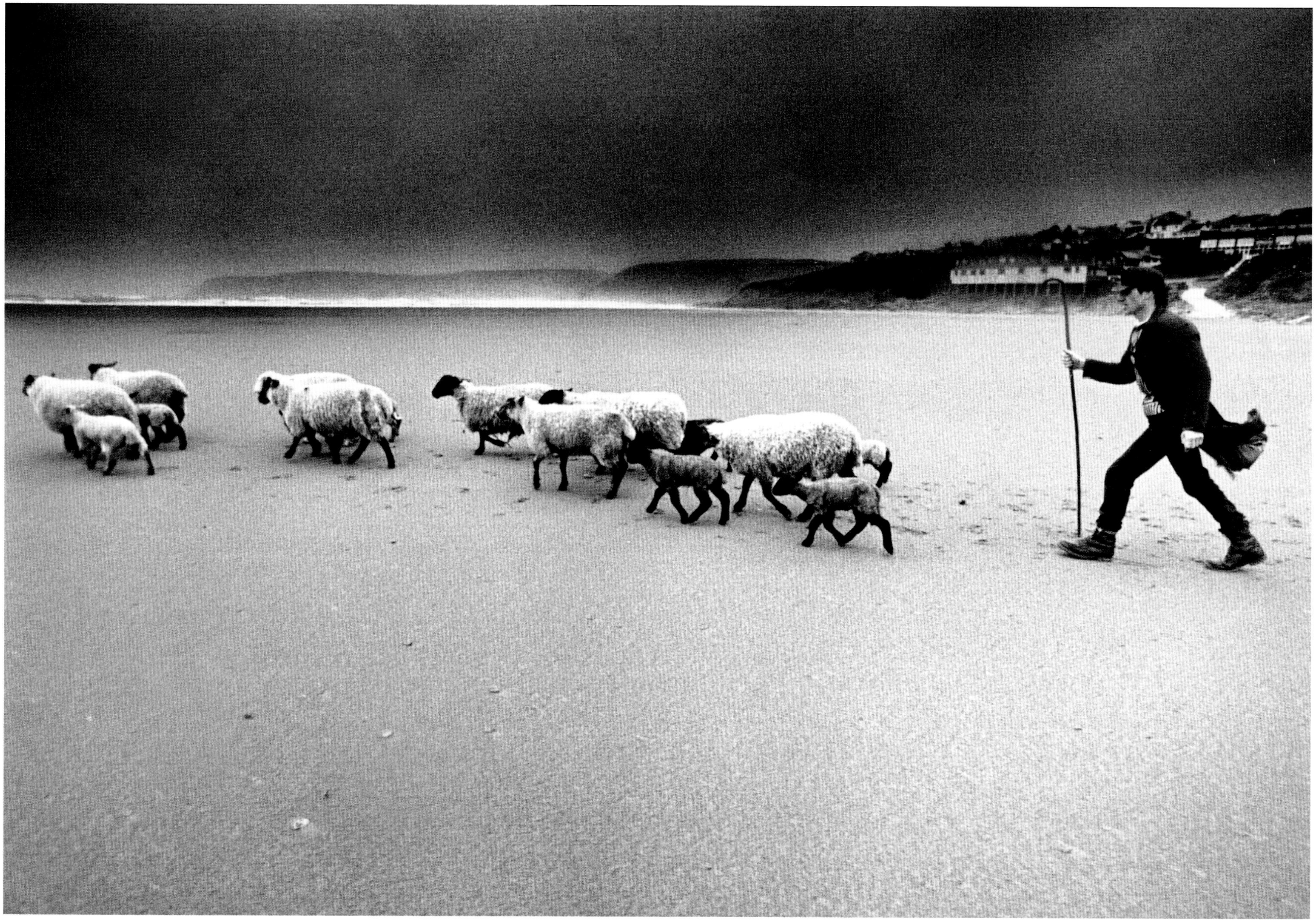

Flocking Over

The Observer, 1990

Shepherd John Stanesby was resuming an old tradition by taking his sheep over a sandy half-mile causeway to graze on the meadows of Burgh Island in Kingsbridge, South Devon. Until he revived the use of the island's pastures sheep had not been herded across for fifty years. It's a big commitment. The island is completely cut off by each high tide and only passable twice a day, so each day has to begin with checking the tide charts to be sure of a safe crossing.

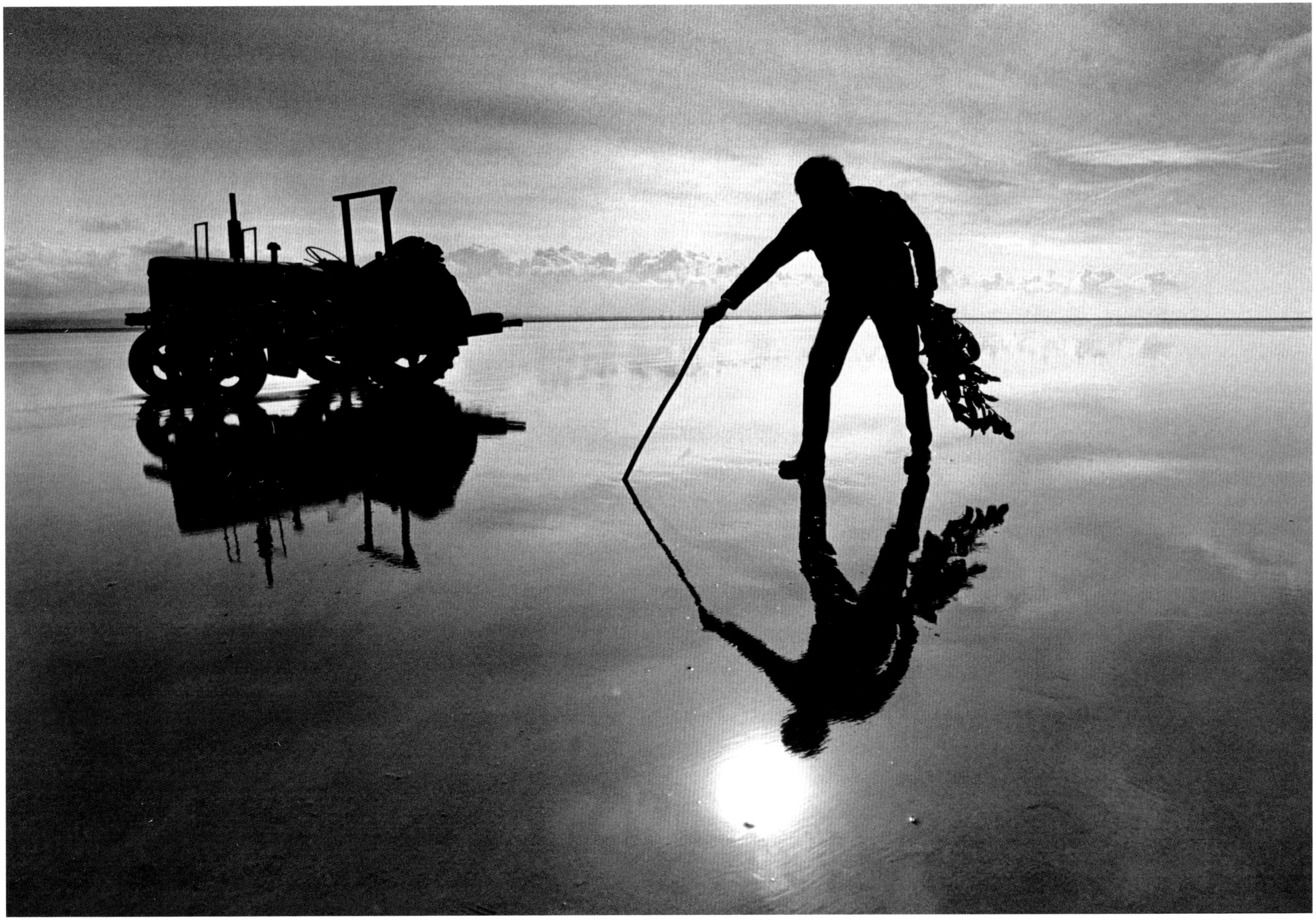

Shifting Sands

The Independent, 1992

Sand pilot Cedric Robinson had been had been the Queen's Guide to the sands at Morecambe Bay for thirty-three years, when I met him in 1992. His job was to guide walkers and to mark quicksand danger areas at low tide with the evergreen branches of laurel trees which would stay put as markers, despite being underwater at high tide. His leafy warning system protected thousands of walkers from the dangers of shifting quicksands between Grange-over-Sands and Morecambe in the Lake District in Lancashire. He didn't retire until 2019, by which time he was eighty-six.

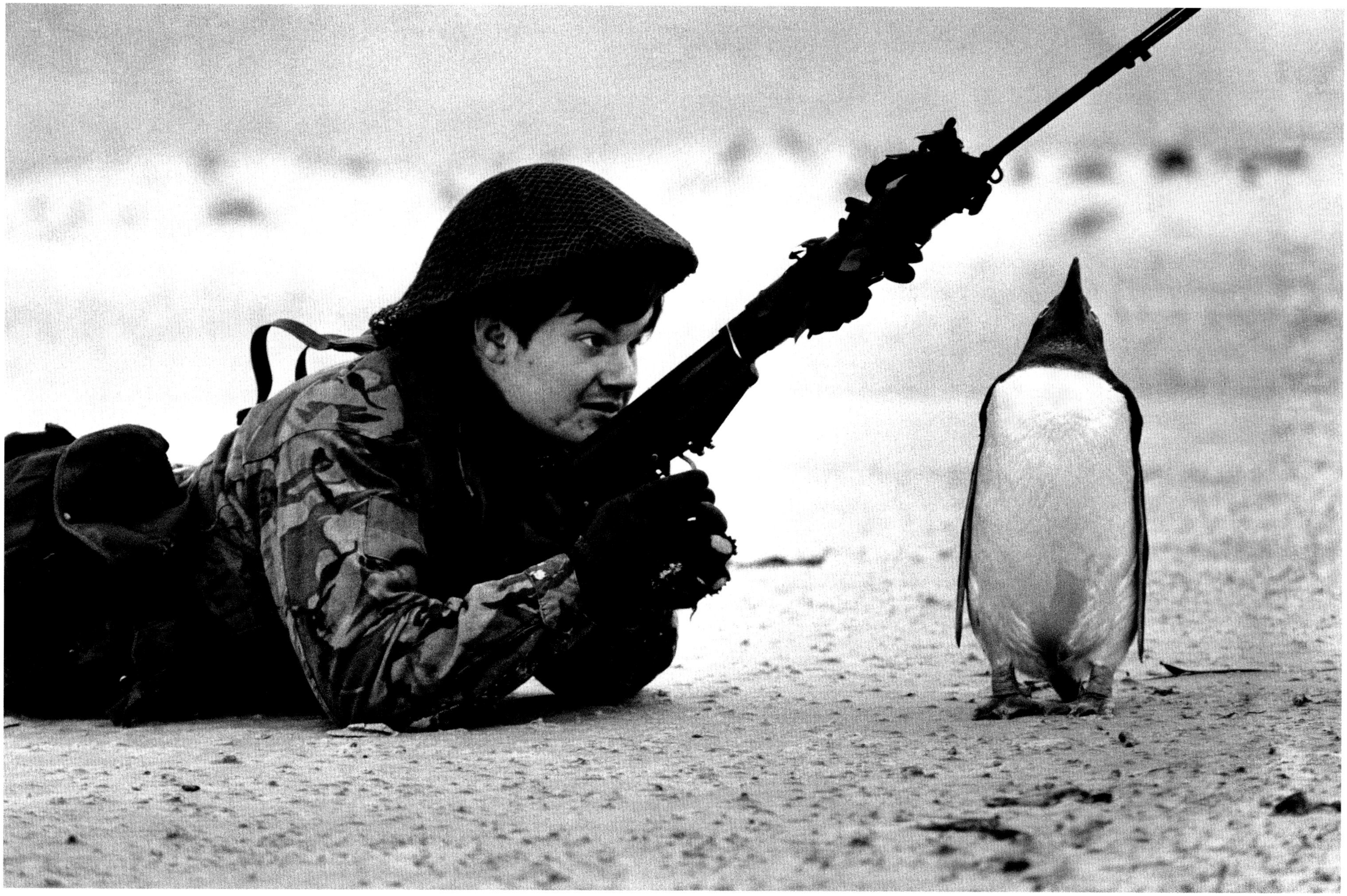

Standing to Attention

The Sun, 1983

On patrol with the British Armed Forces on West Falklands Island. This is Private Jack Frost (yes, that really was his name, poor lad, which is why he was selected for Penguin Patrol on the day) who was serving in the Falklands a year after the conflict, The cunning plan was to have him posing amongst a sea of the local Gentoo penguins. We started with a flock of over one hundred birds but as we approached, they scattered. Two sweaty hours later we had managed to round up precisely one baffled Gentoo. Penguins run faster than you'd think.

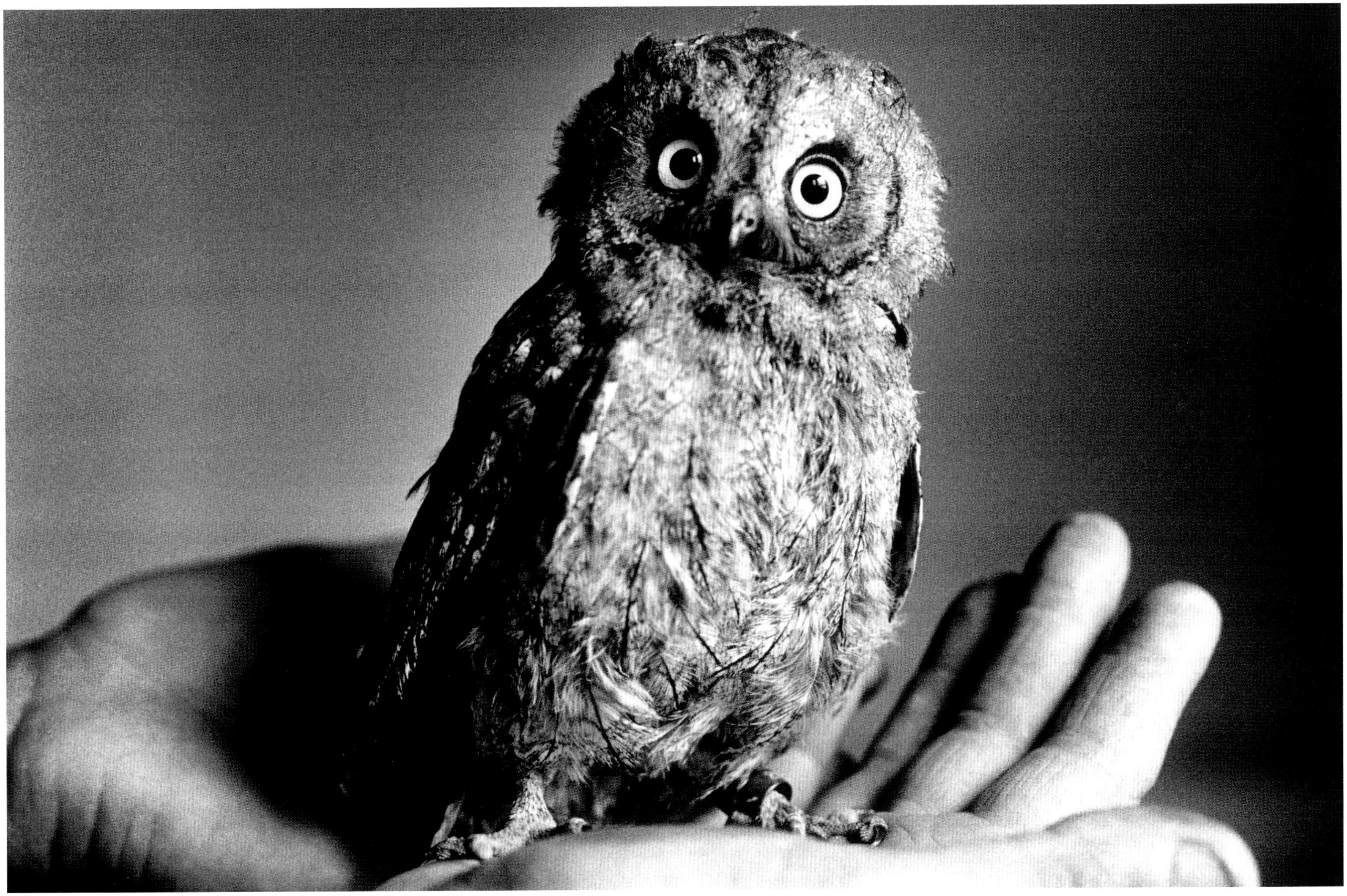

A Bird in the Hand

The Guardian, 1995

A tiny baby European Scops owl nestles in the hand of its keeper at the Gloucester Bird Sanctuary. Scops owls are very rare in Britain and this owlet was the first recorded as born here.

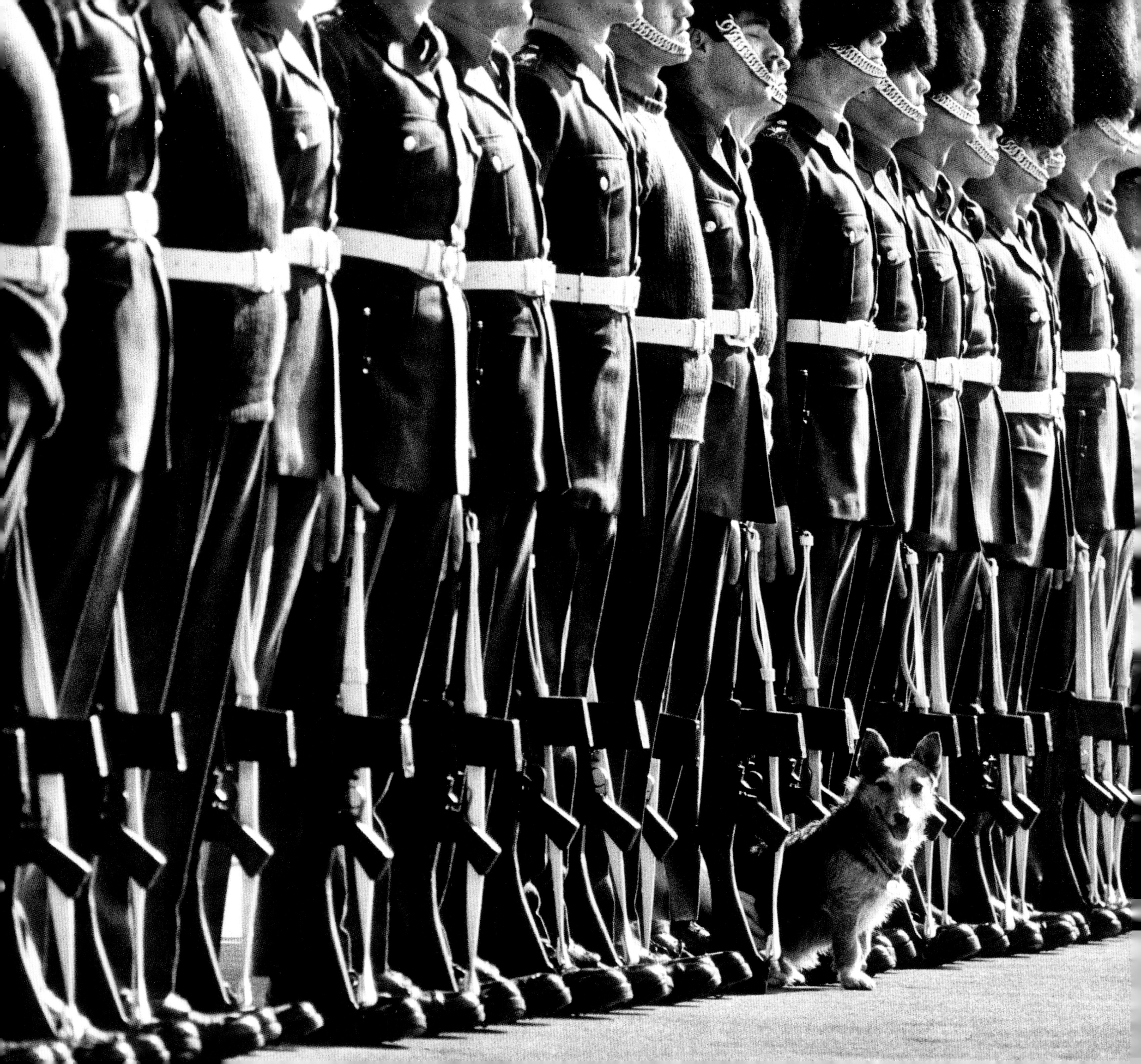

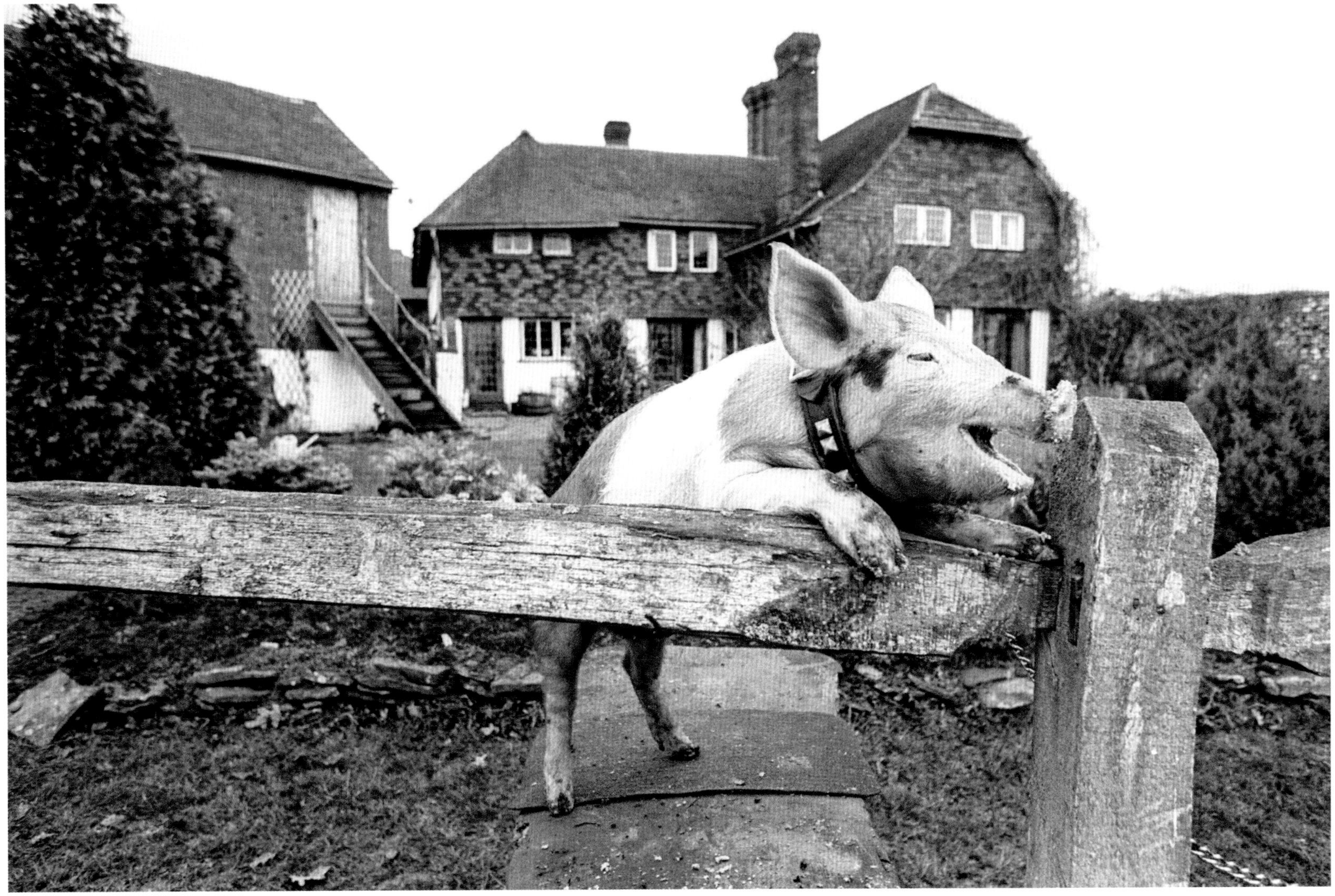

It's a Dog's Life

The Sun, 1980

Farewell parade for Rats, the corgi-terrier cross mascot of the 1st Battalion Welsh Guards, at Pirbright Barracks in 1980. Rats served on several tours of duty in Northern Ireland during the 1970s and came under fire several times as he patrolled in Crossmaglen. He never left the patrols, even when he was shot at or when bombs exploded nearby. He was twice wounded by car bombs, which left four pieces of metal in his body, served on helicopter patrols and in 1979 won a gold medal for his devotion to duty.
He was retired to England for health reasons.
I wanted the lively little dog to look proud and very much part of the team, so I got a guardsmen to lie behind the troop, holding Rats' hind legs so he was perfectly in line with his guard of honour.

Guard Hog

The Guardian, 1994

This Tamworth pig was promoted to guard dog – or perhaps guard hog – duties after disturbing burglars trying to break into the lonely Sussex farm where it lived.
The farmer was so impressed by the way its ear-splitting squeals scared off the intruders, he gave the pig a special collar and allowed it to patrol the farmyard and check out visitors at the gate.

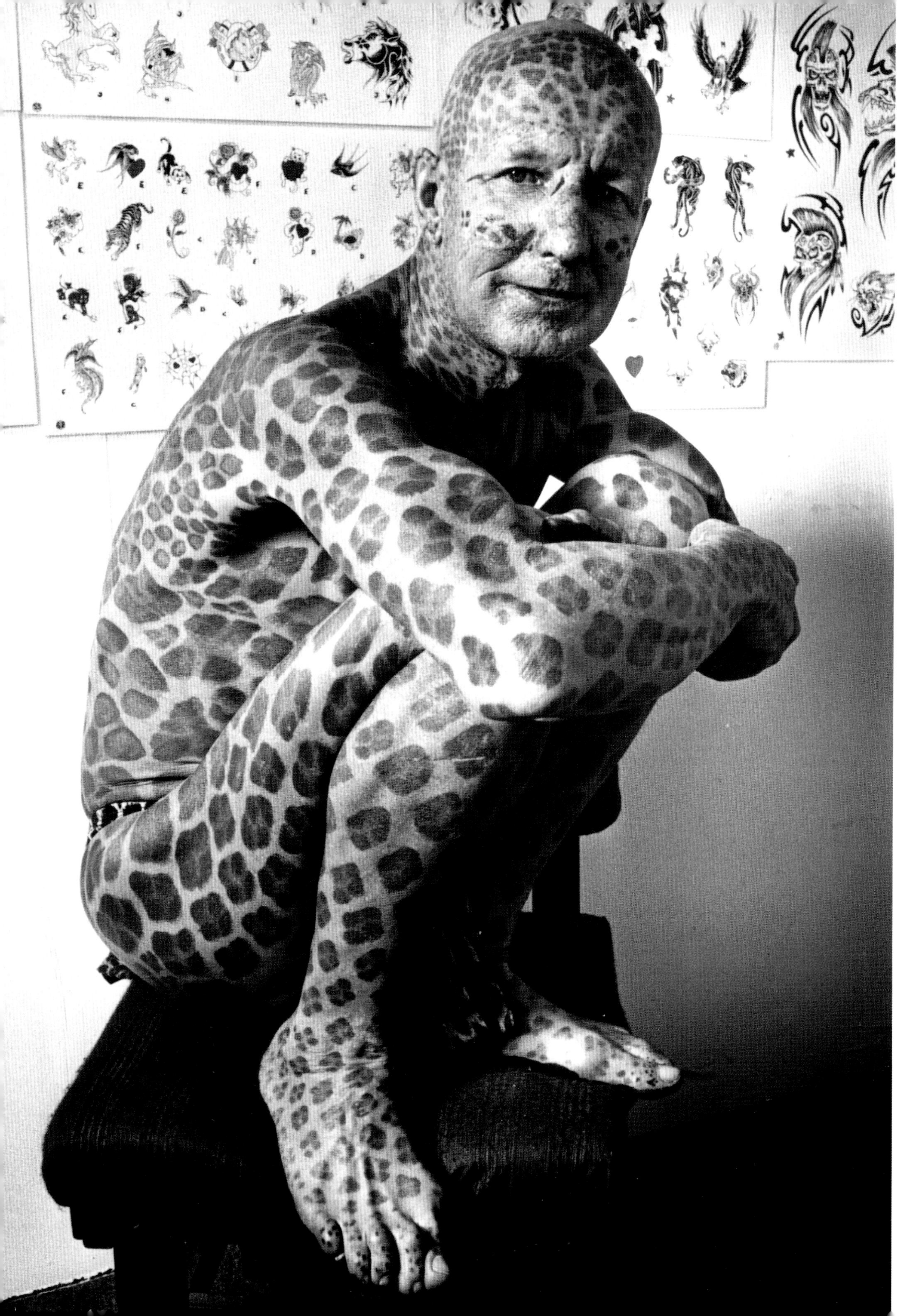

Leopard Spots

The Guardian, 1989

At the time I met Tom Leppard he was, according to the *The Guinness Book Of Records*, the world's most tattooed man. But I found him in a Brighton tattoo parlour having a little bit more work done. He was visiting his favourite tattoo artist for the final touch – the soles of his feet and palms of his hands were going to be inked solid black to match the pads of a live leopard. He had already spent more than £5,000 on the spots covering every inch of his body but this was going to make the whole design perfect.

Surprisingly, he wasn't especially fond of leopards and certainly didn't think he was some sort of big cat himself. He said that he chose the spots because they were easy for tattoo artists to do and looked good as an all-over pattern.

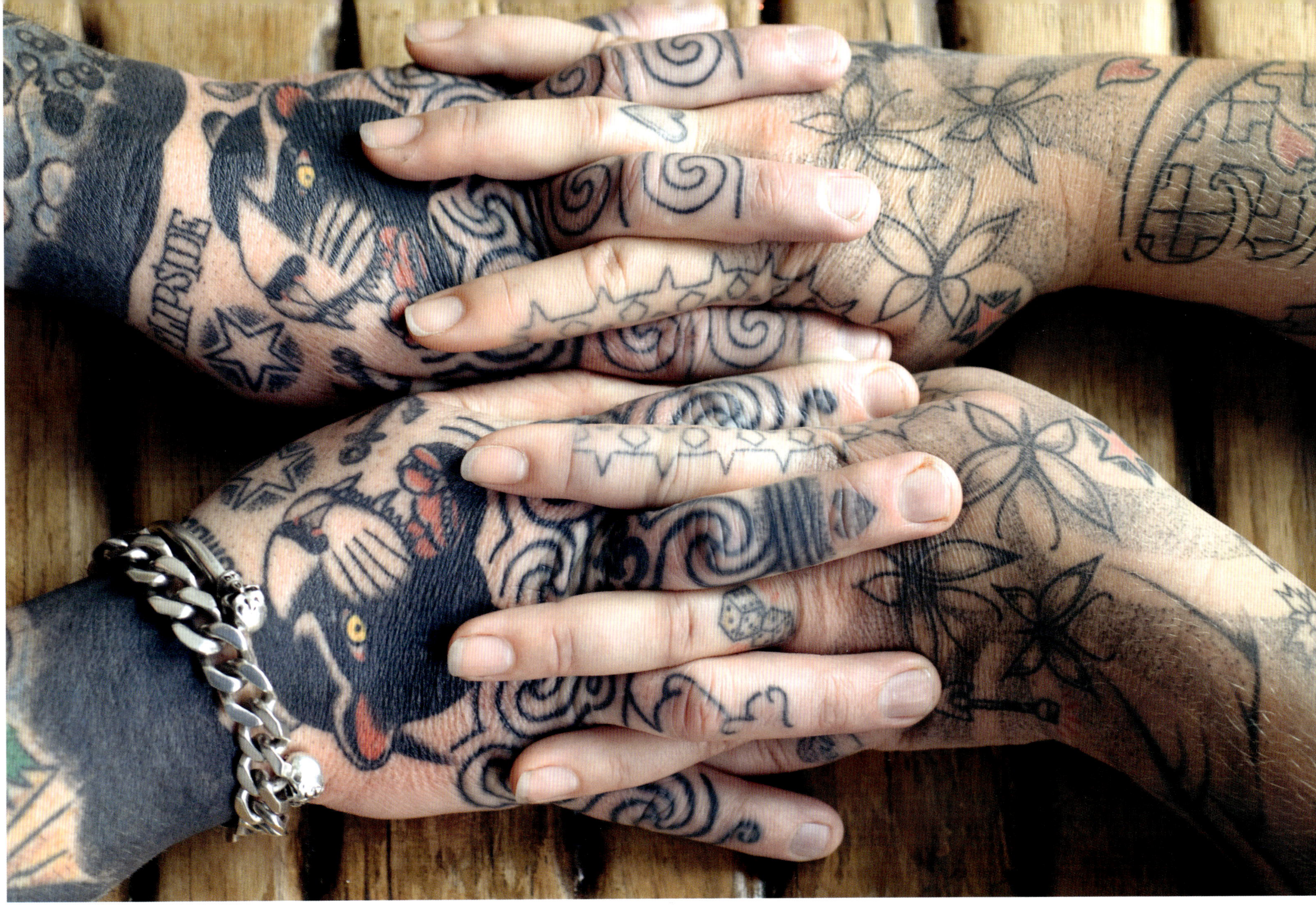

Hands On

The Guardian, 2008

Tattooist Sarah Ormonde and her husband John entwine their fingers to proudly display their his and hers artwork.
John, a Post Office worker and long-time tattoo enthusiast, let his wife use him as a human canvas to experiment on and was almost as inked as Tom Leppard.

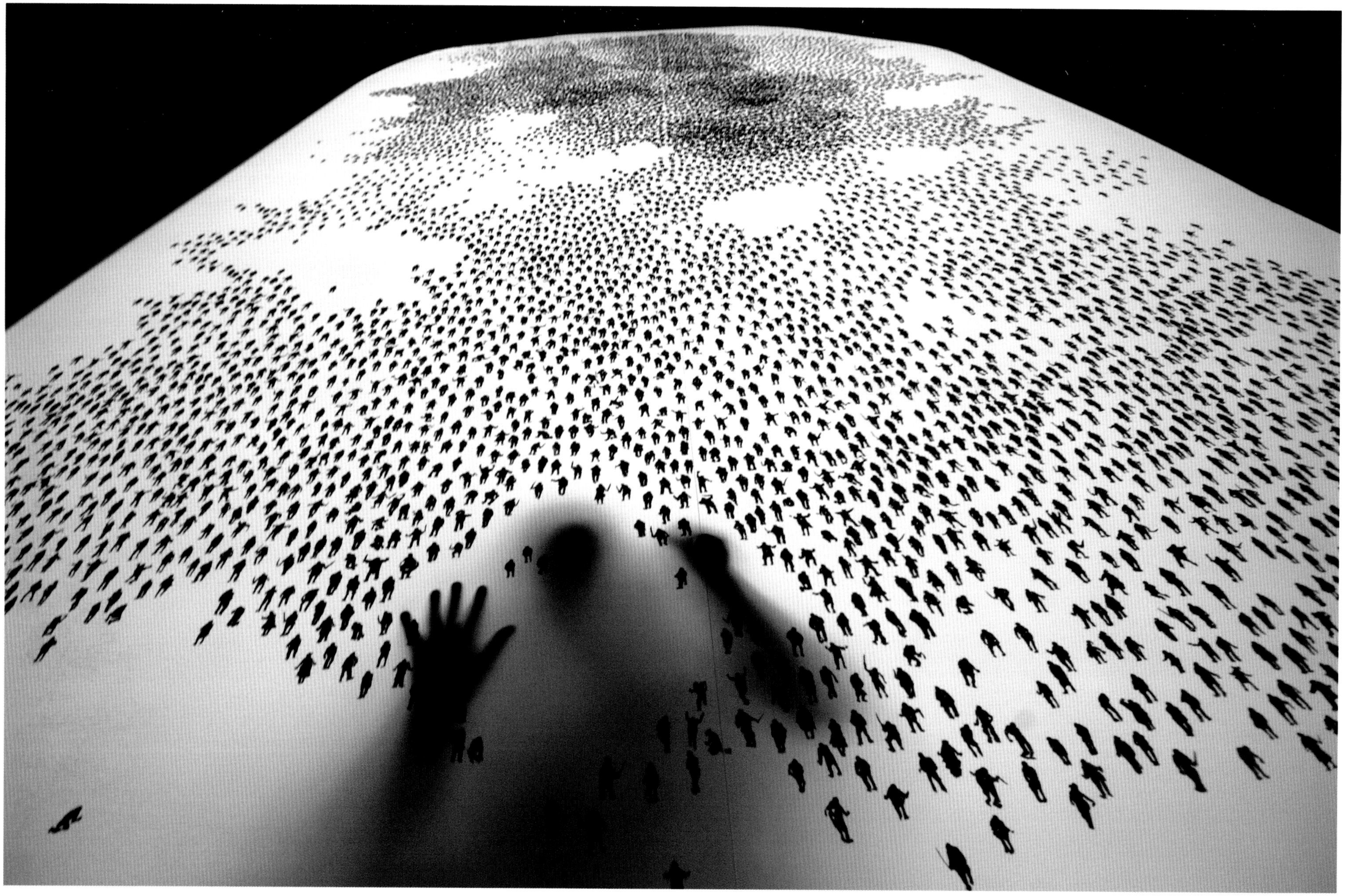

Ten Thousand Figures

The Independent, 2005

Blurred shadows of artist Mark Anstee's head and hands can be seen as he draws 2-in human figures on a vast translucent membrane suspended in the chancel of a former church.
There were eventually 10,000 of the 1/32 scale little figures in his artwork *Early Redemption*. It took him twenty-five days to draw them as he hung from a harness behind the screen.
He was working more than 20ft up and didn't want to stop for me, so I had to wait for the few moments when he was close enough to his artwork to give a really hard shadow and make a picture.

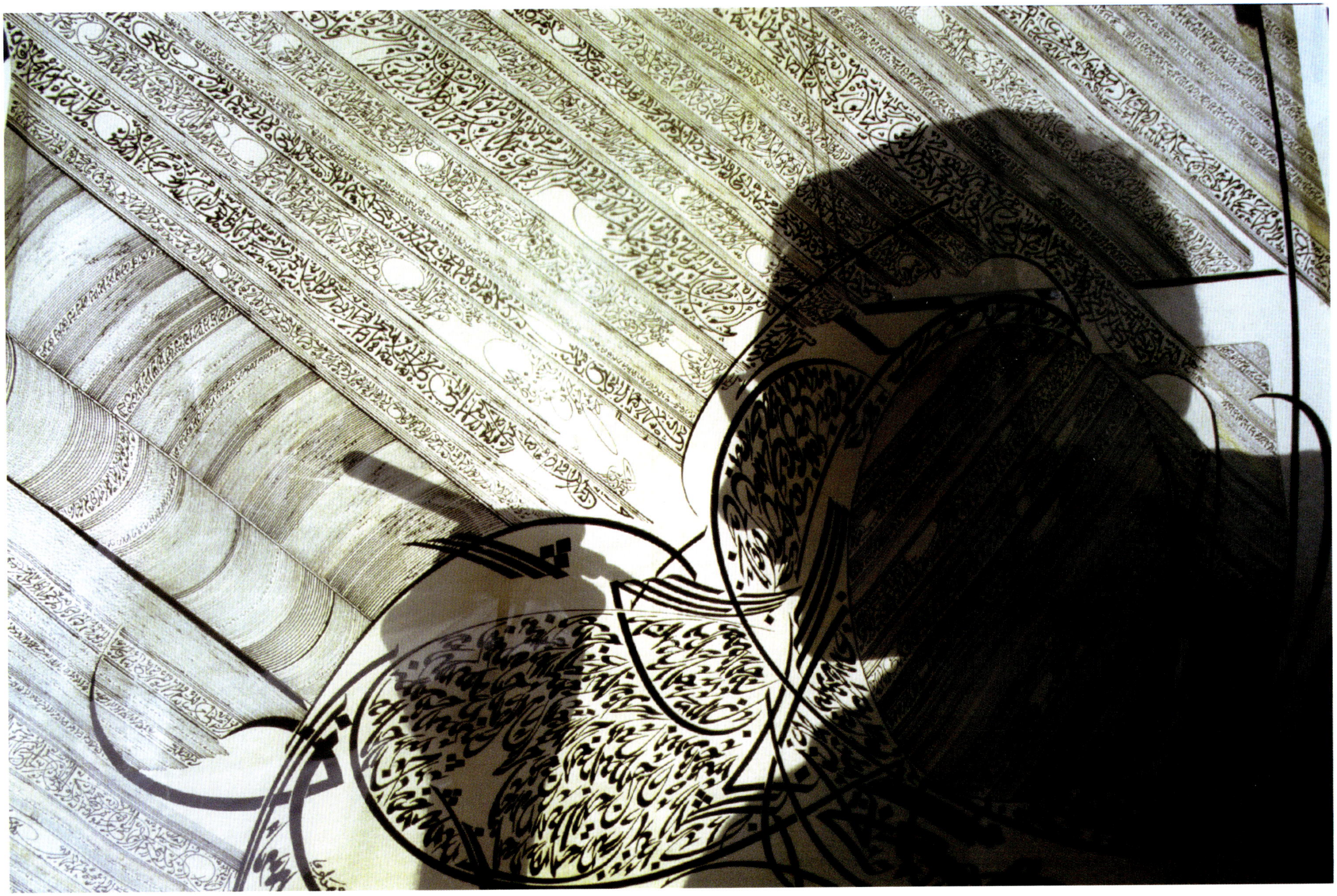

Flowing Lines

The Guardian, 2001

Calligrapher and exhibition curator Ewan Clayton's shadow falls across an exquisite Arabic-inspired manuscript text by Nja Mahdaoui from Tunisia, drawn on goatskin.
It was part of 'Spring Lines', an exhibition of contemporary calligraphy from the East and West at the Museum of Art + Craft, East Sussex, which has a famous collection of calligraphy and works by typographic artists.

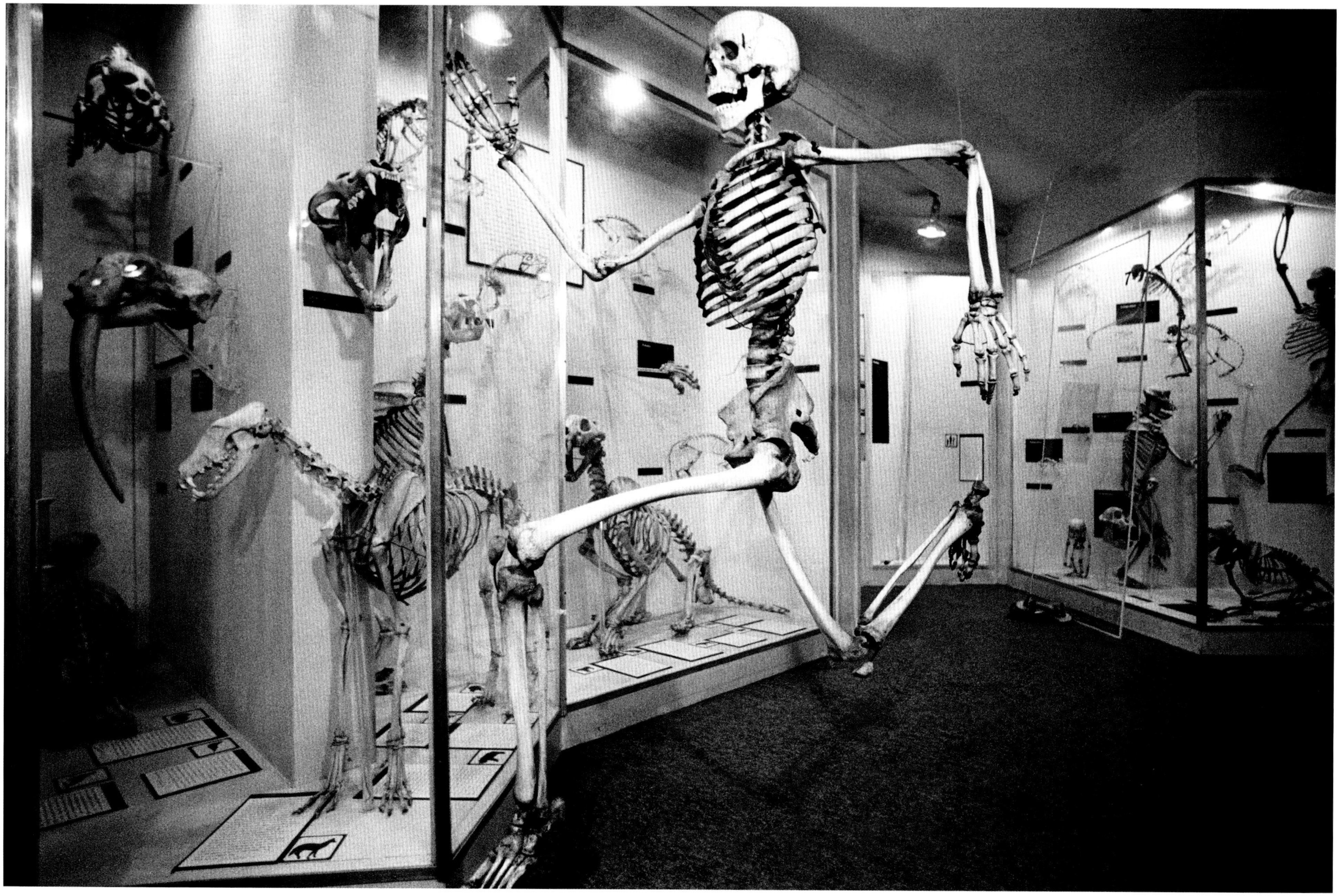

Doing a Runner

The Guardian, Life Magazine and the Encyclopaedia Britannica, 1990

My local museum sent out a flier to announce its forthcoming centenary celebrations for the Booth Museum of Natural History in Brighton, to be hosted by David Bellamy. There was also a picture of the museum's human skeleton walking a monkey skeleton on a lead.

I contacted the museum and suggested marking the big anniversary with a picture of the skeleton instead of a celebrity. At first the curator was reluctant and wanted me to stick to taking a picture of Bellamy, but he saw the funny side when I told him I wanted to photograph the skeleton escaping. Because of the schedule we could only do it at 5.30am and the museum staff were there, ready to go when I turned up. The skeleton had to be hung by piano wire from a plank, attached to a hand operated forklift by G-clamps, then fitted with a Kodak Tri-X film can to wedge its jaws open as if it were laughing. We were all laughing by the time it was finished. It was used in the *Guardian* the next day and many times since.

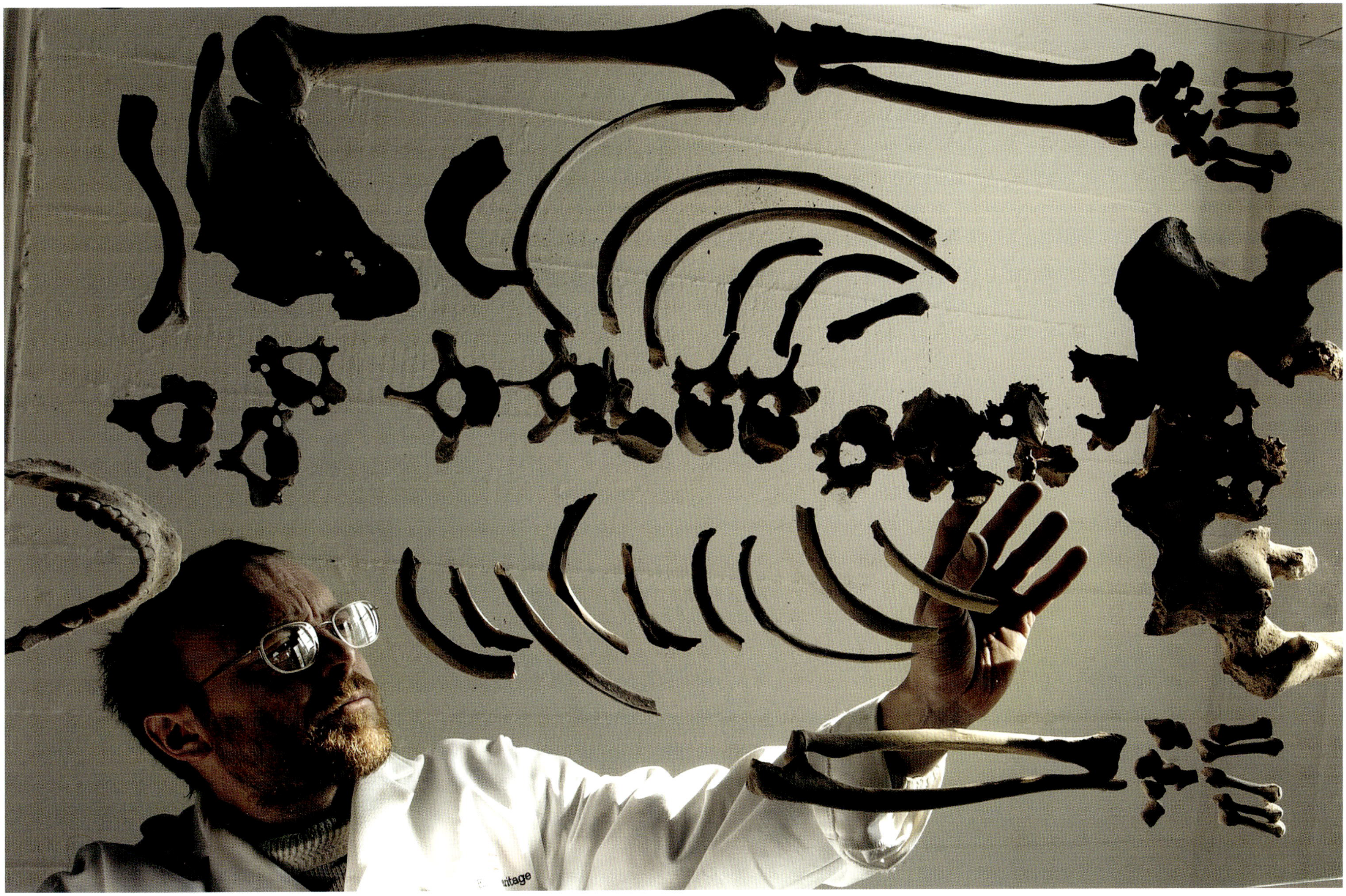

TB or not TB?

The Guardian, 2002

Simon Mays, a human skeletal biologist for English Heritage, had to examine the spine of a thirty-year-old Iron Age man who lived in Devon around 300BC. DNA tests had just confirmed that he had been Britain's earliest known TB victim. I always carried a sheet of toughened glass in my car for jobs like this.

We laid the skeleton out on the glass which was supported by two tables and I lay flat on the floor below it with the camera.

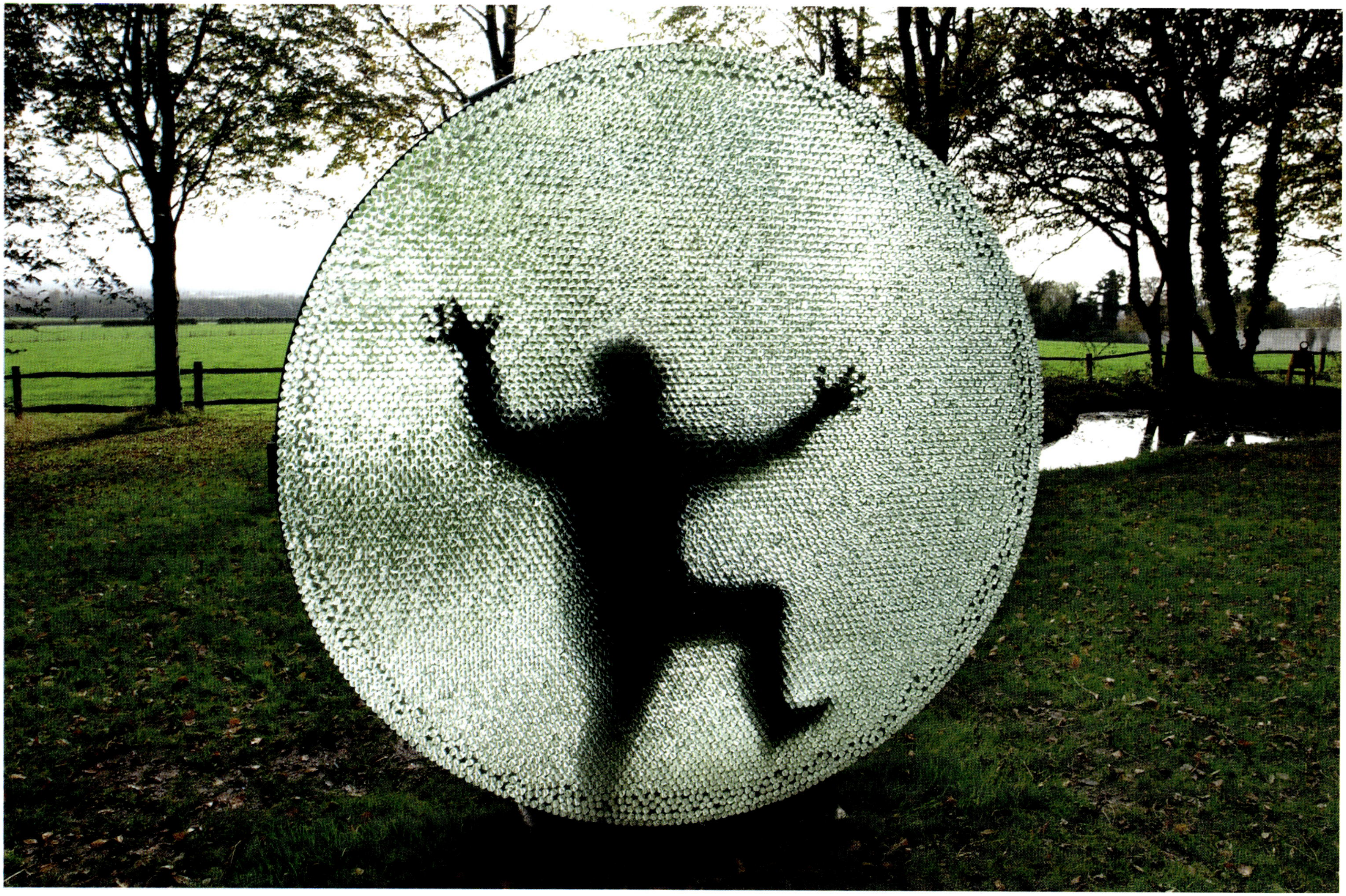

On a Roll

The Guardian, 2004

Wilfred Cass was a small man who loved big art, the bigger the better.
He had just celebrated his eightieth birthday by mortgaging his home to add another 5 acres to the vast sculpture park he'd established ten years earlier, when he retired from a successful business career in London.
Wilfred's idea of a brilliant retirement was to pour millions of pounds into giving British sculptors a showcase at his Sculpture at Goodwod, near Chichester. He was as enthusiastic about every new piece as a child with a new treasure.
I loved working with him. When I asked him to pose for an eightieth birthday picture, he bounced behind an enormous circle of glass rods by Tim Morgan, waving and pretending to walk on it like a treadmill.

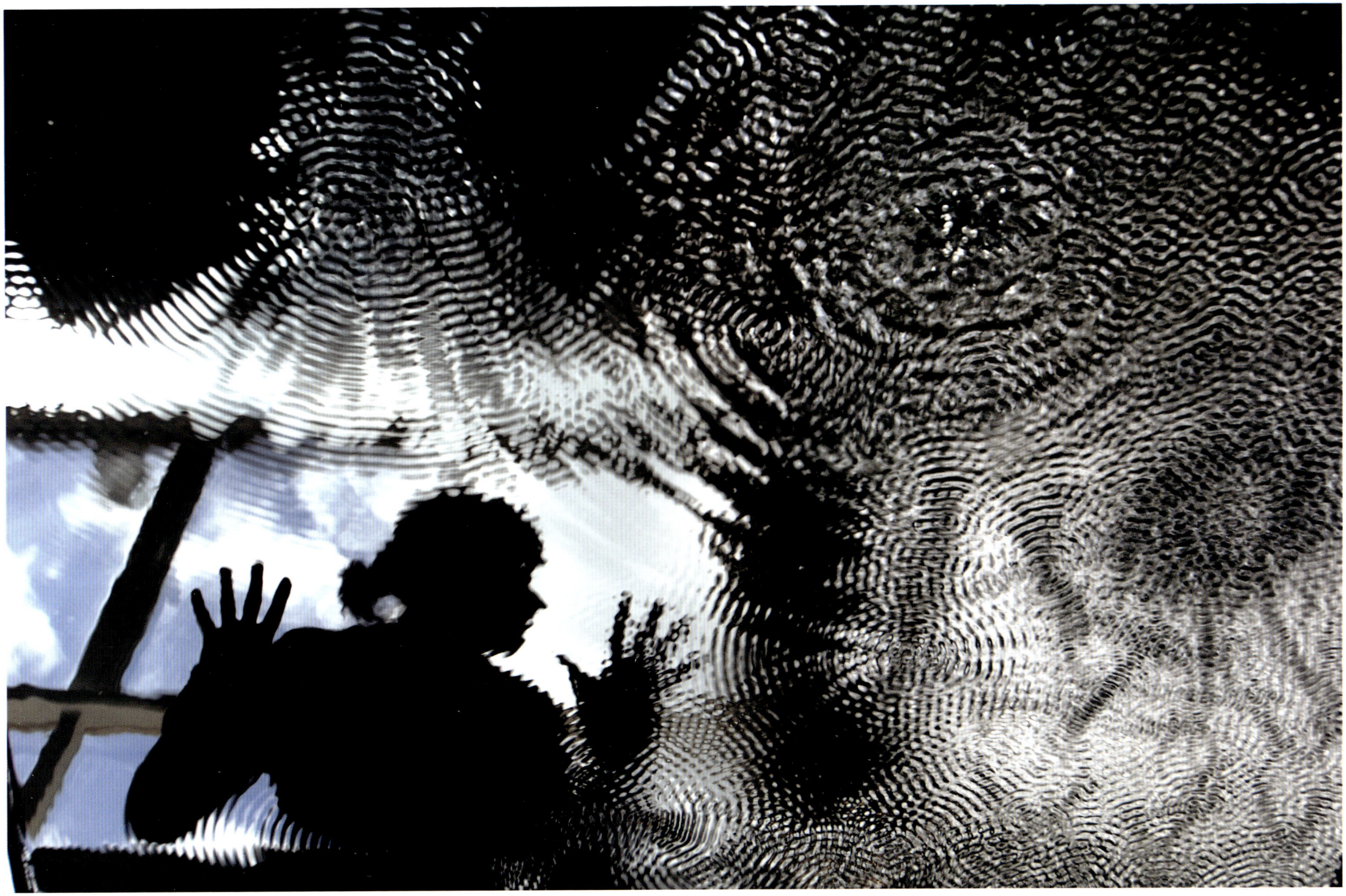

Causing a Ripple

The Guardian, 2006

Art student Alice Cunningham created a stir during the University of Brighton annual sculpture degree show by using sound waves of Martin Luther King's 1965 'We Shall Overcome' speech that caused ripples around the world.
She used tiny underwater speakers to broadcast the speech from the bottom of a circular pool and the vibrations of his voice were visible as ripples spreading across the surface.
It was silent and mysterious and when you realised what it was all about it was strangely moving.
She got her degree. And some years later I was really delighted when the picture was used as the cover of a hefty scientific tome called *The Routledge Companion To Sound Studies.*

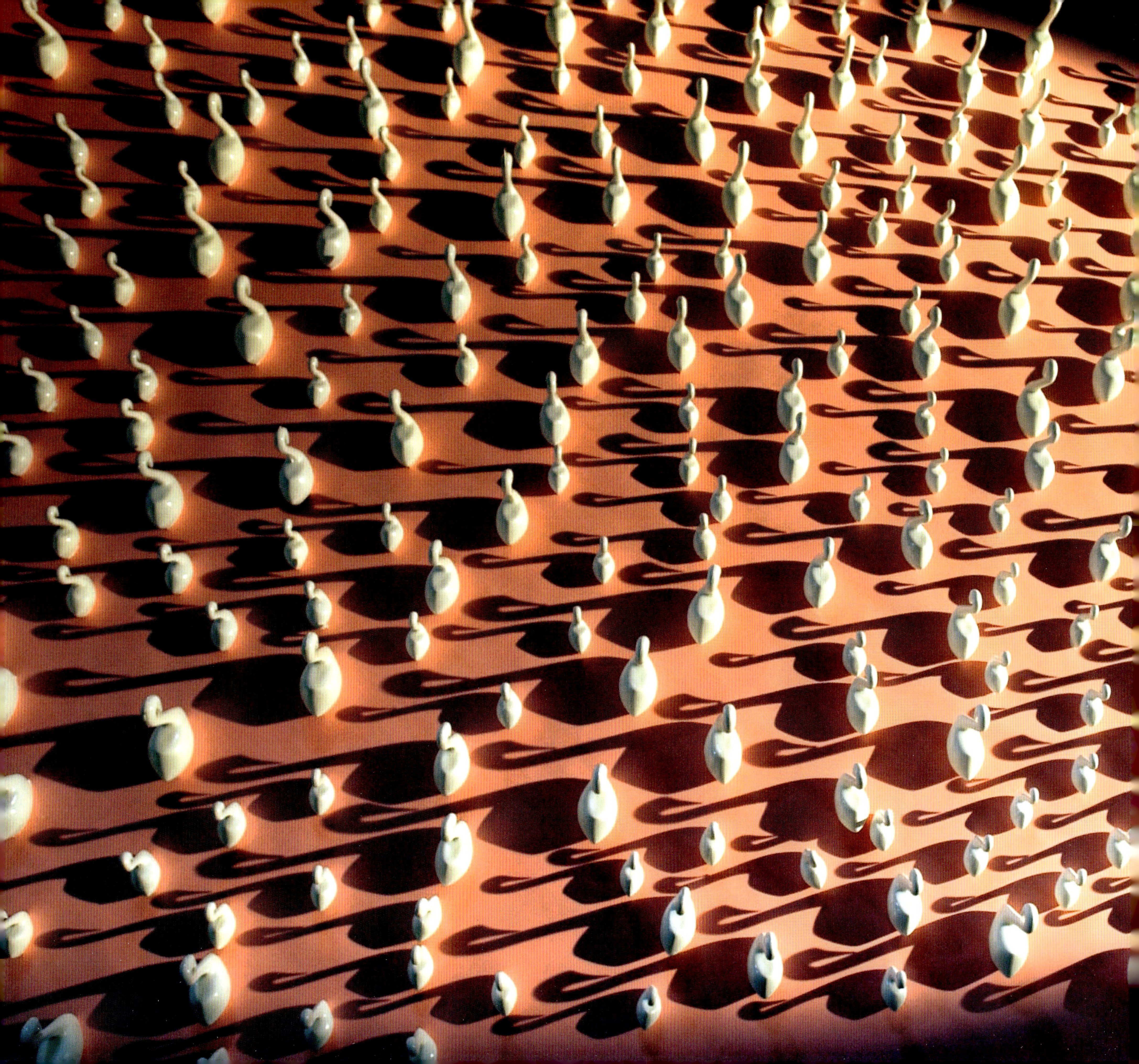

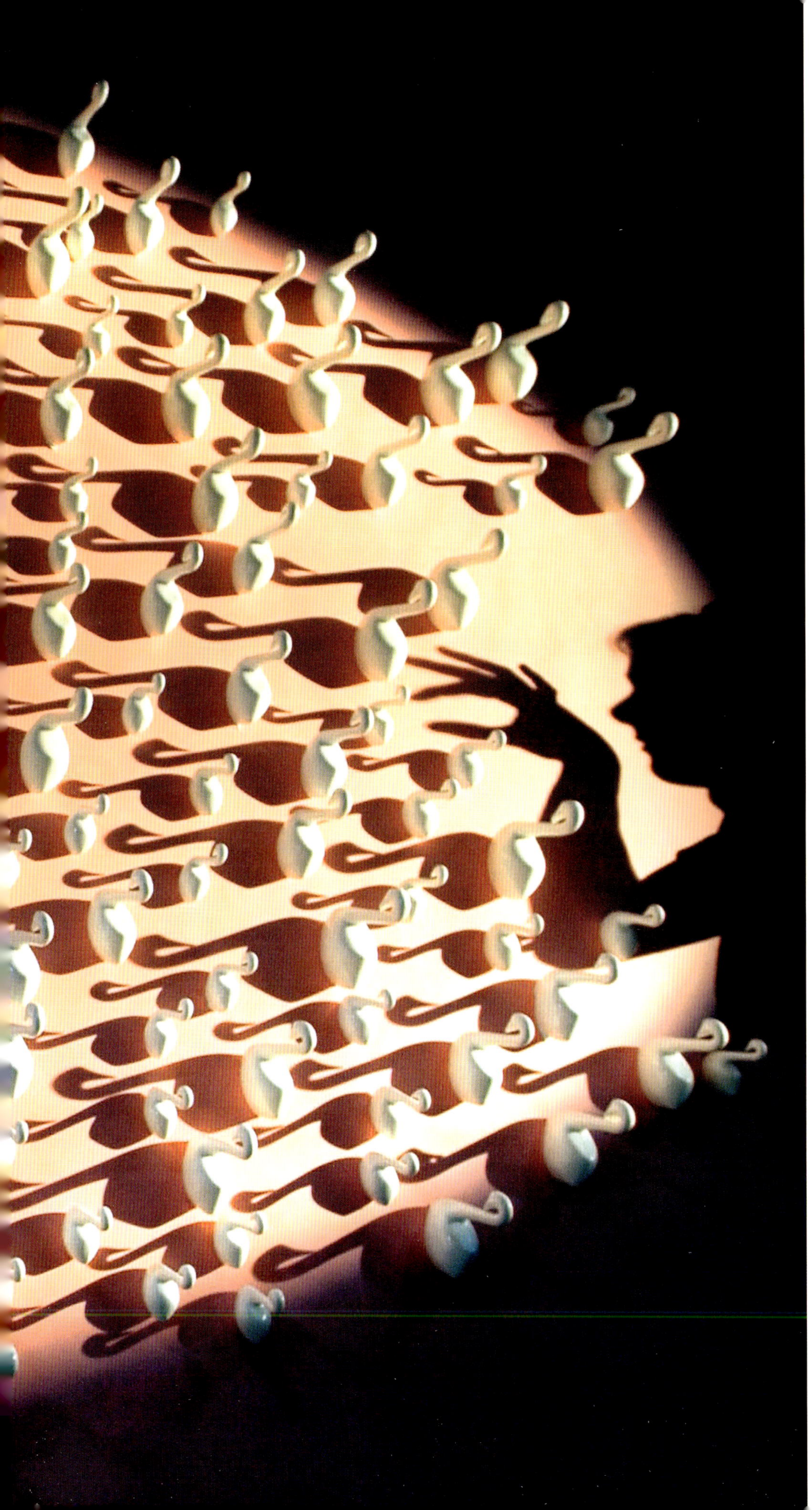

Swan Lake

The Guardian, 2004

Working with students is always interesting. I went to local degree shows every year to look for inspiration and they never let me down.
This was Stephen Johnson, a crafts student at the University of Brighton, who had been busy casting 500 tiny swans in plastic resin for his degree show. The shapes were gorgeous but they needed a bit of punch, so I borrowed a 2000-watt spotlight from the Sallis Benney Theatre downstairs. It created shadows of elongated birds' necks with Stephen's own shadow behind them and made the whole exhibit jump into focus. I still have one of those little swans in my study.

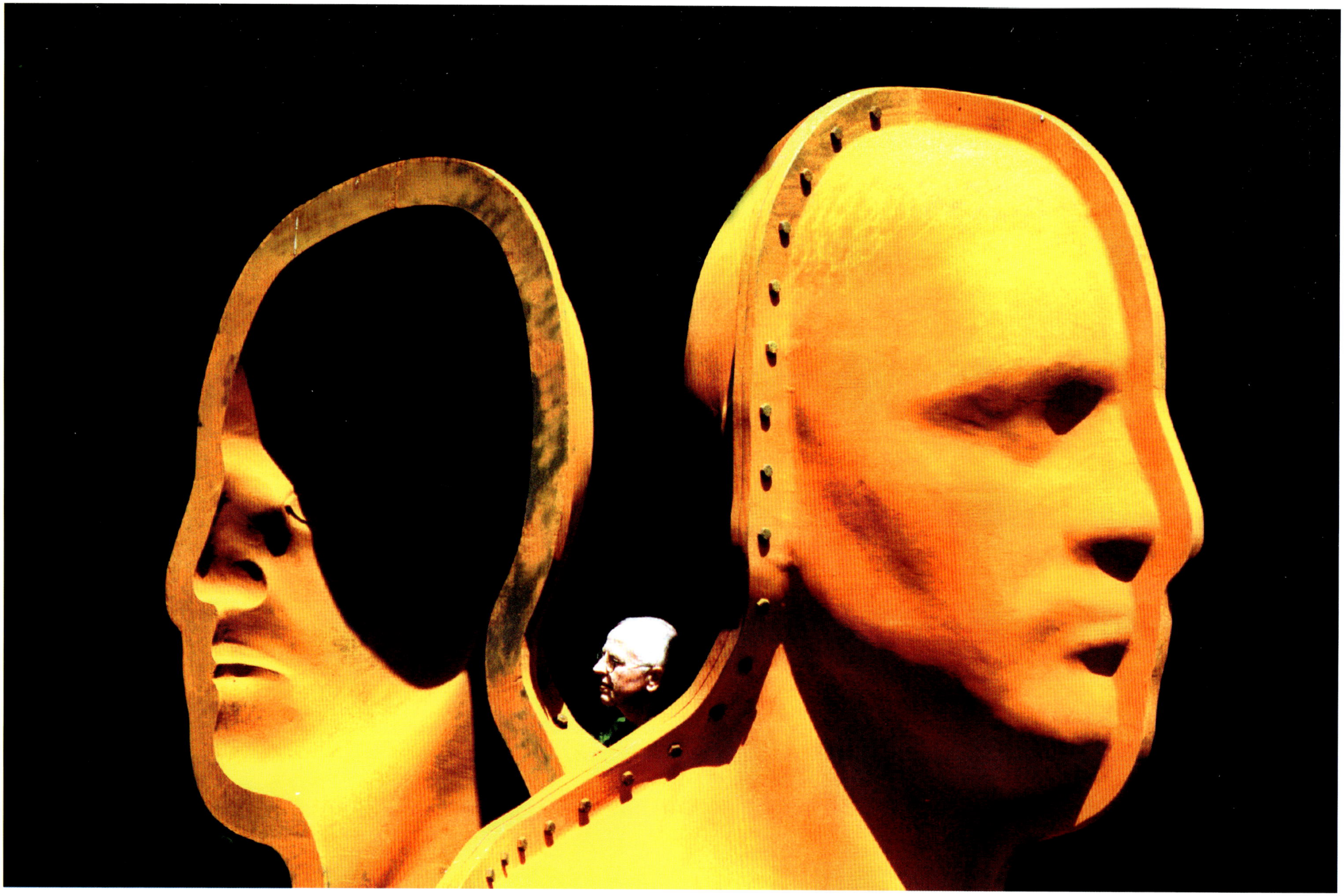

Head to Head

The Guardian, 1999

Sculptor Peter Burke is dwarfed by his giant 8-tonne poured steel sculpture Janus Head. It was being installed at Wilfred Cass's sculpture park, Sculpture at Goodwood, near Chichester, West Sussex. Burke was an apprentice at Rolls-Royce Aero Engines as a school-leaver and I always liked the way his engineering background was applied to his many sculptures based on the human body.

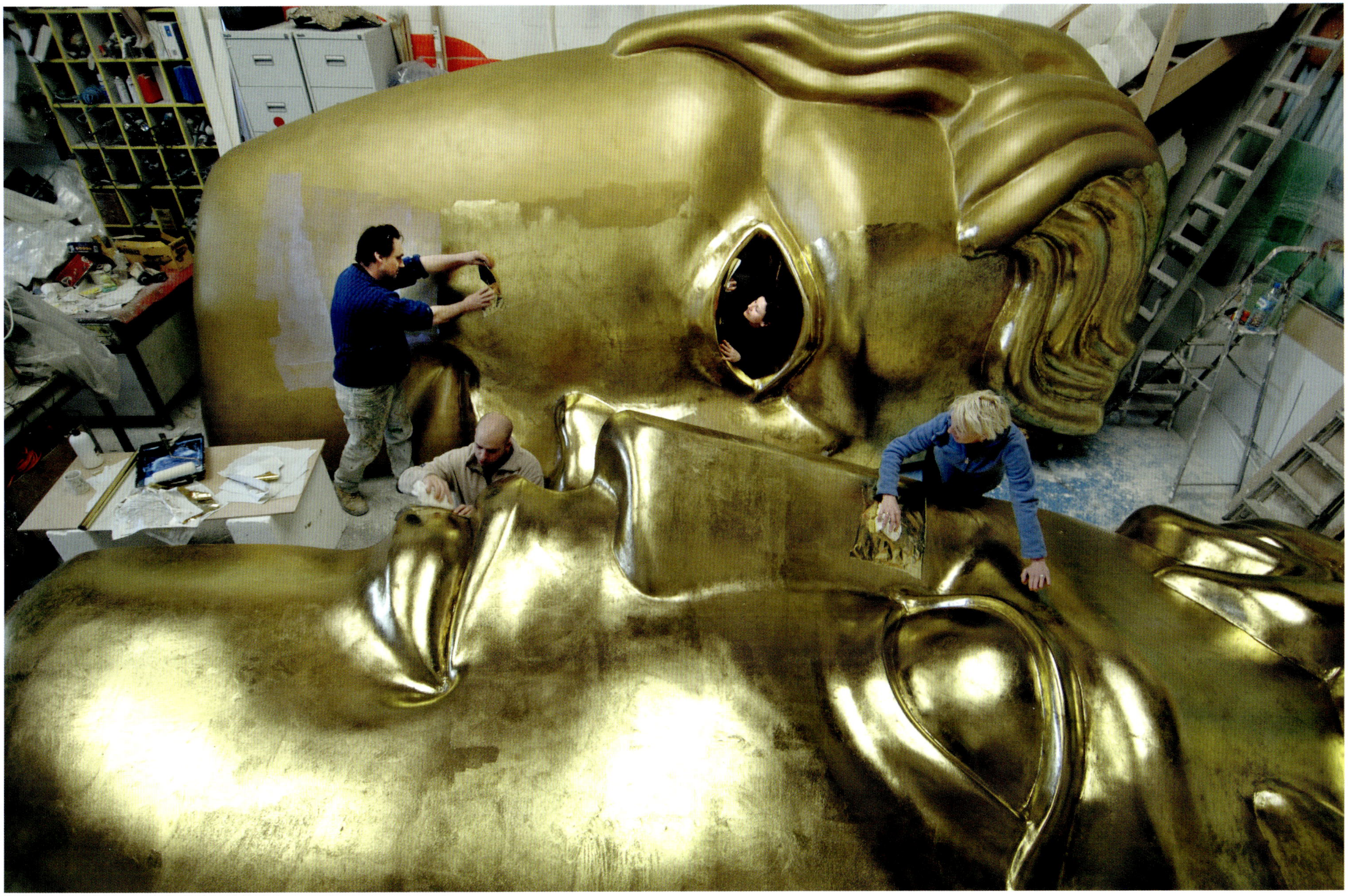

BAFTAS

The Guardian, 2007

Giant masks had to be created especially for the stage of the Royal Opera House in Covent Garden, where the 60th British Academy Film Awards were being held in 2007.
The job was being done by Aden Hynes and his team in Basildon, where I found them barely able to move in the cramped studio. The two huge masks were carved from polystyrene, coated in fibreglass and here they are being gilded with gold leaf before a pair of specially fitted lorries carried them off to London and the awards night.

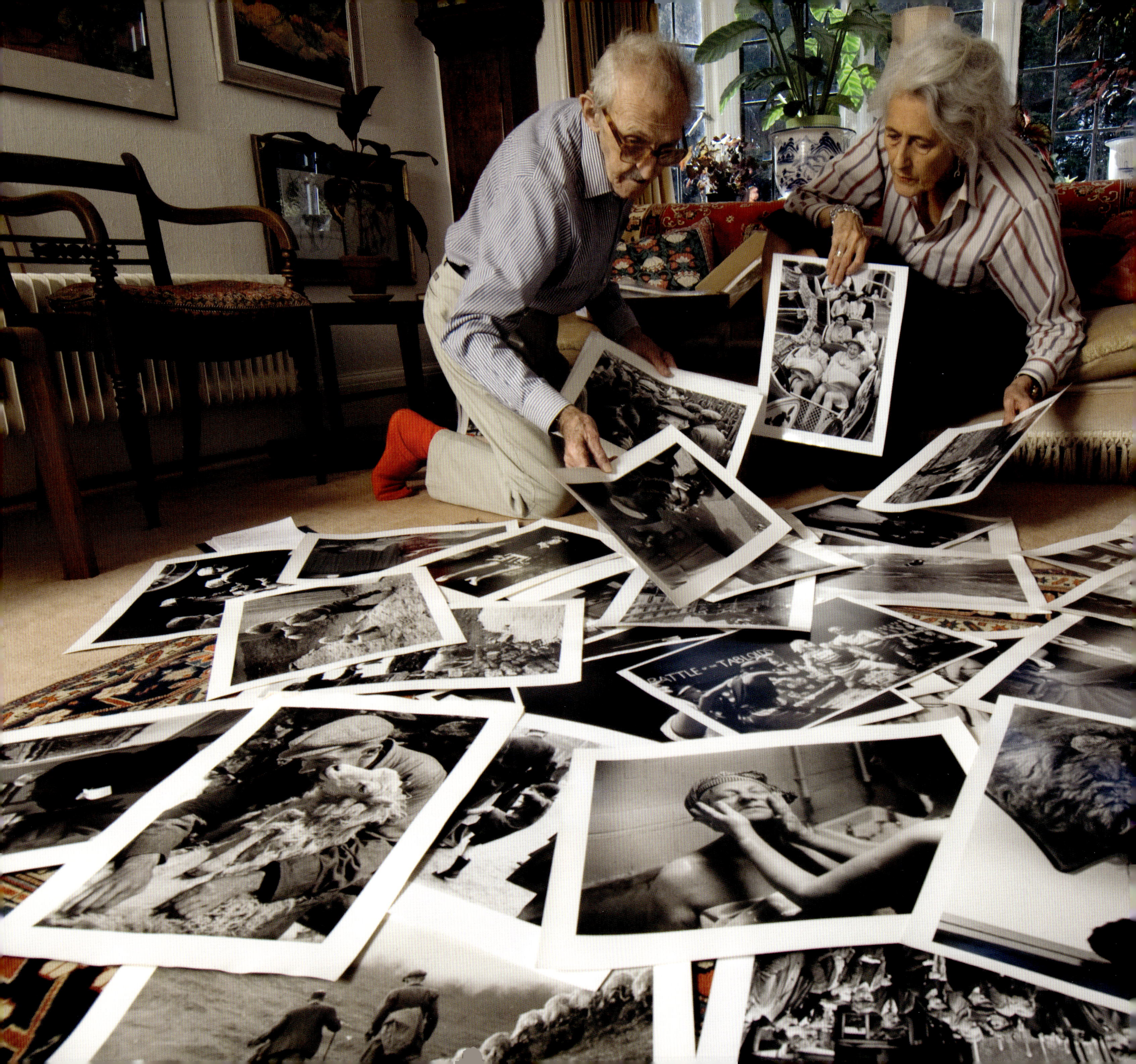
BATTLE TABLOIDS

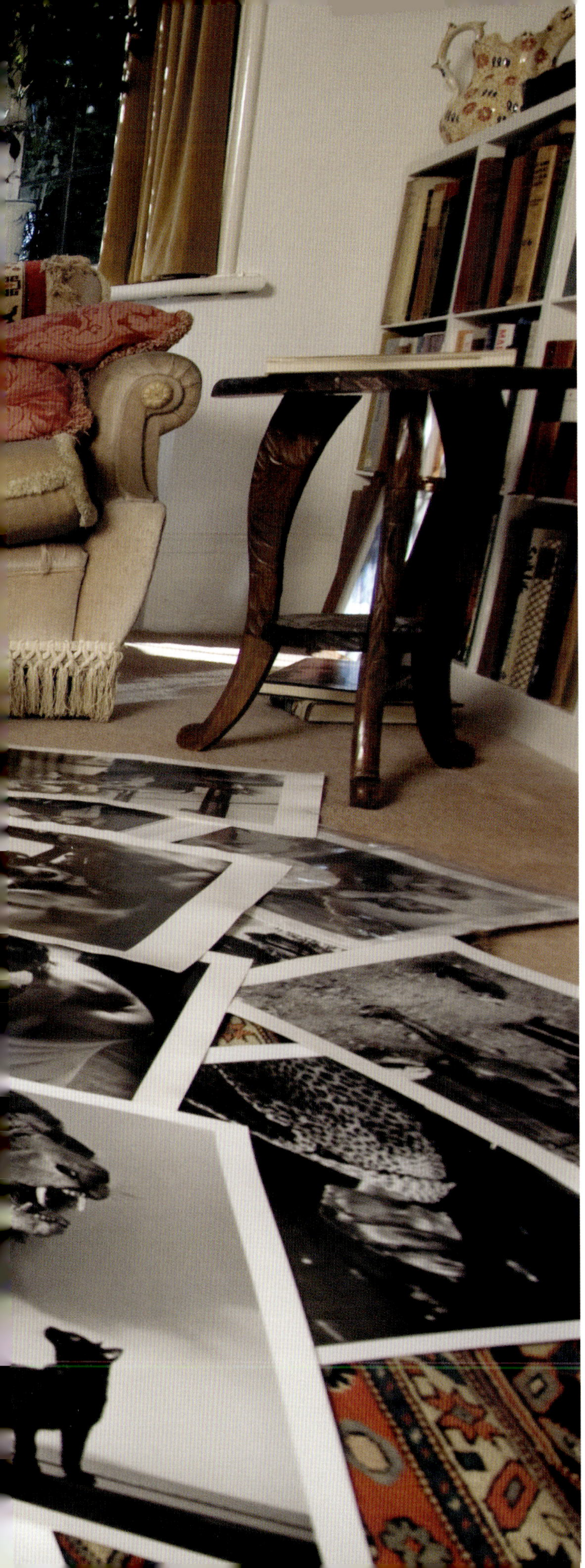

Picture Posts

The Guardian, 2007

The renowned *Picture Post* photojournalists Thurston Hopkins and Grace Robertson were sorting through hundreds of Grace's black and white prints in preparation for an exhibition.
I had asked to photograph them for a book called *UK at Home*.
Both of them were old hands at this sort of thing and helped me set up the shot while reminiscing about their hectic lives in the 1950s and '60s.
I was trying to work out why this situation didn't look quite right and Grace said firmly: 'It needs a pop of colour. Thurston – go and put your red socks on.' Thurston, then 93 years old, went off to change his socks. 'She's right, you know,' he said as he came back downstairs. And she was.

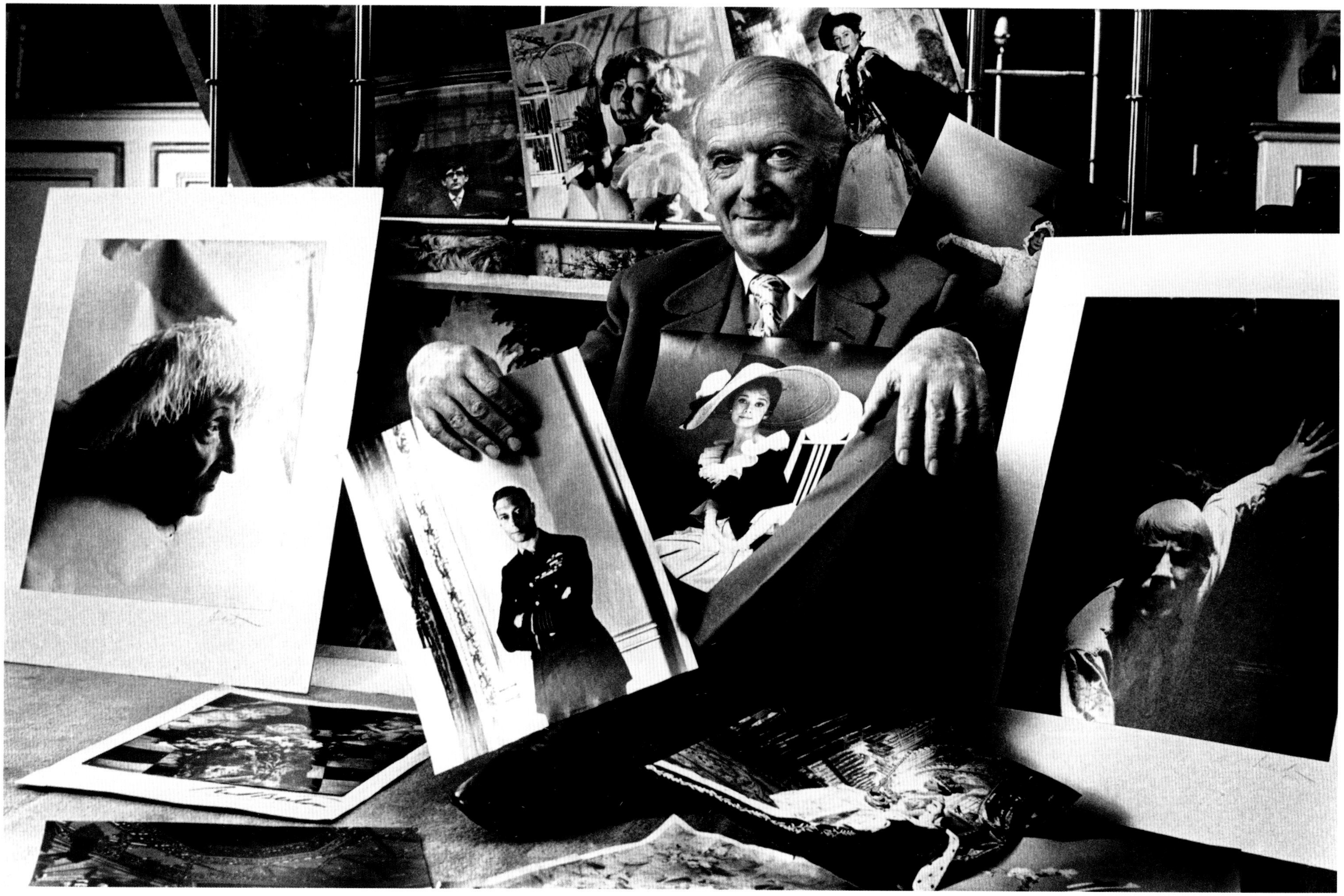

All My Own Work

The Daily Mail, 1967

Just eighteen months into my newspaper career I was sent to photograph the famous society photographer Cecil Beaton at his home in Kensington. He was about to launch a major retrospective of work in a London gallery the next week and I wanted to show him sitting on the floor surrounded by his images of notable people. After sifting through countless boxes of prints of his photographs, he announced that the perfect setting for the portrait would be at the foot of his imposing brass bed.
So we arranged Dame Edith Sitwell, Audrey Hepburn, the late Queen Elizabeth II, her late father, King George VI, and a few others in his bedroom and he composed himself gracefully on the floor. When I finished he picked up my Nikon F and used it to photograph me – and that picture went into the paper too.

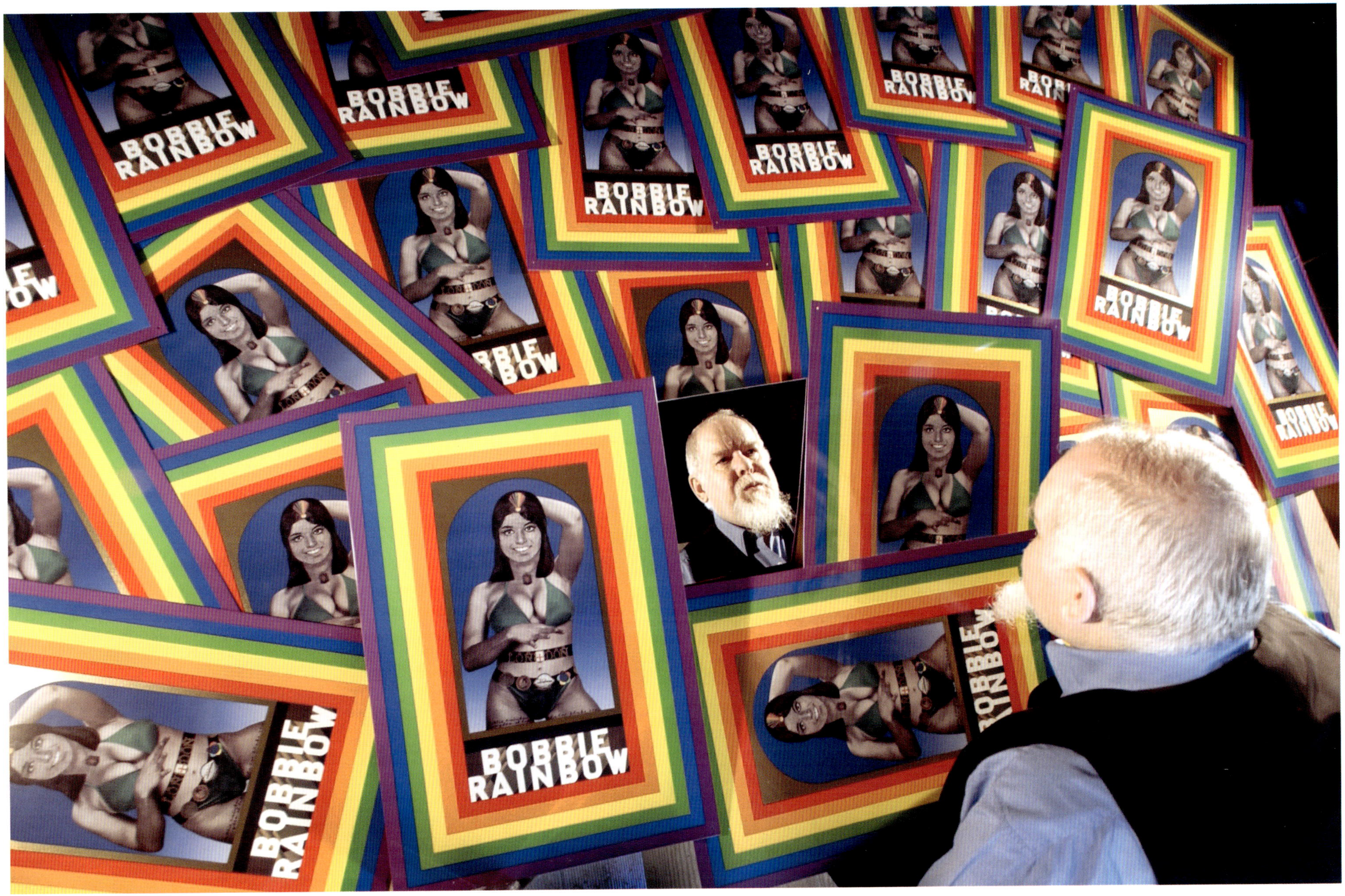

Peter Blake and Bobby Rainbow

The Guardian, 2001

Peter Blake, the godfather of British Pop Art, with some of the 2,000 tinplate prints of Bobbie Rainbow, a fictional lady wrestler he created to raise funds for his favourite art gallery.
The Pallant House Gallery in Chichester houses collections of his most famous pictures and he was giving them the personally initialled Bobbie Rainbow prints to sell at £30 each.
They were a sellout, of course. And now if they come up for sale they fetch about £750 each.

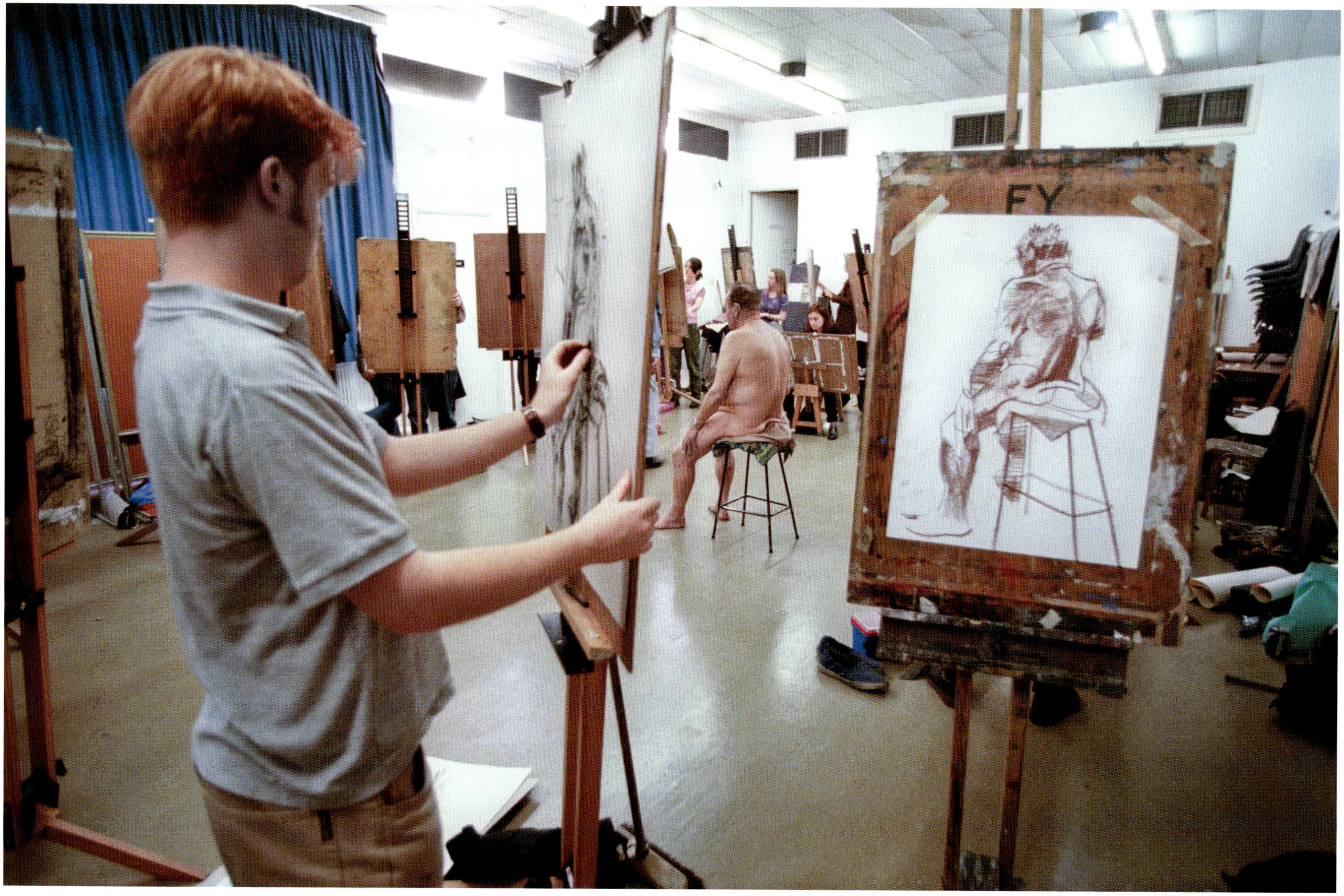

Life Class

2006

I was asked to think about pictures of life drawing classes for a project by a friend, so I went to watch fine art students at the University of Brighton at work. The picture wasn't published but I liked the way it turned out.

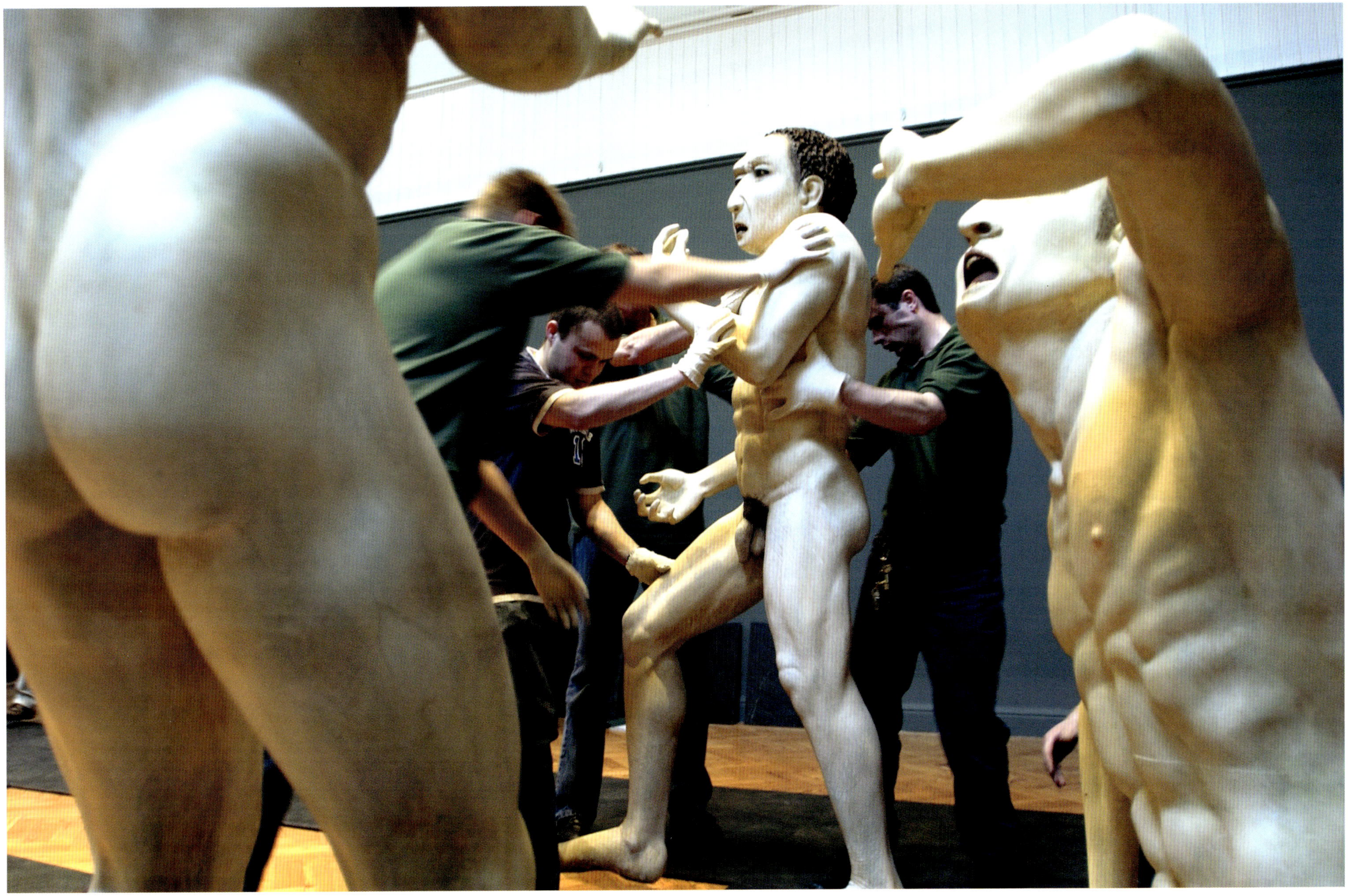

Handle With Care

The Guardian, 2004

Gallery porters carefully manhandling larger than life male nudes by the Brazilian sculptor Ana Maria Pacheco, for the first UK showing of her *Land of No Return* exhibition at Brighton Museum & Art Gallery. Pacheco's dramatic, painted wooden figures were very heavy and very fragile, and everyone involved in getting them in and out of a lift to their gallery space and positioning them correctly felt the tension of moving them. The appalled expressions on the faces of the figures didn't help.

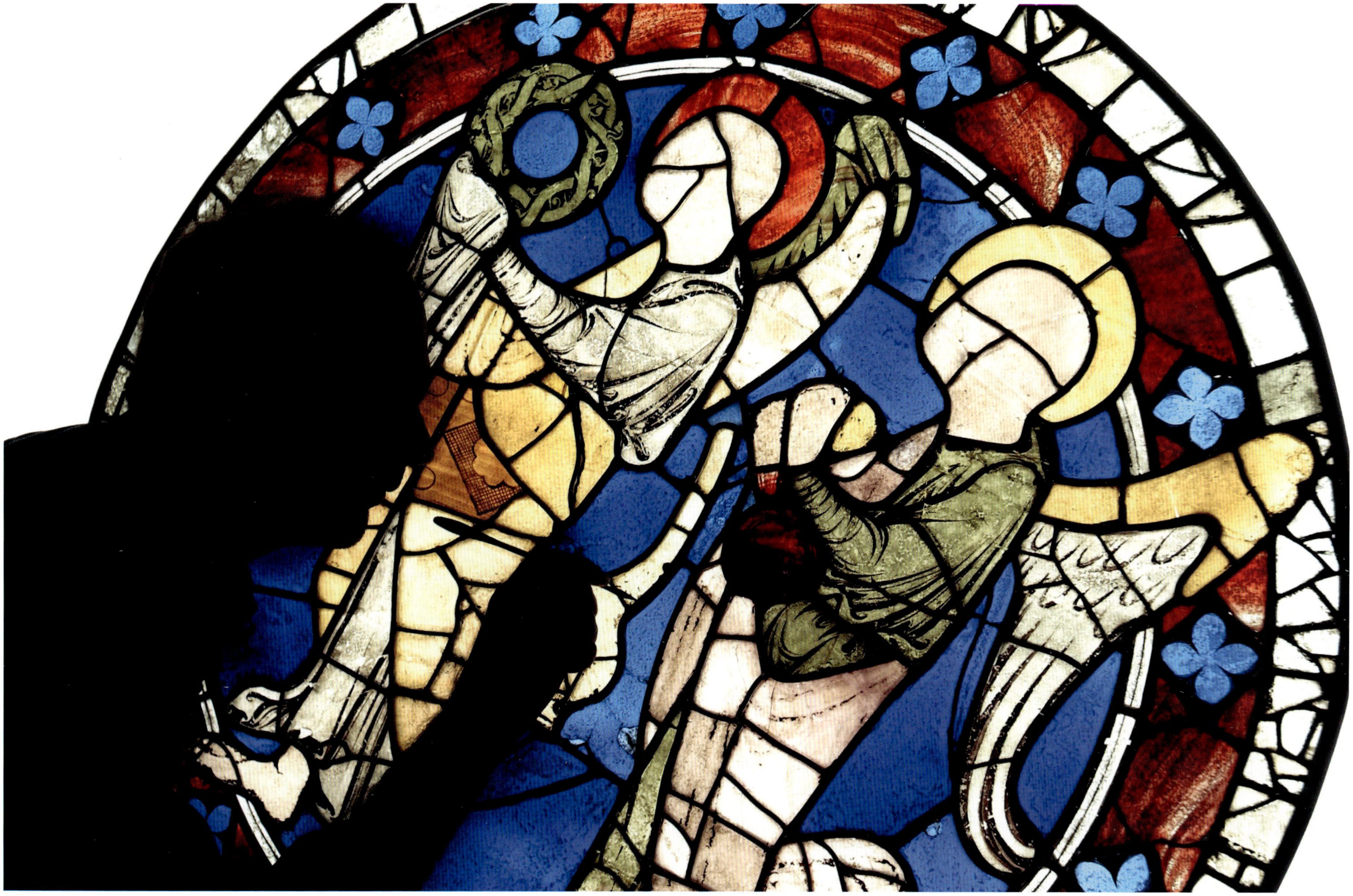

The Dean's Eye

The Guardian, 2003

Tom Küpper, the chief glazier of Lincoln Cathedral, restores one of the original stained-glass roundels of the Dean's Eye rose window. The fragile glass, some of it worn away to fingernail thickness after more than a thousand years of exposure to the weather, was being cleaned, set in new lead and reinforced at the back with matching modern glass where needed.
It was originally set in the window high above the north transept in 1220, yet every detail of the glass was still clear and bright. It is now back in place, glowing in the sunlight, almost as good as new.

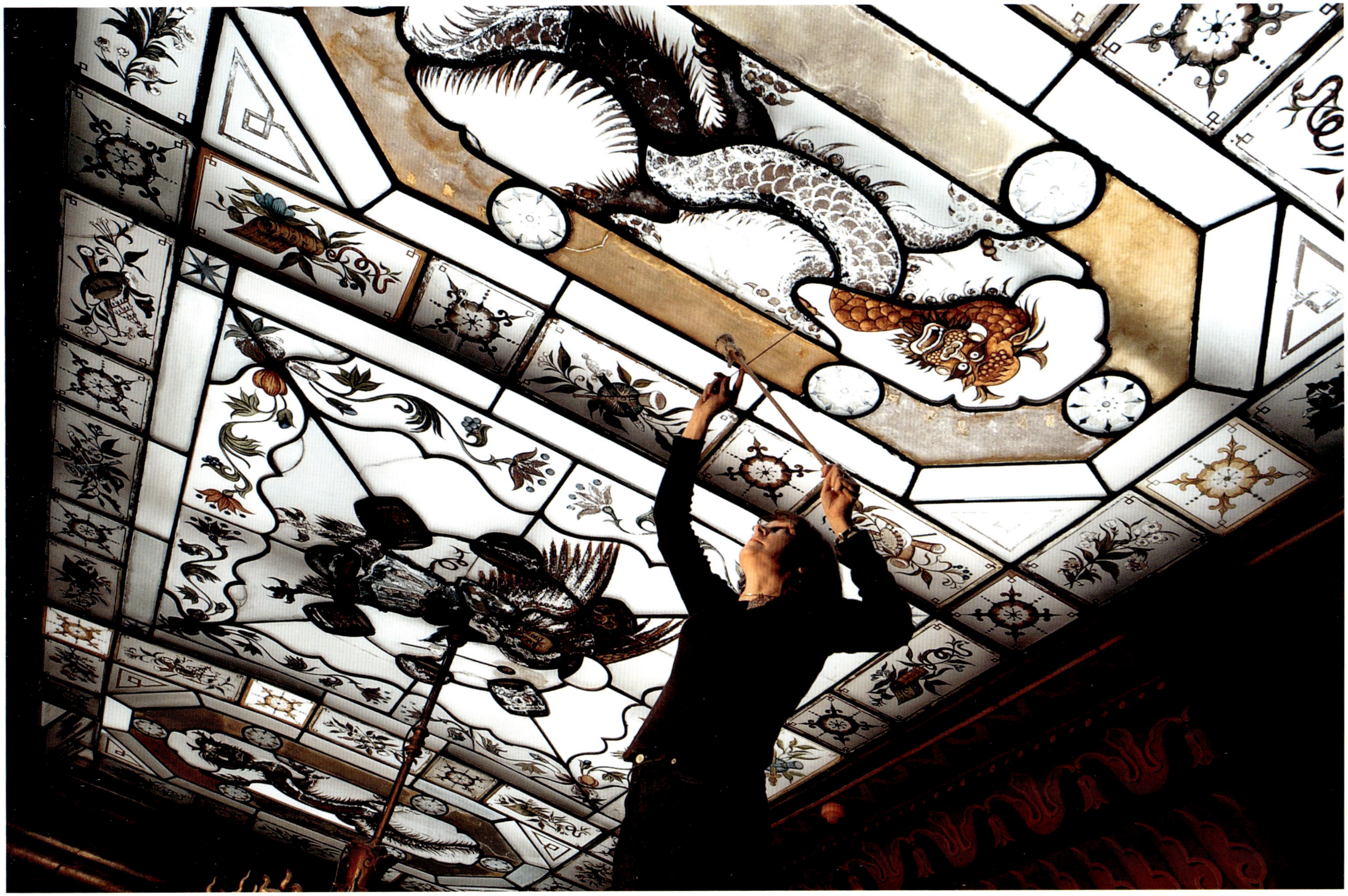

Glass Ceiling

The Guardian, 2003

Decorative artist Anne Sowden worked behind the scenes at Brighton's extravagant, fragile Royal Pavilion as a conservator for thirty-two years. She probably knows more than anyone else about the actual nuts and bolts of combating damp, decay, insects and the impact of thousands of curious visitors.
She has had a hand in repairing and restoring everything from dragon chandeliers to hand-painted wallpaper and watching her at work was always fascinating – here she is starting on the original 1815 Frederick Crace Laylight window above the Long Gallery.

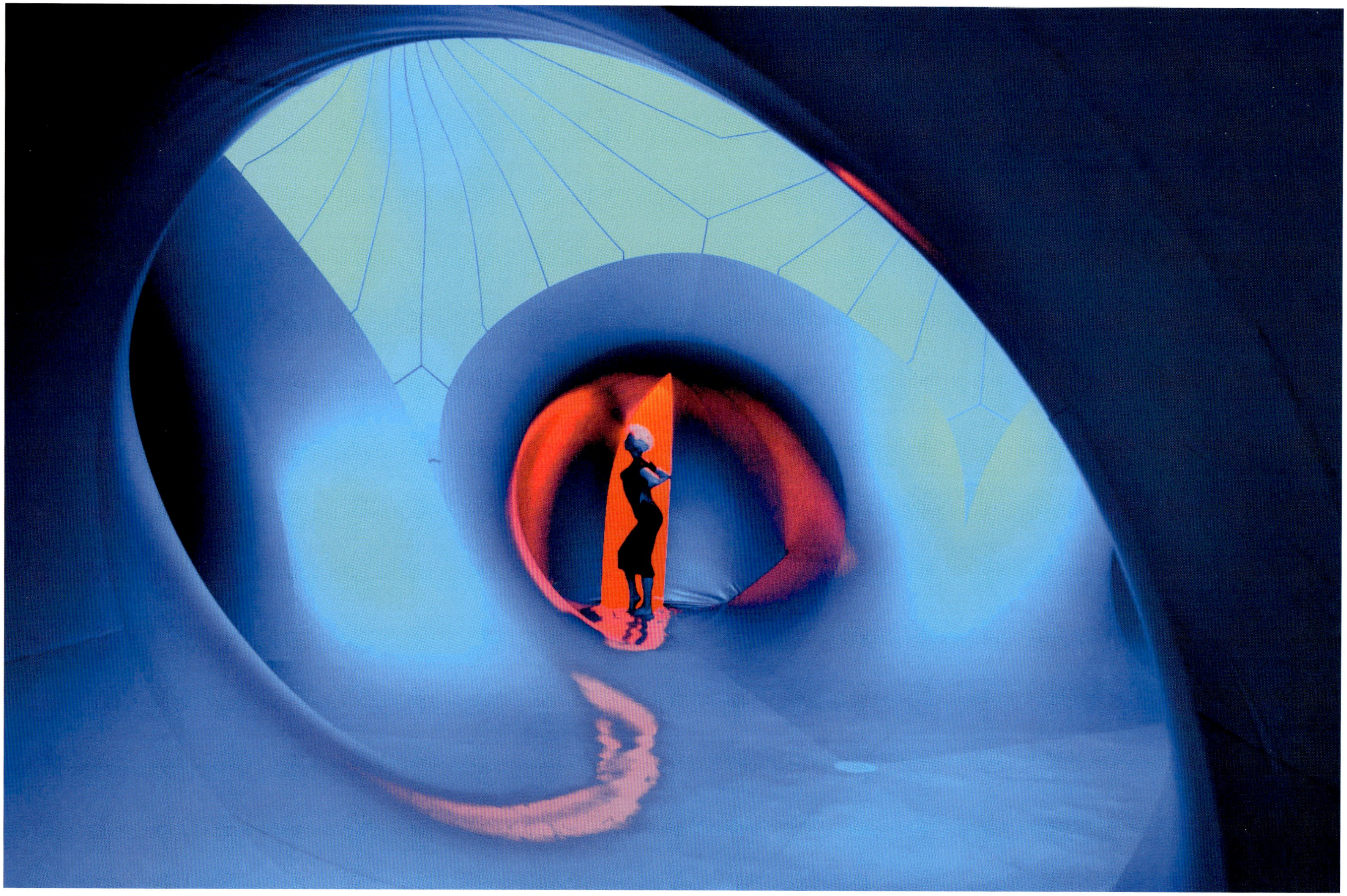

Out of the Blue

The Independent, 2002

Comedian Helen Kane made a beautiful silhouette as she rehearsed her role as Marilyn Monroe for a Brighton Festival show in a giant inflatable tent called a Luminarium.
Daylight shining through the coloured fabric made her shimmer with blues and reds.

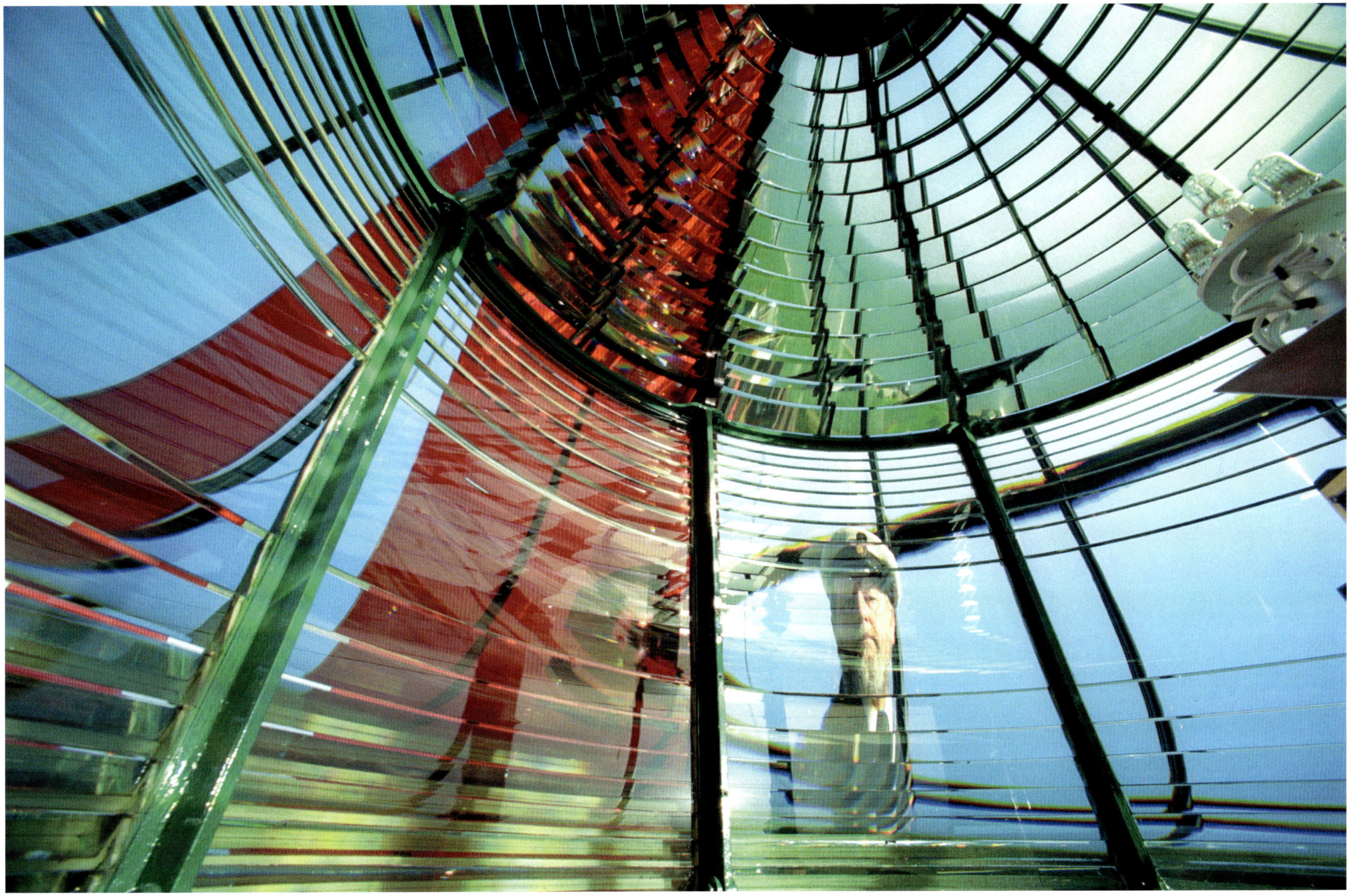

Putting the Light Out

The Guardian, 1998

Lighthouse keeper Dermot Cronin, seen here through the gigantic lens of Britain's last manned lighthouse, North Foreland at Broadstairs, Kent. Dermot was Britain's last lighthouse keeper. When North Foreland was switched to automatic operation a few weeks after this picture was taken, he and the five colleagues who shared the 24-hour-shift rotas were redundant. Dermot did the final shift and left the light in the care of a computer.

Electric Avenue

The Guardian, 2006

I was walking down Madeira Drive in Brighton on a misty, dark evening when I noticed a red glow coming out of one of the shops under the arches. The shop, Fishtail Neon, was owned by lighting artist Andy Doig who was selling his own work alongside scores of neon advertising signs dating from the 1930s to the present day. Some of the rare examples were worth £1,500 or more and together they were dazzling.

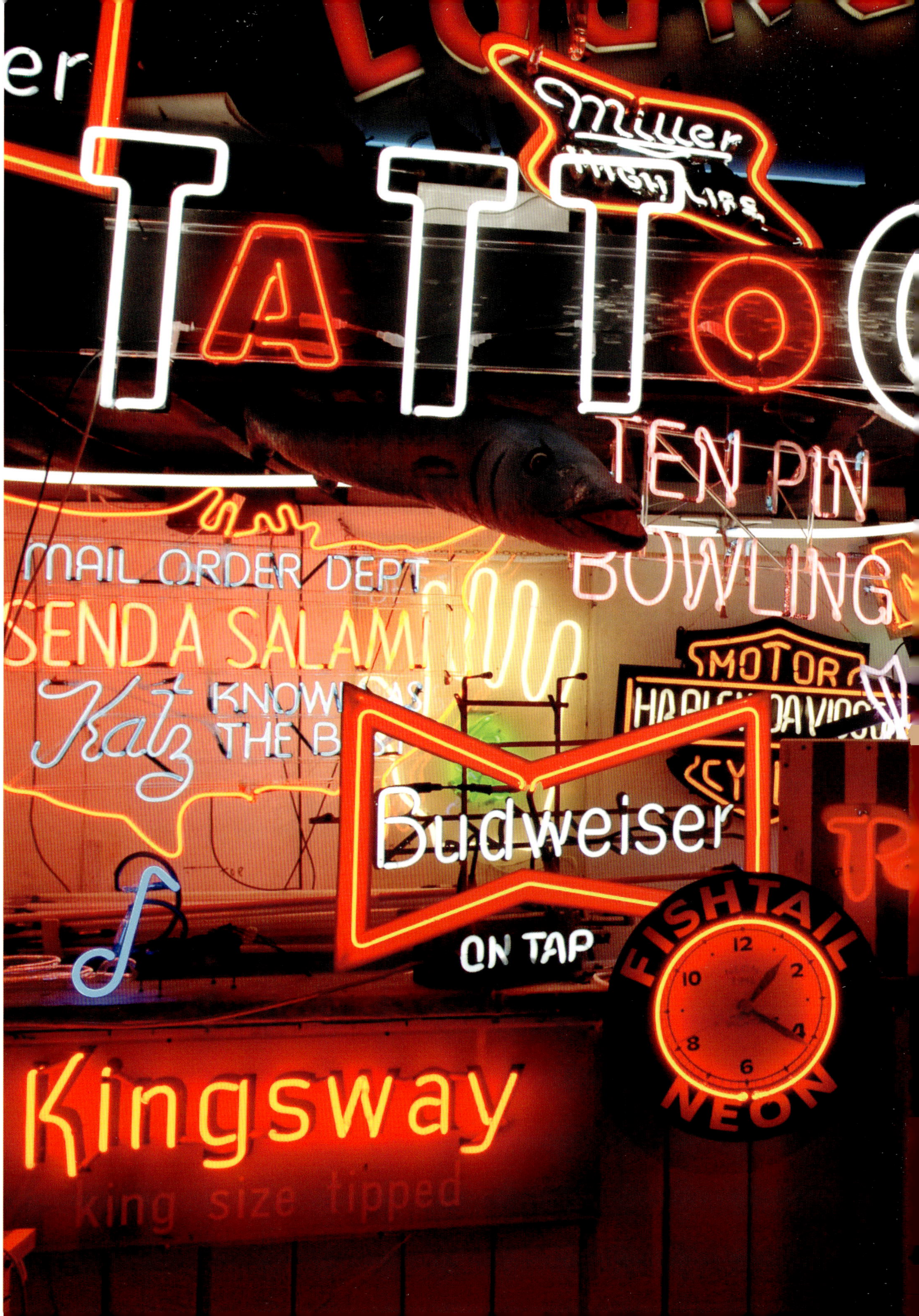

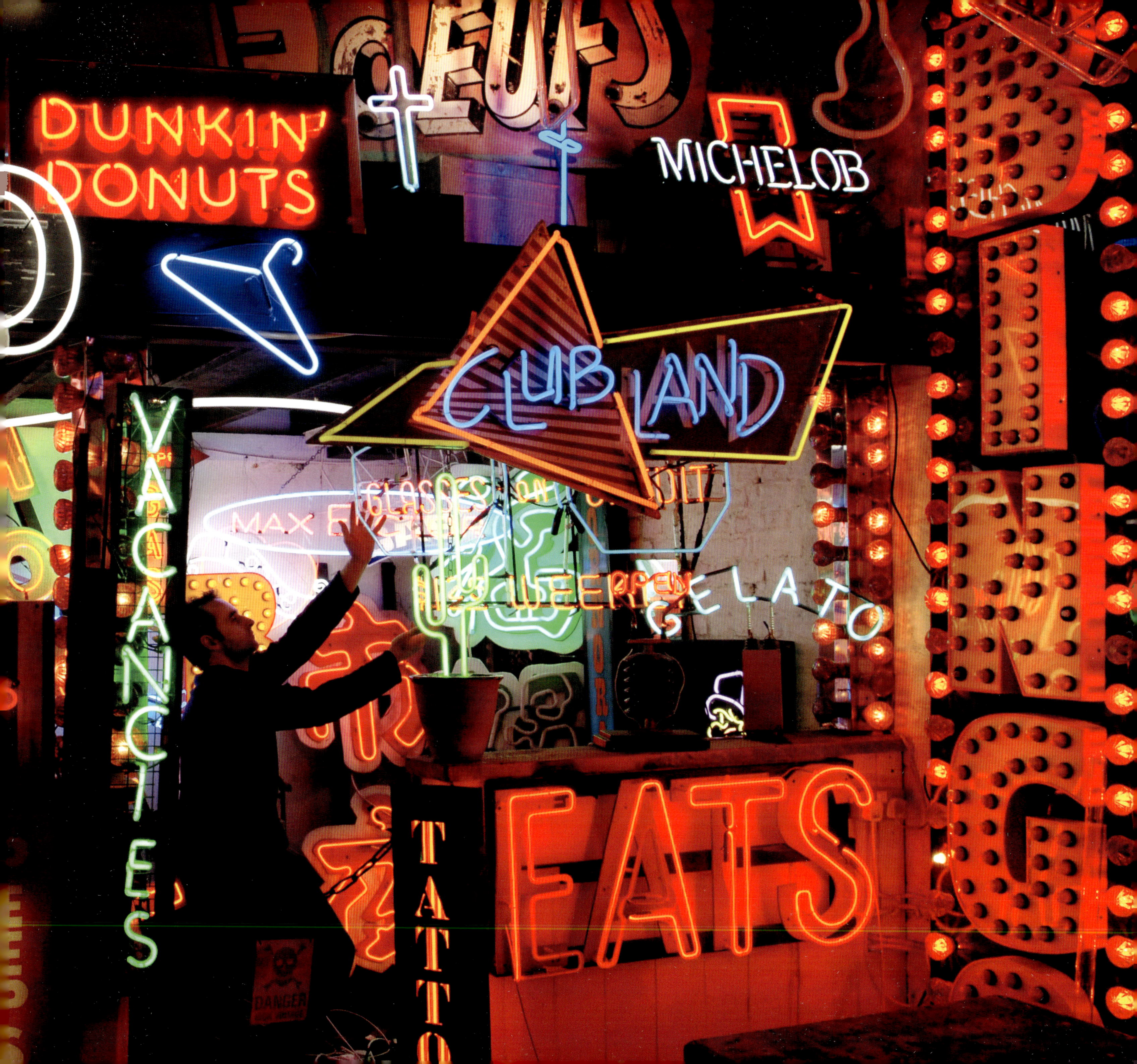

DUNKIN' DONUTS
MICHELOB
CLUB LAND
VACANCIES
MAX
GELATO
EATS
DANGER

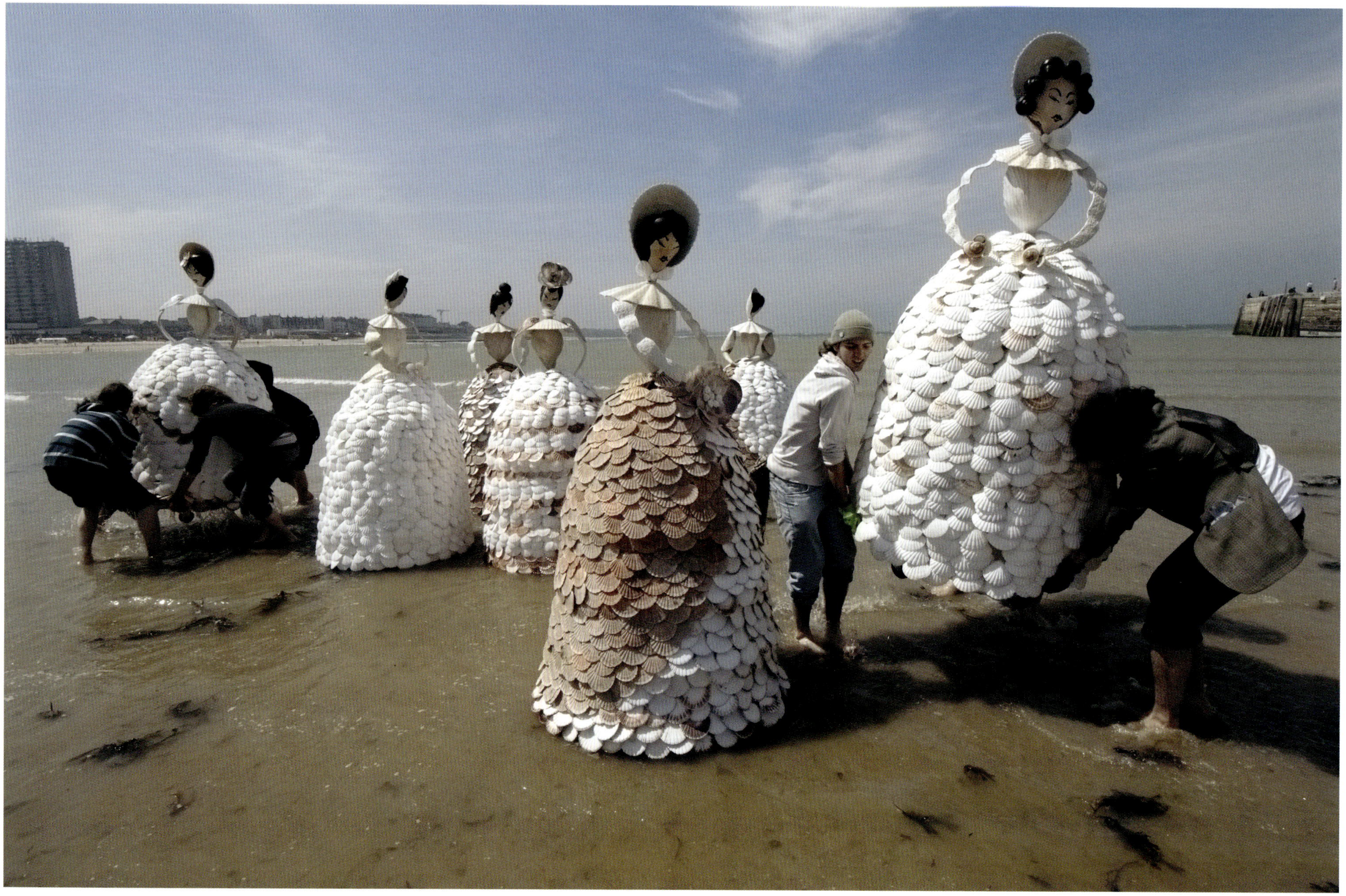

Shell Ladies

The Guardian, 2008

Margate wanted to celebrate some of the famous and infamous women who had personal or literary links with the town, so they commissioned sculptor Anne Carrington to make these 7-ft-tall Shell Ladies, using local scallop shells.
There were twelve of them, from Baroness Orczy, who wrote *The Scarlet Pimpernel* to Phyllis Broughton, the famous Gaity Girl.

I wanted to get them all together on the beach before they were dotted around the town for the summer season and we had to race a fast incoming tide to get the picture.
We just made it. Then I took this image of them being hoisted from the flooding beach afterwards, which was even better.

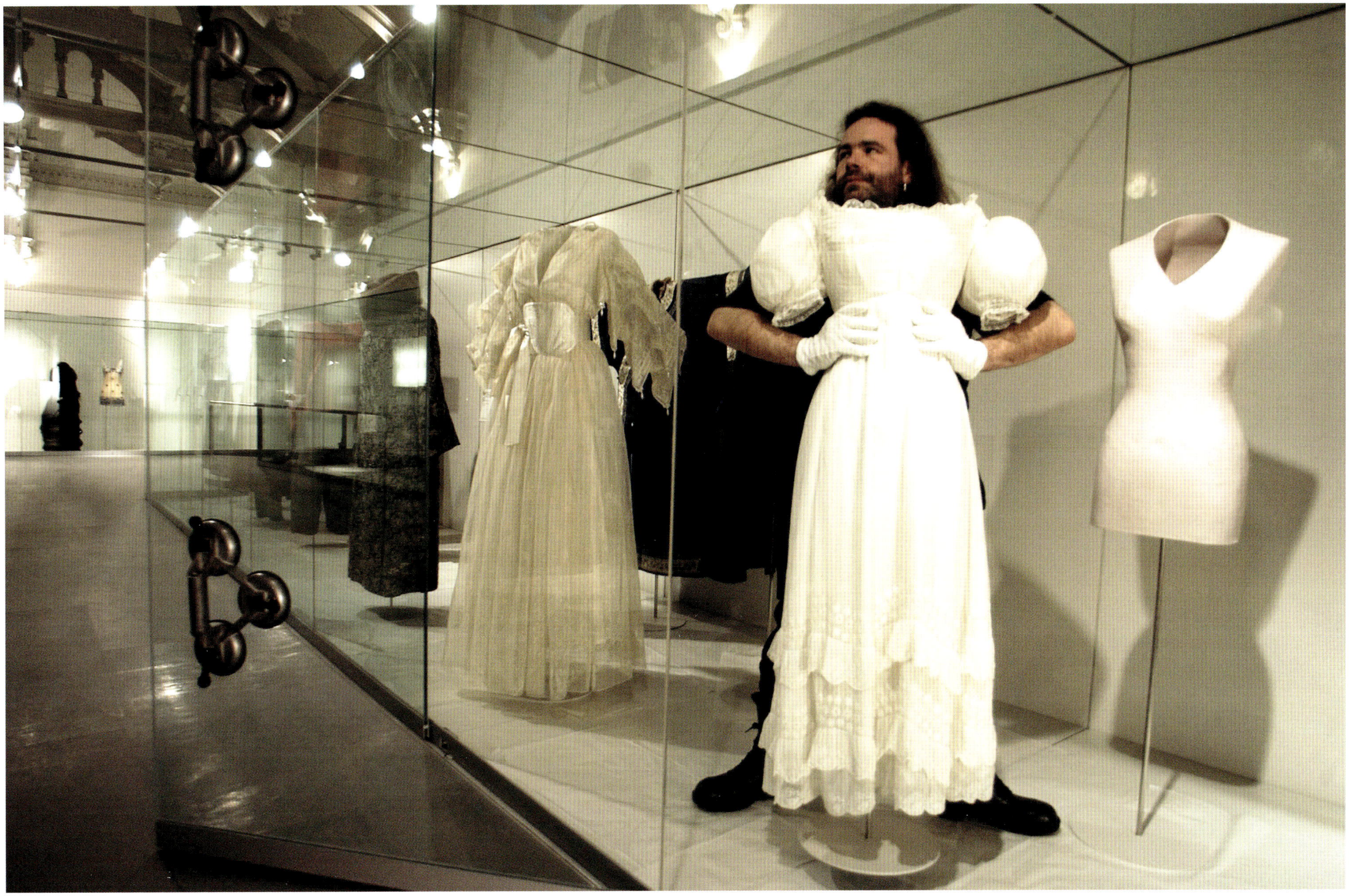

Fashion Show

The Guardian, 2002

Richard Le Saux, Keeper of Local History and Archaeology at Brighton Museum & Art Gallery has never forgiven me for this.
Brighton Museum was about to open a new fashion and costume display after a £10 million, two-year revamp and they offered me Richard or one of the women curators to help set up a picture.
Of course I chose Richard, whose long hair, beard, Motorhead T-Shirt and Dr Martens boots made a brilliant contrast between then and now.
As he was arranging a Regency era white Indian muslin dress it all worked beautifully. Boots and all.
The image was used in the paper and adopted as a poster for the exhibition itself. It appeared on many billboards and in almost every bus shelter in the city. Richard, a football fan, had to withstand ribbing from fellow fans who sang, 'Who's the bloke in the frock?' at him for several games.

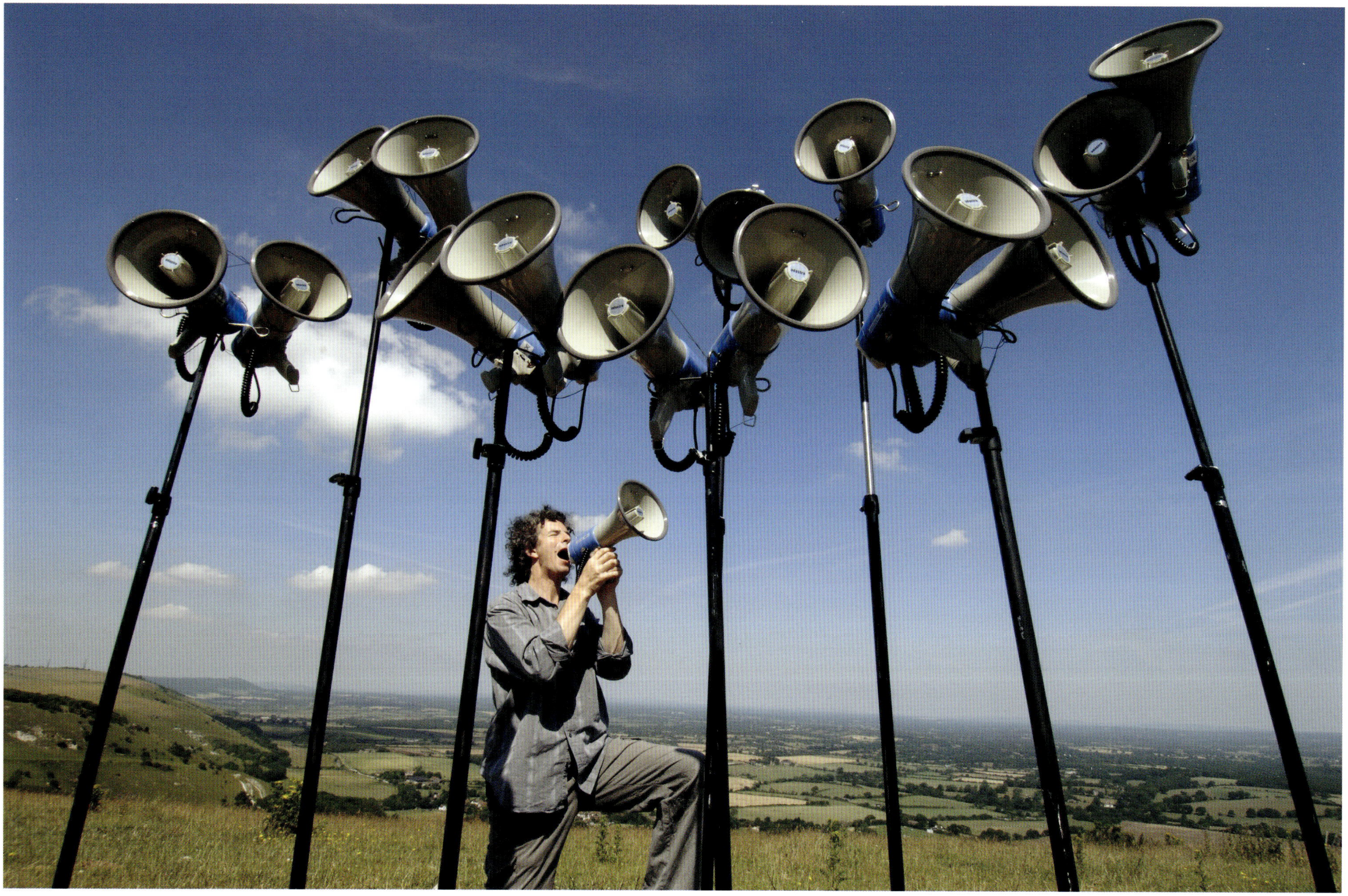

Shouting

The Guardian, 2006

Orlando Gough, a composer and the director of an extraordinary choir called The Shout, prepares for a rehearsal at the top of Devil's Dyke, on the South Downs just north of Brighton.
Megaphones feature large in The Shout's repertoire of concerts, music theatre and outdoor performances, where they regularly use them for their dramatic delivery of all sorts of sounds. I loved seeing them being set up because they made such wonderful shapes.

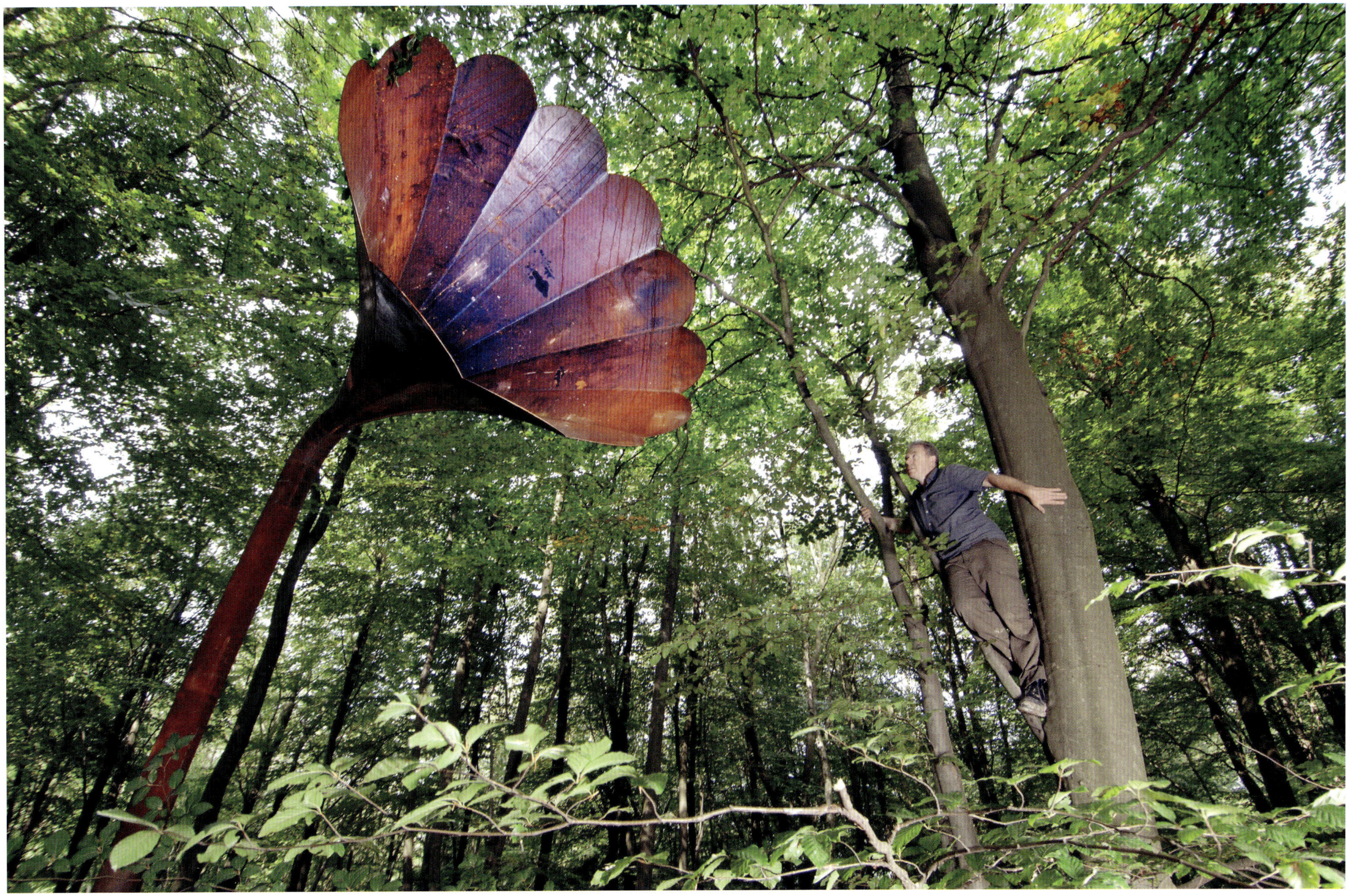

Score for a Hole in the Ground

The Guardian, 2006

Musician and conceptual artist Jem Finer was a founder member of the Pogues. The pieces he composes now could hardly be less like the chaotic banjo solos he used to perform.
Here he is setting up his latest work, *Score for a Hole in the Ground*, where a gigantic horn modelled on an old gramophone trumpet amplifies sounds produced by a slow trickle of water dripping randomly on a rack of steel splines in a deep underground chamber.
The result, broadcast to the birds and anyone who walks past in King's Wood, Challock, Kent, is abstract music generated by nothing more than water and gravity.
It's not easy conveying any, let alone all, of that in a photograph but Jem, 20ft up in the treetops, addressing his giant horn, does capture some of the elegant strangeness of it all.

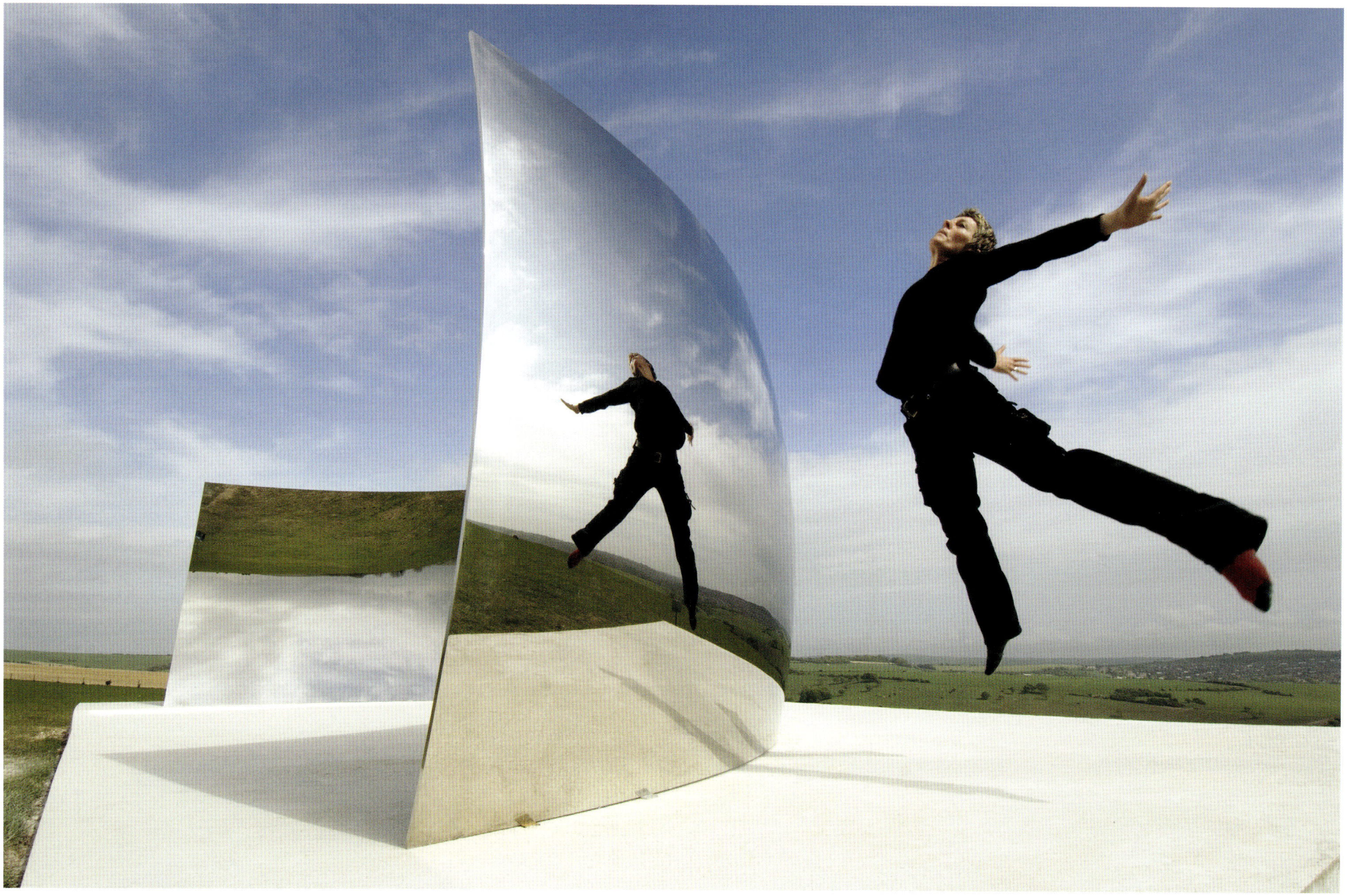

Leaping into Action

The Guardian, 2009

C Curve was a huge concave stainless steel mirror installation by Turner Prize-winning artist Anish Kapoor. It was set high on the South Downs behind Brighton when Kapoor was guest artistic director of the 2009 Brighton Festival, and something about it just made people want to jump for joy.
Hundreds of people made the long uphill trek to see the sculpture, and photograph themselves leaping about in front of its lovely curves.
I asked Brighton Festival Guide Helen Goodwin, on duty to make sure nobody damaged Kapoor's work, to have a go herself and she bounced into action, making a wonderful athletic shape.
Later she was horrified when she saw the picture and realised she was wearing odd socks.

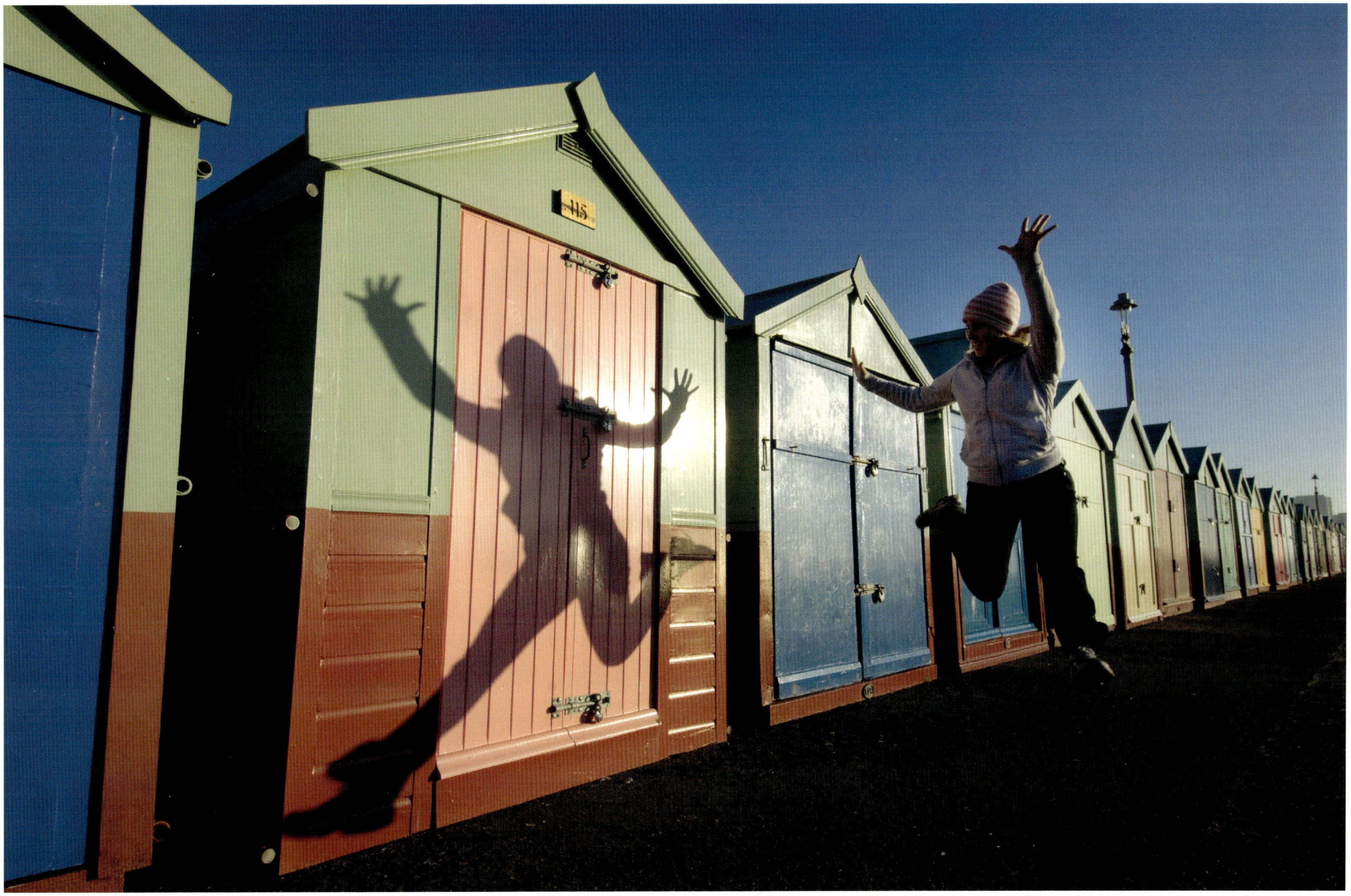

Beach Hut Jogger

The Guardian, 2009

I always carry a camera, just in case I see something that might make a picture. Walking along Hove Promenade, I stopped to mess about with the sharp shadows cast on the beach huts by the low winter sun. Then along came my neighbour, writer Josie Lloyd, on her morning run, in a great mood because her latest book had made a bestseller list.
She said, 'I'll help with that,' and proceeded to leap around like a mad thing. It made a great image and we've been friends ever since.

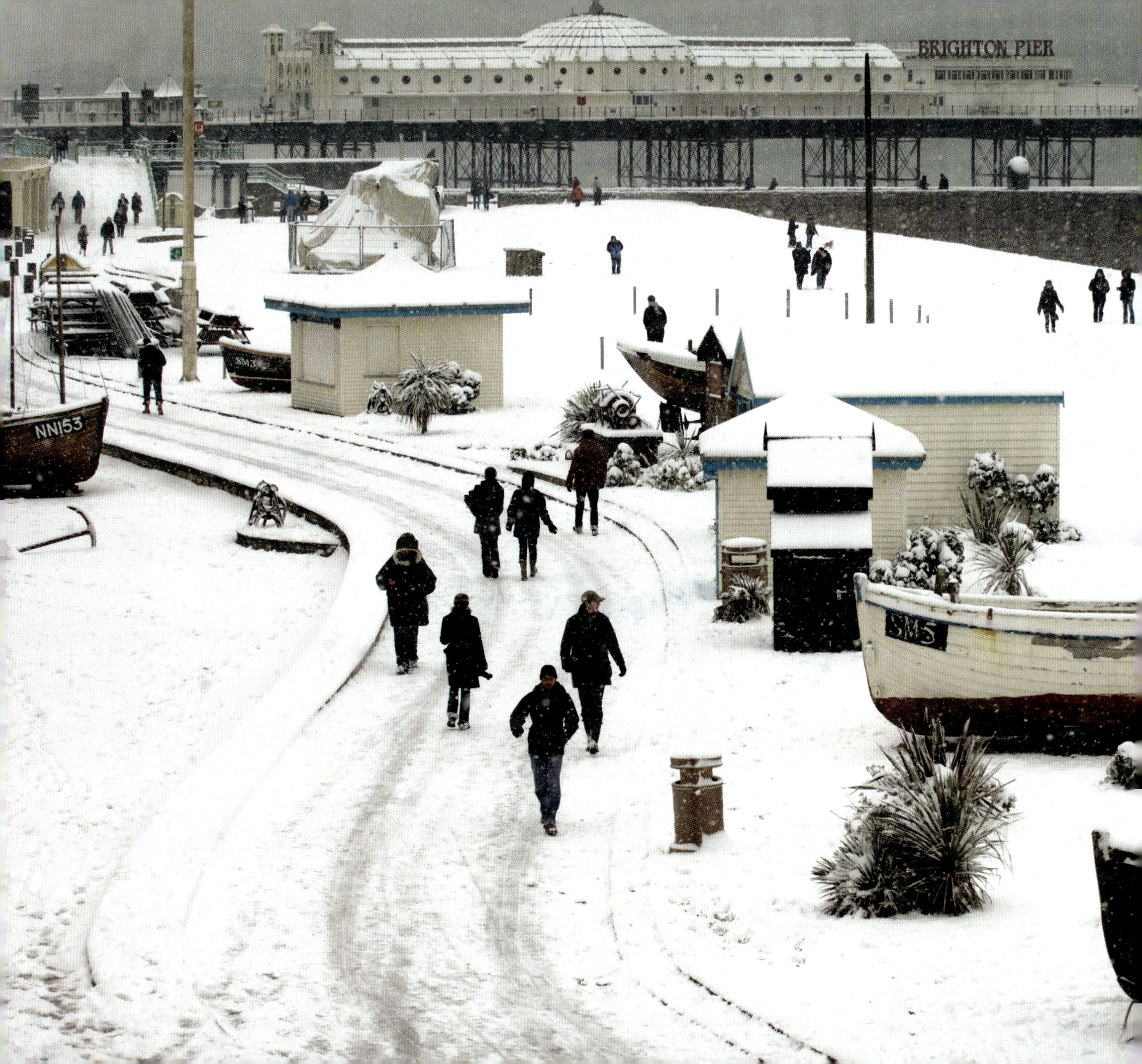
BRIGHTON PIER
SM3
NN153
SM5

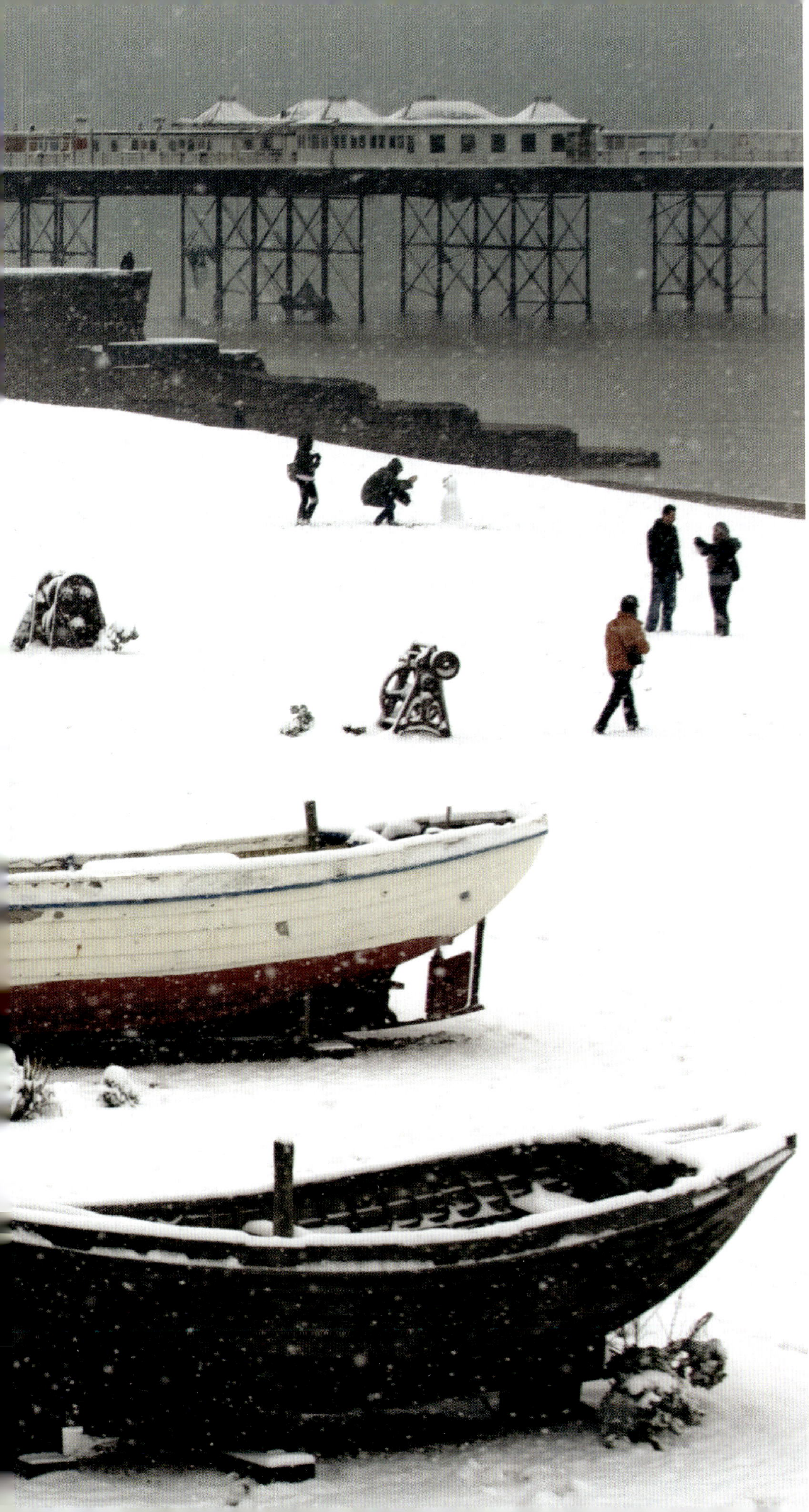

We Can't Believe it's Brighton

The Guardian, 2009

Snow hadn't settled properly on Brighton Beach for over two decades, so when it finally did, in 2009, hundreds of people came down to enjoy it, build snowmen, throw snowballs and just enjoy a day off work. There were over ninety snowmen built on Hove lawns alone. I thought the whole scene was like a Lowry painting.

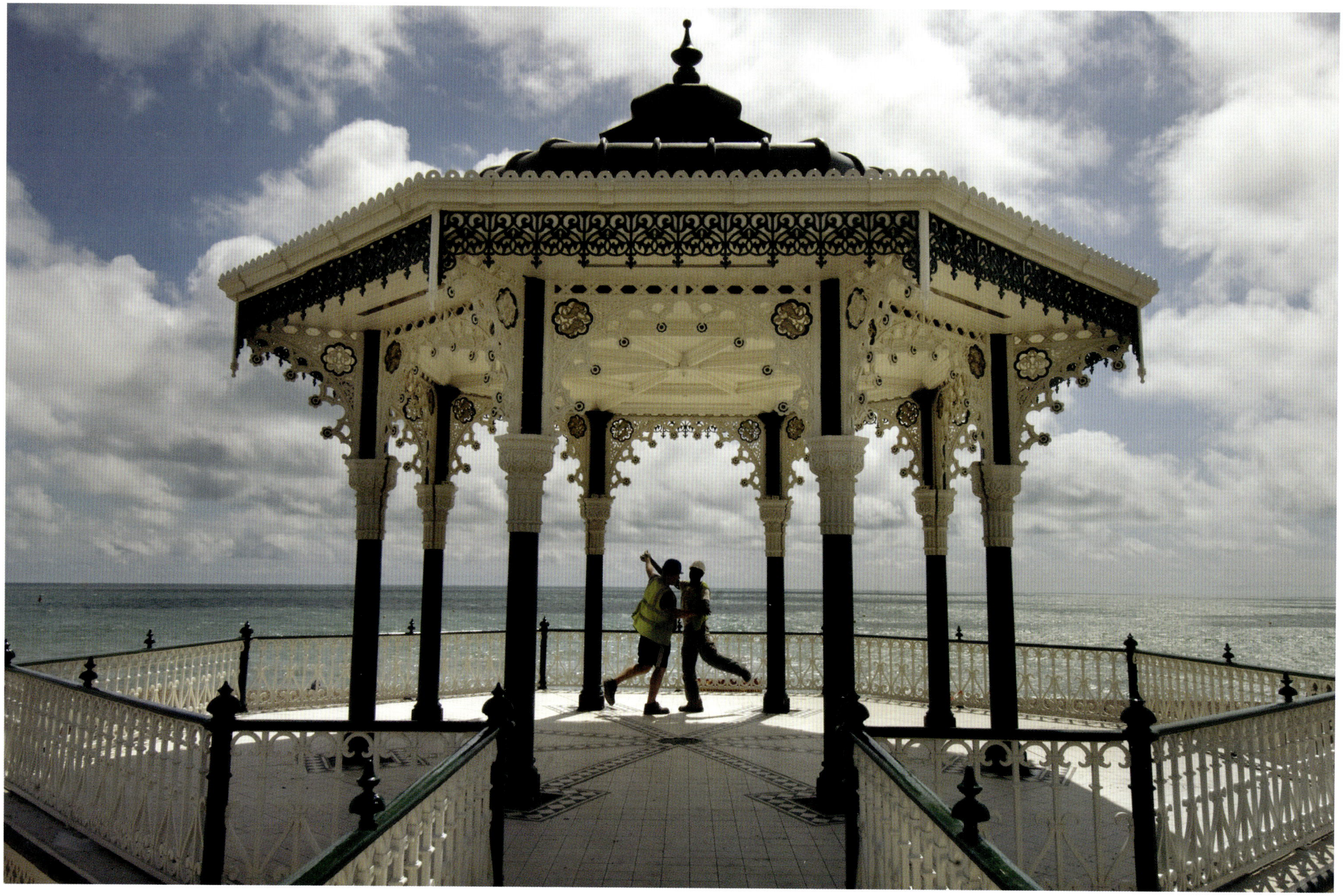

The First Dance

The Guardian, 2009

A double act of two burly builders, Rob Nitman and Lamin Jatta celebrating their work on a million pound restoration of Brighton's Victorian seafront bandstand with a quick twirl.
The pair, in their high-vis vests, hard hats and steel toe-capped boots, waltzed round after finishing the last touches, a couple of hours before the grand opening by local council leaders later that afternoon. The refurbished bandstand caught the public imagination at once and has been busy ever since, used for brass bands, samba and salsa dance classes, jive shakedowns, choirs, concerts of all sorts and countless wedding ceremonies.

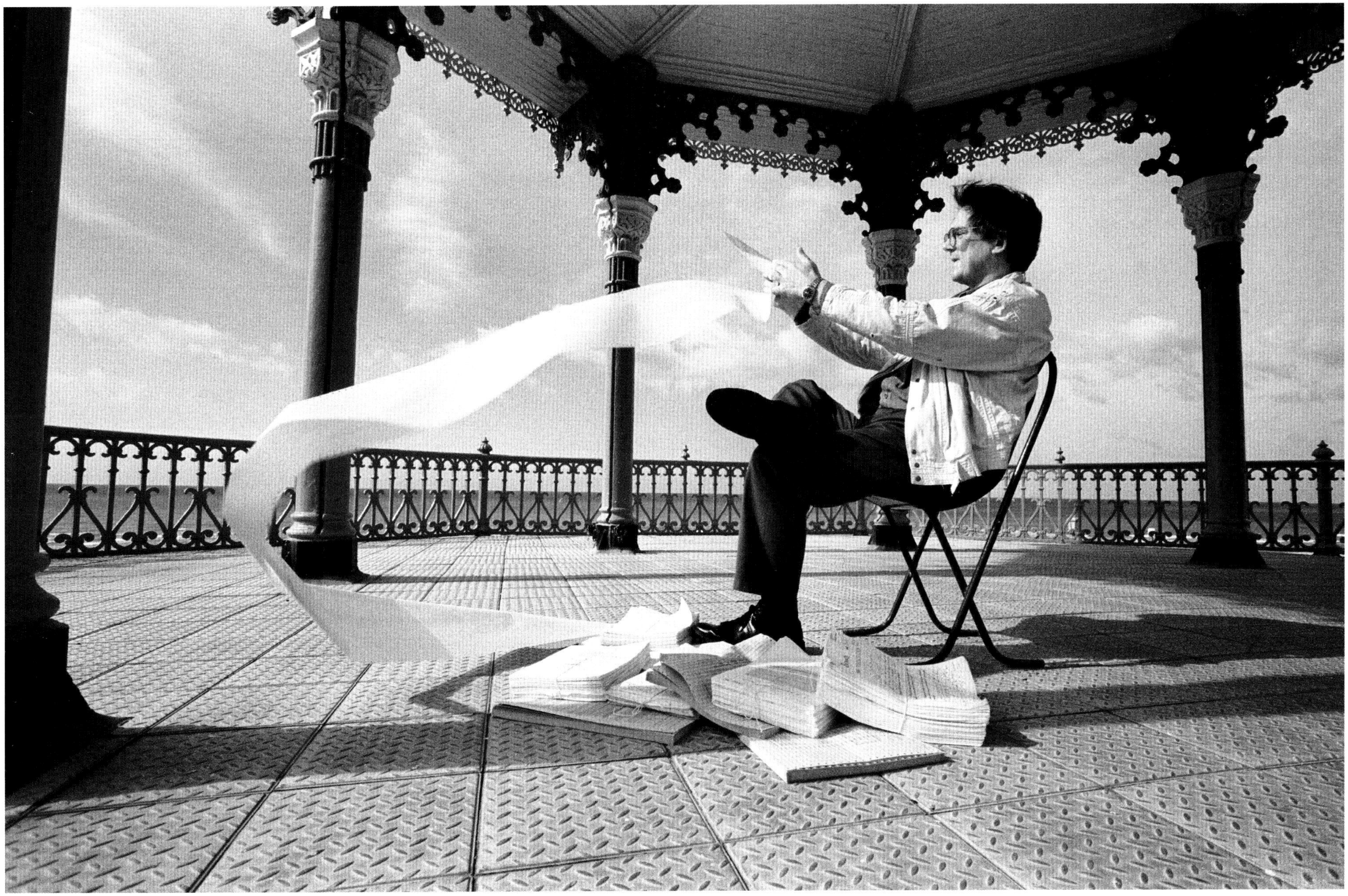

Poet's Corner

The Guardian, 1992

The official caption for this was 'Poet Sebastian Barker sits in the ornate Victorian bandstand on Brighton seafront as he revises the voluminous manuscript of his 4,500 line poem on Nietzsche.' This was not quite the whole story. The epic poem had been prepared for a reading at the 1992 Brighton Festival. Actors Prunella Scales and Timothy West were to perform it onstage and Sebastian, the author of many books of poetry and editor of the *London Magazine* was in town to direct them. My problem was how to show that this was no ordinary poem. It was a HUGE poem.

I borrowed a heap of computer printouts and a little chair from Brighton Council Press Office and took Sebastian to the bandstand. The printouts contained about the same number of lines as his epic work and they billowed out magnificently in the breezy weather.

The picture was a triumph, but I was in trouble when I returned the props. Bits had gone missing. It turned out that this was a rather important list. And some of the pages were last seen heading up the coast in the direction of Eastbourne.

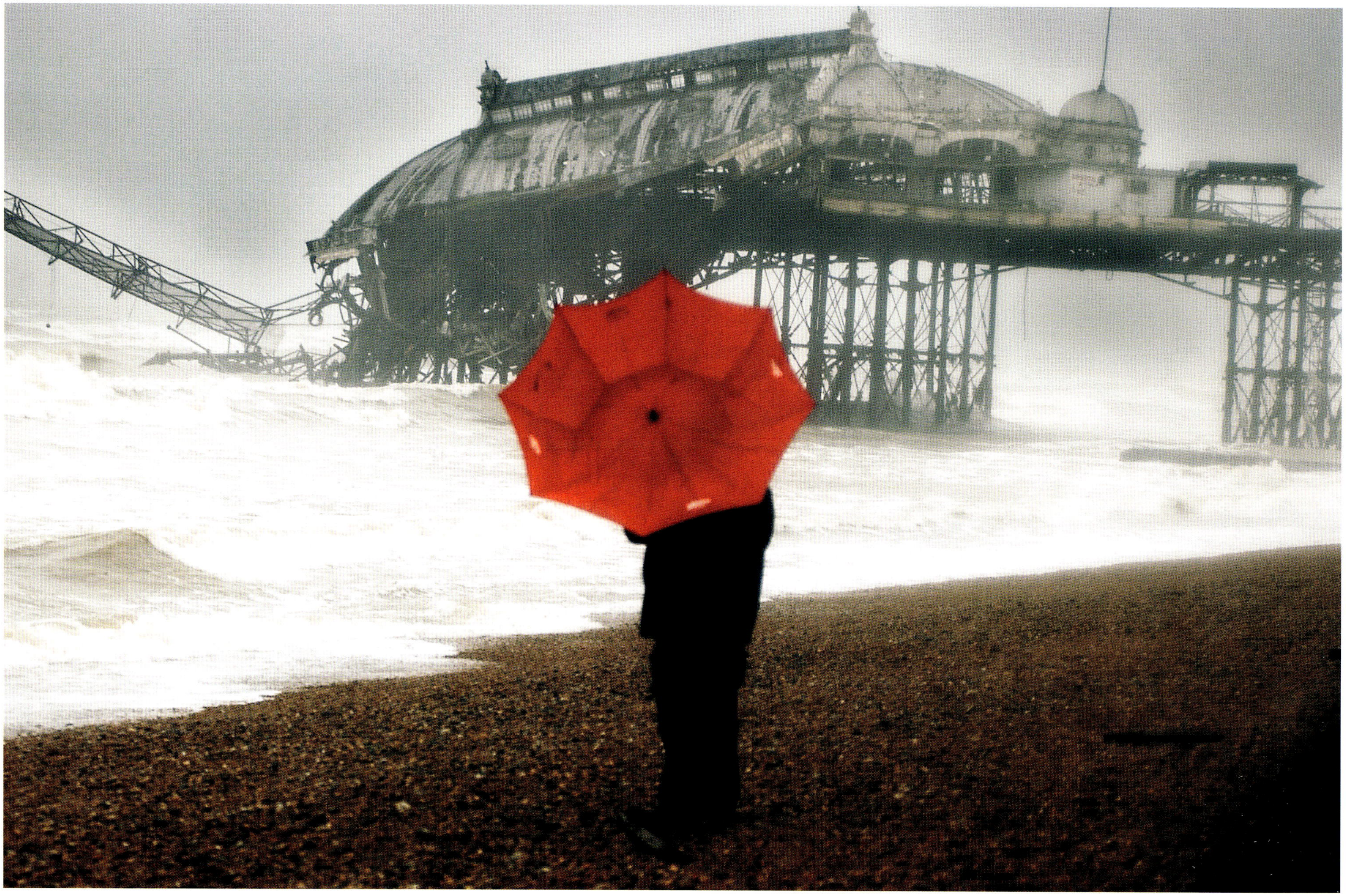

Red Alert

The Guardian, 2000

My boiler had blown up and I was reduced to borrowing the bathroom in a house over the road. On the morning this picture was taken, as I emerged with my towel and toothbrush, a neighbour ran up to say that the West Pier had collapsed in the stormy weather. I rushed back to the house, grabbed my cameras and ran down to the seafront.
The pier was literally falling apart as huge waves crashed against it. A mass of decking and other debris was being washed up on the beach.

The wind was howling, there was a muzzy grey mist of sea spray and countless bounty hunters were scurrying up and down the beach eagerly hunting for souvenirs.
Then, further up the beach beyond the mayhem, I spotted a man in a suit, fighting with his large red golf umbrella in the buffeting wind.
At last a bit of colour... I helped the very damp man wrestle his brolly back from inside out and did my pictures as he continued to combat the wind.

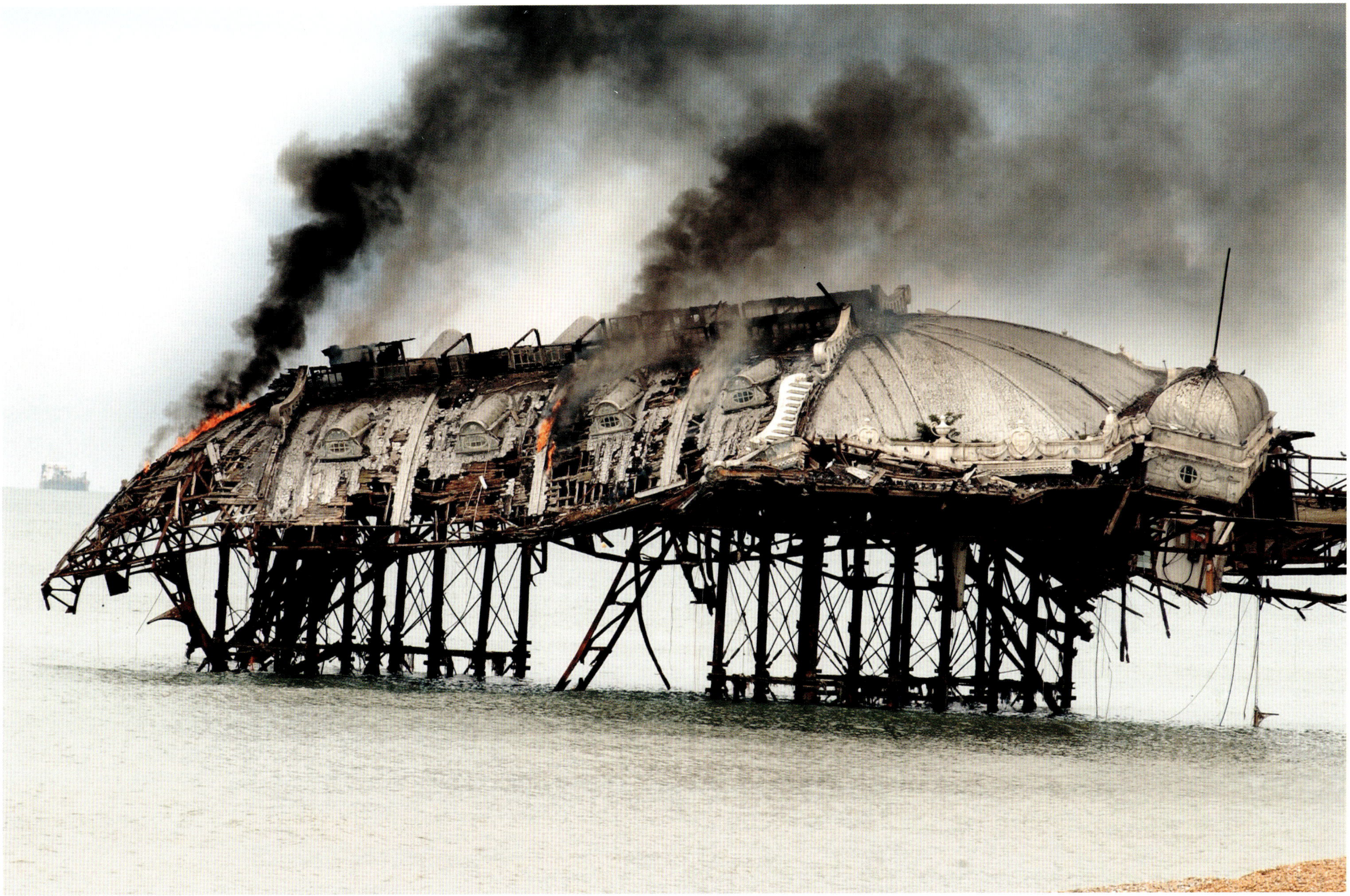

Going Up in Smoke

The Guardian, 2003

Brighton's beautiful Grade I listed pier was in terrible shape at the start of 2003 but there was still hope. A £1.2 million national lottery grant had been approved and restoration work was due to begin within weeks.
Then all hopes of a rescue were dashed by arsonists who targeted it twice – in March it was deliberately set on fire and the damage was bad but not fatal. Then in May another attack destroyed the Concert Hall and Pavilion, leaving the wreckage seen here. The lottery withdrew its funding.
Nobody was ever charged with the mindless arson attacks which left so many of the pier's supporters bitterly disappointed.

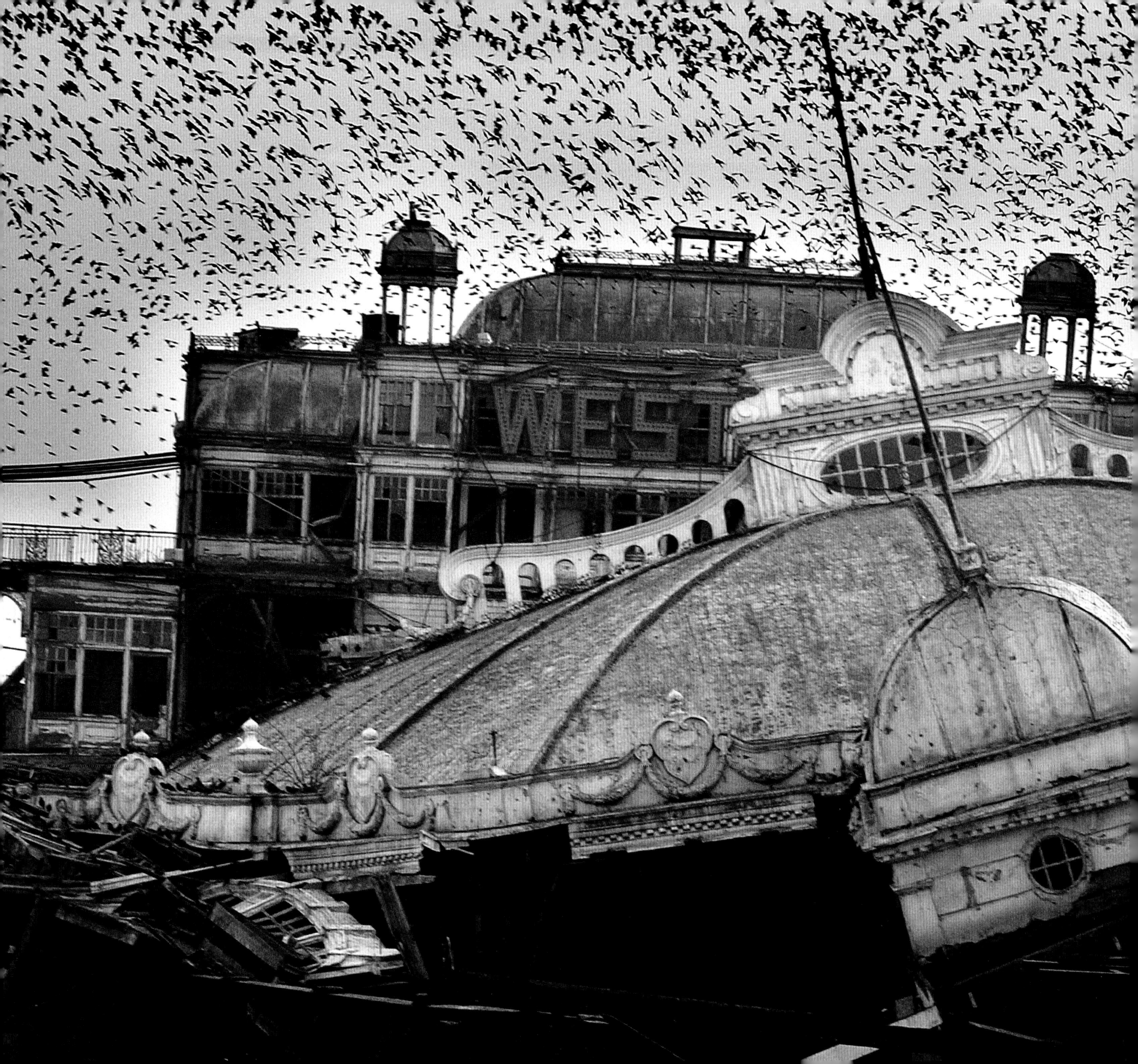
WES

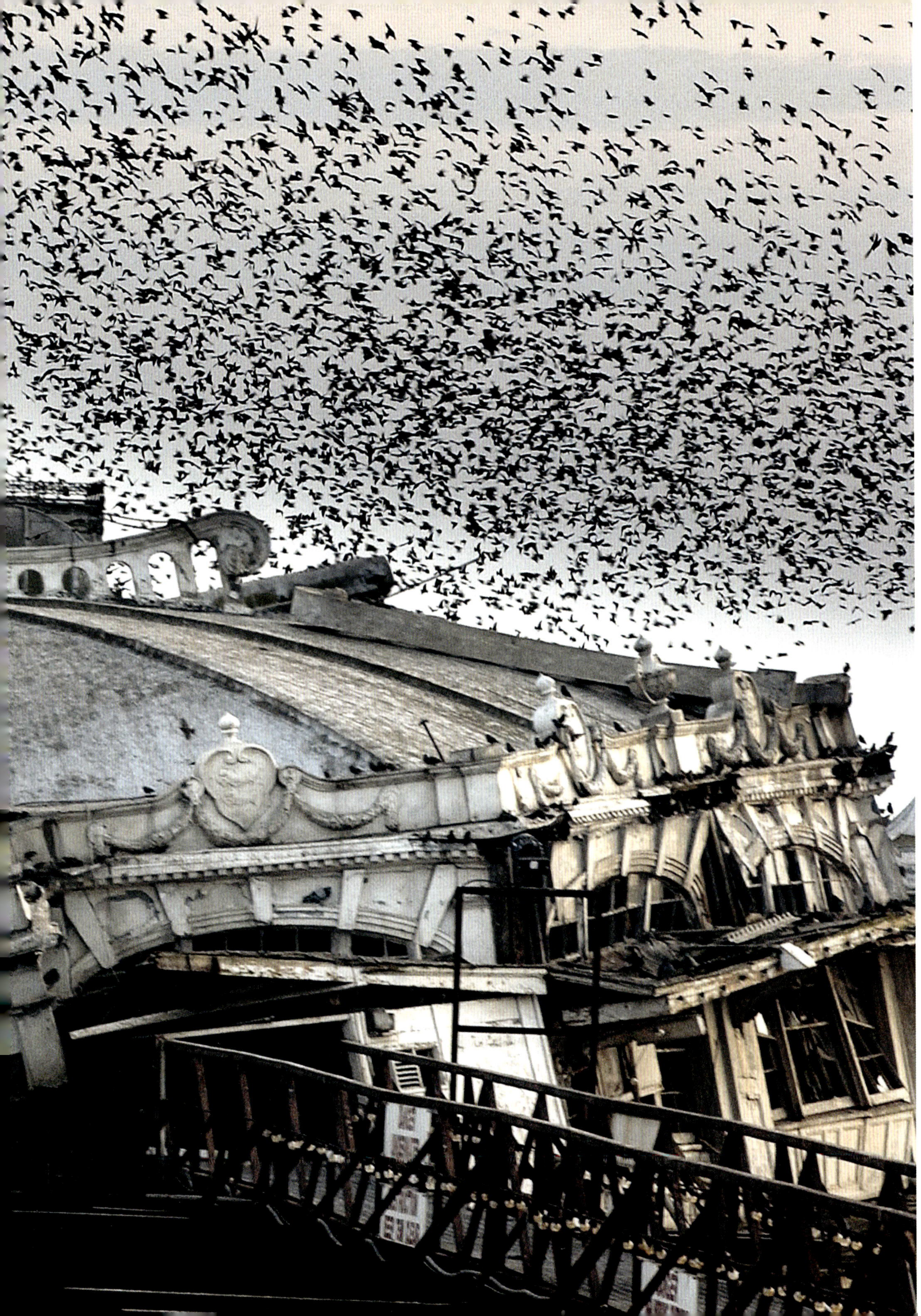

Only for the Birds

The Guardian, 2003

A murmuration of starlings fills the sky above what's left of the once grand concert hall of Brighton's decaying Grade I listed West Pier. The birds were regular visitors, delighting onlookers as they performed mass aerobatics overhead every evening, then swooped down to roost for the night. Few starlings roost there now, fires have reduced the old pier to a skeleton and there is hardly any shelter for the birds. But they still come to swirl and swoop over its remains.

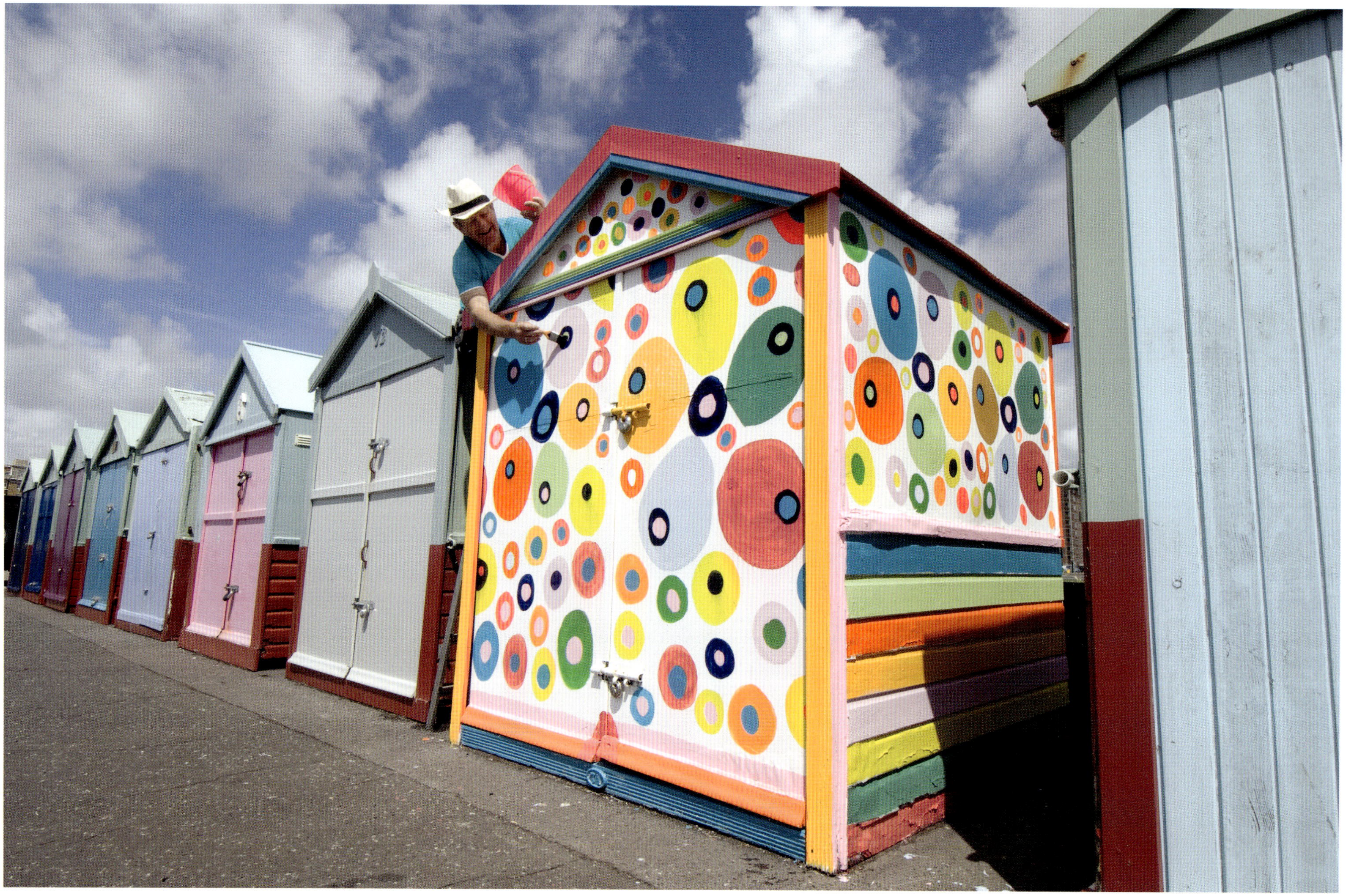

Doing the Polka

The Guardian, 2011

The owner of Hove beach hut No. 71 was a rebel. Hove is very proud of the uniformity of its line of green huts but he decided to defy the rules by painting his beach hut with multicoloured polka dots. He had erected a canvas screen around his hut to hide what he was doing, as he was directly opposite the local council offices, but I poked my nose in to see what he was up to and persuaded him to let me photograph him quickly the next morning, without the screen.
We had only just moved the screen and got started when an appalled seafront officer appeared and ordered the dots to be painted out at once.

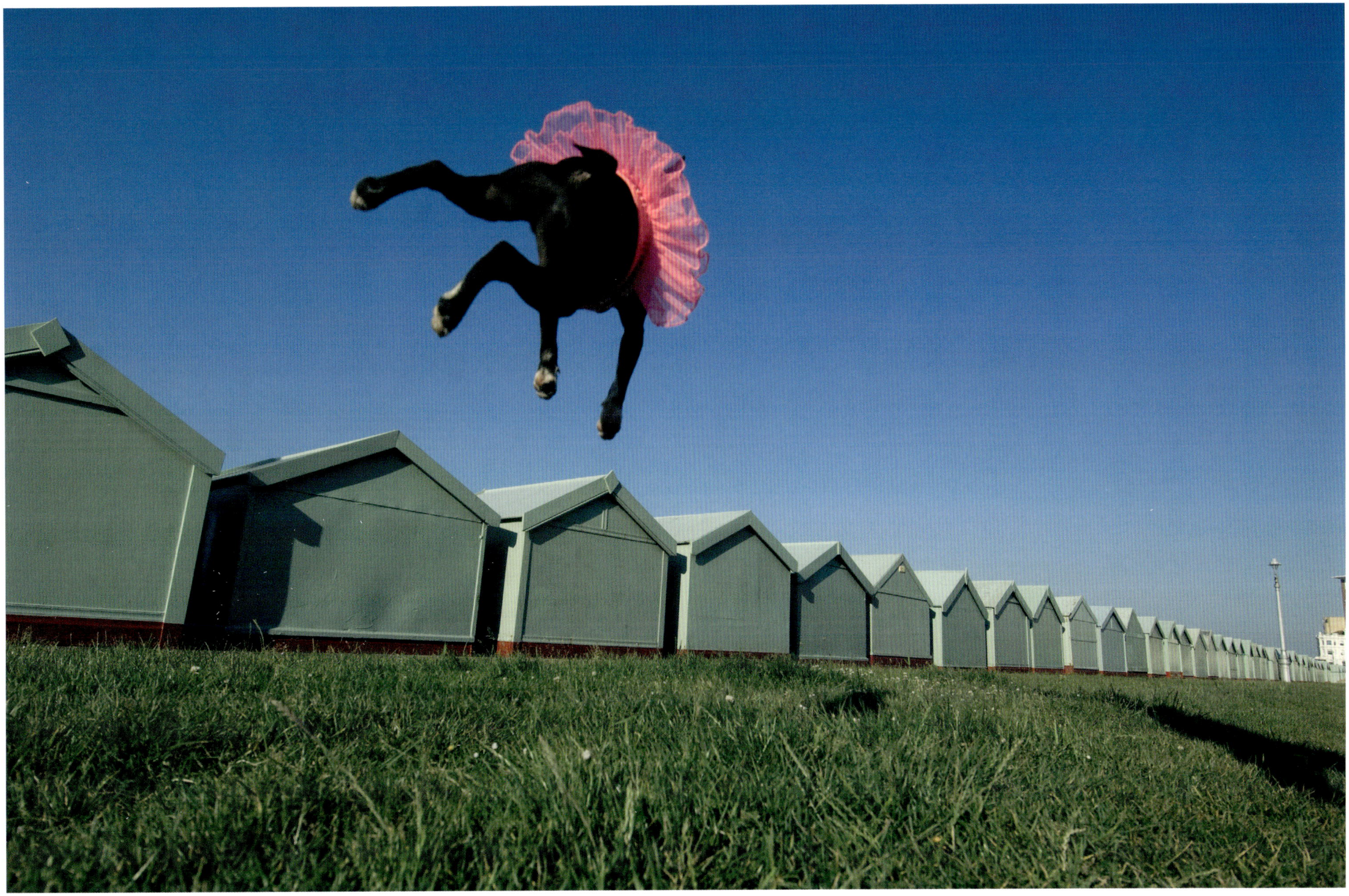

High Flier

The Guardian, 2009

Yoda, a Boston Terrier puppy in his holiday finery for a seafront walk on Brighton and Hove Promenade, was leaping about by the beach huts, chasing his ball.
I'd often noticed him out and about – his owner worked in a pet shop selling doggy dressing up accessories and Yoda usually wore something fetching. The pink tutu, though, specially chosen as it was a Bank Holiday, was something else. I had to take his picture.

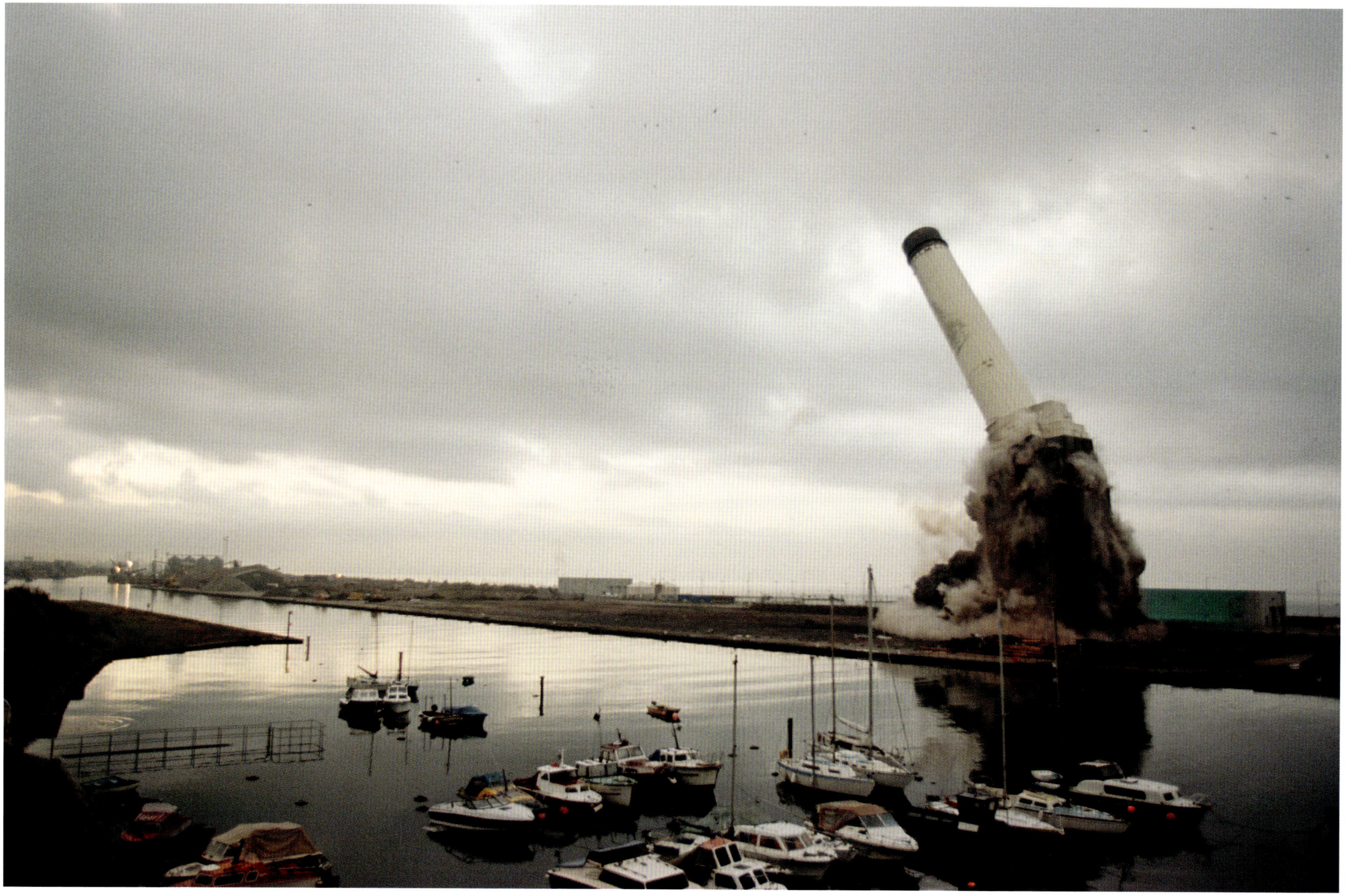

Out with the Old

The Guardian, 1998

The 350-ft-high chimney of a grimy old 1940s coal-fired power station bites the dust at dawn. Brighton B Power Station at Shoreham Harbour was being levelled to make way for a new modern Scottish Power gas-fired replacement.
Long redundant, the old tower had been left to the birds who used it as a nesting site. The moment the explosives went off, hundreds of roosting pigeons took flight from the top.

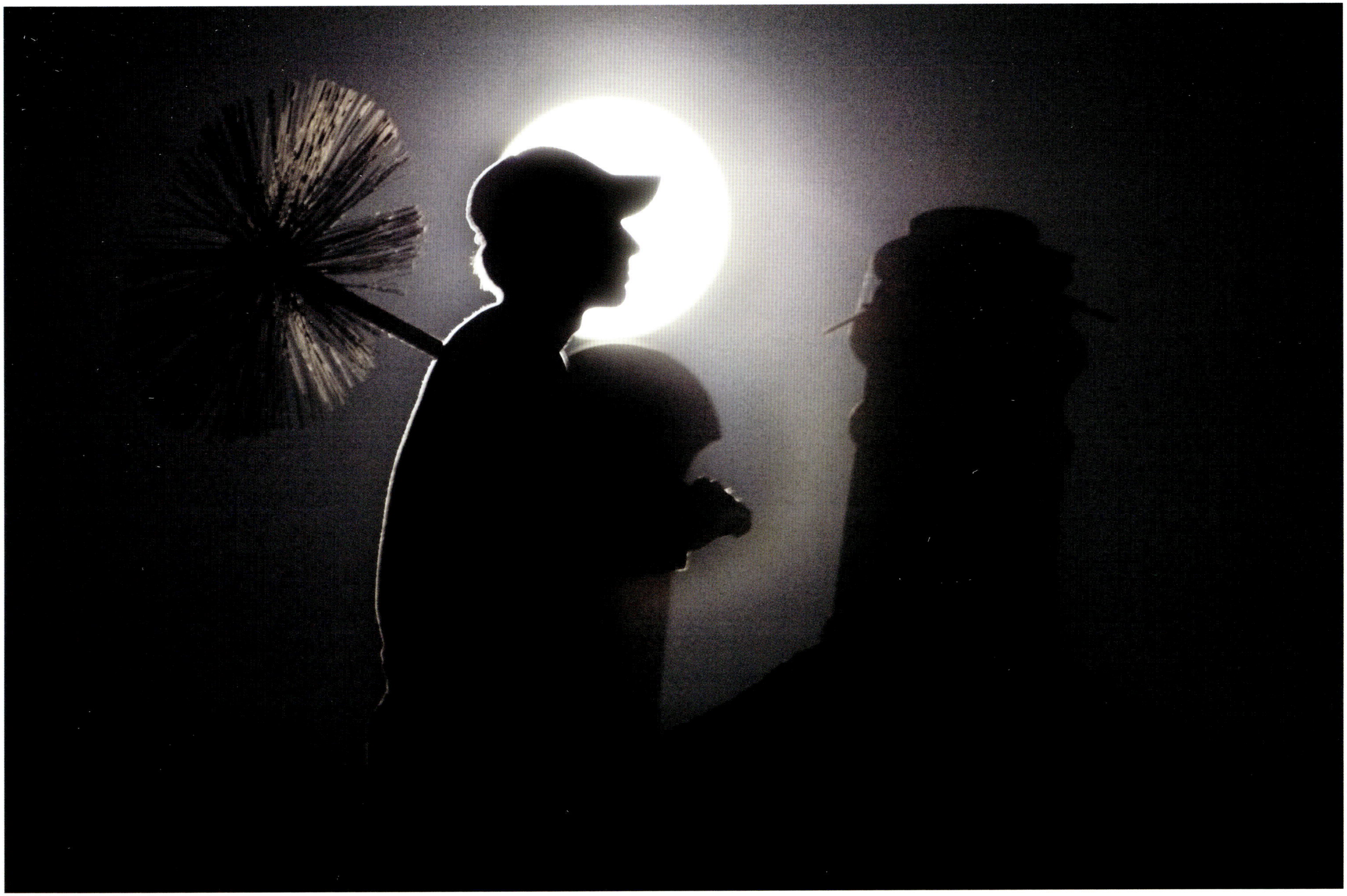

Night on the Tiles

The Guardian, 2002

An especially bright full moon was forecast and we had just had the chimney swept. Inspiration struck. Persuading the sweep to come back with his brushes after sundown for a picture was tricky at first, but when he got the idea he laughed and turned up with all his sooty brushes.
My plan was to use them to create a romantic image. My model was already waiting, a baffled but willing Brazilian exchange student called Pedro who lived in the house where I'd found the perfect chimney and had no fear of heights.
Pedro scrambled on to the roof with the brushes as night fell, and perched by the chimney. After a lot of desperate shouting and arm waving from me at street level, he struck a wistful pose, perfectly in line with the moon as it rose behind him. The picture was taken using a 300mm long lens without the use of a tripod.

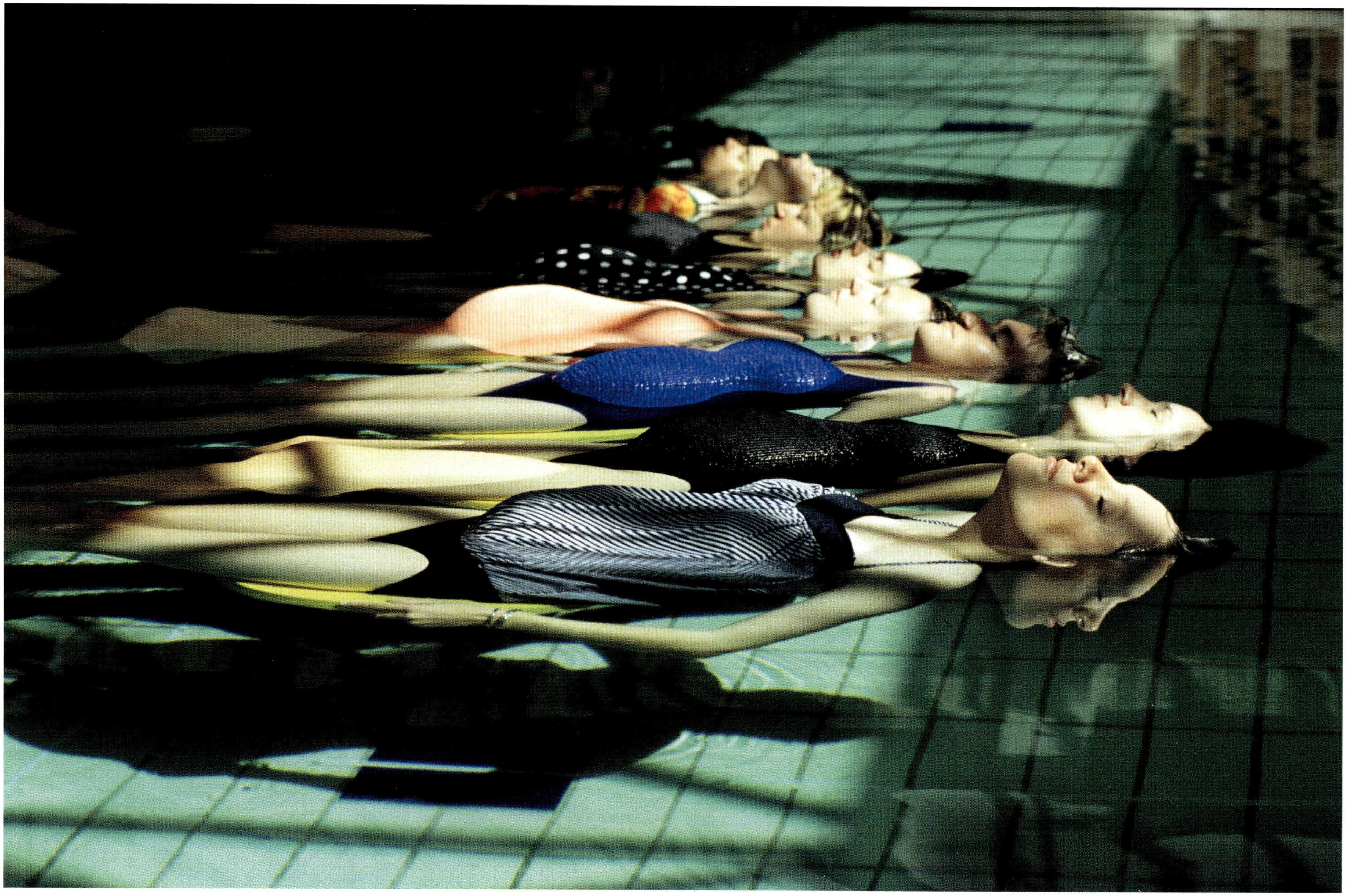

Water Babies

The Guardian and the Sunday Times Magazine, 1992

Ten mothers-to-be were learning to chill out at an ante-natal relaxation and exercise class in the Prince Regent swimming pool in Brighton.
The buoyancy of the water helped them exercise gently and they had foam rubber rings under their bottoms for stability, which let them float about with just their tummies and faces visible above the water.
They floated about patiently until I had them all lined up. Then a shaft of natural sunlight from the glass panels in the roof illuminated their serene faces and I knew we had something really special.

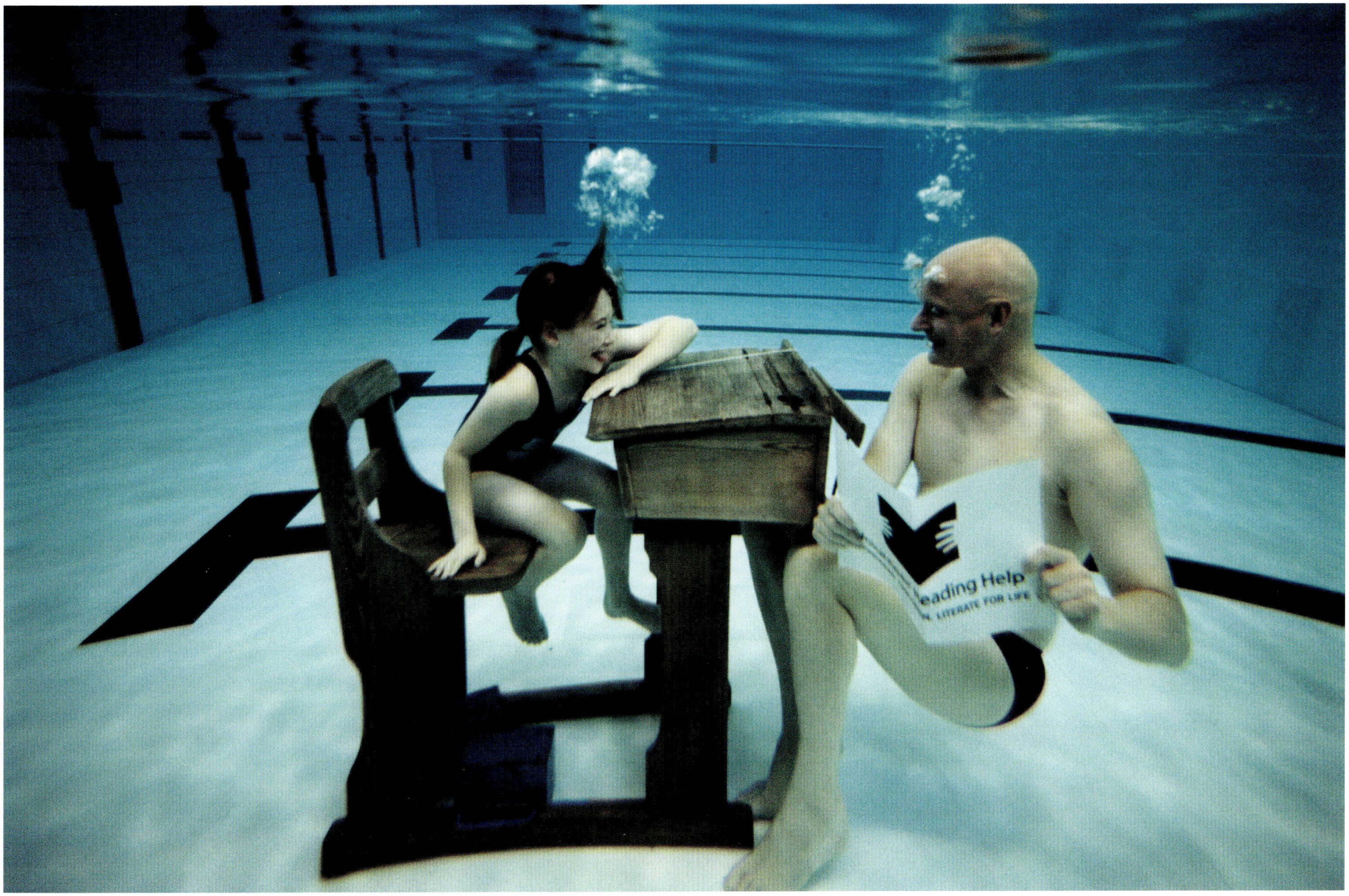

Swimming Lesson

The Guardian, 2000

Olympic gold medal swimmer Duncan Goodhew is dyslexic and had agreed to help promote a reading scheme for kids with similar problems. I suggested that if he really wanted to raise awareness, the best way to do it would be to take to the water.
We set up a classroom at the bottom of a swimming pool in Burgess Hill, Sussex. An old school desk I found in a junk shop was held down by weights. The camera (my usual old Nikon, I've never had a waterproof camera, I can barely swim) was dropped into a clear plastic case, pushed down into the water by burly swimming pool attendants.
Two little girls, great swimmers both of them, took it in turns to hold their breath and sink to sit at the desk with Duncan. Who, of course, was in his element. This picture was the one that clinched it because they just looked so relaxed, as if they were actually breathing underwater.

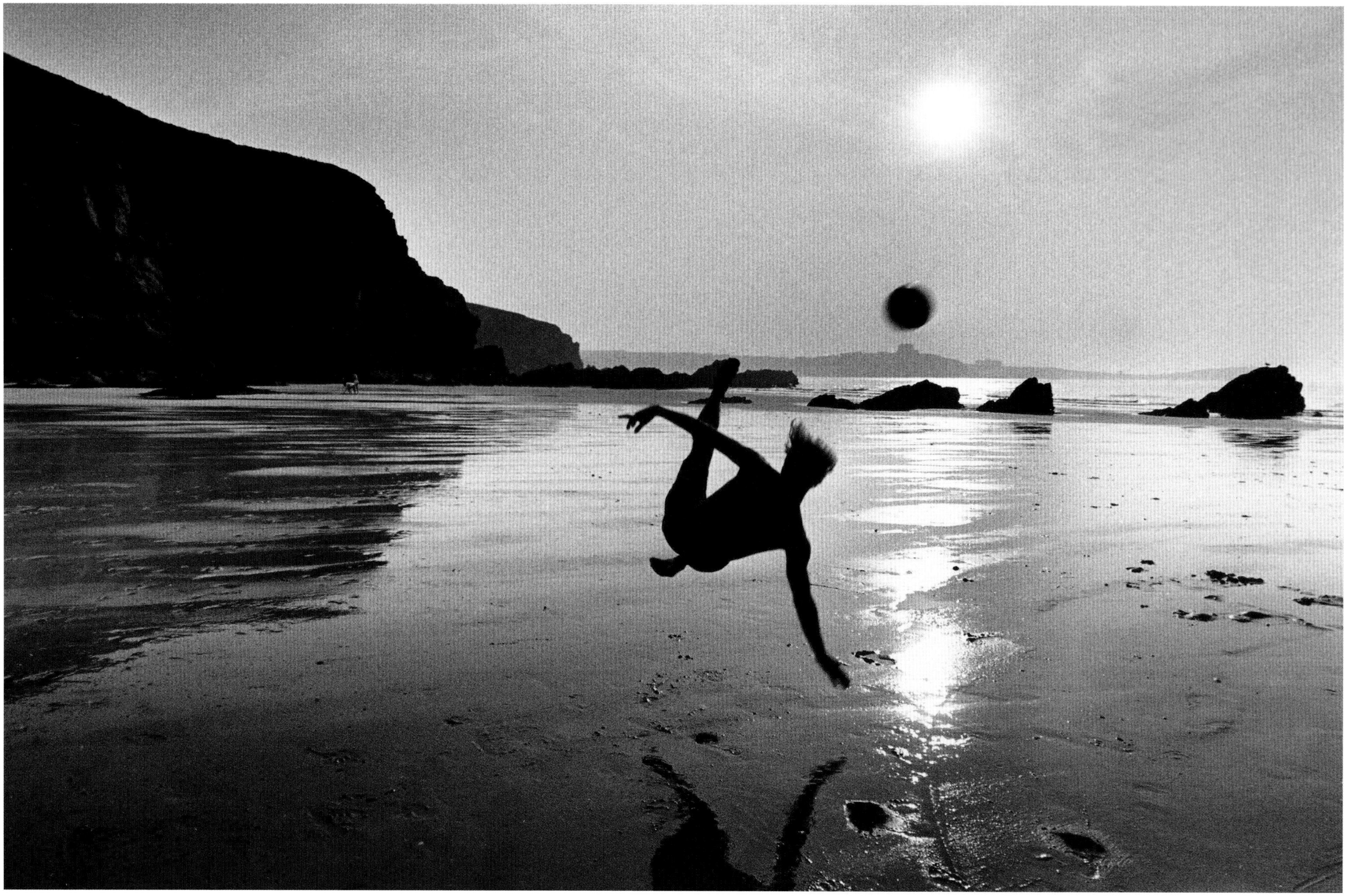

Beach Boy

The Guardian, 1991

I saw a small news item saying beautiful Lusty Glaze Beach near Newquay, North Cornwall had been put up for sale at £250,000, complete with twenty-six beach huts. (And 230 wooden steps up to the main road.) I thought it might make a picture story.
It was late afternoon when I arrived and most of the holidaymakers had straggled off. A group of lads were enjoying a last game of football under the cliff. This young lad was trying to impress his mates with scissor kicks. The image sailed straight into the paper.

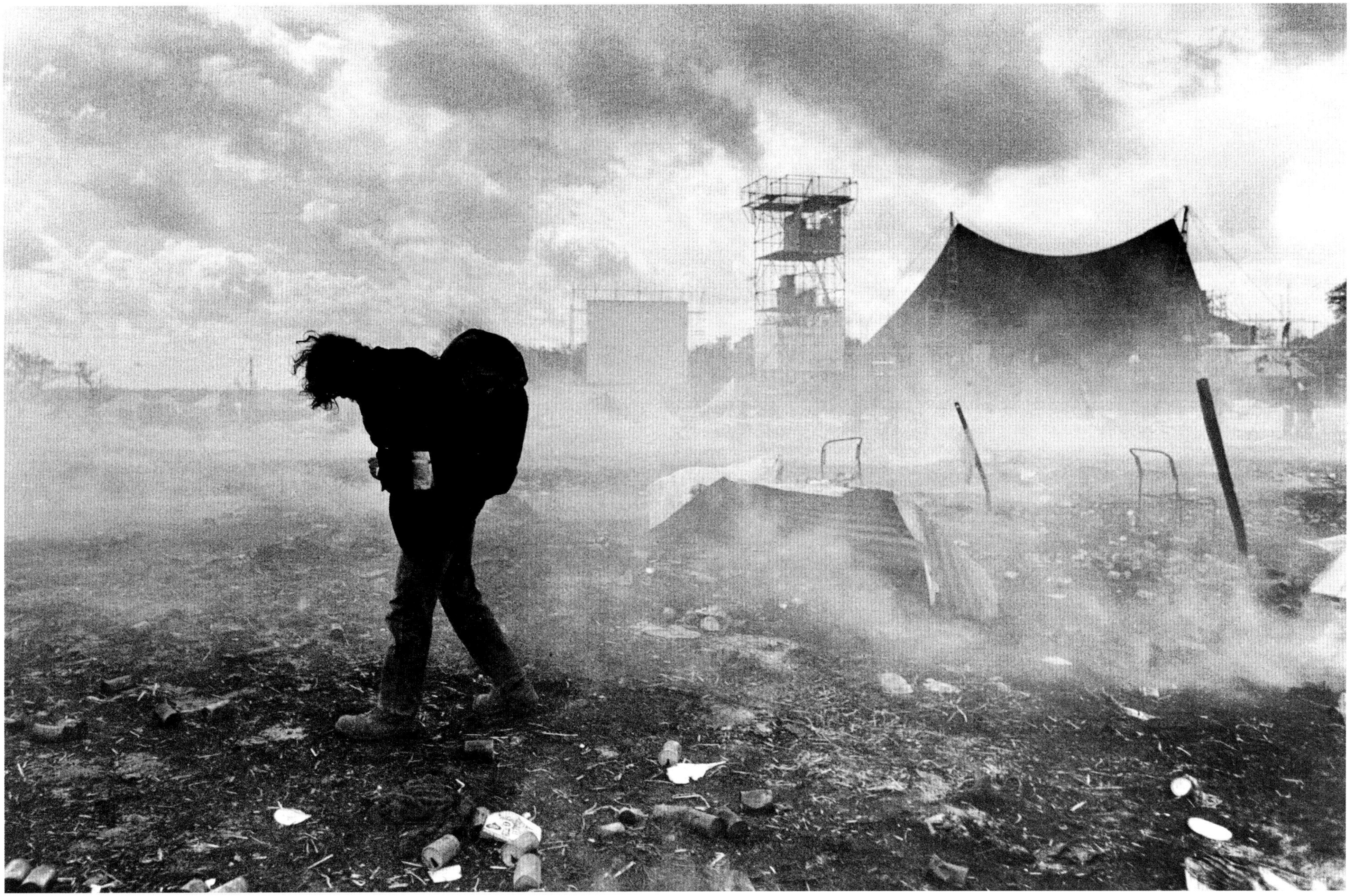

Going Home

The Sun, 1972

A music fan makes his way through the dawn mist after a three-day pop festival at Bardney, Lincolnshire. Outrageous and successful American festivals in Woodstock and their British counterparts in 1969 and 1970 on the Isle of Wight had made these events – and the army of fans who flocked to them – big news.

I often photographed the fans as much as the musicians. Top names such as the Beach Boys, Rod Stewart and Genesis were all at this event but never appeared in the paper.

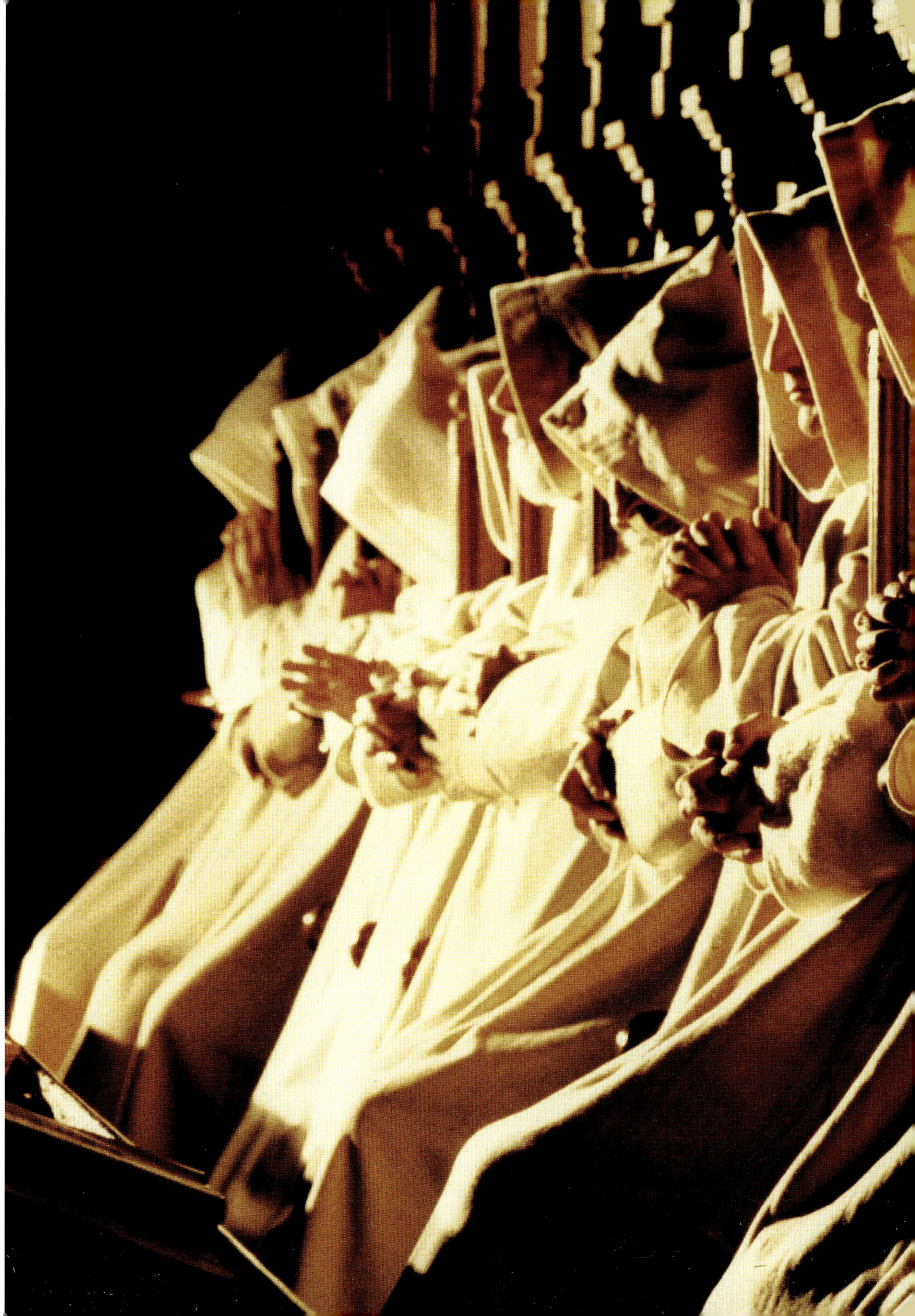

Silent Order

The Guardian, 1998

Carthusian monks from St Hugh's Charterhouse monastery in Cowfold, West Sussex at prayer in vespers, late at night. The prior allowed me into the service and gave me just a few minutes to light and photograph the monks at the end of the prayers. Cameras were usually utterly forbidden but they had made a recording of their Gregorian chants to raise money for the restoration of the monastery and this was to give their project some publicity.

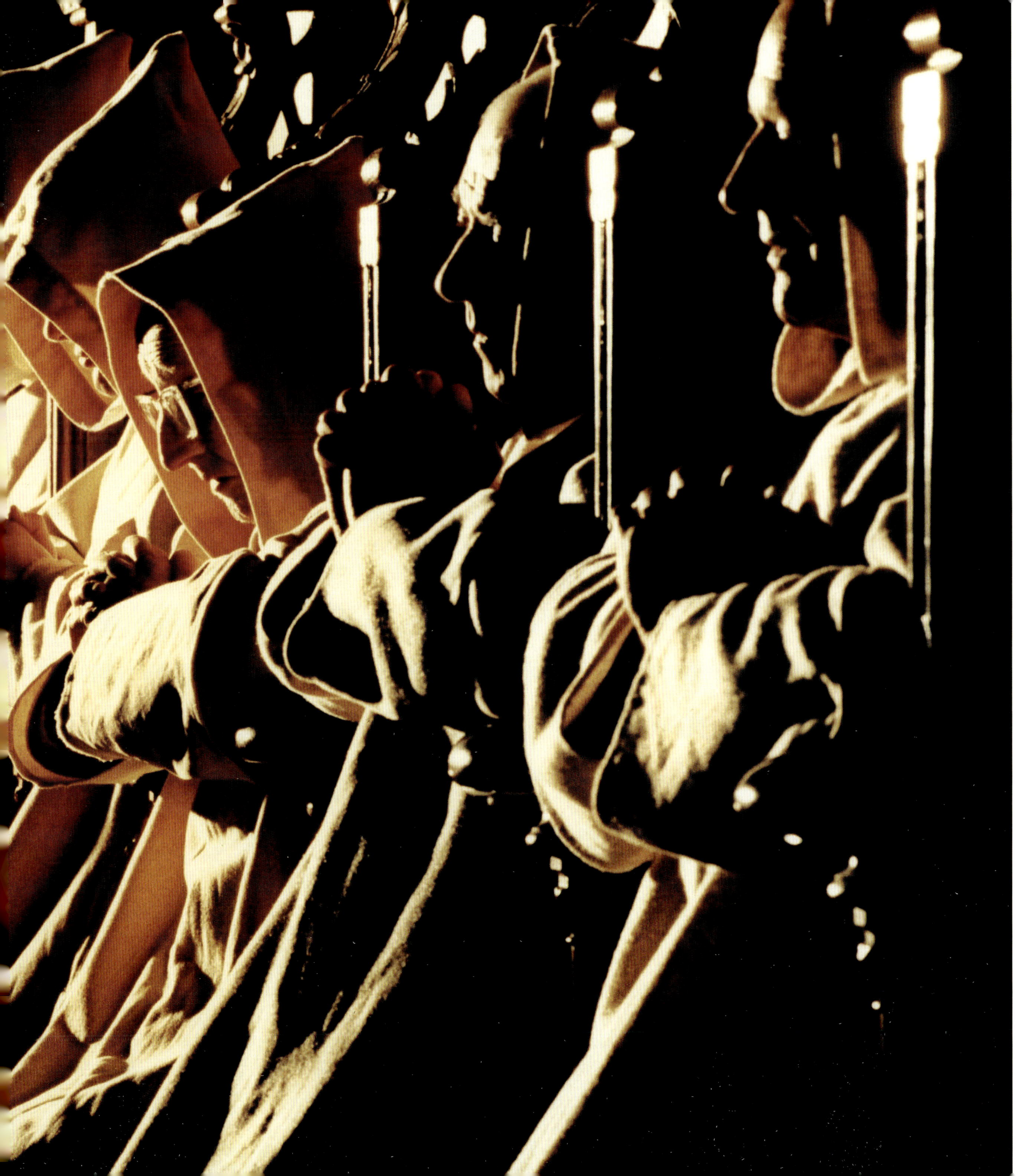

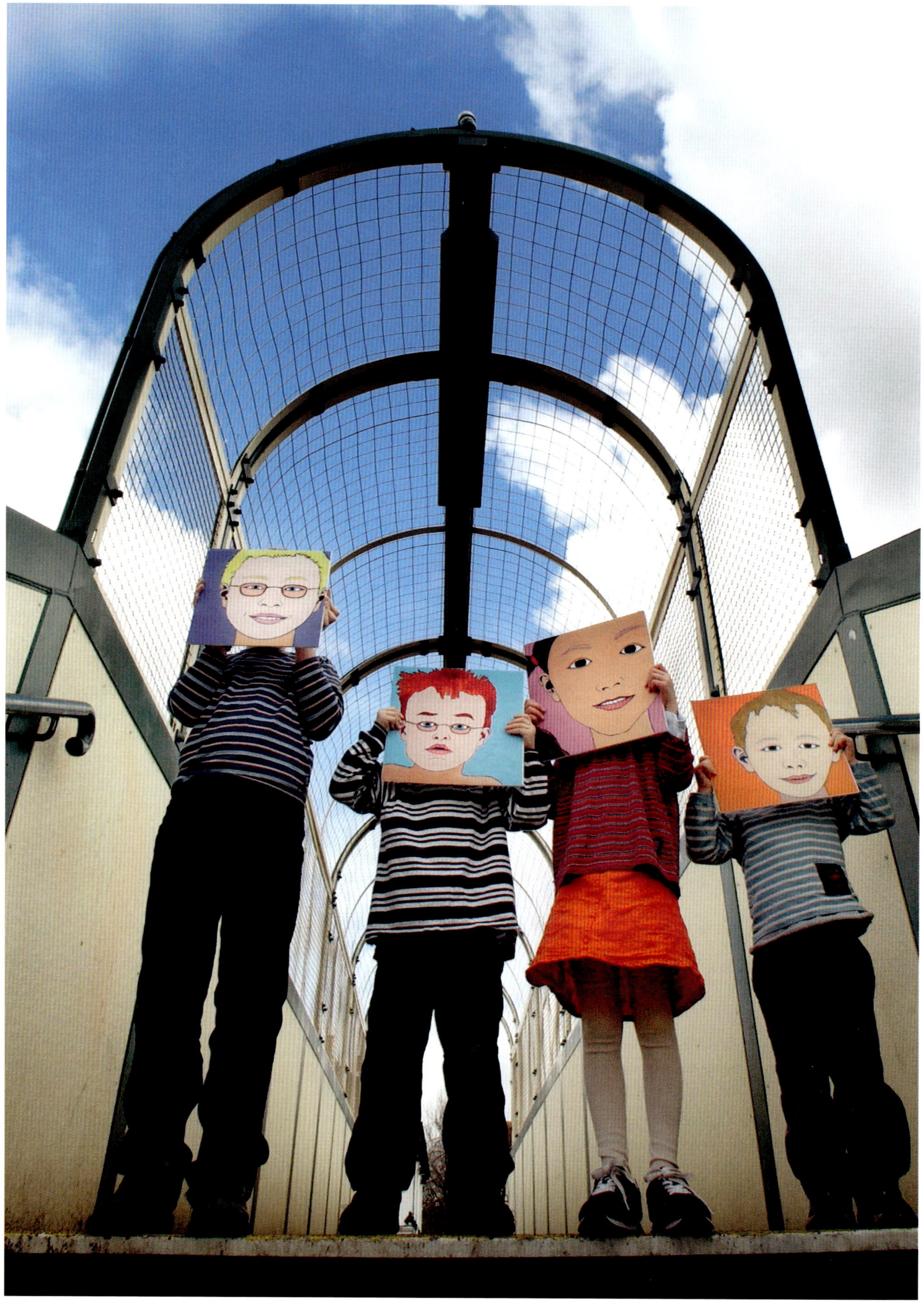

A Family Affair

The Guardian, 2004

The four grandchildren of artists Fran Slade and Colin Ruffell posed on a bridge at London Road Station, Brighton. They were holding portraits of themselves, painted by Fran, which were part of an Open House exhibition during the 2004 Brighton Festival. The whole family – children, parents and grandparents – all showed paintings and sculptures and it was one of the most popular fringe exhibitions of the year. Left to right: Remus and Marlon Gerard, Eden and Lucien Ruffell.

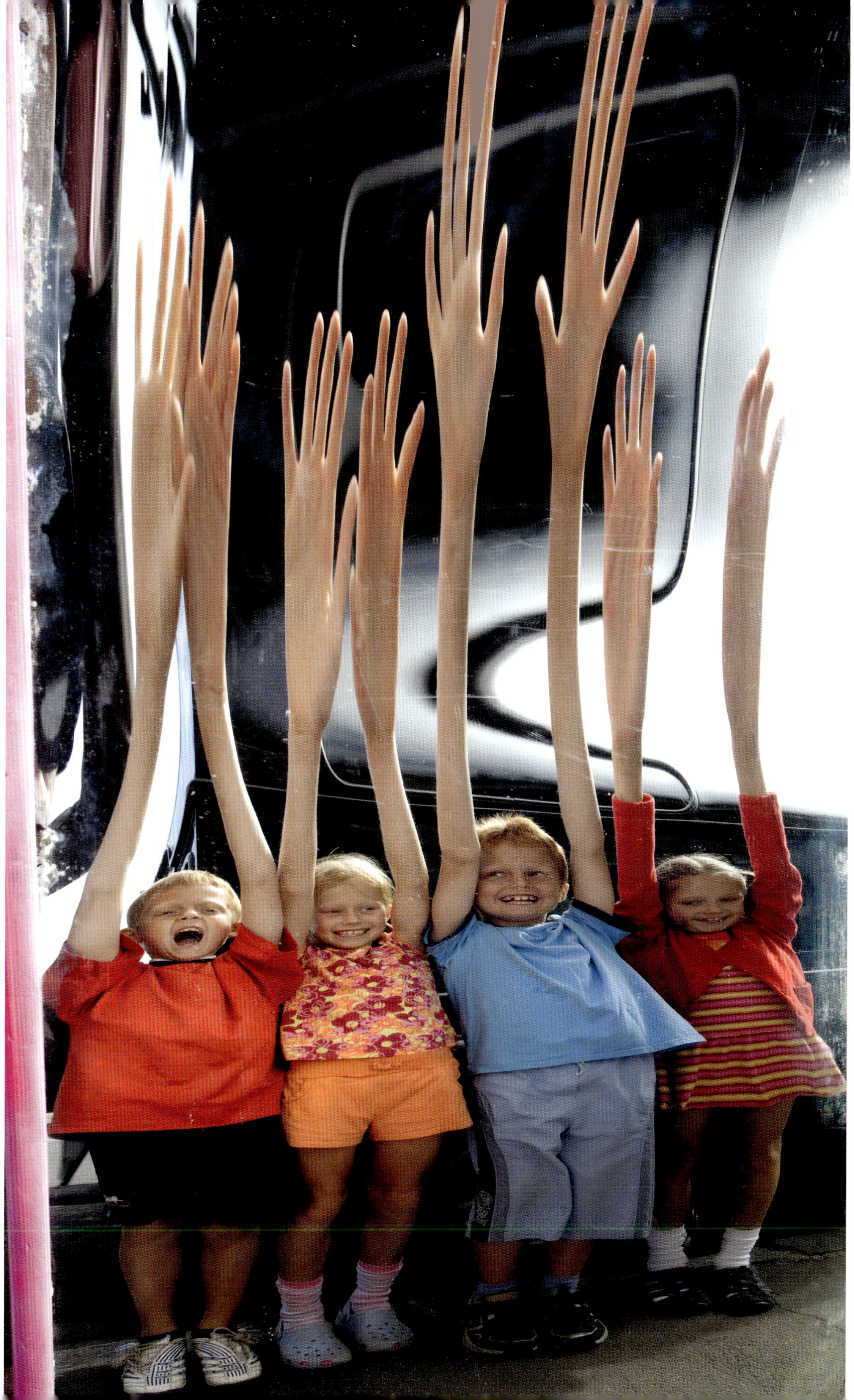

Hands Up!

The Guardian, 2009

Driving down a road in Hove, a friend of mine discovered a tatty old amusement arcade mirror from Brighton Palace Pier dumped in a builders' skip. He managed to hoist it out before the skip was removed and asked me if I'd like to use it for anything. I did, for several projects, but the happiest pictures were of local children larking about during the school holidays.

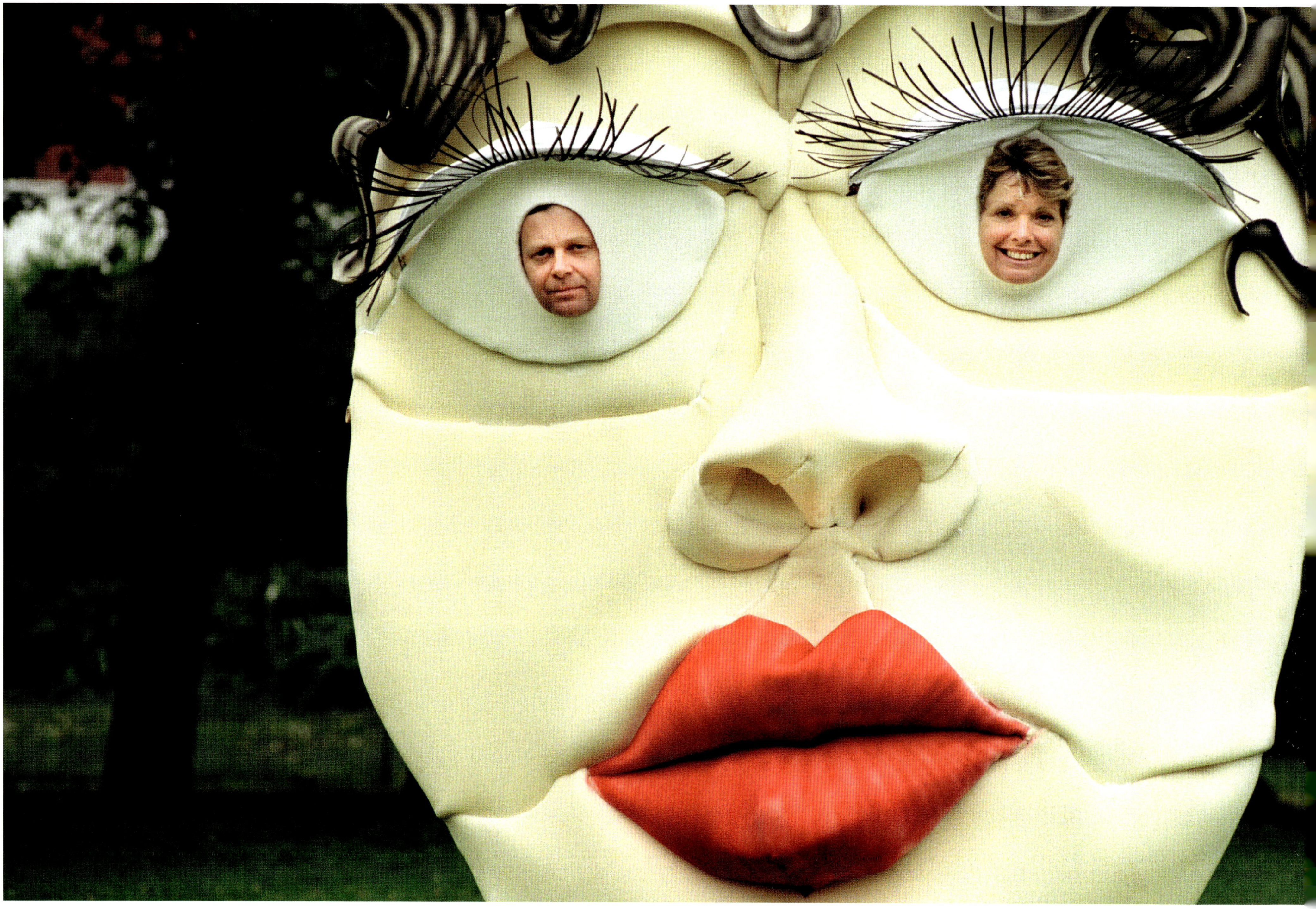

Face to Face

The Guardian. 1996

What can you do with the soberly dressed and sensible looking organisers of arty events to get their faces in the news? In 1996 I took two giant eyeballs out of a foam rubber sculpture and coaxed the Brighton Festival chief Chris Barron and his fellow director Deborah Grubb to clamber up stepladders into the huge head. They popped their heads into the eye sockets which made an eye-catching portrait.

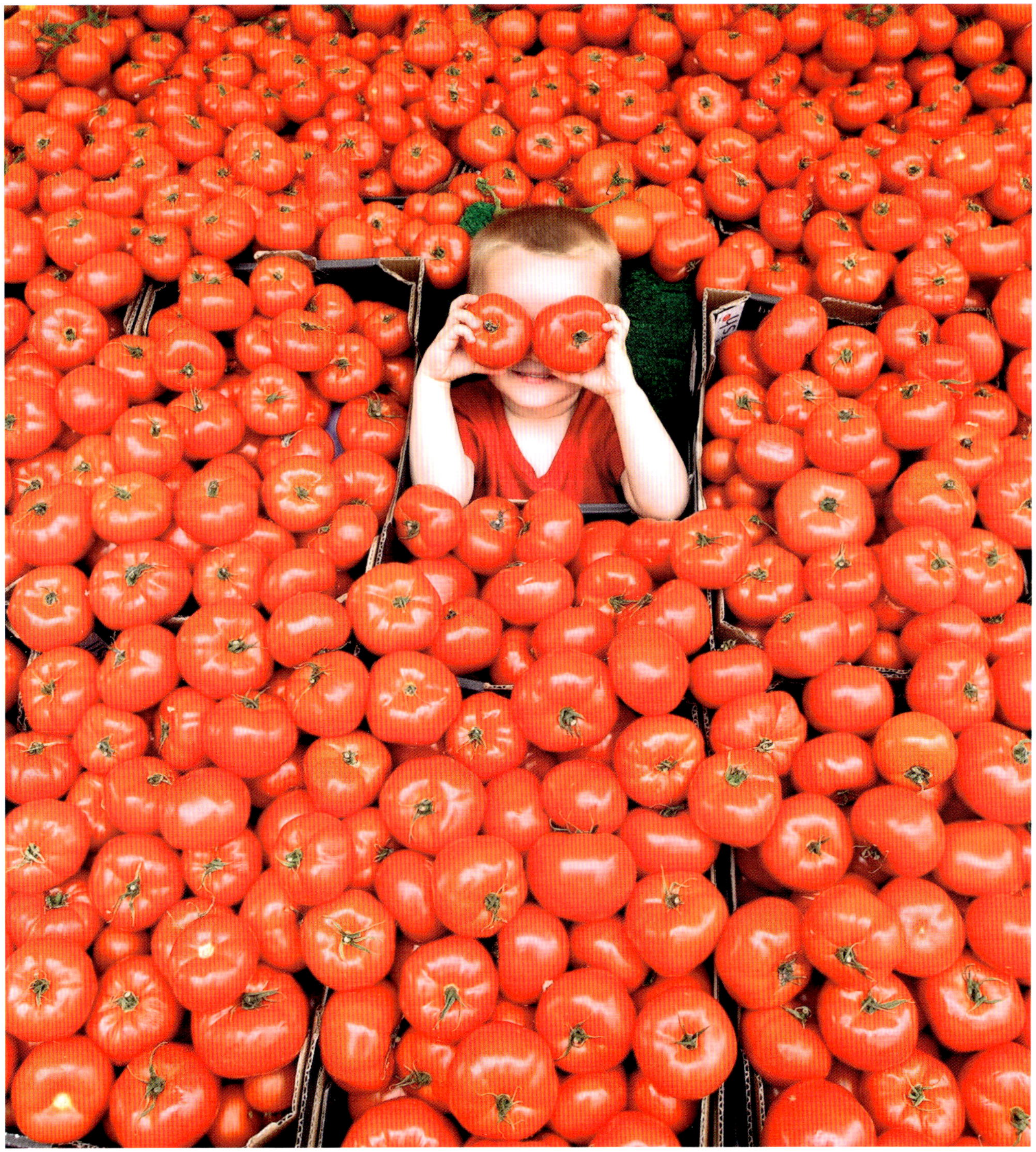

Seeing Red

The Guardian, 2004

I was asked for an image to illustrate a 'Five a Day' fruit and veg feature. The obvious place to start was Brighton Open Market, where I met this little boy out shopping with his mum. I explained I needed to put a child into a big display of fruit, preferably the hundreds of English beef tomatoes on the C H Mears stall nearby.
She agreed to lend me her lad and we dropped him into a space where he started playing with the tomatoes, pretending that they were his eyes. It was his idea, not mine! And he was only three years old. His wonderful mum meanwhile had agreed to crawl under the stall to hold him at the right height for the picture – so this is all very much about the kindness of strangers. And the picture went down so well it was also used as a poster for a food festival.

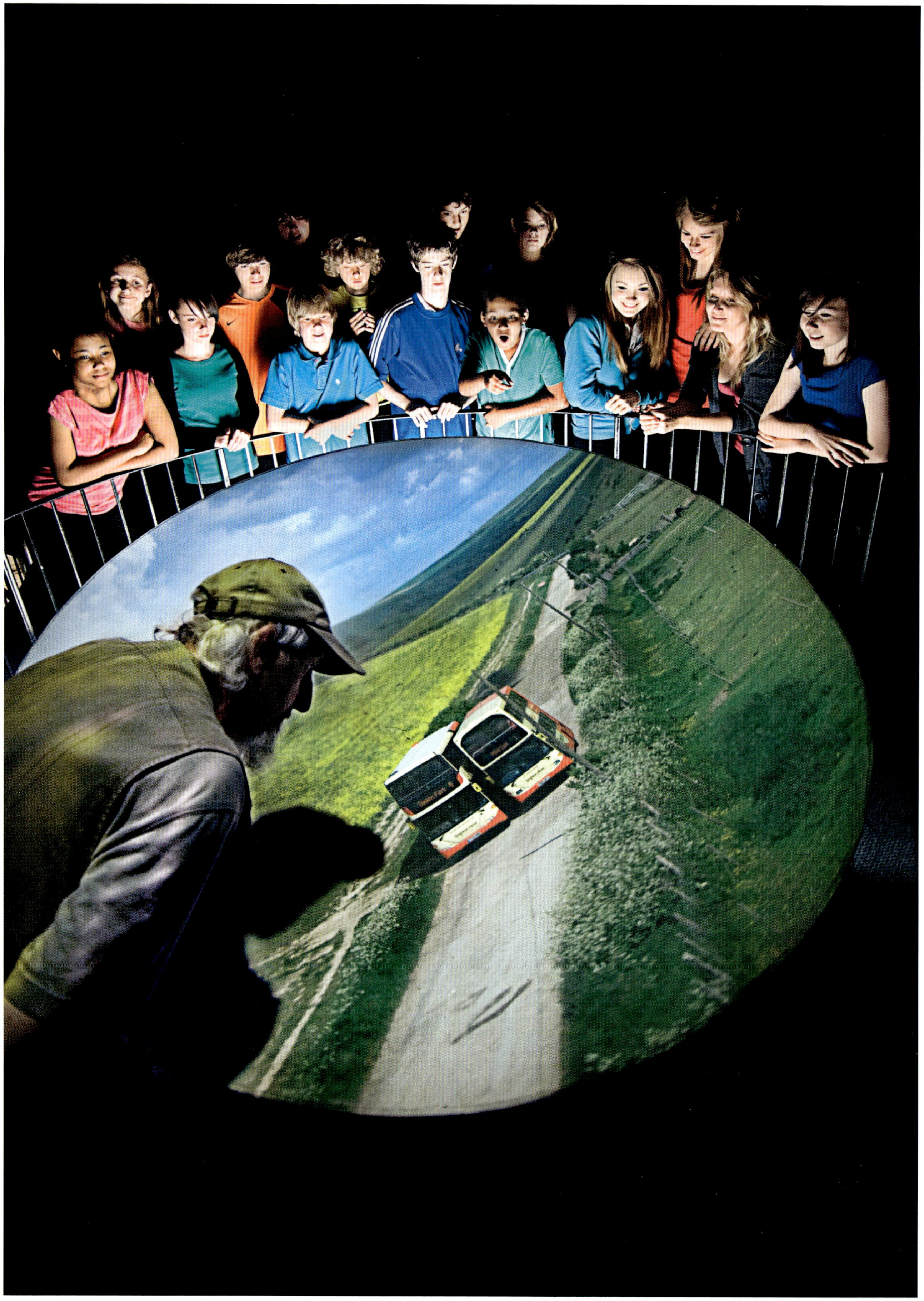

Darkroom

Brighton Bus and Coach Company, 2011

Mick Feist, the curator at Foredown Tower, Portslade, Sussex, was explaining the workings of a camera obscura to eleven to thirteen-year-old schoolchildren from Portslade Community College. Camera obscura means dark room. It's a very ancient forerunner of today's cameras but you can't put it in your pocket. It's a whole room. Light comes in through a tiny hole in a wall, passes through a lens and is reflected on a surface opposite, so you can see the surrounding landscape, sun and sky. In its day it was a big attraction and this one, housed in a converted Edwardian water tower, has a viewing gallery which offers 360 degree views, from the Isle of Wight to the South Downs. Or, as in this case, the road below with two buses passing. The exposure of the image on the screen was so dim that I needed a torch to position the children and curator, then took the picture in what to them seemed to be complete darkness.

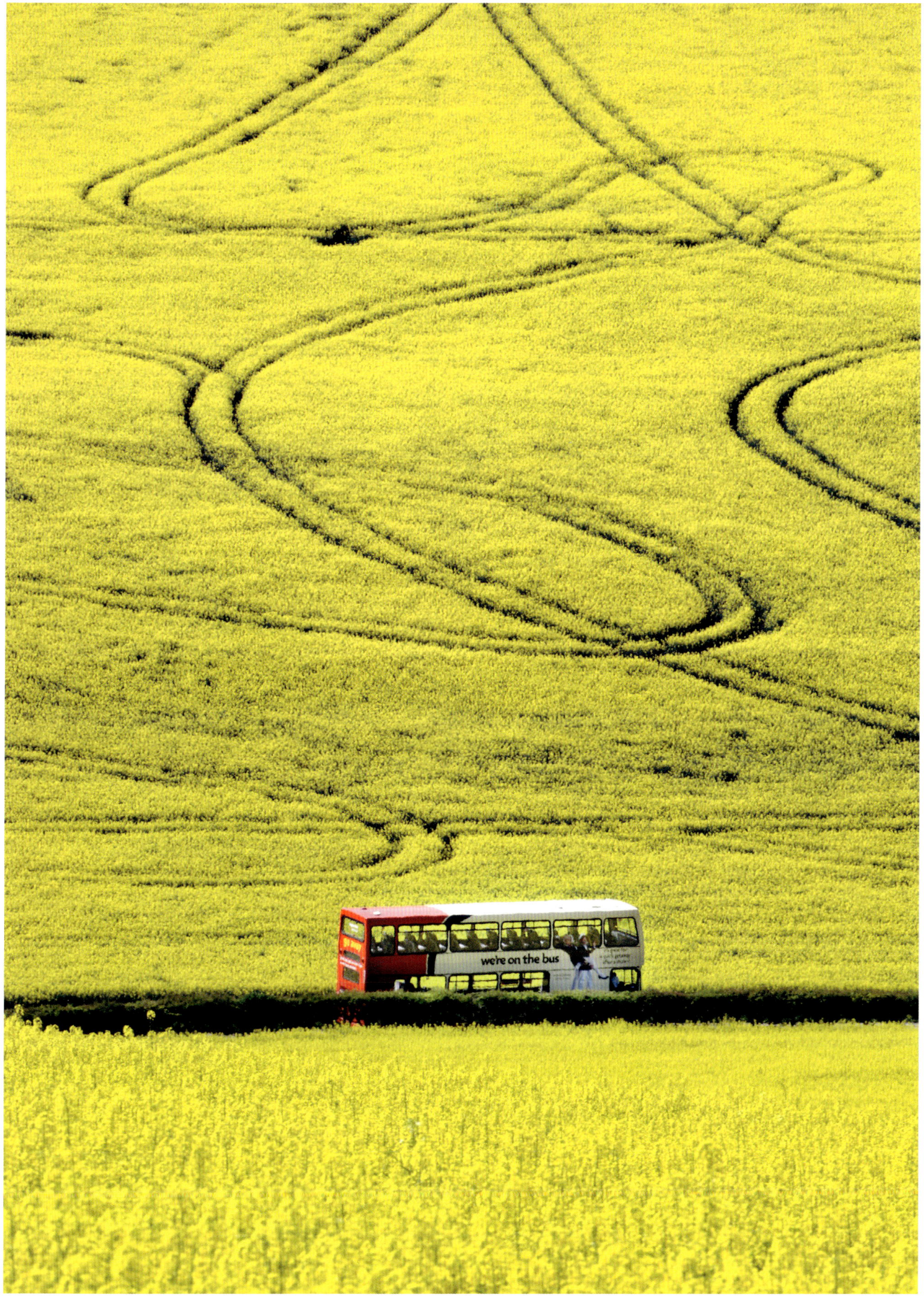

Magic Bus

Brighton Bus and Coach Company, 2009

Transport of all kinds always interested me. Even buses, which are shaped like bricks and are nobody's idea of glamorous travel, have a certain charm when you get to know them. For more than ten years Roger French, the Brighton bus company's managing director, commissioned me to produce covers for the company's *Bus Times* magazine, and let me do anything I liked with his vehicles as long as it wasn't boring.
When I saw these tractor tracks criss-crossing a golden field of rape on the road to Lewes, I knew a little cream and red country bus would complete the picture perfectly. I borrowed a bus, with a driver who patiently went up and down the road until everything lined up just as I'd imagined it.

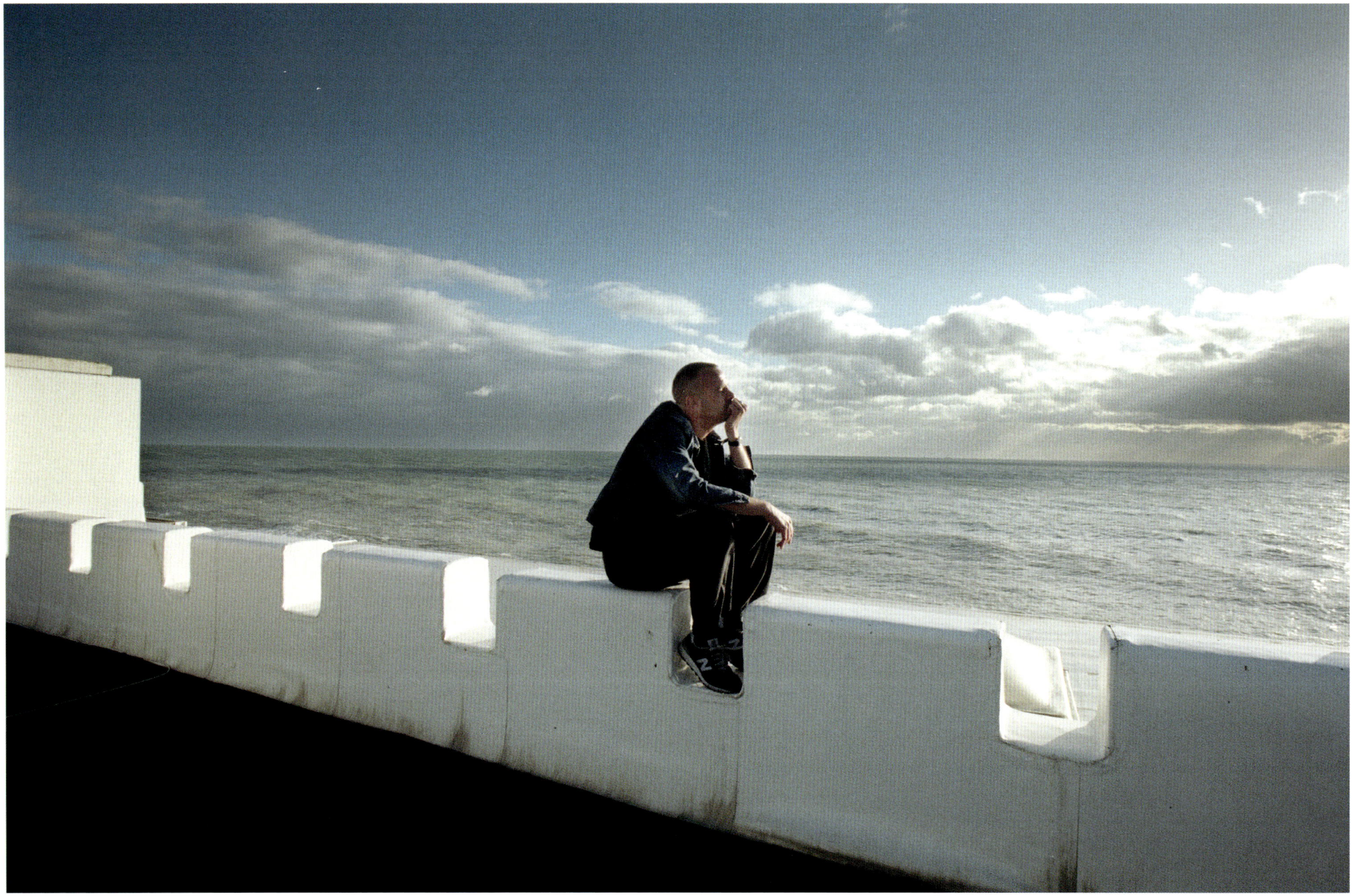

Chilling Out

The Guardian, 1999

Musician, DJ and legendary rave and beach party organiser Norman Cook, aka Fatboy Slim, has a seafront house tucked away behind a scruffy, industrial area in Hove. He likes to sit on the roof terrace and just chill, so that's what he did when I went to photograph him.
It was 1999 – his music had defined the '90s and I expected ... well I'm not sure what I expected but not the very low-key, calm friendly guy I found.
I loved the tranquil setting he chose and whenever he was in the news, with some new monster event at a superclub or opening a vast festival, I always thought of him in his special, peaceful place.

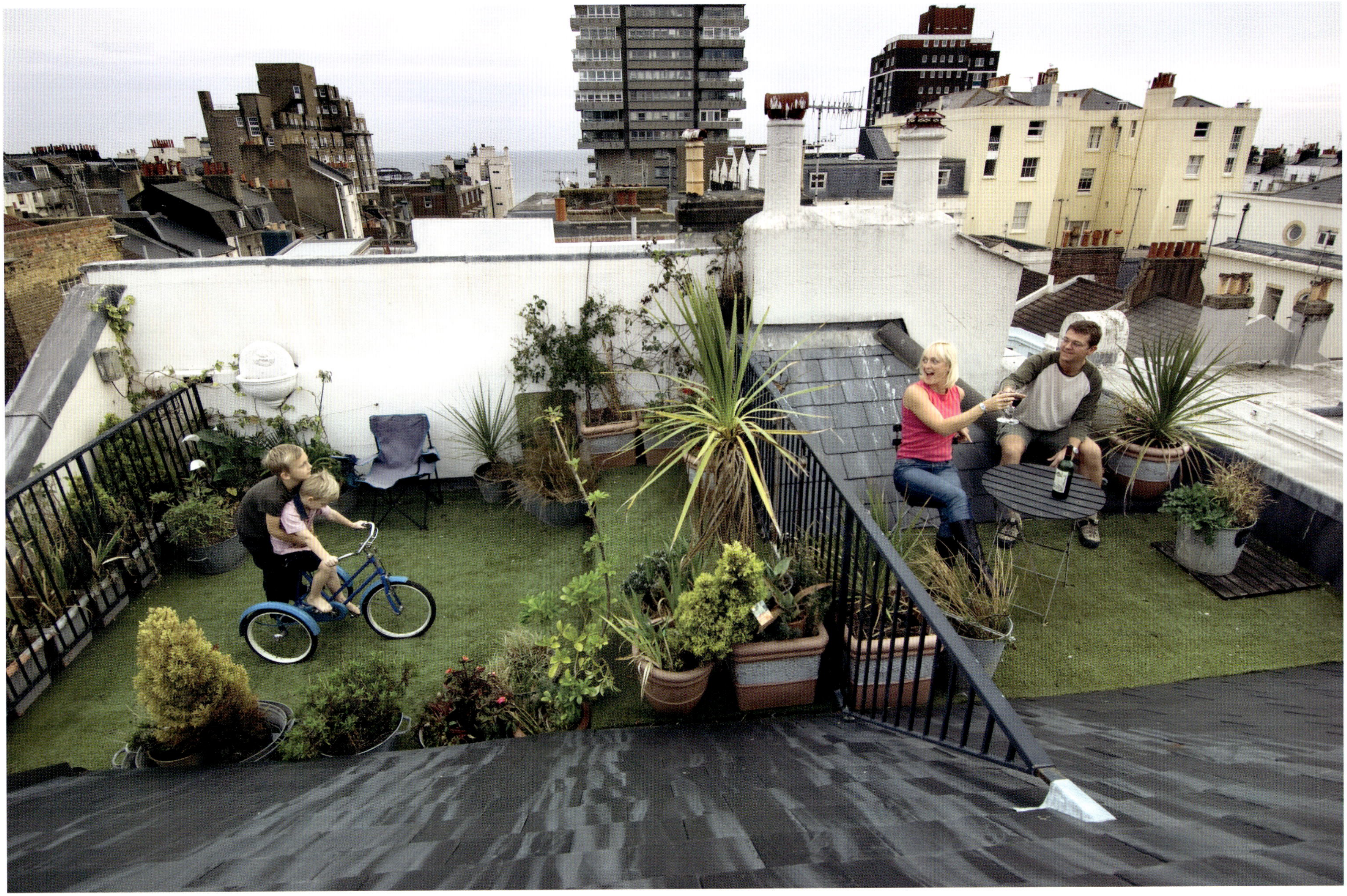

Home Turf

The Times colour supplement, 2007

Tania and Greg Schnuppe only had one scrap of open space for a garden – amongst the chimney pots on the roof of their house in the centre of Brighton. Their sons, Ben (four) and Max (five), had just enough room to play on their tricycle while their parents relaxed with a drink.
In the densely populated city, few residents have conventional gardens. There are a surprising number of these secret little patches, carved out on rooftops, complete with artificial grass, potted plants and, for the lucky ones, sea views.

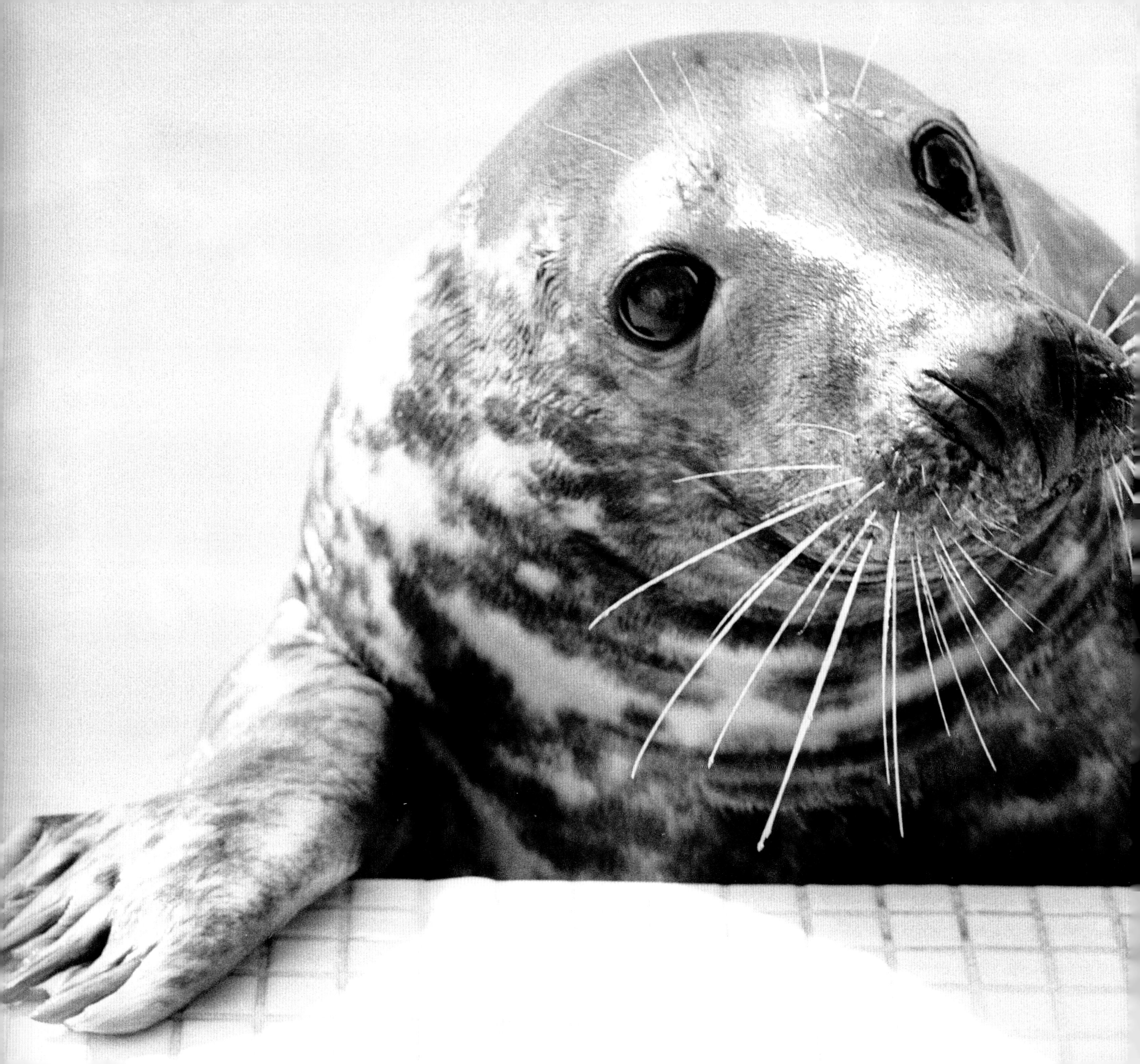

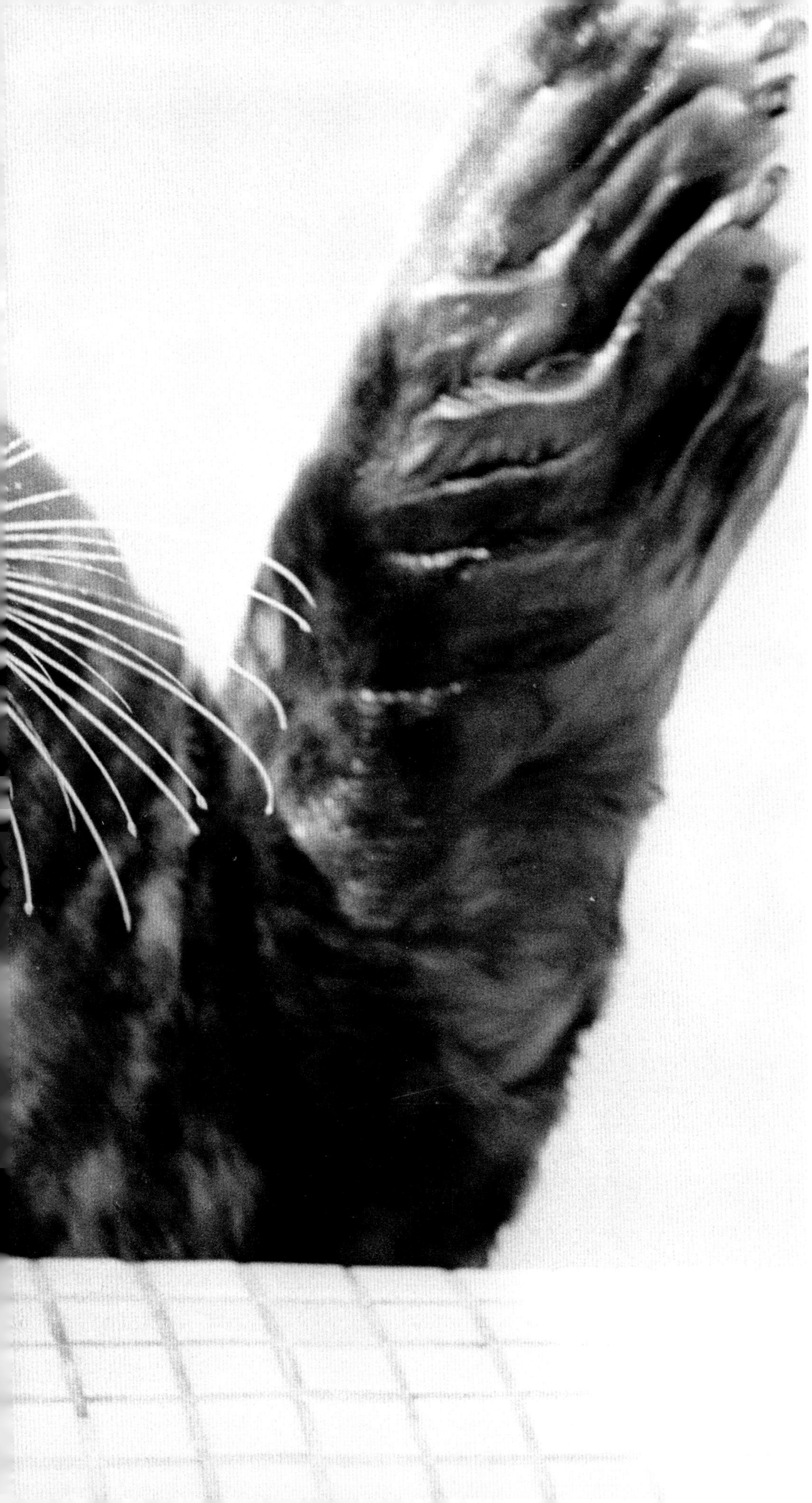

On the waterfront.

The Guardian, 1994

Twiggy was a grey seal captured as a pup and sold to a circus. When the circus closed she was kept for a miserable seventeen years as a curiosity at the back of a pub in Humberside, with only a bathtub as a pool. She was finally rescued by the RSPCA in 1994 and brought to the Cornish Seal Sanctuary at Gweek, where I found her adjusting to life in the nursery pool. She was never able to return to the wild but lived to enjoy nine years of loving care at the Sanctuary, in peace and security.

Roger in his own words

The younger of two children of Vera, who worked in the local textile trade making vests and socks, and Fred, a telephone operator, was born in the Leicester Royal Infirmary on 31 August 1944. That was me.

I did well at school but was a bag of nerves at exams, failed my 11 plus and was relegated to a grim secondary modern, where I was expected to do well, sailed through the mock O Levels, and then spectacularly failed the real exams. There was no question of retakes, and I left the next day.

By then I had been introduced to the world of photography as a thirteen-year-old schoolboy, without knowing it, on Platform 3 of Grantham railway station. It was the down platform for trains to Newcastle and the north, and on an overcast summer's day in 1958 I had cycled the 30-odd miles from home to enjoy a day of watching steam trains. A sleek, streamlined, shiny green machine flashed through the viewfinder of my parents' Kodak Brownie Cresta II plastic camera, at a dashing 70mph. The very basic camera only had a shutter speed of a fortieth of a second which wasn't ideal to capture this speedy beast. Nor was the plastic lens able to produce a quality result, but it was a surprising, atmospheric picture of a steam-hauled express, sharp on the locomotive pulling the train, yet strangely muzzy on the surrounding station. There's a power and an aura about a machine that breathes and wheezes at you and suddenly I'd got it on film.

At the same time I was getting up at six every day to do a paper round. I enjoyed racing up and down the streets on my bike, trying to beat my best time for delivering everything before breakfast and school, and I also liked flicking through all the different papers while I waited in the shop for my load. It was the photographs that interested me – grainy black and white and often as muzzy as my steam train. I tried to work out how they were taken and why they were chosen.

After the O levels disaster my academic career had screeched to a halt, and I was clearly not destined for the school's improbable suggestion of a career as a statistician. My mother thought for a bit about her peculiar sixteen-year-old son, and then marched me round to Leicester College of Art, where that Grantham photograph, along with a few others, got me a place on a graphic art course.

I armed myself with a Rolleicord, almost as good as the photographer's workhorse of the time, a Rolleiflex, and an exposure meter. Halfway through the three year course I discovered the delights of a thrillingly modern single lens reflex Nikon F. I had to have it. At £80 it consumed my student grant for the entire year, but I had part-time jobs selling car and bike bits at Halfords and cameras that I knew absolutely nothing about in Dixons, so I could pay my Mum for my food and buy film.

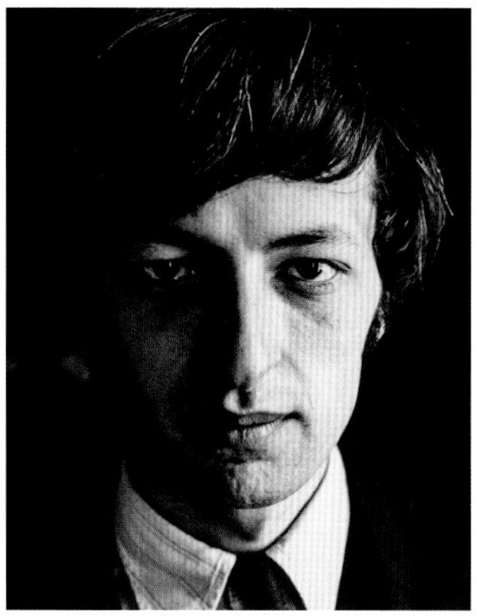

Portrait of Roger Bamber by Cecil Beaton, 1965

College done, my first jobs out in the world without much of a clue how to actually do anything, were as an assistant dogsbody on the small *Women's Mirror* in London that folded nine months later, and after I returned to Leicester, tail between legs, in a small but forceful advertising agency which taught me a lot about lighting but failed to excite me with the subjects – gents' smart slacks and mid-price shoes.

Back at my art college things had changed. A new full-time photography course opened, and the new head asked me to become his deputy, aged nineteen and teaching students mostly older than me. I only did it for a year, but it felt like ten, though it was good fun working with other people. It gave me the confidence to take my portfolio to Fleet Street, having learned that my future wasn't in teaching others.

My first stop in Fleet Street was an unannounced visit to the top paper of the day – the *Daily Express*, housed in a stunning black glass building that looked more like an ocean-going liner than a newspaper. It's hard to believe now but this was the powerhouse paper of the day, using quality pictures, lots of them, by their own stud of top photographers. The picture editor sent an affable man who turned out to be their chief photographer, Terry Fincher, down to the magnificent gold Art Deco lobby, where he looked through my work and informed me that the paper already had a staff of thirty eight photographers plus a squad of freelancers waiting in the wings. The *Daily Mail*, however, was looking for new blood, he said. My portfolio and I left for Tudor Street, home of the *Mail* and a far less glamorous front lobby. This time I was sent straight up to the second floor, where my portfolio did a tour of the picture editor, art editor, news editor, features editor, this editor, that editor. In under three hours I was offered a job.

My salary was £26 a week, in June 1965 a small fortune, and aged twenty I was the youngest staff photographer in Fleet Street.

The twenty or so photographers fought to get their pictures into the *Mail's* new half-page Vision slot, set up as a rival to the *Express* Photonews. One early job which hit the slot was the World Windsurfing Championships in Newquay in 1966. It was a very British disaster. There was no wind for a succession of lovely sunny days. The international champions, flopped on their boards on their bellies, becalmed in a sparkling sea, made the picture.

Industry gave me a few Vision spreads. The closure of the coal mines and the death of steam railways in Britain were both desperately sad but they were a gift for anyone with an eye for stark, graphic black and white images. Coal mine pitheads, and locomotives breathing clouds of smoke and hissing steam, taken up and down the country as the very last of the engines ran their final course before being sold for scrap, all made punchy images for me.

A notable job was being sent to cover an exhibition of Cecil Beaton's work, a day which ended with me persuading the great man to plonk himself on the floor surrounded by piles of his portraits, and Beaton, rather stylishly, choosing the foot of his brass bed to do so. Then he retaliated by grabbing my Nikon F and taking a portrait of me.

Another classic was a 1967 feature on sports day at St Dunstan's home for war-blinded servicemen and women at Ovingdean, which gave me a wonderful image of a powerfully built and totally blind soldier sprinting towards the bleeping noise from a megaphone as he ran flat out to a finish line he had to trust was there. This was the picture which made me realise that one small detail can make people look twice – stop dead and ask, 'What's going on in that picture?'.

Mick Jagger caused a sensation on stage in Hyde Park in 1969 by strutting his stuff in what appeared to be a minidress. It was all ruffles and attitude and it made the *Daily Mail* editor's hair stand on end. The fashion label, Mr Fish, was the culprit and a team was sent to get hold of an identical garment and do a picture of somebody as skinny and hairy as Jagger wearing the damn thing on a busy London street. They didn't have far to look, all eyes pointed at me, so I was forced into Mr Fish's frock (actually a bishop's sleeve tunic according to the fashion editor) and set off for Piccadilly, trailed by a photographer and the fashion editor, where I had to stroll about while passersby gawped. I found it excruciating being on the wrong end of the lens.

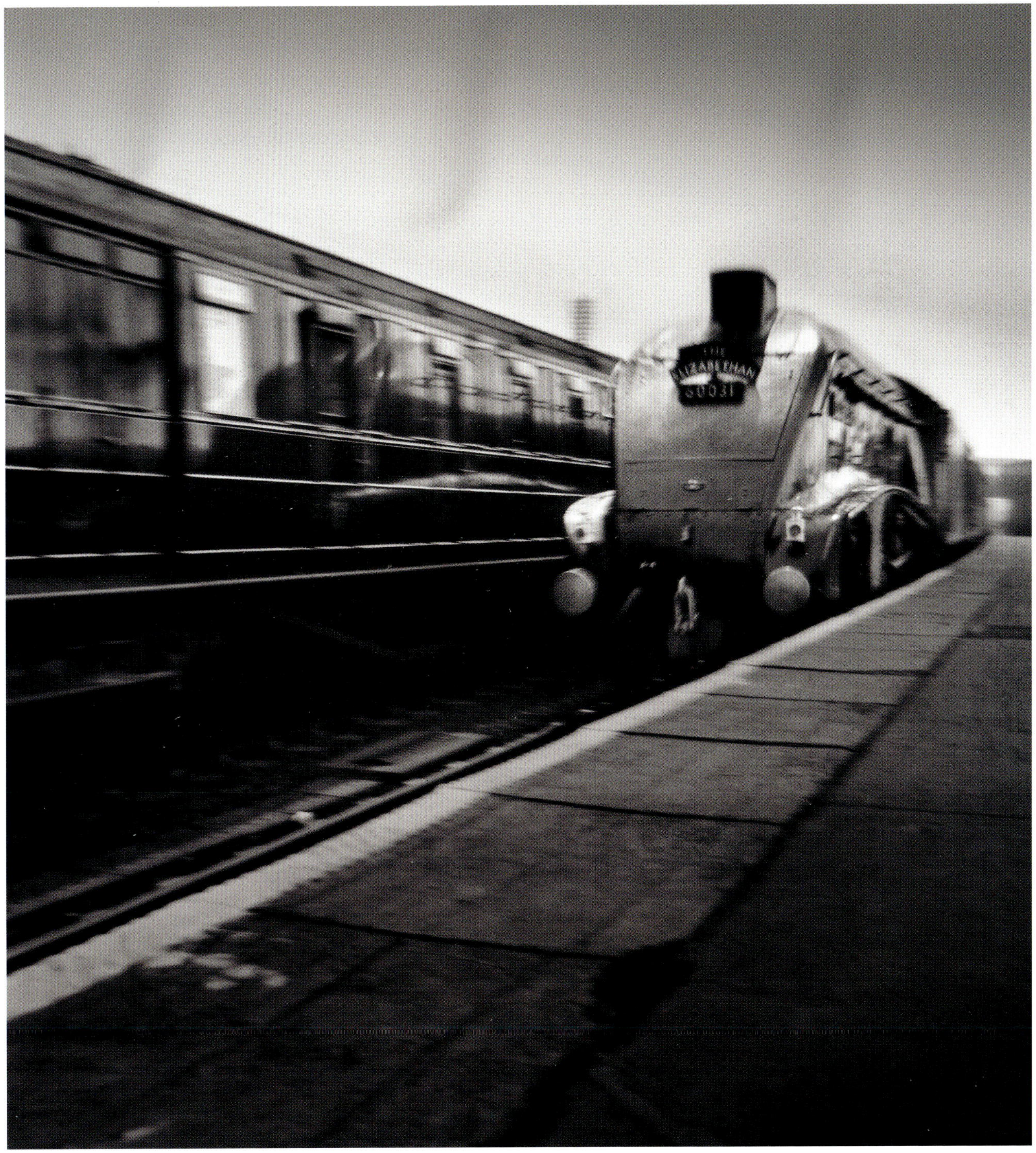

The Golden Plover, photographed by a thirteen-year-old Roger, as it speeds past Platform 3 at Grantham railway station

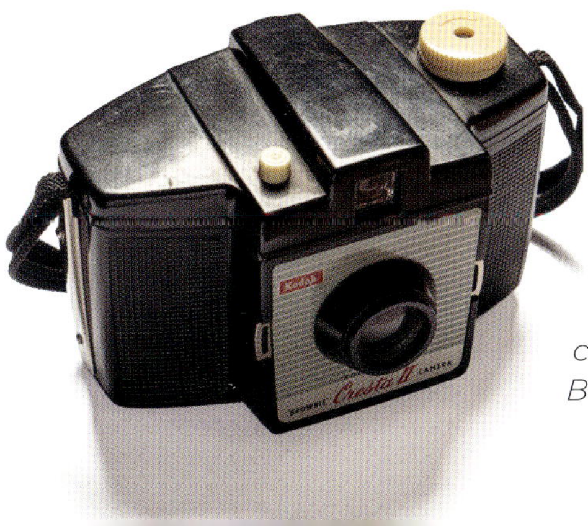

Roger's first camera, a Kodak Brownie Cresta II

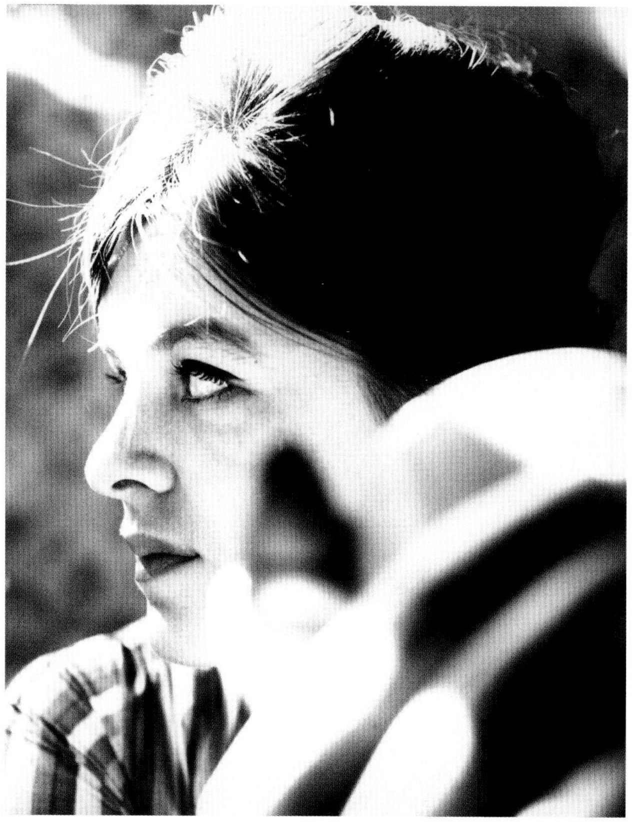

My sister Valerie, 1963. Friend and foe in childhood. My only model as a student, but a stunning one.

Later that year I became the first photographer to report for duty at the *Sun,* headhunted to join pushy Australian newspaper tycoon Rupert Murdoch's new tabloid. As a new paper it hadn't got many adverts, and there was always room for pictures. As no other photographer seemed interested in the modern music scene, I became the pop music snapper as well as hard news. Some of it was very glamorous and some less so. At one festival P.J. Proby got so wasted in the backstage bar that he fell off the stage singing his number one hit 'Hold Me'. Nobody even tried. I doubt if he felt a thing as he landed in the bemused audience.

Among the tours were the Rolling Stones, David Bowie in his Ziggy Stardust days, Marc Bolan and T. Rex, Peter Gabriel, and even the Bay City Rollers. I also borrowed the Page 3 studio whenever a steady stream of artists wanted to come and show off for me, Freddy Mercury and Queen, Brian Ferry, Noddy Holder, Cat Stevens, Suzi Quatro among them.

Sometimes I actually did Page 3 when Bev Goodway, the regular guy, was off: cheerful, charming girls would turn up to strip off in the most matter-of-fact way imaginable. When the *Sun* decided on a pirate theme week for the page, I was a shoo-in so they could by-line me 'Picture by Jolly Roger Bamber'.

In 1973, the IRA set off a car bomb outside Scotland Yard which failed to detonate, another in Whitehall that had little effect, and a car bomb outside the Old Bailey which caused massive damage to buildings and killed one man from a heart attack. In Fleet Street, only a few hundred yards away, people were running around like headless chickens, not knowing where the blast was. I had six pictures in the paper the next morning including a double-page centre spread of two rescuers ushering a shocked and bloodied barrister from the scene, which helped win me News Photographer of the Year.

In 1982, everyone was desperate to cover the Falklands. Every news organisation sent a writer out with the forces, but no photographers were allowed until the prime minister, Margaret Thatcher, intervened and said two Fleet Street photographers should sail with the Task Force. An officer from HMS *Fearless* duly appeared in Portsmouth Dockyard to greet a slavering group of Fleet Street photographers, and invite us all to put our cards in his hat: the Press Association and the *Express* got the golden tickets. The rest of us immediately headed for South America, confident we would find someone insane enough to take us to the Islands by boat or plane: anybody trying that would be blown out of the water and sky, and nobody was keen on risking their lives just for us to take pictures. A grand tour ensued, to Montevideo, on to Buenos Aires, and the world's most southerly city, Punta Arenas. It was a very expensive hiding to nothing: seventy-seven days later and with only one picture in the paper to prove I had been anywhere remotely near the action, the war finished and I was back in a jumbo heading home.

The following year I went back to the Falklands, with reporter Shân Lancaster, to chronicle the changed life of the Islands including troops transporting Rapier missiles up mountain sides on the backs of tiny Falkland ponies, or trailed by excited gaggles of penguins waddling behind them. We reached the Islands by an eighteen-hour flight in a Hercules Royal Air Force plane – essentially a giant flying lorry. This one refuelled in mid-air and I was able to watch and photograph from the cockpit as the pilot inched towards the fuel line being dangled from an aircraft just above us.

I won Photographer of the Year not long after that but I was starting to feel restless. The *Sun* was becoming more and more obsessed with showbiz stories and TV soaps, and less and less interested in the sort of news I enjoyed.

Unrest was brewing in Fleet Street too. First it was the inkies – the printers – striking over pay, then the journos over the dismissal of a staff reporter. Murdoch then played his ace card by moving the *Sun*, *Times*, *Sunday Times* and *News of the World* to his new modern plant in Wapping, leaving the printers out in the cold.

I remember on a Sunday being bused from Bouverie Street over to the new soulless building in Wapping, with computer terminals replacing typewriters and agency printers with no newspaper experience in the darkroom. We had a new room for sixteen photographers, big enough at best to swing two cats. The following day all hell broke out, the start of daily running the gauntlet through the strikers' picket lines – including our much missed photographic printers. It was not a happy time.

It came as a blessing when a meeting of editorial staff was called by the editor Kelvin Mackenzie, trying to persuade us to change our contracts. As the meeting became hostile, he lost his temper and said, 'Anyone who doesn't want to work for a living can take redundancy right now.' By nine the following morning fifty-six staff members had already applied to take the money and run. The management immediately withdrew the offer but the first twenty-two had been accepted: I was applicant twenty-one and the only photographer. I got out with a good payoff for nineteen years' service, my cameras and my office car.

After a short, happy time freelancing in the States, a different and wonderful world for me, I returned to find a new picture editor at the *Observer,* open to any ideas, and for over a year I found idea after idea for the paper. Then out of the blue the *Observer's* sports photographer, Eamonn McCabe, was appointed the new picture editor of the *Guardian*, a job which for me fitted him like a glove, and allowed the paper to challenge the

Cup of Tea: the menu board of a café in Skegness in 1961. We went to Skeggy for our holidays every year and I loved the distinctive lettering that shouted 'Chips' and 'Pot of Tea' as we walked down the road from the station to the sea. This was the very first image I had in an exhibition, a show by Leicester College of Art students in London a couple of years later.

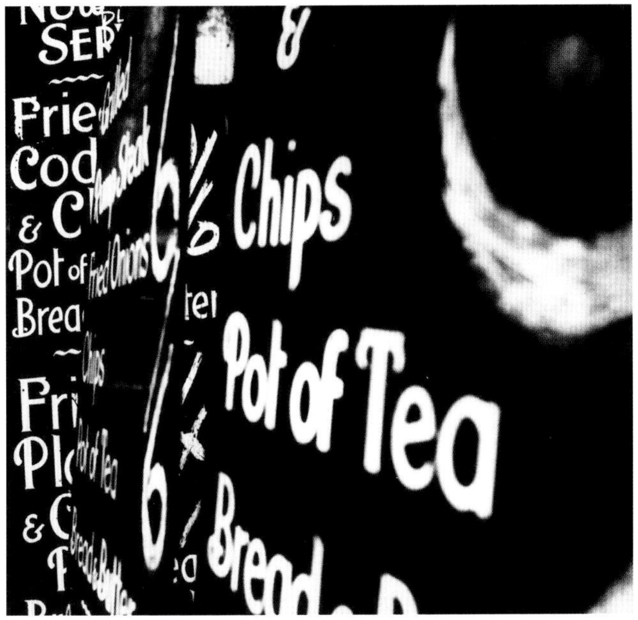

newly launched *Independent* which was making waves with its bold use of pictures. After twenty-five years on a red top tabloid, to get big displays in a quality broadsheet was the icing on the cake. Eamonn's number two was an affable ex-agency man, Alan Sparrow, and number three a computer wizard, Roger Tooth. I felt I was joining the elite in creative photography, not just in London but in Manchester where Denis Thorpe and Don McPhee were friends in the north. An early story in Brighton's intricate brick-lined Victorian sewer tunnels introduced me to the lovely poetic writer Maev Kennedy, and we formed a working relationship for most of my *Guardian* days.

Success seemed to flow through the rest of the '80s and into the '90s, winning me runner-up in the Ilford Press Photographer of the Year in 1991, and the main gong the following year. On one of my few visits to the Farringdon Road HQ of the *Guardian*, I noticed a rack of pigeon holes for photographic prints ready to use on the paper. Each was labelled Education, Politics, Sport, Travel, Finance and so on, every category of pictures needed for editions – then slap bang in the middle was one saying BAMBER PICTURES. Wow, I had my own pigeon hole slot; I knew I must be doing something right.

By 2004 things had changed at the *Guardian*: Alan Sparrow left to open his own business, Eamonn McCabe decided to go back to being a working photographer, specialising in portraits, and the paper had moved to a smaller format and plushy new offices in King's Cross, just around the corner from where I used to go train spotting. My legs were not what they had been – I wish I'd never had that first cigarette – and it was time for me to move on too. I was lucky to live in a place full of artists and quirky people, and I'd got this whopping great beach 200 yards down the road which became my studio. Instead of the stress of supplying newspapers I made local connections, like with a mad hippy called Nigel Swallow who had a gallery and produced a fabulous calendar each year, and Tony Miller of Brighton Council, who had the ambitious idea of producing a council newspaper and commissioned me to do the front covers – the following year it won a Local Government Communication Award. Roger French, the local bus company managing director, so admired my picture of a Brighton & Hove double decker bus overtaking a man who commuted to and from work on a Sinclair C5 three-wheel trike, that I was asked to photograph their timetable covers for the next ten years.

In 2005 the University of Brighton awarded me an Honorary Master of Arts degree. I was spectacularly chuffed, but thought the award would just be a quick handshake and a thank you at the Brighton Pavilion Dome. But ... I learned I was expected to make a long acceptance speech to a sea of gown-clad students wearing mortar boards. My legs turned to jelly as I crossed the stage to the microphone. I started by saying that my name was Roger Bamber, a photographer, and ... after a pause ... that I wasn't used to this and ... that I was BLOODY TERRIFIED. This produced an enormous cheer, and instead of a speech I showed the audience twenty minutes of photographs.

When photographers get together they always talk about their kit, but that doesn't interest me in the slightest. I know how to operate things, but I'm not a wizard – I thought technology peaked with the Nikon F in about 1973. I know never to forget the importance of simplicity, light and shade – and looking for beauty in the ordinary. Going digital took an almighty effort of will but once I adapted I did love the extra range it gave me. I still haven't mastered the TV remote though.

Looking back over a long and lucky life doing a job I love, one thing strikes me straight away. Although I've been able to meet some famous people and travel to some amazing places, many of the most satisfying and successful pictures I've taken have had pretty everyday subjects. This is not a crowd-funded book, but it is a book created by all the crowds of extraordinary people in it who moaned about posing for me – and did it all the same.

Roger Bamber had not completed his account of his own life when he died on 11 September 2022. Shân Lancaster and Maev Kennedy compiled this account from the thousands of words he had written and from the scores of yellow Post-it notes covering his desk.

Roger Bamber 1944-2022

Favourite camera: Nikon F

Awards: News Photographer of the Year 1973
Press Photographer of the Year 1983
News Photographer of the Year 1983
Press Photographer of the Year 1992
(Many others, including Commercial and Industrial Photographer of the Year, Business Photographer of the Year, lots of features gongs and second place in Glamour Photographer of the Year 1972

University of Brighton, Honorary Master of Arts 2005

Favourite music: Stranglers, Supertramp

Favourite films:
Closely Observed Trains (bw, Czechoslovakia, 1966);
Shaun the Sheep (Aardman Animations, 2015)

Favourite colour: Black and white

Met Shân Lancaster in 1979 when both working for the *Sun*; they married at Brighton Pavilion, 2004

Published in 2023 by Unicorn
an imprint of Unicorn Publishing Group LLP
5 Newburgh Street
London
W1F 7RG
www.unicornpublishing.org

ISBN 978-1-911397-16-8

10 9 8 7 6 5 4 3 2 1

Designed by Alex Bamford
Printed in the UK

Majority of images available at TopFoto.co.uk

Acknowledgements

Alex Bamford, The Man Of The Match for countless hours designing and discussing the damn thing, Finn Hopson for making my prints look their best and Nigel Swallow for years of creative input and fun. These three have been fantastic friends and without them this project would never have made it to the press.

I am also grateful to so many other friends for their help and encouragement over the years: Larry Bartlett; Steve Bassam; Robin Bell; Theo Bergström; Tom Buckeridge; Alan Capel; Wilfred and Jeanette Cass; Ewan Clayton; Terry Fincher; Sarah Hayworth; Stuart Higgins; Jim Holden; Thurston Hopkins; Lianne Jarrett; Maev Kennedy; Roger French; Brian Harris; Murdo MacLeod; Eamonn McCabe; Janet Midwinter; Tony Miller; Jeff Morgan; Grace Robertson; Peter Robinson; Joan Sisley; Flora Smith and all at TopFoto; Alan Sparrow; Arthur Steel; Tom Stoddart; Denis Thorpe; Adrian Turner.

Special thanks to Rebecca Smithers for her contribution and support.

And to my sister Val.

This book is
dedicated to my
lovely Shân

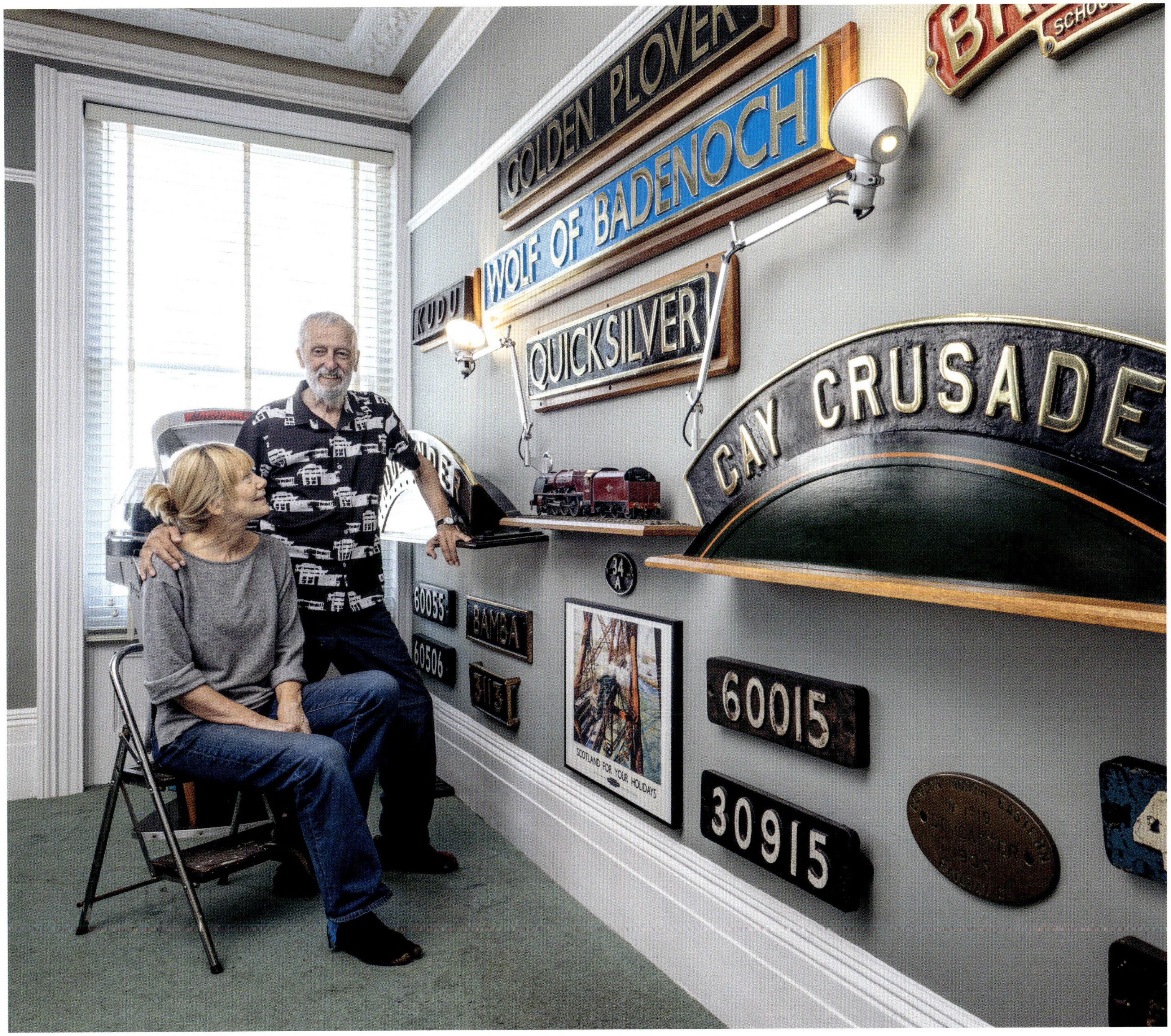

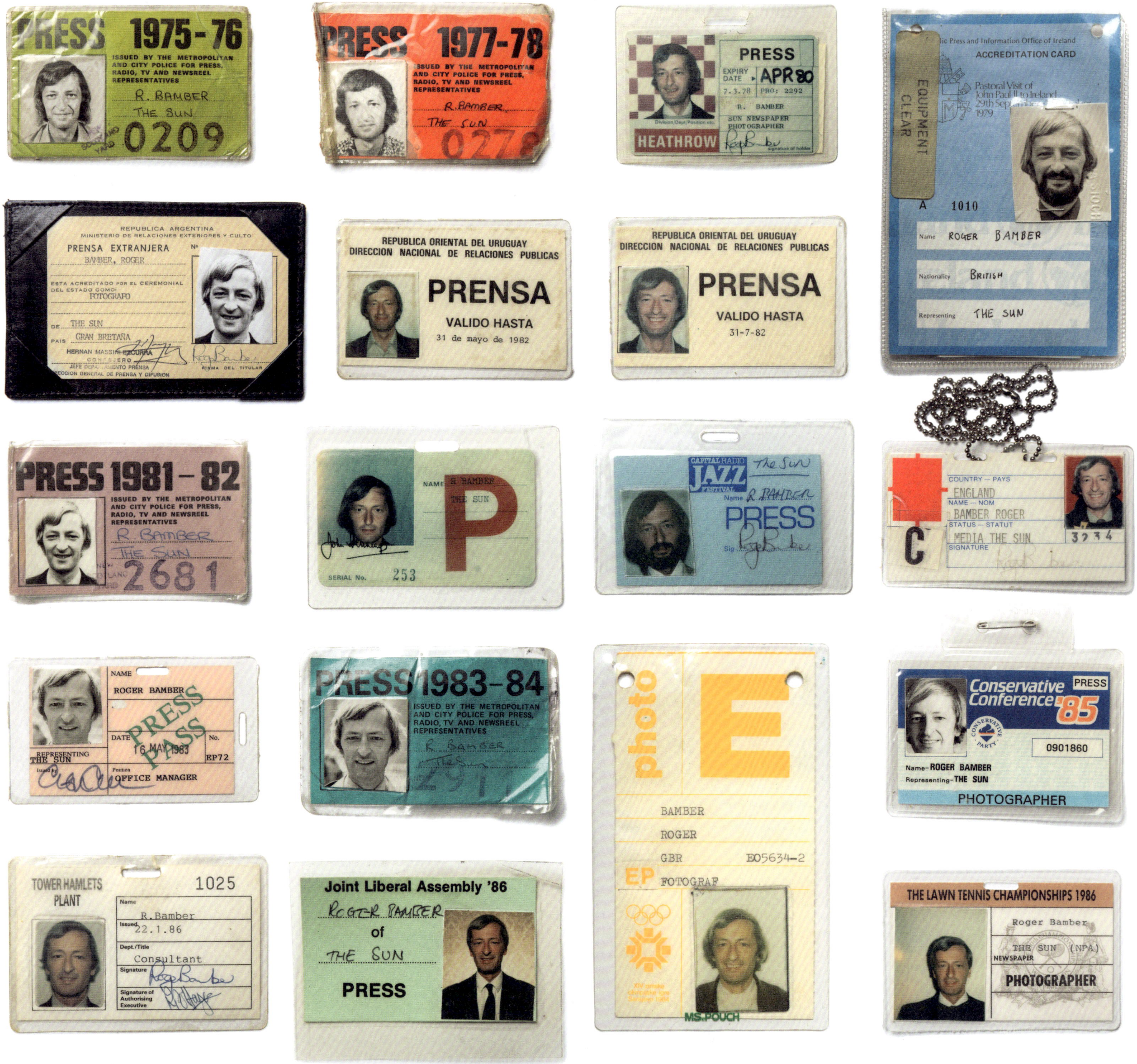
PRESS 1975-76
ISSUED BY THE METROPOLITAN AND CITY POLICE FOR PRESS, RADIO, TV AND NEWSREEL REPRESENTATIVES
R. BAMBER
THE SUN
0209
PRESS 1977-78
ISSUED BY THE METROPOLITAN AND CITY POLICE FOR PRESS, RADIO, TV AND NEWSREEL REPRESENTATIVES
R. BAMBER
THE SUN
PRESS
EXPIRY DATE APR 80
7.3.78
PRO: 2292
R. BAMBER
SUN NEWSPAPER PHOTOGRAPHER
HEATHROW
ACCREDITATION CARD
Pastoral Visit of John Paul II to Ireland 29th September 1979
EQUIPMENT CLEAR
A 1010
Name ROGER BAMBER
Nationality BRITISH
Representing THE SUN
REPUBLICA ARGENTINA
MINISTERIO DE RELACIONES EXTERIORES Y CULTO
PRENSA EXTRANJERA
BAMBER, ROGER
ESTA ACREDITADO POR EL CEREMONIAL DEL ESTADO COMO:
FOTOGRAFO
DE THE SUN
PAIS GRAN BRETAÑA
FIRMA DEL TITULAR
REPUBLICA ORIENTAL DEL URUGUAY
DIRECCION NACIONAL DE RELACIONES PUBLICAS
PRENSA
VALIDO HASTA
31 de mayo de 1982
REPUBLICA ORIENTAL DEL URUGUAY
DIRECCION NACIONAL DE RELACIONES PUBLICAS
PRENSA
VALIDO HASTA
31-7-82
PRESS 1981-82
ISSUED BY THE METROPOLITAN AND CITY POLICE FOR PRESS, RADIO, TV AND NEWSREEL REPRESENTATIVES
R. BAMBER
THE SUN
2681
NAME R BAMBER
THE SUN
P
SERIAL No. 253
CAPITAL RADIO JAZZ FESTIVAL
The Sun
Name R. BAMBER
PRESS
COUNTRY — PAYS
ENGLAND
NAME — NOM
BAMBER ROGER
STATUS — STATUT
MEDIA THE SUN
SIGNATURE
C
NAME
ROGER BAMBER
PRESS PASS
DATE 16 MAY 1983
No. EP72
REPRESENTING THE SUN
Position OFFICE MANAGER
PRESS 1983-84
ISSUED BY THE METROPOLITAN AND CITY POLICE FOR PRESS, RADIO, TV AND NEWSREEL REPRESENTATIVES
R. BAMBER
photo
E
BAMBER
ROGER
GBR E05634-2
EP
FOTOGRAF
MS.POUCH
Conservative Conference '85
PRESS
0901860
Name-ROGER BAMBER
Representing-THE SUN
PHOTOGRAPHER
TOWER HAMLETS PLANT
1025
Name R.Bamber
Issued 22.1.86
Dept./Title Consultant
Signature
Signature of Authorising Executive
Joint Liberal Assembly '86
ROGER BAMBER
of
THE SUN
PRESS
THE LAWN TENNIS CHAMPIONSHIPS 1986
Roger Bamber
THE SUN (NPA)
NEWSPAPER
PHOTOGRAPHER